'Climate change adaptation is political. This is the core message of this timely and potent text. At a world-historical moment in which crises of capitalism, political cynicism, and ecology converge, it reminds us that adapting to these crises is not a technocratic exercise but a deeply political undertaking which demands heightened sensitivity to uneven arrangements of power the world over. A vital contribution to the nascent field of critical adaptation studies, this theoretically informed, empirically rich text offers a much needed analytical arsenal for confronting the relations of power that subtend current conditions of crisis.'

Andrew Baldwin, Department of Geography, Durham University, UK

'This excellent book successfully highlights and critiques the often neutral and apolitical manner in which climate change adaptation is discussed. Through a series of rich empirical case studies from different parts of the world, this book brings politics back in, revealing how actors on global, regional and local levels negotiate different adaptation futures, and what injustices and vulnerabilities emerge around these power dynamics. A must-read for all those – scholars and policymakers – working on climate adaptation.'

Ingrid Boas, Assistant Professor, Wageningen University, The Netherlands

'The lived experience of climate change is not just about transforming landscapes and livelihoods; it is also about navigating and adapting to climate policies that may serve to exacerbate and re-entrench existing inequalities. This new collection of empirically informed research exposes these inequalities and will become an essential part of the climate change literature. Contributions to the collection range from remote villages to the boardroom, and have much to teach students, scholars, and policymakers about the implications not only of a changing climate, but also of the policies designed to address it.'

Heather Lazrus, National Center for Atmospheric Research, Boulder, USA

'In this compelling volume, global experts innovatively confront and respond to a critical concern of contemporary climate change adaptation: the apolitical nature that seems to pervade discourse, governance efforts and scholarship. The first of its kind, the book offers powerful insights into potential ways to account for the multiple evolving social dynamics that are critical within the framework of climate change adaptation in various spaces. It is destined to become a key reference for those interested in interrogating the political implications behind climate change adaptation.'

Louis J. Kotzé, Research Professor of Law, North-West University, South Africa,
and Marie Curie Research Fellow, University of Lincoln, UK

'This diverse and enriching peer-reviewed volume exposes climate change adaptation to an overtly critical gaze. This book provides an urgently needed and empirically grounded critique of climate adaptation's purported neutrality, and, by resisting the ideological erasure of the politics at the heart of contemporary adaptation projects, pushes back against the "naturalisation" of climate and adaptation discourses and strategies. "Denaturalising" climate adaptation could scarcely be more important for resisting patterns of climate injustice. This volume makes that case, and makes it persuasively.'

Anna Grear, Professor of Law and Theory, Cardiff University, UK

'The destructive potential of climate change is one of the most complex human issues of the present century. Taking into account different regional contexts, the works included in this volume provide an urgently needed critical perspective on power relations and on the different types of injustices that are present in the global agendas of adaptation to climate change.'

Gabriela Merlinksy, Researcher at Institute Gino Germani,
University of Buenos Aires, Argentina

A Critical Approach to Climate Change Adaptation

This edited volume brings together critical research on climate change adaptation discourses, policies, and practices from a multi-disciplinary perspective. Drawing on examples from countries including Colombia, Mexico, Canada, Germany, Russia, Tanzania, Indonesia, and the Pacific Islands, the chapters describe how adaptation measures are interpreted, transformed, and implemented at grassroots level and how these measures are changing or interfering with power relations, legal pluralism, and local (ecological) knowledge. As a whole, the book challenges established perspectives of climate change adaptation by taking into account issues of cultural diversity, environmental justice, and human rights, as well as feminist or intersectional approaches. This innovative approach allows for analyses of the new configurations of knowledge and power that are evolving in the name of climate change adaptation.

This volume will be of great interest to students and scholars of climate change, environmental law and policy, and environmental sociology, and to policymakers and practitioners working in the field of climate change adaptation.

Silja Klepp is a professor of geography at Kiel University, Germany.

Libertad Chavez-Rodriguez is a researcher at the Center for Research and Advanced Studies in Social Anthropology (CIESAS) in Monterrey, Mexico.

Routledge Advances in Climate Change Research

www.routledge.com/Routledge-Advances-in-Climate-Change-Research/
book-series/RACCR

A Critical Approach to Climate Change Adaptation

Discourses, Policies, and Practices

Edited by Silja Klepp and
Libertad Chavez-Rodriguez

Routledge
Taylor & Francis Group

LONDON AND NEW YORK

earthscan
from Routledge

First published 2018
by Routledge

2 Park Square, Milton Park, Abingdon, Oxfordshire OX14 4RN
52 Vanderbilt Avenue, New York, NY 10017

Routledge is an imprint of the Taylor & Francis Group, an informa business

First issued in paperback 2020

British Library Cataloguing-in-Publication Data
A catalogue record for this book is available from the British Library

Library of Congress Cataloging-in-Publication Data
Names: Klepp, Silja, editor. | Chavez-Rodriguez, Libertad, editor.
Title: A critical approach to climate change adaptation : discourses,
policies, and practices / edited by Silja Klepp and Libertad Chavez-
Rodriguez.
Description: Abingdon, Oxon ; New York, NY : Routledge, 2018. |
Series: Routledge advances in climate change research | Includes
bibliographical references and index.
Identifiers: LCCN 2018004522| ISBN 9781138056299 (hardback :
alk. paper) | ISBN 9781315165448 (ebook : alk. paper)
Subjects: LCSH: Climatic changes–Research. | Climate change
mitigation–Research.
Classification: LCC QC903 .C75 2018 | DDC 363.738/745612–dc23
LC record available at https://lccn.loc.gov/2018004522

ISBN: 978-1-138-05629-9 (hbk)
ISBN: 978-0-367-45904-8 (pbk)

Typeset in Sabon
by Wearset Ltd, Boldon, Tyne and Wear

Contents

Illustrations

Contributors

Salvador Aquino Centeno is a professor and researcher at the Center for Research and Advanced Studies in Social Anthropology in Oaxaca, Mexico. His areas of interest include indigenous peoples and the state; neoliberalism, indigenous peoples' territorialities and global environmental politics; social memory and representations of the past; and historical and contemporary anthropology of legal and illegal processes. He has conducted collaborative research among the Zapotec indigenous communities of the Northern Sierra of Oaxaca, Mexico over the past 16 years.

Sybille Bauriedl is a geographer, working as a senior researcher at the Sustainability Research Centre at the University of Bremen, Germany. Her research combines the approaches of political ecology, feminist geography, and critical urban studies with current projects on bioeconomy in East Africa, local energy transition in Germany, and digitalised urban infrastructures. She also runs a blog on climate debates (klimadebatte. wordpress.com).

Leigh-Anne Buliruarua is the regional coordinator for the European Union Pacific Technical Vocational Education and Training on Sustainable Energy and Climate Change Adaptation Project (EU-PacTVET). She holds a postgraduate diploma in environmental science from the University of the South Pacific in Fiji, and a BSc in biology from Victoria University, Melbourne, Australia. She has over ten years' experience as a project manager on climate change/natural resource management. She is currently pursuing an MSc in climate change to evaluate the alignment of the competencies developed under the EU-PacTVET with regional and global frameworks for climate change and disaster risk reduction.

Libertad Chavez-Rodriguez is a researcher and lecturer at the Center for Research and Advanced Studies in Social Anthropology in Monterrey, Mexico, and a member of the Mexican National Researchers' System. In 2014, she was awarded a PhD in social sciences from the University of Bremen, Germany, for her thesis *Climate Change and Gender: The* *significance of gender in the social vulnerability to extreme weather events in regions under flood risk in Mexico and Germany*. She holds an MSc in regional science/regional planning from the University of Karlsruhe, Germany. Her current research focuses on socio-spatial segregation and social vulnerability to hydro-meteorological hazards in urban areas, mainly using socio-anthropological methodology. Her areas of interest include social vulnerability to hazards; gender and environment; intersectionality and disasters; and socio-environmental issues from a political ecology perspective.

Susan A. Crate is a professor of anthropology in the Department of Environmental Science and Policy at George Mason University, USA. She specialises in environmental and cognitive anthropology, with a focus on anthropology and climate change. She has worked with indigenous communities in Siberia since 1988, with a research agenda that now extends to Canada, Peru, Wales, Kiribati, Mongolia, and Chesapeake Bay, Virginia, USA. She currently engages in creating community-based narratives on climate change to empower and bring about positive social change, an effort inspired in part by her role in *The Anthropologist*, a documentary taking an anthropological approach to climate change. She served on the American Anthropology Association's Task Force on Climate Change and is currently a lead author on the IPCC Special Report on Oceans and Cryosphere.

Sara de Wit is a postdoctoral research fellow at the Institute of Science Innovation and Society at the University of Oxford, UK. She is currently part of the Forecasts for Anticipatory Humanitarian Action Project. Trained in anthropology and African studies, she has a strong empirical orientation, with long-term fieldwork experience in southeast Madagascar, the Bamenda Grassfields in Cameroon, and Maasailand in northern Tanzania. She has undertaken 'ethnographies of aid' – at the intersection of science and technology studies development theories, environmental anthropology, and post-colonial studies – in which she broadly focused on how globally circulating ideas, such as climate change and notions of development, travel and what happens when they are translated by different actors along the translation chain.

Michael Flitner is a professor of geography at the University of Bremen, Germany. He holds a cooperation chair at the Sustainability Research Centre and the Leibniz Centre for Tropical Marine Ecology, both in Germany. He studied geography, biology, and education, with a specialisation in development research. His work concerns environmental issues from a social science perspective, and environmental and nature conservation policy in regional and international contexts. He focuses on conflict lines between environmental/nature conservation and public opinion to environmental justice and civic engagement, as well as on climate change questions and the historical and cultural perspectives of political ecology.

Heiko Garrelts is a researcher on environmental governance and is currently a member of the Sustainability Research Centre at the University of Bremen, Germany. He holds diplomas in political science and landscape planning. His research addresses decision-making processes in different policy fields, especially nature protection and climate change policy.

Jonas Hein is a postdoctoral researcher in the working group Social Dynamics in Coastal and Marine Areas at the Institute of Geography at Kiel University, Germany. He previously worked at the German Development Institute in the department for Environmental Policy and Management of Natural Resources. His areas of interest include the political ecology of conservation and development, peasant resistance, forest carbon offsets, and international forest and climate policies.

Sarah Louise Hemstock is an author and adviser to the Alofa Tuvalu Small Is Beautiful project – recognised by UNESCO as a Decade of Achievement project. She is currently leading the European Union Pacific Technical Vocational Education and Training on Sustainable Energy and Climate Change Adaptation Project (EU-PacTVET) at the South Pacific Community, is an adjunct fellow of the University of the South Pacific, Fiji, and was a visiting fellow at Nottingham Trent University, UK. Her interest in the Pacific region began as a consultant at Imperial College, University of London, UK, when she researched biomass resources in several Pacific small island development states. In 2010, she was made Government of Tuvalu Honorary Ambassador – Officer for Environmental Science.

Johannes Herbeck has studied human geography, political sciences, and sociology at the Technical University of Munich and the Ludwig-Maximilians-University of Munich, Germany. Since 2008, he has been working as a researcher at the Sustainability Research Centre at the University of Bremen, Germany. In 2014, he was awarded a PhD for his thesis *Geographies of Climate Change: Vulnerability, security, translocality*. Since then, he has been a researcher and scientific coordinator within the project *New Regional Formations: Rapid environmental change and migration in coastal regions of Ghana and Indonesia*, funded by the Volkswagen Foundation, Germany.

Helene Jacot des Combes is the senior lecturer in climate change adaptation at the University of the South Pacific, Fiji. She is currently a member of the UNISDR Scientific and Technical Advisory Group, and works on the European Union Pacific Technical Vocational Education and Training on Sustainable Energy and Climate Change Adaptation Project

(EU-PacTVET). She is a member of several Pacific regional committees: the Regional Working Group on Education, Climate Change and Disaster Risk Management; the Pacific Climate Change Roundtable; and the Technical Working Group for the Development of the Regional Integrated Strategy on Climate Change and Disaster Risk Management, called the Framework for Resilient Development in the Pacific (FRDP). She is also a member of the International Association of Emergency Managers.

Emilia Kennedy works for the Government of Alberta Climate Change Office. She is a geographer with research interests in political theory, climate and energy policy, and carbon-reduction technologies in Canada.

Silja Klepp is a professor of geography at Kiel University, Germany. She is a trained social anthropologist. In her current research on climate change migration and adaptation, she integrates post-colonial perspectives and critical theories in the study of climate change effects. She has published research on issues of climate justice and climate migration in Oceania, on boat people in the Mediterranean Sea, and on EU refugee and border politics. She has conducted field research in Kiribati, Vanuatu, New Zealand, Italy, Libya, Malta, and Zambia. One of her recent articles is 'The politics of environmental migration and climate justice in the Pacific region'.

Yvonne Kunz studied human geography and cultural anthropology at the University of Trier, Germany. In 2016, she was awarded a PhD in human geography from the Georg-August-University Gottingen in Germany, where she is part of the German Research Foundation (DFG)-funded Collaborative Research Centre on Ecological and Socioeconomic Functions of Tropical Lowland Rainforest Transformation Systems (Sumatra, Indonesia). She heads the Environment and Climate Desk of the Berlin-based non-governmental organisation *Watch Indonesia!* focusing on human rights, democracy, and the environment in Indonesia and East Timor.

Kevin Maitava holds an MSc in climate change and a BA in environmental studies. He has interests in food security, disaster risk management, and climate change-induced relocation. Originating from Fiji, he is committed to using his education and professional experience to contribute towards building a better Fiji.

Tess Martin is a researcher and senior academic working with the Pacific Centre for Environment and Sustainable Development at the University of the South Pacific, Fiji. Over the past eight years she has worked in ten Pacific Island countries. Her recent work has been instrumental in developing the first technical and vocational education and training

(TVET) regional qualifications in climate change adaptation and sustainable energy for the Pacific region. Her publications focus on education and climate change adaptation in the Pacific region.

Daniel Morchain is a global adviser in climate change adaptation and resilience with Oxfam, as well as co-investigator in the Adaptation at Scale in Semi-Arid Regions project, which aims to make research more inclusive, more participatory, and to recognise social impact as researchers' ultimate objective. He views the climate change debate as one that should be embedded in social justice, transformation, gender equality, and leadership – and believes that success will depend on how we all engage with it at an emotional level.

Detlef Müller-Mahn is a professor of development geography at the University of Bonn, Germany, and spokesperson of the collaborative research centre Future Rural Africa: Future-making and Social-Ecological Transformation, in Germany. His research addresses questions of environmental governance and risk in the context of global change, with a focus on pastoralists and peasants in Eastern Africa. He edited *The Spatial Dimension of Risk: How geography shapes the emergence of riskscapes* (2013).

Alejandra Navarro-Smith is a research professor in the Department of Sociocultural Studies at ITESO University, Guadalajara, Mexico. She is a trained social anthropologist using visual media, and has undertaken fieldwork for more than a decade (2006–17) among Cocopah fishers in the Colorado River Delta. Her current work focuses on the production of vulnerability threatening the well-being of Cocopah fisher households. Climate change, rising sea temperature, and a lack of public policies on these issues in the Mexican seas are some of the factors generating high risks for Cocopah fishers. One of her recent articles is *Dilemmas of sustainability in Cocopah territory: an exercise of applied visual anthropology in the Colorado River Delta* (2016).

Ignacio Rubio C. is a professor at the School of Social and Political Sciences of the National University of Mexico. His research focuses on disasters, risks, and environmental conflict. He coordinates a research project on the sociology of risk and uncertainty. He is part of the Mexican National Researchers' System and a board member of the International Sociological Association's thematic group 04.

Celia Ruiz de Oña Plaza is an associate researcher at the Multidisciplinary Research Centre of Chiapas and the South Border of Mexico, of the National Autonomous University of Mexico. Her current research focuses on topics related to mitigation and adaptation policies in the field of political ecology and science technology studies in the coffee sector of Chiapas and in the conservation sphere. For the past ten years she has been involved in various rural development projects in Chiapas dealing with sustainable productive systems.

Ruth Senikula is the gender and vulnerable groups inclusion consultant for the European Union Pacific Technical Vocational Education and Training on Sustainable Energy and Climate Change Adaptation Project (EU-PacTVET) based at the Pacific Community in Nabua, Fiji. She completed a joint degree in applied psychology and education from the University of the South Pacific, Fiji. She is now pursuing postgraduate studies at the same university in the area of climate change.

Roy Smith is course leader for an MA in international development at Nottingham Trent University, UK, and vice chairman of the Pacific Islands Society of the UK and Ireland. He has conducted fieldwork in Micronesia, Melanesia, and Polynesia. His current research concerns food security and marine conservation, with a focus on coral reefs.

Astrid Ulloa is an anthropologist and professor in the Department of Geography at the Universidad Nacional de Colombia. Her main research interests include indigenous movements, indigenous autonomy, gender, climate change, territoriality, extractivisms, and anthropology of the environment. She is author of *The Ecological Native: Indigenous peoples' movements and eco-governmentality in Colombia* (2013). Recent articles include *Perspectives of environmental justice from indigenous peoples of Latin America: a relational indigenous environmental justice* (2017), *Geopolitics of carbonized nature and the zero carbon citizen* (2017) and *Environment and development: reflections from Latin America* (2015). She is currently writing about gender and mining and territorial feminisms in Latin America.

Luz María Vázquez is a research coordinator and lecturer at York University, Canada, where she was also awarded a PhD in the Department of Sociology. She worked for over ten years in a research centre at the National Autonomous University of Mexico, where she acquired strong research skills based on extensive ethnographic and qualitative work. Her research interests include environmental sociology, local governance, resource management, conservation, and climate change.

Sophie Webber is a lecturer in geography in the School of Geosciences at the University of Sydney, Australia. She is an economic and environmental geographer. She studies climate change adaptation and resilience in South East Asia and the Pacific region and the development agencies and institutions that work there.

Chapter summaries

Chapter 1 Governing climate change: the power of adaptation discourses, policies, and practices

Silja Klepp and Libertad Chavez-Rodriguez

This book presents the outcome of a workshop on climate change adaptation discourses, policies, and practices held in Oaxaca, Mexico, in 2016. Participants were mostly from and/or undertaking research in the Global South. Two main themes arose: that cultural, social, and political diversity is largely absent from climate change adaptation and that the overwhelming social inequalities under which adaptation to climate change is taking place are not only ignored, but are often naturalised or even strengthened. The various chapters of this book explore a number of questions: Which social dynamics can evolve within the framework of climate change adaptation in various spaces? Which assumptions and rationalities are inherent in mainstream climate change adaptation discourses, policies, and practices? Which patterns of use and misuse can we observe regarding climate change adaptation? Which social processes are initiated or hindered through climate change adaptation?

Chapter 2 A clash of adaptations: how adaptation to climate change is translated in northern Tanzania

Sara de Wit

This chapter explores how the nascent idea of Adaptation to Climate Change is translated in northern Tanzania. By interrogating how nongovernmental organisations and other actors in northern Tanzania adapt to the idea of adaptation itself we gain insight into the ways in which a new development paradigm comes into being. Based on 14 months of multi-sited ethnographic fieldwork this chapter reveals the politics of adaptation that emerge in the encounter between global ideas of adaptation and what it means for different stakeholders on the ground.

Chapter 3 Rethinking the framing of climate change adaptation: knowledge, power, and politics

Daniel Morchain

This chapter explores the existing institutional arrangement driving the thinking and action behind climate change adaptation, as well as development more broadly. It argues that it is an unfair arrangement, where Northern academic and political institutions exert disproportionate influence over the sector. It also finds that there is a bias towards understanding climate change as an overly biophysical challenge – not as a social issue. Climate change adaptation and development should, instead, be founded on inclusive, representative and consultative principles that enable the amalgamation of various sources of knowledge and that support otherwise marginalised groups to become increasingly influential and the owners of their own development pathways.

Chapter 4 Climate change economies: denaturalising adaptation and hydrocarbon economisation

Sophie Webber and Emilia Kennedy

A vibrant literature investigates marketised attempts to limit climate change impacts. This literature has exposed the failures of market-based policies, but has also overlooked equally important components of climate governance. This chapter speaks to this gap by examining adaptation economies in the Pacific Islands, and hydrocarbon economies in Alberta, Canada. Drawing connections between climate change knowledge services to inform adaptations and attempts to create carbon capture and storage programmes, we extend existing understanding of how actors are attempting to manage climate change, and we demonstrate the contours and connections of a more broadly conceived category of climate change economies.

Chapter 5 Tourism, environmental damage, and climate policy at the coast of Oaxaca, Mexico

Ignacio Rubio C.

Tourism is a human activity sensitive to climate. This chapter provides a brief description of some of the problems that underlie tourism development in one particular town – Zipolite – a small town on the coast of Oaxaca, Mexico. Discussion focuses on how climate change adaptation policies portray and evaluate the environmental risks that jeopardise tourism development and create environmental fragility and damage. The chapter provides insight into these critical issues and shows that the expansion of political economies based on massive investment in infrastructure can involve marginalisation of local communities from development.

Chapter 6 Vulnerability factors among Cocopah fishers: climate change, fishery policies, and the politics of water in the delta of the Colorado River

Alejandra Navarro-Smith

This chapter examines the consequences of climate change on the daily lives of the fishing Cocopah families in Baja California, with a focus on public policy regarding climate change adaptation in northwestern Mexico and the southwestern USA. Climate change, as well as the politics of water management, and rigorous fisheries and environmental protection policies, are some of the factors endangering the quality of life for Cocopah fisher households in Baja California and may also be exacerbating their existing social vulnerability. The chapter includes a range of personal reflections from Cocopah elders.

Chapter 7 Ruling nature and indigenous communities: renewed senses of community and contending politics of mitigation of climate change in the northern Sierra of Oaxaca, Mexico

Salvador Aquino Centeno

Accepting the international agenda of climate change mitigation policy, the Mexican government has created a top–down institutional framework of environmental laws and discourses of justification for climate change prevention. This chapter examines how indigenous communities of the northern Sierra of Oaxaca have become involved in the politics of climate change mitigation, through lessons learned from several years of environmental impact due to forest extraction. The chapter focuses on how these communities have incorporated this climate policy while contesting the institutional and official policies of climate change. Based on their own experiences of sustainable management, the indigenous communities have advanced very effective practices of climate change mitigation.

Chapter 8 Adapting in a carbon pool? Politicising climate change at Sumatra's oil palm frontier

Jonas Hein and Yvonne Kunz

We investigate climate policy and its impacts on Sumatra's peasant communities using two case studies for Jambi province: one on the expansion of oil palm cultivation and one on the challenges for peasant agriculture posed by the development of a conservation forest. The associated conflicts centre on often-neglected aspects of climate politics. They illustrate trade-offs between different objectives of the UNFCCC, namely between mitigation and adaptation. We argue that marginalised actors face triple exposure. They are not only negatively affected by climate change and neoliberal globalisation but are also increasingly by attempts to reduce greenhouse gas emissions.

Chapter 9 Adapting in the borderlands: the legacy of neoliberal conservation on the Mexican–Guatemalan border

Celia Ruiz de Oña Plaza

In the Global South, incipient adaptation projects in territories that have for several years experienced mitigation strategies based on environmental payments, encounter significant inertia towards maintaining a monetised approach to combat climate change. This chapter reflects on the implications of this in the Tacaná Volcano Biosphere Reserve, in the borderland between Mexico and Guatemala. By reviewing historical and current trends for a landscape where coffee plantations and conservation strategies are the target of climate change mitigation and agro-ecological adaptation strategies, this chapter argues that it is necessary to reach a close understanding of the uniqueness of the regions where they are to be implemented.

Chapter 10 Climate change adaptation narratives in the Gulf of Mexico

Luz María Vázquez

This chapter uses a case study on fishing communities in the Gulf of Mexico to analyse the potential challenges the that Mexican government may face when implementing climate change adaptation initiatives in the region. A narrative analysis approach shows how actors understand and frame problems. Discussion of two adaptation measures – community relocation and the establishment of protected areas – demonstrates how government climate change initiatives are not designed to address the structural factors that are determining people's vulnerabilities to climate change, such as poverty or lack of environmental planning. By ignoring such issues and focusing only on how to face impacts, government adaptation initiatives could exacerbate existing conflicts and reinforce inequalities.

Chapter 11 Leaving the comfort zone: regional governance in a German climate adaptation project

Heiko Garrelts, Johannes Herbeck, and Michael Flitner

This chapter reflects on a climate change adaptation project in northwest Germany – nordwest2050 – against the backdrop of debate around new forms of regional governance. These are bound up with hopes for improved effectiveness, wider participation and new integration and innovation processes. The broad-based participatory processes of nordwest2050 enabled the collaboration of actors whose voices are seldom heard in conventional policy processes. The project also showed that adaptation to climate change is a contested, political process. Nevertheless, the differences and conflicts revealed in the course of the project could play a productive role in the future, as a catalyst for further discussions and transformation processes.

Chapter 12 Reconfiguring climate change adaptation policy: indigenous peoples' strategies and policies for managing environmental transformations in Colombia

Astrid Ulloa

This chapter analyses conceptual discussions about 'adaptation' as a strategy for responding to climate change. The analysis indicates a wide range of interpretations on its meaning and scope. It highlights the political dimension of adaptation strategies, due to the inequalities that are generated, both in access and in their implementation in diverse cultural contexts. It starts from the idea that the culturally given causes and answers respond to conceptions about the non-human. The analysis is based on the results of work carried out in indigenous contexts in Colombia.

Chapter 13 Atlases of community change: community collaborative–interactive projects in Russia and Canada

Susan A. Crate

This chapter describes a community–collaborative partnership to develop intranet (within-community) atlases of community change, to empower local communities to monitor change in all its forms (including unprecedented local change due to climate perturbations), develop plans of action and move forward with appropriate responses. Pilot studies took place in two arctic contexts: a post-Soviet community in northeastern Russia and a coastal community in Labrador, Canada. The chapter explores whether this approach for community self-monitoring of change will improve local adaptation to climate change. The chapter concludes that the prototypes developed drove enough community interest to warrant further development.

Chapter 14 Professionalising the 'resilience' sector in the Pacific Islands region: formal education for capacity-building

Sarah Louise Hemstock, Helene Jacot Des Combes, Leigh-Anne Buliruarua, Kevin Maitava, Ruth Senikula, Roy Smith, and Tess Martin

Practitioners and policymakers are recognising the importance of integrating climate change adaptation and disaster risk management. This approach has been adopted in the European Union Pacific Technical Vocational Education and Training on Sustainable Energy and Climate Change Adaptation Project (EU PacTVET). A key barrier to improving national resilience to climate change impacts and disaster risk has been identified as a lack of capacity and expertise due to the absence of sustainable accredited and quality-assured training programmes that guarantee access to people. TVET modules and tools developed under the EU PacTVET project will establish a community of practitioners supporting community resilience in Oceania.

Chapter 15 Conclusion: the politics in critical adaptation research

Sybille Bauriedl and Detlef Müller-Mahn

This concluding chapter focuses on the political aspects of critical adaptation research by discussing the key arguments of the various case studies presented in this book. In particular, the chapter asks why we need critical adaptation research, since is not adaption always an act of criticism on the unsustainable use of nature? The chapter argues that adaptation is not a neutral driver of action but an outcome of a contested political process. Yet, adaptation is mostly told as a single story, disregarding multifaceted knowledge systems and global environmental justice. To make adaptation research truly critical, it must be more socially and politically reflective.

Part I
Introduction

1 Governing climate change

The power of adaptation discourses, policies, and practices[1]

Silja Klepp and Libertad Chavez-Rodriguez

Introduction

Climate change adaptation is an influential discourse and a powerful political concept linked to many material practices. It has the power[2] to set political agendas and policies and to reframe development programmes on different scales – from global to local. 'Adaptation' – and linked to this the concepts of 'vulnerability' and 'resilience' – is currently the main notion mediating ideas on anthropogenic climate change and society. Nevertheless, it is often difficult to understand what various scholars have observed: that despite its significant political effects, most of the discussions concerning 'adaptation' are effectively framed in an apolitical manner (Cameron 2012; Gesing *et al.* 2014; Eriksen *et al.* 2015; Taylor 2015). This means that the political implications behind climate change adaptation are not explicitly addressed, and so remain invisible. Why is this so? And what do we learn if we focus our analysis on the political aspects, on changing power relations, growing vulnerabilities, and different kinds of injustices linked to climate change adaptation rather than the apolitical aspects of the process? This book aims to contribute to a better understanding of how climate change adaptation politics is evolving, to provide a more accurate account of what is happening on the ground, and to discuss what is needed to set free potentials for change in climate change adaptation to make it a more just and fair tool of governance.

This may be illustrated using the example of Kiribati (Oceania), where adaptation narratives are especially powerful. These Pacific islands – 33 low-lying atolls and reef islands extending just a few feet above sea level and with a permanent population of just over 110,000 – have been identified by climate scientists as highly vulnerable to climate change because of sea-level rise, more intense storms, and drought.

National budgets and aid programmes are being reframed and adaptation projects and policies are today crucial for national and regional household budgets and aid programmes in Oceania and elsewhere. In Kiribati, adaptation thinking informs political decision-making on all scales. In contexts from national to local, the people of Kiribati (the *I-Kiribati*) receive, appropriate, and transform adaptation measures. Here, climate change adaptation has emerged as a powerful assemblage (Deleuze and Guattari 1987; Head 2009) where different interests, worldviews, and futures are negotiated. One such example is the Kiribati Adaptation Project (KAP) (Storey and Hunter 2010; Webber 2013; Donner and Webber 2014). This exemplifies those features of large adaptation projects that are most criticised: it is financed by the World Bank, it has been running since 2002, and it was established because Kiribati was seen as the 'vulnerable of the vulnerable'. To date, the project has cost around US$10 million and has recently (2015) entered phase III. Numerous consultants have been contracted since 2002, many knowing little about the country and staying in Kiribati for a couple of days only. Even World Bank managers agree that a lot of money has been wasted and that the needs of the population were not sufficiently considered (Klepp 2014). Meanwhile, Kiribati has changed socio-economically on various levels. Arguably, this change is mainly due to aid programmes having been reframed as climate change adaptation programmes, which in turn has often resulted in a shift in responsibility from the Kiribati Government to a more abstract and ever-changing assemblage associated with climate change effects. This process is referred to by some as the 'garbage can effect', metaphorically being used to contain and pose diverse and often previously existing social and socio-ecological problems. Other programmes, such as those concerning domestic violence, may no longer be financed. One researcher has coined the phrase 'performative vulnerability' (Webber 2013), which must be enacted to receive funding from major donors. The former president of Kiribati, Anote Tong, has been especially masterful at enacting performative vulnerability in international fora, drawing on images of vulnerable sinking islands partly linked to colonial legacies of perceived weak, isolated, small islands in the Pacific (Farbotko 2010). However, Kiribati's international standing has also increased (Klepp 2014) and this has resulted in adaptation funds for many positive things, such as sanitation infrastructure, health programmes, and education. Kiribati is clearly undergoing profound change – owing to both the direct effects of the changing climate (environmental effects) and the so-called second-order effects of the changing climate (social effects) that are often also bound to discursive formations (UFZ 2008: 18). Although climate change adaptation, as realised by international donors seems to be the only viable option for survival (de Wit 2014: 57), what is missing in Kiribati are discussions about what this means for the development of the country as a whole. For example, which adaptation concepts and goals would be most appropriate and how should the growing funds for climate change adaptation be spent. These political implications, although fundamental to the future of the country, are not yet openly debated in any public fora.

Motivated by this situation and by what is happening elsewhere in the world regarding politics of climate change adaptation (Chavez-Rodriguez

Figure 1.1 Kiribati Adaptation Project's placard, Kiribati.
Source: photo: Silja Klepp.

2014; Klepp 2014; Klepp and Herbeck 2016; Klepp 2017), around 20 scholars – the majority from and/or undertaking research in the Global South – met in Oaxaca, Mexico, in September 2016 for intensive discussions on climate change adaptation discourses, policies, and practices. Two main themes arose: that cultural, social, and political diversity is more or less absent from climate change adaptation (Bravo 2009; Cameron 2012; Eriksen *et al.* 2015; Taylor 2015) and that the overwhelming social inequalities under which adaptation to climate change is taking place are not only ignored, but are often naturalised (Gesing *et al.* 2014: 5) or even strengthened (Bravo 2009; Dietz and Brunnengräber 2016). In this book we discuss how social science approaches can be used to move away from the prevailing viewpoints and so capture under-represented perspectives. We also discuss how to use these findings to imagine different possible futures.

To show how the politics of climate change adaptation can be addressed rather than ignored, an academic 're-politicising' of climate change adaptation could create a more holistic perspective: referred to by von Benda-Beckmann *et al.* (2009: 9) as a 'multi-sited arena of negotiation'. This includes the structural aspects, namely the networks of interactions connecting various actors and different kinds of actants (Latour 1996; Ingold 2008) and the power relations and rationalities that organise these interactions and are reproduced or changed by them (von Benda-Beckmann *et al.* 2009). Our approach implies a process-oriented analysis and more attention to the socio-political context (Eriksen *et al.* 2015; Moloney *et al.* 2018). It promotes climate change adaptation as a 'travelling idea' that is interpreted, localised, and modified in different settings (Weisser *et al.* 2014) or as 'mobile policy' locally translated through practice (Cochrane and Ward 2012: 7). We also recognise the idea that climate change is a neutral, apolitical, and universal imaginary projected by climate science, and detached from local responses to climate (Jasanoff 2010: 235) and a global imaginative resource (Hastrup and Fog Olwig 2012: 2). The various chapters of this book will explore a number of questions: which social dynamics can evolve within the framework of climate change adaptation in various spaces? Which assumptions and rationalities are inherent in mainstream climate change adaptation discourses, policies, and practices? Which patterns of use and misuse can we observe regarding climate change adaptation? Which social processes are initiated or hindered through climate change adaptation?

The rest of this introductory chapter summarises the different strands of discussion regarding a political analysis of climate change adaptation. These ideas are examined in greater detail in Chapters 2 to 15. We start by providing a short history of the term 'adaptation', in order to better understand its dramatic revival (Taylor 2015: 6) in the context of climate change, especially under the United Nations Framework Convention on Climate Change (UNFCCC) and the Intergovernmental Panel on Climate Change (IPCC) (Head 2009; Bassett and Fogelman 2013; Watts 2015). We then examine those perspectives and lines of research that seem fruitful in scrutinising given terminologies and assumptions in climate change adaptation projects and policies and that are effective in politicising climate change adaptation. This will help us to establish how and why climate change adaptation can become such a powerful tool in the hands of the elites and, to a lesser extent, of the subaltern.

Reinventing and de-politicising adaptation through climate change

Academic understanding of socio-economic and political processes for transforming the environment first emerged in the mid-twentieth century in the context of American geography and anthropology: the Berkeley School of Cultural Geography was developing particular interest in empirical, often ethnographic, research on the interlinkage between culture, land, and environment (Watts 2015: 23). Borrowed from evolutionary biology, where it meant constant adjustment by organisms to newly arising challenges from their external environment (Taylor 2015: 3), the term adaptation or 'adaptational strategies' was first used in cultural ecology and then found its way into the social sciences as a whole in the 1960s (Watts 2015: 28). Cultural aspects, ecological principles, and eco-system analysis approaches were combined in writings about adaptation, for example those concerning Native Americans and their environmental history in the southwest USA (Steward 1955), the practices of ethnic groups managing their resources on the prairie of Alberta, Canada (Bennett 1969), or the padi rice systems that organise society in Bali, Indonesia (Geertz 1963). Again, shaped largely by American anthropology and geography, natural hazards literature and its notions of vulnerability (which focused on how natural hazards created social vulnerabilities) and adaptation began to appear in the 1970s and was soon criticised by a developing political ecology in ways that still sound familiar today (Bassett and Fogelman 2013).

Debate about hazards, risks, and vulnerabilities and an emphasis on social root causes such as poverty and lack of rights in colonial contexts, or on the so-called natural sources of disaster, shaped a discussion that led to fundamentally different views on adaptation (Bassett and Fogelman 2013: 44). These varying conceptualisations are an integral part of the different understandings of vulnerability that exist within international fora, in the field of development aid, and in academia. The natural-hazard approach dates back to the 1960s and is based on a long tradition of disaster research. It was particularly influenced by the early work of Gilbert F. White (a prominent American geographer), who began to analyse natural hazards and human responses (Kasperson *et al.* 2005: 259). By integrating knowledge of natural sciences, engineering, and social sciences, an attempt was made to explain the connections between physical system elements, such as exposure, probability, and impact of hazards (Adger 2006: 271). Nevertheless, the natural hazards literature of the 1970s and 1980s was still relatively apolitical, seeing the vulnerability of a system as the result of the intensity, frequency, and nature of external events (Dietz 2006: 14), that is, primarily implying biophysical vulnerability (Füssel 2005). The 'environment as hazard' work of Burton *et al.* (1978) brought together the most important elements of the natural-hazard approach. With regard to vulnerability, it established that almost all types of hazard have different effects on different social groups (Burton *et al.* 1978). Nevertheless, the approach was dominated by problem analysis and solutions from engineering science. As a consequence, an explanation for the differences in vulnerability shown by different groups of people, and within social groups at any one geographic location, the focus of later human-ecological research, was not addressed for some years (Adger 2006: 271; Dietz 2006: 15).

In the 1970s, critiques coming mainly from a political-economy background and following social-constructivism approaches considered that nature and society should not be analysed as separate entities. They analysed context-dependent aspects such as social structures and power relations and underlined that adaptation cannot be based on too simplistic *homo economicus* considerations of human behaviour (Dietz 2006: 14; Bassett and Fogelman 2013: 44). In the 1980s and 1990s, political ecology and researchers such as Blaikie *et al.* (1994), Dow and Downing (1995), Hewitt (1997) and Watts and Bohle (1993) began to address social vulnerability, thereby focusing on causal structures. They suggested that the vulnerability of individuals or communities to environmental change is mainly based on their position in social and political contexts (Watts and Bohle 1993; Clark *et al.* 2005).

Even if new conceptual approaches to vulnerability analysis are committed to combine social and biophysical vulnerability in an effort to overcome the separation between natural/biophysical sciences and social science analysis[3] (see for example Peluso and Watts 2001), this 'great divide' (Bassett and Fogelman 2013: 44) in the conceptualisation of vulnerability was taken up again after the re-introduction of 'adaptation' to climate change after the Rio Summit in 1992 (Pelling 2011). It still persists today and leads to different understandings of legitimate adaptation strategies.

Multiple de-politicising factors in climate change adaptation

Many factors make it difficult to consider political dynamics in mainstream adaptation approaches. In this section, we address those that appear most important. Later, we discuss analytical perspectives and tools to deconstruct these factors and shed light on the politics of climate change adaptation.

What adaptation means is still open to debate. It is used in a highly contested way (Arnall *et al.* 2013; Taylor 2015) and how it is interpreted, for example in development projects, is often unclear. Following its re-introduction to the social sciences and policy debate after the Rio Summit in 1992 (Pelling 2011), Bassett and Fogelman (2013) identified three different concepts in the climate change literature: *adjustment*, *reformist*, and *transformative* approaches to adaptation. Each of the three approaches implies different strategies for reducing vulnerability.

The *adjustment* approach mostly implies top–down solutions (see Schipper 2007: 6; Hillmann *et al.* 2015: 6). The socio-political root causes of vulnerability and anthropogenic climate change are not addressed under this approach because they are hidden behind the measurable, quantifiable, and predictable global effects of climate change (Dietz and Brunnengräber 2016). Adaptation strategies comprise technological innovation and infrastructure, a growing body of knowledge, and optimising the governance and management of society (Dietz and Brunnengräber 2016). In contrast, there are approaches that define vulnerability as being far more dependent on context, and regard more radical system change, sustainable development

(Watts and Bohle 1993; Fankhauser 1998), and societal transformation as the most viable way to reduce vulnerability and strengthen adaptation capacity (Schipper 2007). Bassett and Fogelman (2013) refer to these as *reformist* or *transformative* approaches. The latter includes the idea of resolving the internal contradiction caused by an economic system that promotes growth that is energy-intensive and accelerates climate change, and that has adverse consequences for growth and human well-being now and in the future (Harvey 2010). In their analysis of IPCC reports and adaptation-focused articles in leading global change journals, Bassett and Fogelman (2013) found that the so-called adjustment approach is by far the most influential, and is used by 70 per cent of authors.

Pelling (2011) saw the debate as being driven by four main questions: what to adapt to? Who or what adapts? How does adaptation occur? What are the limits to adaptation? All of these questions have political implications linked to questions of power and resources, social inequality, and access to decision-making and information that are not easy to answer. Although the critique of the 1970s and 1980s had found its way into aspects of development aid and disaster risk reduction (such as through grassroots or empowerment approaches), it seems that many of the criticised aspects returned via the 'back door', that is, via climate change discourses and adaptation aid projects (Bassett and Fogelman 2013; Taylor 2015; Watts 2015). The rationalities that characterise current adaptation concepts are criticised as being primarily shaped by the natural sciences (Cannon and Müller-Mahn 2010; Hastrup and Fog Olwig 2012) and as ignoring aspects of climate justice as well as social, cultural, political, and economic conditions on the ground (de Wit 2014; Gesing *et al.* 2014; Eriksen *et al.* 2015; Klepp and Herbeck 2016). What seems new in the climate change adaptation literature, compared with the critique of the natural hazards literature of the 1970s and 1980s, is the focus on the agency and empowerment of vulnerable groups and a pro-poor development planning (Bassett and Fogelman 2013: 51). This is probably due to a trend to the mentioned foci that we can see in social science and development aid generally and can be seen as a politicising factor.

However, an inherent de-politicising factor of climate change adaptation and the reason why such projects are mostly linked to concepts of adjustment and not to a deeper understanding of societal change is closely linked to development aid functioning as an 'anti-politics machine' (Ferguson 1990). In order to be accepted as supposedly 'neutral' agents that have a humanitarian mission, development agencies 'disguise what are, in fact, highly partial and interested interventions as universal, disinterested and inherently benevolent' (Ferguson 1994: 181). This characterises the entire development aid apparatus (Ferguson 1994: 178) and replaces discussions and interventions on social and political inequalities and power relations with crisis narratives that describe 'development' in terms of the well-being of entire regions being threatened by a phenomenon such as famine or climate change (Bravo 2009: 262). This reframes political questions of resource distribution and access as technical problems that must be addressed by technical 'development' interventions (Ferguson 1994: 180). Furthermore, these crisis narratives legitimise elites and decision-makers on the ground as main receivers of development aid that is often used in their own political interests (Bravo 2009). In the case of the Arctic, Bravo argued that an expert elite that comes as an 'army of consultant climate modellers, ecologists and anthropologists' (Bravo 2009: 269) together with local elites is sustaining the climate change crisis narrative. They legitimise the belief that local people must be guided by techno-managers and gain growing access to the resources that are at the core of the crisis narrative (Bravo 2009: 269). As the chapters of this book will show, the contested assets in adaptation settings are mostly land (Chapters 2, 7, 8, 9, and 11) and water (Chapters 6 and 10).

Nevertheless, we want to stress that we are not denying the risks that anthropogenic climate change poses for people, or claim that climate change exists only on a discursive level. On the contrary, we believe that all of these factors contribute to a bundle of de-politicising factors in climate change adaptation that shape our societal responses to climate change. This can make people on the ground much weaker and vulnerable to its effects, as answers and adaptive strategies must be complex and multidimensional, including our socially, politically, and culturally diverse realities. Moreover, climate change adaptation strategies should face the deeper roots of global inequalities, as Dietz (2009) reminded us.

If we speak about multiple de-politicising factors that are inherent to climate change adaptation on different scales, we must consider the 'multi-dimensional inequalities' (Dietz 2009) in the context of global climate change that are adversely affecting developing countries. With very low per capita emissions, these countries bear little responsibility for anthropogenic climate change and yet they remain heavily impacted by actual and expected environmental change. One important aspect that constitutes the multidimensional inequalities that Dietz is observing in the context of climate change is the violent, disempowering, and impoverishing heritage of colonialism. Nonetheless, as reported by Cameron (2012: 110), serious consideration of the colonialised context in which climate change adaptation is evolving is currently non-existent in the literature on the human dimensions of climate change. Although several authors have written about the importance of employing a colonial perspective, in Cameron's opinion they fail to account for the colonial dimensions of societal problems (Cameron 2012: 110) or to include these dimensions in climate change adaptation:

> If the very factors cited as undermining Inuit capacities to adapt to climatic change are themselves a legacy of colonial interventions, then re-framing Inuit vulnerability as a matter of enhancing 'local capacities',

rather than attending to the structural and systemic processes by which those capacities are continually undermined, must be challenged.

(Cameron 2012: 110)

This is even more the case when it comes to aspects of knowledge and power, as we can see in various chapters of this book (Chapters 2, 3, and 12). The dominant role of Western (natural) science in climate change adaptation often seems to sweep away local knowledge structures. As Logan Cochrane put it in his recent blog entry on Linda Tihuiwai Smith's book *Decolonizing Methodologies: Research and indigenous peoples*, 'even when exploitation is not explicit, there is [...] "a cultural orientation, a set of values, a different conceptualization of such things as time, space and subjectivity, different and competing theories of knowledge, highly special-ized forms of language, and structures of power" (Smith 1999: 42), which act to reinforce the dominance of one way of knowing over another' (de Sousa Santos 2010; Mignolo 2012; Cochrane 2017). In Chapter 3, Daniel Morchain states that in the case of climate change adaptation, rather than climate science taking the lead, a multitude of knowledge, inside and outside academia, must be foundational. Currently, the imbalance of knowledge 'is used by powerful actors worldwide to maintain control and ownership over the development agenda' (Morchain 2017).

Moreover, in the context of knowledge and climate change adaptation, there is another pitfall: 'good' adaptation must take local contexts, values, and interpretations of 'good living' into consideration in order to make adaptation meaningful and successful in terms of assisting the most vulner-able. The inclusion of the populations affected by changes in adaptation planning and the relativisation of the dominant role of climate change sci-ences in favour of local (environmental) knowledge and climate change interpretations is urged by many authors (Crate and Nuttall 2009; Lazrus 2009; Kelman 2010; Crate 2011; Rudiak-Gould 2012). However, the focus on 'local' and on indigenous people and their knowledge is often accompanied by assumptions concerning 'intellectual and spatial confine-ment' (Appadurai 1988, quoted in Cameron 2012: 105) of this very know-ledge that we must challenge in our thinking on climate change adaptation. Issues of scale that must be problematised as well as handled with care and sensitivity can remind us that our understandings of the local and the global in climate change adaptation are themselves relational productions (see Cameron 2012).

One last crucial factor in de-politicising climate change adaptation that needs to be raised here, and which is closely related to a restricted under-standing of knowledge and vulnerability, is how our climate is understood as existing separately from human beings living in the world. As Taylor wrote, 'the Cartesian foundations of adaptation that dichotomise climate and society as separate yet mutually influencing systems or domains' (Taylor 2015: xiii) are responsible for a widespread understanding of climate change as an external shock to an otherwise well-functioning society. As Hulme (2010), Taylor (2015) and others described in the 'socio-technical apparatus' that underlies the concept of climate of the IPCC and the UNFCCC and other mainstream understandings, climate seems to be an exclusively physical process that can be measured in local places that create indications for regional or global-scale climatic conditions (Bravo 2009; Taylor 2015: 27). Historically experienced and represented as an entanglement of physical conditions and human knowledge and practices, today an abstract and de-politicised understanding of climate forms the condition in which narratives of climate change adaptation are evolving, as Astrid Ulloa shows in Chapter 12. She examines why it seems so difficult to inscribe questions of power, inequalities, and politics into climate change adaptation. One answer comes from political ecology: because contrary to binary understandings of human/environment relations, concepts of how we act in the world in relationship with the environment, the climate, and its changes are inherently political.

Climate change adaptation politics on a global level

The IPCC and the UNFCCC, themselves informed by science, have always greatly influenced research and implementation of climate change adaptation projects and policies at various levels (Pelling 2011: 17). The IPCC was founded in 1988 and its assessment reports are based on a procedure of scientific consensus. It was mainly created for consolidating knowledge for decision-makers. Since its first assessment report in 1990, adaptation has played an ever-growing role and IPCC definitions have formed the adaptation agenda of the UNFCCC. Since the second IPCC assessment report in 1995, the idea that the severity of the threats posed by climate change to people and ecosystems is dependent on their 'vulnerability' has grown in importance (Liverman 2009: 284). In the course of this development:

> the locus of western moral concern moved (and not for the first time) from temperate to tropical and polar geographies, and the threatened worlds of other species of plant and animal as a sign for life on earth as whole.
> (Cosgove 2008, as quoted in Daniels and Endfield 2009: 216)

Here we find another aspect that made and makes climate change adaptation an 'urgent' matter, where in a type of modernist backlash technical solutions are transferred from the Global North to countries of the Global South without much negotiation.

Although mentioned in UNFCCC documents since the Rio Summit in 1992, it is following the 2001 UNFCCC Conference of the Parties that adaptation to climate change, particularly in the Global South, has become a fundamental principle of global climate policy (Bassett and Fogelman 2013: 42). The UNFCCC established a governance and management structure to support low- and middle-income countries in adapting to climate change. Bilateral and multilateral institutions, such as the development banks and other UN agencies, are included in this structure. In 2001, the Adaptation Fund was established to finance adaptation projects and programmes in countries of the Global South that are parties to the Kyoto Protocol. The Adaptation Fund is financed through a share of proceeds from the Clean Development Mechanism project activities and other sources of funding. The Global Environment Facility is one of the main financial mechanisms that serves as a delivery body for adaptation projects under the UNFCCC, including small-scale projects and programmes. Another milestone is the Cancun Adaptation Framework that was adopted at the 2010 Climate Change Conference in Cancun, Mexico (COP16/ CMP6). In the agreements, member countries affirmed that adaptation must be addressed with the same level of priority as mitigation. The national adaptation plan (NAP) process was established to support member countries in formulating and implementing national adaptation plans (NAPs) and to identify adaptation needs. National adaptation programmes of action (NAPAs) provide a process for least developed countries to recognise priority activities to adapt to climate change. All such programmes and institutions have great political influence on different levels. For example, Dietz (2009) described how NAPAs can set and reset political agendas of national elites in the name of climate change adaptation (de Wit, Chapter 2). A general criticism is that the emerging management and infrastructure for supporting climate change adaptation at the UNFCCC level is organised around existing power structures and favours banking interests and technical-fix solutions. Instead of being a driver for change or transformative action, these mechanisms are supporting the status quo (Pelling 2011).

Particularly since the shift from mitigation to adaptation in the climate change discourse of the early 2000s (Smith 2013: 28), ideas of adaptation have been regarded as supposedly neutral drivers of action and appear to be the only possibility for ensuring the continuation of the human species on earth (de Wit 2014: 57). The refashioning from stopping climate change towards adapting to it is itself profoundly political (Cameron 2012: 107). Even if that does not mean that mitigation is completely abandoned, the focus on adaptation has changed thinking about the human dimensions of climate change from a problem of environmental politics and justice on the global scale to something that should be tackled at a more local level, for example in 'community-based focus groups' (Cameron 2012: 109). In this case, actions would be concentrated in the local, as if adaptation capacities were only a matter of enhancing local resilience, targeted through technical intervention and expertise by Western consultants, ignoring structural and systemic processes (frequently linked to legacies of colonial intervention) of climate change and vulnerability (Cameron 2012: 110). It has also made the social effects of climate change accessible and 'governable' for international politics and development aid (Cameron 2012: 110).

In 2007, the IPCC defined adaptation as 'the adjustment in natural or human systems in response to actual or expected climatic stimuli or their effects, which moderates harm or exploits beneficial opportunities' (IPCC 2007: 27). Here the root causes of social vulnerabilities are framed in terms of exogenous environmental drivers that must be dealt with. Dietz and Brunnengräber saw this 2007 IPCC definition as the most influential reference for climate policy today (2016: 128). However, the critical literature associated with different perspectives on climate change adaptation has grown rapidly since 2000, with a clear recent trend for understanding this more and more as a complex social process (Eriksen *et al.* 2015). More differentiated and contextual understandings of vulnerability to climate change found their way into different chapters of the latest (2014) IPCC assessment report, while other chapters still understood adaptation to be 'the adoption of specific technologies, programs, policies or measures to address climate risk' (Eriksen *et al.* 2015: 525). These conceptual tensions will probably endure (ibid.: 526). They are accompanied by different understandings of climate change as an inherently political problem that calls us to change lifestyles and politics on different scales or, in contrast, as a local or regional problem to which people on the ground should adapt (see Cameron 2012; Klepp and Herbeck 2016). Generally, the historically high greenhouse gas emissions of industrialised countries and commensurate responsibilities for observable and expected changes in global climate have been subsumed under the notion of 'shared, but differentiated responsibilities'. This has not, however, resulted in far-reaching political concessions towards the so-called developing countries of the world. Rather, global power structures themselves have complicated negotiations about 'fair' goals of climate politics and about compensatory payments for adaptation measures (Parks and Roberts 2010). It remains to be seen whether newer concepts such as 'loss and damage' (McNamara *et al.* 2018) or the Paris Agreement (which establishes new instruments such as the nationally determined contributions [NDCs]) will bring fundamental change.

Operationalising climate change adaptation through vulnerability and resilience thinking

At present, the impact of climate change on society is primarily framed in terms of adaptation, vulnerability, and resilience. In terms of operationalising adaptation concepts, notions of vulnerability and resilience are particularly powerful in their practical meaning for governance on the ground. They are translated into political measures and adaptation projects, which are implemented at the local, national, regional, and transnational level

(Bravo 2009: 258). Concepts of vulnerability and resilience were used to describe the choices available to people and ecosystems in response to (and adaptation to) natural events well before discussion of climate change began (Gaillard 2007: 522). These concepts are closely associated with each other and are difficult to disentangle. In the context of climate change, both concepts are the subject of competing definitions, which are often not made transparent when they are used (Fog Olwig 2009: 314; Kelman 2010). They define the social and cultural effects of climate change using a vocabulary of ecological risks and within an ecosystemic perspective, which fails to reflect the complexity of human societies (Bravo 2009: 259). As a result, the primarily political and normative issues raised by climate change adaptation are framed in de-politicising natural science and eco-system terms (Hastrup 2009: 26; Felli and Castree 2012; Gesing *et al.* 2014). In the context of climate change, they frame the categories within which adaptation thinking takes place. These concepts must be challenged to allow space for alternative ideas about tackling climate change or for alternative societal reactions to be developed (Dreher and Voyer 2014).

The following discussion outlines and examines the discourses relating to the concepts of vulnerability and resilience. The focus is on outlining the main points of criticism of these concepts, and on illustrating the conditions that they have created for negotiating climate change adaptation mainly in countries of the Global South. The chapter authors adopt such perspectives, and several case studies reflect the influence of the conceptualisations of vulnerability and resilience in shaping climate change adaptation.

Vulnerability and climate change

Abundant use has been made of the concept of vulnerability since the very beginnings of climate change research. In its 2007 assessment report, the IPCC defined vulnerability as:

> the degree to which a system is susceptible to, and unable to cope with, adverse effects of climate change, including climate variability and extremes. Vulnerability is a function of the character, magnitude, and rate of climate change and variation to which a system is exposed, its sensitivity, and its adaptive capacity.
>
> (IPCC 2007: 27)

In the following, we trace some of the vulnerability narratives that connect to the effects of global climate change. Why are these narratives so powerful? The historical importance of climate change discourses is seen by Liverman to lie 'in their impact on the environmental, energy and economic development of many countries, [...] and the structuring of a new set of international relations around responsibility for causing and solving climate change' (Liverman 2009: 282).

Numerous authors have criticised the way in which discussion of appropriate adaptation to climate change is dominated by the supposedly objective, hard-data-based, neutral solutions offered by the natural sciences (e.g. Barnett and Campbell 2010; Tanner and Allouche 2011) and 'geographic objects' (Barnett and Campbell 2010: 2), such as coastlines, sea-level rise or precipitation data. The devastating consequences of climate change predicted by natural scientists also shape media and academic discourses on climate change, for example in Oceania and Africa. Very little attention is paid to inhabitants' own interpretations of climate change or to the potential strategies for responding which they have traditionally used or are currently using (Barnett and Campbell 2010: 21; de Wit 2014, Chapter 12 (this volume); Ulloa Chapter 12 (this volume)). Development states are pictured by Western media, academics, and international cooperation as marginalised, vulnerable and in need of development, as well as poor and not equipped for economic growth. These constructions are an expression of constellations of knowledge and power, which have been reconfigured in the context of climate change.

The vulnerability discourses linked to the effects of climate change tend to emphasise the internal deficits of countries of the Global South. The threat of climate change, it is implied, can only be averted and the problems of powerless groups solved by an active 'invulnerable expert' (Barnett and Campbell 2010: 162) who interprets what would be good for them. The behaviour of industrialised countries, whose emissions are considered to have caused climate change in the first place, is blended out by shifting the locus of the problem to the countries of the Global South (Barnett and Campbell 2010: 2). In this way, it becomes clear how concepts of vulnerability, which are implemented as part of international cooperation, produce and reproduce unequal power relationships within the knowledge–power nexus. Ideas about adaptation to climate change, which do not necessarily correlate with the needs and preferences of people on the ground, can be forced through into practice.

Resilient citizens?

In parallel form, since the beginning of the century discourses of adjustment to climate change have increasingly moved away from the concept of vulnerability to privilege the concept of resilience instead (Walker *et al.* 2002, 2006; Smith 2013: 28; Weichselgartner and Kelman 2015). In contrast to the widely criticised concept of vulnerability, resilience appears to have the potential to cope more effectively with the uncertainties inherent in climate science (Barnett 2001: 984), is better able to take account of specific local features (Bravo 2009), and allows for greater conceptual flexibility (Hastrup 2009: 28).

The concept of resilience in the context of ecological systems was first introduced by Crawford S. Holling in an article published in 1973

(Barnett 2001: 984; Bravo 2009: 260). This ecological context was subsequently important for transplanting the concept to climate change discourse. In its 2007 assessment report, the IPCC defined resilience as 'the ability of a social or ecological system to absorb disturbances while retaining the same basic structure and ways of functioning, the capacity for self-organization, and the capacity to adapt to stress and change' (IPCC 2007: 880). The 2012 IPCC Special Report on extreme weather events recognised resilience – together with coping – to be one of the essential conditions for the alleviation of the adverse impacts of disasters. Resilience is understood as:

> the ability of a system and its component parts to anticipate, absorb, accommodate, or recover from the effects of a potentially hazardous event in a timely and efficient manner, including through ensuring the preservation, restoration, or improvement of its essential basic structures and functions.
>
> (IPCC 2012: 34)

One of the advantages of resilience is that the term provides a shared vocabulary which enables policies and initiatives in various areas and at different levels to be brought together and compared (Bravo 2009: 258). The concept has been used since the 1970s as a technical term in several disciplines, such as engineering and child psychology. It has also been used in the field of disaster research (Gaillard 2010: 220). In the field of ecology, it is trendsetting mainly because of the resilience theory developed through the later theoretical and empirical work of Holling, and in collaboration with other researchers such as Lance Gunderson and Brian Walker. The resilience theory has been further developed and expanded to comprise social-ecological systems (see Gunderson and Holling 2002; Walker *et al.* 2006). This was mainly accomplished through the work of the international research network *ResilienceAlliance*, founded by Holling in 1999 (ResilienceAlliance 2015). The danger, however, is that a concept is seen to have emerged from ecology, which is rooted in a common, worldwide understanding of the framework and interpretation of climate change (Bravo 2009: 258). This implies a systemic perspective which understands ecosystems as being closed systems (Hastrup 2009: 20; see also Crate 2011: 186).

Cannon and Müller-Mahn (2010) regarded the concept as being insufficiently differentiated in relation to the effects of climate change and as inadequate for capturing people's multifaceted, dynamic livelihoods. As is the case with the concept of vulnerability,[4] the concept of resilience excludes the possibility of rethinking the relationships and processes of co-production of natural and social orders (Ingold 1996, quoted in Bravo 2009: 260) and of resolving the dichotomies between nature and humans. This fundamentally functionalist narrative framing of the effects of climate change is criticised for taking material causes as its starting point, the rational human response to which is to take adaptive action (Bravo 2009: 260; Cannon and Müller-Mahn 2010). The concept of resilience obscures power relationships and socio-economic factors, such as the impact of colonialism, which play a major role in connection with environmental risk (Cannon and Müller-Mahn 2010).

Around the discourses on climate change and migration, the concept of resilience now seems to have taken a further neoliberal turn which emphasises the individual responsibility of 'more resilient' climate change subjects and migrants (Felli and Castree 2012; Klepp 2017). The 'resilient lives' (Felli and Castree 2012: 4) of individuals and communities are discussed in terms of their ability to be absorbed by foreign labour markets. The 'resilient subject' will be compelled to continually adapt to dangers supposedly beyond their control, in contrast to a subject that considers itself capable of changing the world, its structures and conditions (Evans and Reid 2013). This neoliberal thinking sees, for example, climate-induced migration as successful adaptation and a solution rather than, as was previously the case, a problem of securitisation within a discourse of environmental migration (Herbeck and Flitner 2010; Klepp and Herbeck 2016; Klepp 2017). The danger here is that the populations concerned may find themselves being selected into groups of the resilient and non-resilient, and may experience new forms of discrimination and control as the non-resilient 'others' (Gesing *et al.* 2014: 11), in which aspects of climate justice are excluded altogether. In the resilience discourse linked to climate change adaptation, the responsibility for successfully adapting to climate change is generally shifted to the regions, communities, and individuals that are suffering from the effects of climate change, disguising the responsibility of industrialised countries as the originators of anthropogenic climate change (see Chandler 2014; Davoudi 2016).

How does power operate in climate change adaptation? Alternative concepts, useful tools

The climate change adaptation literature today offers various alternatives to the mainstream concepts discussed above and paves multiple ways for re-politicising climate change and climate change adaptation, and puts people, their agency, and their living conditions back in the focus of analysis. They highlight the 'geographies of inequality' (Daniels and Endfield 2009: 219) in climate change adaptation in opposition to the across-the-board de-politicising of climate change and climate change adaptation, through the climate change sciences (Bravo 2009; Bettini 2013; Gesing *et al.* 2014; Methmann and Oels 2015), through international cooperation (Tanner and Allouche 2011), and to some extent as a result of disempowering concepts such as vulnerability and resilience. A standpoint that goes even further aims to supplant current vulnerability and resilience concepts with a broader 'citizenship approach' which emphasises agency and political aspects in adaptation debates (Bravo 2009) as well as futures that show alternatives to a nation-state system that is refusing solidarity with people that are experiencing the adverse effects of climate change (Klepp and Herbeck 2016, Klepp 2017).

As previously mentioned, we suggest that re-politicising climate change adaptation should create a more holistic perspective – one of a 'multi-sited arena of negotiation' (von Benda-Beckmann *et al.* 2009: 9). This implies understanding climate change adaptation as a social process (Eriksen *et al.* 2015) that produces winners and losers. The 'processes of prioritisation and exclusion' (ibid.: 526) that are inherent in every climate change adaptation choice, 'necessarily have positive and negative effects distributed socially, spatially and through time' (ibid.: 526). Knowledge plays a crucial role in the social dynamics of prioritisation and exclusion. Western and northern scientific institutions mainly produce the knowledge that forms the basis of and validates a certain type of climate change adaptation; one that fits into international aid schemes and is often connected to or directly sells Western technical knowledge and products.

Research on a more systematic way to understand the failures of climate change adaptation projects and the rationalities of climate change adaptation more generally is about to start (see Sovacool and Linnér 2016: 2). This book contributes by collating empirical insights from a variety of settings, where climate change adaptation is studied as a powerful concept and tool in socially, culturally, and politically diverse contexts. Nonetheless, numerous approaches from critical social sciences have recently been applied in critical climate change adaptation research. Some appear to be especially popular and effective for re-politicising climate change adaptation and are addressed in this book, mainly political ecology (e.g. Taylor 2015), political economy (e.g. Sovacool and Linnér 2016), critical development studies (e.g. Cameron 2012), and science and technology studies, in relation to questions of knowledge, climate science, and technology (e.g. Jasanoff 2010).

We assume that a first step in re-politicising climate change adaptation must be to question and discuss the biopolitical implications of adaptation concepts (Cameron 2012; Taylor 2015). In our empirical research, we ask the 'classical' questions of governmentality (Foucault 1979; Walters 2012): which hidden ontologies can be found that must be carved out and historicised? What can they tell us about power relations, interests, and rationalities in adaptation settings? Which are the actors, actants, interests, and practices involved in climate change adaptation? Which worldview and mission is behind an adaptation project or policy?

At the workshop in Oaxaca we also discussed that scrutinising adaptation policies and practices and de-constructing the multiple de-politicising factors mentioned above might not be enough. In settings regarding the Global South especially, there is a need for approaches sensitive to cultural diversity and which have post-colonial and de-colonising research perspectives. This is also linked to different ontologies regarding naturecultures and an overcoming of dichotomies between humans and their environments in our research perspectives.

Feminist approaches are also needed to explore the various and often intersectional discriminations that can be reinforced through adaptation policies and projects on the ground. Power and gender relations are often persuasive and persistent, indicating that elites frequently profit most from politics and adaptation projects implemented by international donors. From a gender perspective there are at least two important issues to consider in climate change adaptation: the representation level of women in climate change negotiations and the still widespread representation of women as victims of climate change impacts. Although women's representation does not imply gender awareness, the overwhelming lack of representation of women (such as in disaster risk management), a highly relevant policy field for climate change adaptation, reveals prevailing gender stereotypes about activities related to physical risk exposure and strength mostly assigned to men (Chavez-Rodriguez 2014: 182). Also, in international and national negotiations on climate change, particularly senior officers and decision-making posts are held by men (GenderCC 2017; see UN Women and Mary Robinson Foundation 2013). For example, at the UNFCCC COP16 in Cancun, women accounted for only 30 per cent of all delegation parties, and between 12 per cent and 15 per cent of all heads of delegations; since COP21 in Paris, the increased number of party delegates has been accompanied by a strong decrease in the share of women – to 19 per cent and 17 per cent in 2016 COP22 in Marrakesh (GenderCC 2017). This reflects the entanglement of power and gender relations, and the frequent exclusion of women from learning and working with technical issues, from socialisation to vocational guidance and professional profiles linked to climate change adaptation. Furthermore, this has consequences in terms of gender and social vulnerability to climate change; there is a danger that the over-representation of men in climate change adaptation tasks limits or prevents a consideration of experiences, views, political interests, and (alternative) perspectives of solutions of women (Röhr *et al.* 2008). It is therefore also unlikely that the diverse needs of men and women in highly vulnerable social groups (such as people in need of special health care) will be taken into account. The low representation of women can also be criticised from the human rights perspective, since it reveals the low level of realisation of 'climate and gender justice'. There is an unfair distribution of political participation possibilities between men and women in climate change adaptation, and an unfair distribution of damage and burdens due to climate change-related impacts among groups of different social vulnerability. The inclusion of women is of the utmost importance, but inclusion alone, particularly at the local level, is a double-edged sword: although it can lead to empowerment for women, which can in turn promote overall gender equity, it can also hide the risk of feminising participation at the local level, while women's workloads increase and their participation at higher levels of decision-making beyond their community is not encouraged to the same extent (Röhr *et al.* 2008). Debates on victimisation or agency of women are also highlighted in discussions on gender and climate change adaptation (Enarson 2007; Arora-Jonsson 2011). As Seema Arora-Jonsson (2011) suggested, it is necessary to overcome dichotomous positions in which women can only be considered as defenceless victims or as agents of change, for example in situations of disaster. Women, just like other human beings, can occupy both positions at once, which means being agents of change and being immersed in situations of disadvantage that determine their greater vulnerability compared with men (Kleinman 2007; Arora-Jonsson 2011). Thus, it is not necessary to deny such disadvantages to consider them important players in climate change adaptation at all policy levels.

The notion of intersectionality from the field of gender studies allows for a differentiated analysis of the social vulnerability to natural hazards (Chavez-Rodriguez 2014: 64) and to climate change impacts, considering a differential exposure according to socio-economic variables such as income level, education, housing and transportation conditions, and access to urban services. Furthermore, intersectionality also differentiates according to attributes inherent to the individual such as gender, age, physical and mental dis/abilities, ethnicity, and migratory condition. Intersectional approaches specially acknowledge the entangled relationships among the aforementioned lines of difference and differentiation (West and Fenstermaker 1995; Walgenbach 2007; Lykke 2010) and their role in the configuration of social vulnerability. The approach of 'processes of accumulation of disadvantages' by Mercedes González de la Rocha feature the configuration of social vulnerability (González de la Rocha 2007). According to this approach, for people with high social vulnerability, the disadvantages are generally multiple, feed back onto each other, and tend to accumulate. Examples of commonly accumulating disadvantages are little or no schooling, low income, subordination and dependency in terms of gender and generation, and difficulties in maintaining social relationships (see Wolff and De-Shalit 2007). The intersectionality concept – together with the notion of accumulation of disadvantages – seems to be necessary for a deep comprehension of the social vulnerability to climate change in order to take account of social differences and its interrelations.

Finally, post-colonial perspectives and subaltern studies offer powerful thinking alternatives for the challenge of re-politicising climate change adaptation, by urging the necessity of theoretical and epistemological distance of the Global South to Western thinking, and by fundamentally challenging deep-rooted dynamics of knowledge construction and international power relations shaped by influential historical processes of colonialisation and imperialism articulated by notions of race and racism (Quijano 2000; Dussel 2001; see de Sousa Santos 2010; Mignolo 2012). Regarding the highly diversified human experience, Boaventura de Sousa Santos suggested that the comprehension of the world is broader than the occidental comprehension of the world (de Sousa Santos 2010: 8). He claims for the establishment of 'intercultural post imperial human rights', some of which are of critical relevance for a re-politicisation of climate change adaptation such as the rights of recognition of entities that are actually unable to bear duties, specifically nature and future generations, the right of knowledge, and the right of transformation of property rights based on solidarity notions (de Sousa Santos 2010). In the pursuit of taking theoretical and epistemological distance, Arturo Escobar (2017) – together with other Latin American scholars – explored and synthesised several voices and approaches related to notions of transformation coming from the Global South (e.g. *Buen Vivir*, post-development, civilisational transitions, and transitions to post-extractivism), some of which are approached in different chapters of this book. The suggestion to 're-socialise' the climate in the politics of representation of climate change in order to question the de-politicising effects of the 'rationalist account of abstract climate' (Taylor 2015: 37) connects closely to these approaches of an ontological opening in the debates on climate change and climate change adaptation. Florian Weisser *et al.* (2014) demanded more ontological and epistemological reflections in all climate change adaptation research, as it is mostly absent.

Broadly, what this book shows is that the mechanisms of 'prioritisation and exclusion' (Eriksen *et al.* 2015: 526) that are shown by a variety of different analytical tools follow similar rationalities, in different social, cultural, and political settings all over the world. For example in Chapter 11, Heiko Garrelts and co-authors analyse a German climate change adaptation project in terms of the power relations of different status groups. Stakeholders from a regional economic interest group managed to dominate the agenda with their economic benefits connected to regional development and partly took over the participatory decision-making process. The tendency for climate change adaptation to be dominated by economic drivers and by economically strong actors can be observed in most of the chapters.

Conclusion and chapters

This book collates a variety of perspectives on climate change adaptation. Although these perspectives vary widely in terms of subject matter, they all focus on climate change adaptation as a social process where actors on different levels are negotiating knowledge, power, and different possible futures. In synthesis, it seems to us that climate change adaptation can be seen as a magnifier – a contemporary phenomenon (Sovacool and Linnér 2016) that, also in the form of a biopolitical tool, is connected closely to the most powerful narratives of our time. It represents a new paradigm in North–South cooperation (Weisser *et al.* 2014) and a new arena in which North–South relations are negotiated and reconfigured. In the field of climate change adaptation, humanity is called to deal with the socio-ecological crisis that it has produced. To theorise climate change adaptation and climate change more generally in a better way, we need new understandings in the socio-theoretical conceptualisation of 'locality, sociality and connectivity', as is asked for by Kirsten Hastrup (in press). We need to grasp, first, the increasing complexity of decision-making processes; second, the intensified (transnational) interactions, locally and globally; and third, the increasing dynamics of technological and scientific developments in the climate change and climate change adaptation context.

However, these pathways/understandings that are explored in many chapters of this book should not only be questioned on a theoretical-analytical level, but must also be manifest on a societal level. The latest turn in climate change adaptation concepts are notions of transformation in various contexts and at different scales. Transformative adaptation can become just another buzzword in climate change adaptation, or it can become a real driver for more radical socio-ecological system change (Klepp and Herbeck 2016). All chapters of this book make it very clear that climate change cannot be left to natural science; it is a deeply political, naturecultural phenomenon, and dealing with it must always be multi-dimensional and multidisciplinary. As Daniel Morchain put it: 'Adaptation needs to be transformational, but it can't be so unless the actors driving it radically change their own ways and become more inclusive. Adaptation without transformation is dangerous' (Morchain 2016). Its manifold effects can be observed throughout this book: adaptation without transformation means business as usual in development aid and a cementation of power relations, including a worsening of social inequalities. It remains to be seen as to which direction climate change adaptation will take.

This book comprises five parts. A brief overview of each major section and its component chapters now follows; this includes the geographical focus. Part I contains this chapter – the introduction.

The different conceptualisations of climate change adaptation and their uses and misuses are examined in Part II by Sara de Wit and Daniel Morchain. Sara de Wit (Chapter 2) shows how non-governmental organisations in northern Tanzania are interpreting ideas of adaptation. Her work explores emerging geographies of climate change adaptation as well as sedimented practices that replicate old power structures in the context of what she calls an 'adaptation imperative'. De Wit offers insights into the politics of adaptation that are brought about in the encounter between global ideas of adaptation and what it means for people on the ground. She states that '[w]hereas the government of Tanzania sees the Maasai both as environmental destroyers as well as the most vulnerable people in the face of climate change, the NGOs representing them argue that they are *masters of adaptation instead*' (de Wit, Chapter 2: 43). Daniel Morchain (Chapter 3) outlines an alternative framing of climate change adaptation that takes into account the interplay of knowledge, power, and politics. He examines the implications of the existing institutional set-up and power dynamics on adaptation debates, for example the strong influence of the IPCC versus the weaker representation of local and indigenous knowledge, and the effects of this on the adaptive and developmental potential of the targeted populations.

Part III addresses the many political economies of climate change adaptation and illustrates trade-offs between mitigation and adaptation on various scales. A vibrant literature investigates marketised attempts to limit climate change impacts. This literature has exposed the failings of market-based policies, but has also overlooked equally important components of climate governance. Chapter 4 by Sophie Webber and Emilia Kennedy refers to this gap by examining adaptation economies in the Pacific islands, and hydrocarbon economies in Alberta, Canada. The authors extend existing ideas of how actors are attempting to manage climate change in order to increase understanding of the new carbon economy and the economisation processes and logics involved in governing climate change. They demonstrate the contours and connections of a more broadly conceived category of climate change economies.

Three Mexican authors contribute to Part III: Chapter 5, authored by Ignacio Rubio C., discusses the problems arising through massive investment in tourism infrastructure. Taking the example of a small Mexican town on the coast of Oaxaca (Zipolite), he highlights the missing political and social understanding of environmental risks in times of global change. Climate change adaptation policies as they are applied in Zipolite are therefore condemned only to deliver few results.

In Chapter 6, Alejandra Navarro-Smith asks how climate change and public policy regarding climate change adaptation in the Baja California region of northwestern Mexico and southwest USA influences everyday life for the fishing Cocopah families. In addition to climate change, public water management and strict fisheries and environmental protection are aggravating their social vulnerability.

In Chapter 7, Salvador Aquino Centeno delineates the contestation of climate change mitigation politics by indigenous communities with solid experience in forest conservation and administration in the northern Sierra of Oaxaca, Mexico – a region historically impacted by forest extraction. He shows how a top–down institutional framework (including environmental laws, discourses of legitimation of climate change mitigation, and the enforcement of carbon sequestration strategies and forest degradation prevention measures) has been incorporated and indeed contested by indigenous communities through new forms of social organisation and a renewal of their community sense.

The final chapter of Part III, by Jonas Hein and Yvonne Kunz (Chapter 8), considers trade-offs between climate change mitigation and adaptation, and between mitigation policy objectives and violent conflicts, water scarcity, and biodiversity loss at Sumatra's oil palm frontier in Jambi province. Using two case studies, the authors show how climate policy changes geographies of resource access and control and how certain actors may become marginalised, making them more vulnerable to environmental change.

Different adaptation settings and conflicting meanings and understandings of climate change adaptation are analysed in Part IV: in Chiapas, in the Gulf of Mexico, in Germany, and in Colombia. The failures of adaptation projects are given particular attention in Part IV.

In Chapter 9, Celia Ruiz de Oña Plaza reviews historical trends in coffee plantations and conservation strategies in the Tacana Volcano Biosphere Reserve, located at the Mexican–Guatemalan border. The author argues that incipient climate change adaptation projects in territories that have for years experienced mitigation strategies (based on environmental payments) encounter significant inertia towards maintaining a monetised approach to combat climate change.

Focusing on fishing communities in the Gulf of Mexico, Luz María Vázquez (Chapter 10) analyses Mexican government climate change adaptation narratives through the study of five coastal communities located in the Mexican state of Tabasco, identifying a discrepancy between what government initiatives propose as potential strategies to promote climate change adaptation, and the views of fishers about interrelated local issues. She argues that government initiatives that are presented as neutral strategies to help communities become better equipped to face climate change impacts are contentious, and that their implementation may face challenges of which the government is unaware when they define the climate change problem.

In Chapter 11, Heiko Garrelts, Johannes Herbeck, and Michael Flitner use a case study in northwest Germany to explore the chances and challenges of regional broad-based participatory governance projects relevant to climate change adaptation. They also point to the productivity of the conflicts that emerge once stakeholders 'leave the comfort zone'. Customary practices and political narratives were questioned during the project, and the possibility raised for new approaches towards climate change and climate change adaptation.

Astrid Ulloa (Chapter 12) contributes to conceptual discussions about adaptation, questioning fixed notions of climate change adaptation and raising the importance of historical, political, and cultural dimensions. Ulloa asserts that the culturally given causes and answers to climate change respond to conceptions about the non-human. Her analysis draws on work carried out in indigenous contexts in Colombia and she argues for the need to include cultural perspectives on climate change in public policy.

The book concludes with Part V, in which Crate (Chapter 13) and Hemstock and co-authors (Chapter 14) describe concrete ideas and practices for change in development aid and climate change adaptation research, to show how those aspects of climate change adaptation that were criticised in preceding chapters can be tackled.

Susan A. Crate (Chapter 13) describes a community collaborative partnership to develop intranet atlases of community change, to empower local communities to monitor change in all its forms, develop plans of action, and move forward with appropriate responses. She based her ideas on pilot studies undertaken in two Arctic contexts – a post-Soviet community in northeastern Russia and a coastal community in Labrador, Canada – and concluded that this approach for community self-monitoring of change drove enough community interest to warrant further development.

In Chapter 14, Sarah Hemstock and co-authors describe how a regional project financed by the European Union tackles different problems in the realm of disaster risk reduction and climate change adaptation in Oceania. Based on technical vocational training and capacity-building, a community of practitioners is trained in strategies of disaster risk reduction and climate change adaptation. In this way, local communities get formal education certificates, resources can be used for staff with local knowledge (often making foreign consultants superfluous), and the overall resilience of communities is strengthened.

In the concluding chapter to the book, Chapter 15, Sybille Bauriedl and Detlef Müller-Mahn focus on the political aspects of critical adaptation research, by discussing the key arguments of the various contributions and asking why we need a critical adaptation research. Is not adaptation always an act of criticism on unsustainable use of nature? What are the specific perspectives of critical approaches? What is the political in critical adaptation research?

Although the material presented here may be approached from the perspective of individual chapters and their focus on a particular aspect of the current debate, for a more complete understanding of the difficulties and shortcomings of climate change adaptation and the interconnections between different discourses, politics, and practices, it is better to approach the book differently – it is recommended to approach the book from a more holistic perspective viewing the chapter-specific material more as part of a whole. Nonetheless, what is most important to us at this point is an invitation to our readers to question conceptualisations of climate change adaptation in different adaptation settings, to further advance critical research approaches on climate change adaptation, and to develop solutions for our collective futures that are based on solidarity, emancipation, and fairness, and which take climate justice aspects into account.

Notes

1 This introduction has profited very much from the work of our colleagues who were so kind as to review it: Alejandro Camargo, Hartmut Fuenfgeld, Florian

Dünckmann, Robert Hassink, and Jonas Hein. Thank you for this! We are also grateful to our student assistants Cynthia Aurich, Lucas Wogawa, Sarah Hartwig, and Ana González.

2 Following Lukes (2005), Gaventa (2006), and Hein (2016), we understand power as a dynamic social relationship which operates across scales, space and time. Lukes (2005) differentiates between three dimensions of power: visible power, hidden power, and invisible power. Put simply, visible power 'may be understood primarily by looking at who prevails in bargaining over the resolution of key issues' (Gaventa 1982: 14). It refers to resources, such as financial and natural resources and social and political capital, such as being part of or the leader of a (more or less powerful) political party. Hidden power can be described as the ability to set the agenda, to influence the values, beliefs, and procedures that are thinkable and practicable. This often means the exclusion of certain actors and mechanisms of disciplining others. The third dimension of power, invisible power, refers to internalised domination, subordination, and the acceptance of social inequalities as the order of things. The third dimension refers also to the Gramscian concept of hegemony (Hein 2016). It is mostly invisible power that influences how marginalised people interpret and accept the dominant social production of nature, space, and resources (Gaventa 1982: 16–19).

3 This understanding of vulnerability is known as cross-scale integrated vulnerability. Integrative approaches take into account comprehensive definitions of vulnerability (Füssel 2005). Several new conceptual frameworks for analysing vulnerability have emerged; within the more influential ones are the model of 'double structure of vulnerability' from Hans-Georg Bohle (Bohle 2001), the approach 'environmental criticality' by Kasperson *et al.* (2005), the analytical work 'Syndromes of Global Change' of the research group led by Hans Joachim Schellnhuber (Schellnhuber *et al.* 1997), the work on the vulnerability of coupled social-ecological systems of the research network ResilienceAlliance around Crawford S. Holling (Gotts 2007; Gunderson and Holling 2002; Walker *et al.* 2002, 2006), and the hazard-of-place framework, established by Susan L. Cutter (1996).

4 According to Clark *et al.* (2005), vulnerability can be defined 'as people's differential incapacity to deal with hazards, based on the exposition of groups and individuals within both the physical and socials worlds'. It is a function of two characteristics as follows: 'Exposure (the risk of experiencing a hazardous event)' and 'Coping ability, subdivided into resistance (the ability to absorb impacts and continue functioning) and resilience (the ability to recover from losses after an impact)' (Clark *et al.* 2005: 198). Both characteristics are considered, at least partly, as socially constructed:

> exposure [...] is partly socially constructed in that existing land use and daily commuting patterns, to name but two exposure variables, are social and temporal phenomena [...]. Coping ability [...] is influenced by a large list of variables identified by sociologists, geographers, political scientists and other investigators.
>
> (Clark *et al.* 2005: 199)

These variables include age, disability, family structure and social networks, housing and built environment, income and material resources, lifelines (including transportation and communication, building equipment and appliances, emergency response, and hospitals), employment, as well as race and ethnicity (Clark *et al.* 2005: 199, 204).

References

Adger, W.N., 2006. Vulnerability. *Global Environmental Change*, 16 (3), 268–81.

Appadurai, A., 1988. Putting hierarchy in its place. *Cultural Anthropology*, 3, 36–49.

Arnall, A., Kothari, U., and Kelman, I., 2013. Introduction to politics of climate change: discourses of policy and practice in developing countries. *The Geographical Journal*, 18 (43), 11.

Arora-Jonsson, S., 2011. Virtue and vulnerability: Discourses on women, gender and climate change. *Global Environmental Change, Special Issue on the Politics and Policy of Carbon Capture and Storage*, 21 (2), 744–51.

Barnett, J., 2001. Adapting to climate change in Pacific island countries: The problem of uncertainty. *World Development*, 29 (6), 977–93.

Barnett, J., and Campbell, J., 2010. *Climate Change and Small Island States: Power, knowledge and the South Pacific*. London: Earthscan.

Bassett, T.J., and Fogelman, C., 2013. Déjà vu or something new? The adaptation concept in the climate change literature. *Geoforum*, 48, 42–53.

Benda-Beckmann, F. v., von Benda-Beckmann, K., and Griffiths, A., 2009. Mobile people, mobile law: An introduction. *In:* F. von Benda-Beckmann, K. von Benda-Beckmann, and A. Griffiths, eds, *Mobile People, Mobile Law: Expanding legal relations in a contracting world*. Farnham: Ashgate.

Bennett, J., 1969. *Northern Plainsmen: Adaptive strategy and agrarian life*. New York: Aldine.

Bettini, G., 2013. Climate barbarians at the gate? A critique of apocalyptic narratives on 'climate refugees'. *Geoforum*, 45, 63–72.

Blaikie, P., *et al.*, 1994. *At Risk: Natural hazards, people's vulnerability and disasters*. New York: Routledge.

Bohle, H.-G., 2001. Vulnerability and criticality: Perspectives from social geography. *IHDP-Update*, 2, 1–5.

Bravo, M.T., 2009. Voices from the sea ice: The reception of climate impact narratives. *Journal of Historical Geography*, 35 (2), 279–96.

Burton, I., Kates, R.W., and White, G.F., 1978. *The Environment as Hazard*. Oxford: Oxford University Press.

Cameron, E.S., 2012. Securing indigenous politics: A critique of the vulnerability and adaptation approach to the human dimensions of climate change in the Canadian Arctic. *Global Environmental Change*, 22 (1), 103–14.

Cannon, T., and Müller-Mahn, D., 2010. Vulnerability, resilience and development discourses in context of climate change. *Natural Hazards*, 55 (3), 621–35.

Chandler, D., 2014. Beyond neoliberalism: Resilience, the new art of governing complexity. *Resilience*, 2 (1), 47–63.

Chavez-Rodriguez, L., 2014. *Climate Change and Gender: The significance of intersectionality in the social vulnerability in regions under flood risk* (Orig. German title: Klimawandel und Gender: Zur Bedeutung von Intersektionalität für die soziale Vulnerabilität in überflutungsgefährdeten Gebieten). Opladen, DE: Budrich UniPress.

Clark, G.E., *et al.*, 2005. Assessing the vulnerability of coastal communities to extreme storms: The case of Revere, Massachusetts, US. *In:* J.X. Kasperson and R.E. Kasperson, eds, *The Social Contours of Risk: Volume II: Risk analysis, corporations and the globalization of risk*. London: Earthscan.

Cochrane, A., and Ward, K., 2012. Researching the geographies of policy mobility: Confronting the methodological challenges. *Environment and Planning A*, 44, 5–12.

Cochrane, L., 2017. Decolonizing methodologies, *Logan Cochrane*. Available from: www.logancochrane.com/index.php/decolonizing-methodologies [Accessed 19 June 2017].

Cosgove, D., 2008. Images and imagination in twentieth-century environmentalist: From the Sierras to the Poles. *Environment and Planning A*, 40 (8), 1862–80.

Crate, S., 2011. Climate and culture: Anthropology in the era of contemporary climate change. *Annual Review of Anthropology*, 40, 175–94.

Crate, S.A., and Nuttall, M., 2009. Introduction: Anthropology and climate change. *In*: S.A. Crate and M. Nuttall, eds, *Anthropology and Climate Change*. Walnut Creek, CA: Left Coast Press, 9–39.

Cutter, S.L., 1996. Vulnerability to environmental hazards. *Progress in Human Geography*, 20 (4), 529–39.

Daniels, S., and Endfield, G., 2009. Narratives of climate change. *Journal of Historical Geography*, 35 (2), 215–22.

Davoudi, S., 2016. Resilience and the governmentality of unknowns. *In*: M. Bevir, ed., *Governmentality after Neoliberalism*. New York: Routledge, 210–49.

de Sousa Santos, B., 2010. *Descolonizar el saber, reinventar el poder*. Montevideo: Trilce.

de Wit, S., 2014. Denaturalizing adaptation, resocializing the climate: Theoretical and methodological reflections on how to follow a travelling idea of climate change. *In*: F. Gesing, J. Herbeck, and S. Klepp, eds, *Denaturalizing Climate Change: Migration, mobilities and spaces*. Artec paper No. 200. Bremen: University of Bremen, 56–65.

Deleuze, G., and Guattari, F., 1987. *A Thousand Plateaus*. Minneapolis, MN: University of Minnesota Press.

Dietz, K., 2006. Vulnerabilität und Anpassung gegenüber Klimawandel aus sozial-ökologischer Perspektive. *In*: BMBF, ed., *Global Governance und Klimawandel*. Berlin: BMBF.

Dietz, K., 2009. Prima Klima in den Nord-Süd-Beziehungen? Die Antinomien globaler Klimapolitik: Diskurse, Politiken und Prozesse. *In*: H.-J. Burchardt, ed., *Nord-Süd-Beziehungen im Umbruch. Neue Perspektiven auf Staat und Demokratie in der Weltpolitik*. Frankfurt: Campus, 183–218.

Dietz, K., and Brunnengräber, A. 2016. Klimaanpassung. *In*: S. Bauriedl, ed., *Wörterbuch Klimadebatte*. Bielefeld: transcript Verlag, 326.

Donner, S.D., and Webber, S., 2014. Obstacles to climate change adaptation decisions: A case study of sea-level rise and coastal protection measures in Kiribati. *Sustainability Science*, (9) 3, 331–45.

Dow, K., and Downing, T.E., 1995. Vulnerability research: Where things stand. *Human Dimensions Quarterly*, 1, 3–5.

Dreher, T., and Voyer, M., 2014. Climate refugees or migrants? Contesting media frames on climate justice in the Pacific. *Environmental Communication*, 9 (1), 58–76.

Dussel, E., 2001. Eurocentrismo y modernidad. Introducción a las lecturas de Frankfurt. *In*: W. Mignolo, ed., *Capitalismo y geopolítica del conocimiento. El eurocentrismo y la filosofía de la liberación en el debate intelectual contemporáneo*. Buenos Aires: Ediciones del Signo.

Enarson, E., 2007. *Gender Matters: Talking points on gender equality and disaster risk reduction.* Available from: www.gdnonline.org/resources/gendermatters-talkingpoints-ee04.doc [Accessed 28 November 2017].

Eriksen, S.H., Nightingale, A.J., and Eakin, H., 2015. Reframing adaptation: The political nature of climate change adaptation. *Global Environmental Change*, 35, 523–33.

Escobar, A., 2017. Diseño para las transiciones. *Etnografías Contemporáneas*, 3 (4), 32–63.

Evans, B., and Reid, J., 2013. Dangerously exposed: The life and death of the resilient subject. *Resilience*, 1 (2), 83–98.

Fankhauser, S., 1998. *The Costs of Adapting to Climate Change.* Global Environment Facility (GEF) Working Paper No. 16. Washington, DC: GEF.

Farbotko, C., 2010. Wishful sinking: Disappearing islands, climate refugees and cosmopolitan experimentation. *Asia Pacific Viewpoint*, 51 (1), 47–60.

Felli, R., and Castree, N., 2012. Commentary: Neoliberalising adaptation to environmental change: foresight or foreclosure? *Environment and Planning A*, 44 (1), 1–4.

Ferguson, J., 1990. *The Anti-Politics Machine: 'Development', depoliticization, and bureaucratic power in Lesotho.* Minneapolis, MN: University of Minnesota Press.

Ferguson, J., 1994. The anti-politics machine: Development and bureaucratic power in Lesotho. *The Ecologist*, 24 (5), 176–81.

Fog Olwig, M., 2009. Climate change = discourse change? Development and relief organizations' use of the concept of resilience. *In*: K. Hastrup, ed., *The Question of Resilience: Social responses of climate change.* Copenhagen: Royal Danish Academy of Sciences and Letters, 314–36.

Foucault, J.M., 1979. *The Birth of Biopolitics: Lectures at the Collège de France. In*: M. Senellart, ed., 2004. New York: Palgrave.

Füssel, H.-M., 2005. Vulnerability in climate change research: A comprehensive conceptual framework. *Breslauer Symposium*. International and Area Studies, University of California.

Gaillard, J.-C., 2007. Resilience of traditional societies in facing natural hazards. *Disaster Prevention and Management*, 16 (4), 522–44.

Gaillard, J.-C., 2010. Vulnerability, capacity and resilience: Perspectives for climate and development policy. *Journal of International Development*, 22 (2), 218–32.

Gaventa, J., 1982. *Power and Powerlessness: Quiescence and rebellion in an Appalachian valley.* Champaign, IL: University of Illinois Press.

Gaventa, J., 2006. Finding the spaces for change: a power analysis. *IDS bulletin*, 37 (6), 23–33.

Geertz, C., 1963 [1974]. *Agricultural Involution: The process of ecological change in Indonesia.* Berkeley, CA: University of California Press.

GenderCC, 2017. Gender@UNFCCC [webpage]. Available from: http://gendercc.net/genderunfccc.html [Accessed 9 November 2017].

Gesing, F., Herbeck, J., and Klepp, S., eds, 2014. *Denaturalizing Climate Change: Migration, mobilities and spaces.* Artec paper No. 200. Bremen: University of Bremen.

González de la Rocha, M., 2007. The construction of the myth of survival. *Development and Change*, 38 (1), 45–66.

Gotts, N.M. 2007. Resilience, panarchy, and world-systems analysis. *Ecology and Society*, 12 (1), 24. [online] Available from: www.ecologyandsociety.org/vol.12/iss1/art24/ [Accessed 29 December 2017].

Gunderson, L.H., and Holling, C.S., eds, 2002. *Panarchy: Understanding transformations in human and natural systems.* Washington, DC: Island Press.

Harvey, D., 2010. *The Enigma of Capital.* London: Profile Books.

Hastrup, K., 2009. Waterworlds: Framing the question of human resilience. *In*: K. Hastrup, ed., *The Question of Resilience: Social responses to climate change.* Copenhagen: Royal Danish Academy of Sciences and Letters, 11–31.

Hastrup, K., in press. Towards a global imaginary? Climate change and the end of an era in the social sciences. *In*: M. Knecht, *et al.*, eds, *Decentering Europe: Postcolonial, postbloc perspectives for a reflexive European ethnology.* Bielefeld, DE: Transcript.

Hastrup, K., and Fog Olwig, K., eds, 2012. *Climate Change and Mobility: Global challenges to the social sciences.* Cambridge: Cambridge University Press.

Head, L., 2009. Cultural ecology: Adaptation: retrofitting a concept? *Progress in Human Geography*, 34 (2), 234–42.

Hein, J., 2016. *Rescaling Conflictive Access and Property Relations in the Context of REDD+ in Jambi, Indonesia.* Thesis (PhD). Georg August Universität Göttingen.

Herbeck, J., and Flitner, M., 2010. 'A new enemy out there?': Der Klimawandel als Sicherheitsproblem. *Geographica Helvetica*, 65 (3), 198–206.

Hewitt, K., 1997. *Regions of Risk: A geographical introduction to disasters.* London: Longman.

Hillmann, F., *et al.*, 2015. *Environmental Change, Adaptation and Migration: Bringing in the region.* New York: Palgrave Macmillan.

Hulme, M., 2010. Cosmopolitan climates: Hybridity, foresight and meaning. *Theory, Culture and Society*, 27 (2–3), 267–76.

Ingold, T., 1996. The optimal forager and economic man. *In*: P. Descola and G. Pálsson, eds, *Nature and Society: Anthropological perspectives.* London: Routledge.

Ingold, T., 2008. When ANT meets SPIDER: Social theory for arthropods. *In*: C. Knappett and L. Malafouris, eds, *Material Agency.* Berlin: Springer Science + Business Media.

IPCC, 2007. *Climate Change 2007: Impacts, adaptation and vulnerability.* Contribution of Working Group II to the Fourth Assessment Report of the Intergovernmental Panel on Climate Change. *In*: M.L. Parry, *et al.*, eds. Cambridge: Cambridge University Press.

IPCC, 2012. *Managing the Risks of Extreme Events and Disasters to Advance Climate Change Adaptation (SREX): A special report of Working Groups I and II of the Intergovernmental Panel on Climate Change. In*: C.B. Field, *et al.*, eds. Cambridge: Cambridge University Press.

Jasanoff, S., 2010. A new climate for society. *Theory, Culture & Society*, 27 (2–3), 233–53.

Kasperson, J.X., *et al.*, 2005. Vulnerability to global environmental change. *In*: J.X. Kasperson and R.E. Kasperson, eds, *The Social Contours of Risk. Volume II: Risk analysis, corporations and the globalization of risk.* London: Earthscan.

Kelman, I., 2010. Hearing local voices from small island developing states for climate change. *Local Environment*, 15 (7), 605–19.

Kleinman, S., 2007. *Feminist Fieldwork Analysis.* Qualitative Research Methods Series. London: SAGE.

Klepp, S., 2014. Small island states and the new climate change movement: The case of Kiribati. *In*: M. Dietz and H. Garrelts, eds, *Routledge Handbook of the Climate Change Movement.* New York: Routledge, 308–19.

Klepp, S., 2017. Climate change and migration. *Oxford Research Encyclopaedia of Climate Science* [online]. Available from: http://climatescience.oxfordre.com/view/10.1093/acrefore/9780190228620.001.0001/acrefore-9780190228620-e-42 [Accessed 3 April 2017].

Klepp, S., and Herbeck J., 2016. The politics of environmental migration and climate justice in the Pacific region. *Journal of Human Rights and the Environment*, 7 (1), 54–73.

Latour, B., 1996. On actor-network theory: A few clarifications. *Soziale Welt*, 47 (4), 369–82.

Lazrus, H., 2009. The governance of vulnerability: Climate change and agency in Tuvalu, South Pacific. *In*: S.A. Crate and M. Nuttal, eds, *Anthropology and Climate Change: From encounters to actions*. Walnut Creek, CA: Left Coast Press, 240–49.

Liverman, D., 2009. Conventions of climate change: Constructions of danger and the dispossession of the atmosphere. *Journal of Historical Geography*, 35 (2), 279–96.

Lukes, S., 2005. *Power: A radical view*. 2nd edition. New York: Palgrave.

Lykke, N., 2010. *Feminist Studies: A guide to intersectional theory, methodology and writing*. New York: Routledge.

McNamara, K.E., *et al.*, 2018. The complex decision-making of climate-induced relocation: Adaptation and loss and damage. *Climate Policy*, 18 (1), 111–17.

Methmann, C., and Oels, A., 2015. From 'saving' to 'empowering' climate refugees: Rendering climate-induced migration governable through resilience. *Security Dialogue*, 46 (1), 51–68.

Mignolo, W.D., 2012. *Local Histories/Global Designs*. Princeton, NJ: Princeton University Press.

Moloney, S., Fuenfgeld, H., and Granberg, M., eds, 2018. *Local Action on Climate Change: Opportunities and constraints*. New York: Routledge.

Morchain, D., 2016. Why must climate change be de-naturalised and re-politicised and what does that mean? [online]. Available from: www.climateprep.org/stories/2016/10/13/why-must-climate-change-be-de-naturalised-and-re-politicised-and-what-does-that-mean?rq=daniel%20morchain [Accessed 20 June 2017].

Morchain, D., 2017. Does power push knowledge when it comes to development in arid and semi-arid areas? [online]. Available from: www.assar.uct.ac.za/news/does-power-push-knowledge-when-it-comes-development-arid-and-semi-arid-areas [Accessed 19 June 2017].

Parks, B.C., and Roberts, J.T., 2010. Climate change, social theory and justice. *Theory, Culture and Society*, 27 (2–3), 134–66.

Pelling, M., 2011. *Adaptation to Climate Change: From resilience to transformation*. Milton Park: Routledge.

Peluso, N.L., and Watts, M., eds, 2001. *Violent Environments*. Ithaca, NY: Cornell University Press.

Quijano, A., 2000. Colonialidad del poder y clasificación social. *Journal of World-Systems Research*. Festschrift for Immanuel Wallerstein, part I, VI.2, 342–86.

ResilienceAlliance, 2015. About [webpage]. Available from: www.resalliance.org/index.php/about_ra [Accessed 28 November 2017].

Röhr, U., *et al.*, 2008. *Gender Justice as the Basis for Sustainable Climate Policies: A feminist background paper*. Bonn: Genanet – focal point Gender, Environment, Sustainability, German NGO Forum on Environment and Development.

Rudiak-Gould, P., 2012. Promiscuous corroboration and climate change translation: A case study from the Marshall Islands. *Global Environmental Change*, 22 (1), 46–54.

Schellnhuber, H.-J., *et al.*, 1997. Syndromes of global change. *GAIA – Ecological Perspectives for Science and Society*, 6 (1), 18–33.

Schipper, E.L., 2007. Climate change adaptation and development: Exploring the linkages. *Tyndall Centre for Climate Change Research*, WP 107.

Smith, L.T., 1999. *Decolonizing Methodologies: Research and indigenous peoples*. London: Zed Books.

Smith, R., 2013. Should they stay or should they go? A discourse analysis of factors influencing relocation decisions among the outer islands of Tuvalu and Kiribati. *Journal of New Zealand and Pacific Studies*, 1 (1), 23–39.

Sovacool, B.K., and Linnér, B.-O., 2016. *The Political Economy of Climate Change Adaptation*. Basingstoke: Palgrave Macmillan UK.

Steward, J., 1955. *The Theory of Culture Change*. Urbana, IL: University of Illinois Press.

Storey, D., and Hunter, S., 2010. Kiribati: An environmental 'perfect storm'. *Australian Geographer*, 41 (2), 167–81.

Tanner, T., and Allouche, J., 2011. Towards a new political economy of climate change and development. *IDS Bulletin*, 42 (3), 1–14.

Taylor, M., 2015. *The Political Ecology of Climate Change Adaptation: Livelihoods, agrarian change and the conflicts of development*. London: Routledge.

UFZ, 2008. *Deutsche Anpassungsstrategie (DAS) an den Klimawandel – Bericht zum Nationalen Symposium zur Identifizierung des Forschungsbedarfs, 27–28 August 2008*. Conference proceedings. Leipzig, DE: Helmholtz-Zentrum für Umweltforschung.

UN Women and Mary Robinson Foundation – Climate Justice, 2013. *The Full View: Advancing the goal of gender balance in multilateral and intergovernmental processes*. UN Women [online]. Available from: www.mrfcj.org/pdf/2013-06-07_The-Full-View.pdf [Accessed 9 November 2017].

Walgenbach, K., 2007. *Gender als interdependente Kategorie: neue Perspektiven auf Intersektionalität, Diversität und Heterogenität*. Opladen, DE: Budrich.

Walker, B., *et al.*, 2002. *Resilience Management in Social-ecological Systems: A working hypothesis for a participatory approach conservation ecology* [online], 6. Available from: www.consecol.org/vol. 6/iss1/art14/ [Accessed 16 April 2013].

Walker, B., *et al.*, 2006. Exploring resilience in social-ecological systems through comparative studies and theory development: Introduction to the special issue. *Ecology and Society*, 11 (1): 12. [online] Available from: www.ecologyandsociety.org/vol. 11/iss1/art12/ [Accessed 28 November 2017].

Walters, W., 2012. *Governmentality: Critical encounters (Vol. 3)*. New York: Routledge.

Watts, M.J., 2015. Now and then: The origin of political ecology and the rebirth of adaptation as a form of thought. *In*: T. Perreault, G. Bridge, and J. McCarthy, eds, *The Routledge Handbook of Political Ecology*. New York: Routledge, 19–51.

Watts, M.J., and Bohle, H.G., 1993. The space of vulnerability: The causal structure of hunger and famine. *Progress in Human Geography*, 17 (1), 43–67.

Webber, S., 2013. Performative vulnerability: Climate change adaptation policies and financing in Kiribati. *Environment and Planning A*, 45 (11), 2717–33.

Weichselgartner, J., and Kelman, I., 2015. Geographies of resilience – Challenges and opportunities of a descriptive concept. *Progress in Human Geography*, 39 (3), 249–67.

Weisser, F., *et al.*, 2014. Translating the 'adaptation to climate change' paradigm: The politics of a travelling idea in Africa. *The Geographical Journal*, 180 (2), 111–19.

West, C., and Fenstermaker, S., 1995. Doing difference. *Gender & Society*, 9 (1), 8–37.

Wolff, J., and De-Shalit, A., 2007. *Disadvantage*. Oxford: Oxford University Press.

Part II
Conceptualising climate change adaptation

2 A clash of adaptations

How adaptation to climate change is translated in northern Tanzania

Sara de Wit

Introduction: on the emerging geographies of adaptation

Since 'adaptation' has made its way into the international climate change regime of the United Nations Framework Convention on Climate Change (UNFCCC) alongside mitigation – as one of the two fundamental pillars of global action – an increasing tone of urgency has come to dominate both the policy and research agenda. While it is acknowledged that adaptation needs to take place at all scales to complement mitigation efforts, it is argued that those populations with the least resources have the least capacity to adapt (IPCC 2001: 8). Largely underpinned by the several scientific assessment reports of the Intergovernmental Panel on Climate Change (IPCC), it is now widely recognised that, in order to cope with the effects of climate change, for many communities in the most vulnerable parts of the world, planned and strategic adaptation planning is not just an option but a sheer necessity (IPCC 2014a). It can be said therefore that the adaptation to climate change paradigm has reached the status of being the *sine qua non* for the survival of the Global South. If we take a closer look at the (expected) uneven distribution of the consequences of climate change worldwide, we are immediately confronted with the stark opposition between the developed world on the one hand, and the developing world on the other (nowadays this distinction is more often subsumed under the Global North versus the Global South). The profound inequality entailed by climate change on a global scale has led some authors and policymakers to conclude that climate change has become one of *the* defining contemporary international development issues (Tanner and Allouche 2011: 1). It comes therefore as no surprise that climate change adaptation has been appropriated by the realm of development cooperation. In addition, the United Nations Development Programme (UNDP) has stated that climate change is the defining human development issue of our generation (UNDP 2007/2008: 1).

In part due to the Global North's historical responsibility and concomitant international pressure to compensate and support the Global South in its adaptation pursuit – as outlined by the convention principles (Article

3.1, UNFCCC 1992) – billions of dollars have been pledged for adaptation finance. In response to the anticipated bleak future for the world's poorest populations – and linking global development targets such as the United Nations 2030 Agenda and its associated sustainable development goals (SDGs) – the related policy imperative has addressed what kind of adaptation policies are needed, and how they can best be developed, applied, and funded. Furthermore, a vast body of literature has simultaneously emerged that, although diverse and broad, has largely addressed the basic questions of how and to what extent adaptation can reduce the impacts of climate change (Burton *et al.* 2002: 145). Considering the increasing scholarly engagement with the concept of adaptation, it is striking to find that the majority of studies aim to contribute to a better understanding of (how to enhance) adaptation, while a glaring absence exists of enquiries into the ideological underpinnings of this question (de Wit 2015, 2017). As such, in part due to the urgency of the adaptation pursuit, questions related to the political economy and thus the structural or systemic considerations about what made people vulnerable to climate change in the first place are by and large left unscrutinised. It is worth mentioning that recently an emerging body of work from the social sciences has called for the need to critically interrogate the discursive framings within which adaptation emerges, or looks at the politics of adaptation in the developing world (see Tanner and Allouche 2011; de Wit 2014; Gesing *et al.* 2014; Weisser *et al.* 2014; Arnall *et al.* 2015; Taylor 2015). Before elaborating on this point, let us first briefly explore some potential reasons for the naturalising impetus that drives adaptation.

It is obvious that there is a fine line between what constitutes adaptation to climate change and what is generally understood as a 'conventional' development issue. Hence the debate about whether adaptation should be treated as additional to, or rather as an integral part of, development has received much attention but is far from settled (for a systematic literature review on this topic, see Sherman *et al.* 2016). For instance, some authors have argued that it is highly problematic to subsume the one under the other (Cannon and Müller-Mahn 2010); others have emphasised that 'doing adaptation' will inevitably feed positively into general development aims or vice versa (e.g. Ayers and Huq 2009), which supports the idea that adaptation and development could be tackled in the same way (Sherman *et al.* 2016: 708). However, in a recent critique of adaptation, Marcus Taylor has noted that in the haste to unite development with adaptation, the idea of adaptation that underpins these governing efforts has received relatively little scrutiny. This is in part due, Taylor argues, to the fact that adaptation – with its roots in evolutionary biology – is seen as part and parcel of, and common to, all forms of life. This seemingly natural response entailed by the discourse of adaptation – that treats climate as an externality – provides a fertile ground for a technocratic politics of intervention (Taylor 2015: xi). In addition to this evolutionary principle, it will be argued in the following, that there are other ideological underpinnings of this paradigm that tend to *naturalise* adaptation as the only and indispensable way forward. In fact, some of the recent critique that has been directed at adaptation – largely from the social sciences – bears similarities to the body of post-colonial critique of development, such as Ferguson's 'anti-politics machine of development' (Ferguson 1990), or more implicitly, Escobar's critique of development that conceives of social life as solely a technical problem (Escobar 1995).

Notwithstanding the disputed nature of conceptualisations over adaptation vis-à-vis development, in line with Taylor, this chapter forecloses this debate and argues that there is fertile ground to explore adaptation as a new field of development discourse and practice. Not just because it has given rise to an array of complex new knowledge regimes, operating frameworks for non-governmental organisations (NGOs) and civil society organisations (CSOs), adaptation projects, and research institutions etc. that all seek to enhance the adaptation capacities of the most vulnerable populations in the Global South, but all the more so owing to the apocalyptic aura with which this paradigm is imbued. In other words, the adaptation discourse is not just a scientific measurement mirroring a society's vulnerability to an external climate, but it is also a cultural discourse revealing certain predispositions and values of the knowledge regimes within which the idea has emerged. For instance, we clearly hear the echoes of time of certain Western discourses of 'tropicality' and development in which faraway places epitomised danger and 'otherness', both environmentally and culturally. It is in a similar vein that geographer Andrew Baldwin has argued that the cultural discourse on climate change and migration operates, in part, as a function of the security apparatus, and can be located within the registers of race (or 'white' affect) and difference (Baldwin 2016). By dividing the world into those who can and those who cannot adapt, this imagery is perpetuated by the looming catastrophe of climate change, which renders the Global South once more 'vulnerable', disaster-ridden, poverty-stricken and disaster-prone (see Bankoff 2001). Moreover, it is the same discourse that puts the 'salvation' of the Global South in the hands of the industrialised nations by sharing their expertise and technology and making funds available. As Bankoff (2001) has compellingly argued, Western discourses on disasters form part of a wider historical and cultural geography of risk that generates and maintains a specific image of large parts of the world as dangerous places. Drawing on Bankoff's critique of natural disasters as cultural discourse, Table 2.1 shows that we can meaningfully transpose the table on 'hazard as cultural discourse' to the realm of vulnerability as a concept that renders particular regions of the world as 'adaptation deficient'.

Considering that in many parts of the Global South the adaptation paradigm is already running its own course as a complex field of knowledge and power, translated by, and embedded within, both existing and

Table 2.1 Adopted from *Rendering the World Unsafe: 'Vulnerability' as Western discourse* (Bankoff 2001: 28)

Concept	Period	Condition	Cure/technology
Tropicality	17th – 19th/early 20th century	Disease	Western medicine
Development	Post-Second World War	Poverty	Western investment/aid
Natural disasters	Late 20th century	Hazard	Western science
Adaptation	21st century	Climate change (exacerbating a range of societal ills)	Science, technology (expertise) and funds provided by the 'developed nations'

emerging institutions, it is a timely exercise to scrutinise the discursive framework within which this paradigm unfolds, as well as to examine the 'truth effects' (i.e. how truth is created in discourse, see Foucault 1980) that it brings into being. Against this background, therefore, this chapter seeks to contribute to the emerging body of critical scholarship that explores adaptation not just as a normative concept that asks how people are supposed to adapt to an externally changing environment, but rather how people adapt to the *idea* of adaptation itself. It will do so by exploring adaptation as a travelling idea (Hulme 2009; Weisser *et al.* 2014; de Wit 2014, 2015) that is continuously translated and interpreted by different actors along its journey in rather contingent and unpredictable ways.

This chapter begins with briefly scrutinising the historical roots of the discursive framings as the background to the ways in which adaptation discourses are currently advancing, particularly as far as sub-Saharan Africa is concerned. My basic argument is that this new type of crisis narration risks concealing the truth effects and political nature of making claims to crisis in the first place (on the financial crisis see Roitman 2014). Furthermore, by employing the concept of a travelling idea, in this chapter I seek to move beyond the mere post-colonial critique that takes adaptation as a 'Western' and 'hegemonic' discourse that is imposed upon the rest of the world, but rather as an idea that is continuously brought into being through encounters, as it is translated by manifold actors and embedded within a range of networks and material–semiotic assemblages. The notion of a material–semiotic assemblage clearly draws on science and technology studies (STS)-inspired approaches and takes as a basic point of departure that ideas themselves cannot travel, but that they always need to be materialised (either in speech, persons, or artefacts) before they can be conveyed and put into motion (see for instance Czarniawska 2002, cited by Czarniawska and Sevón 2005). From this more general discussion, I will move to an in-depth and ethnographic exploration of the ways in which the adaptation paradigm is translated in northern Tanzania. Based on 14 months of fieldwork, I interrogate the power dynamics that are entailed by this translation process, which leads to conflicting notions of adaptation between the government of Tanzania on the one hand and the Maasai (agro)pastoralists and NGOs representing them, on the other. As such, it will be argued that the adaptation paradigm deserves critical scrutiny well beyond its normative outlook (how people can or should adapt), and more attention is needed to the ideological workings (its discursive and material structures) that might empower some actors while disempowering others.

On Africa's horizon: between adaptation and the apocalypse

The ways in which the discourse on adaptation to climate change concerning Africa is advancing can largely be characterised by the language of vulnerability, disaster, hazard, inequality, poverty, and lack of adaptive capacity. Let us consider a few findings from the IPCC assessment reports (specifically, the regional chapters on Africa). In its fourth assessment report, the IPCC stated that:

> Africa is one of the most vulnerable continents to climate change and climate variability, a situation aggravated by the interaction of 'multiple stresses', occurring at various levels, and low adaptive capacity. Some adaptation to current climate variability is taking place; however, this may be insufficient for future changes in climate.
> (High confidence, Boko *et al.* 2007, Executive Summary)

In its most basic sense it is thus predicted that the current level of 'autonomous adaptation' will be insufficient for the expected harmful effects brought about by future (anthropogenic) climate change – hence the need for strategic and coordinated adaptation planning. This worrying trend is asserted in the fifth assessment, in which the IPCC stated:

> Climate change and climate variability have the potential to exacerbate or multiply existing threats to human security including food, health, economic insecurity, all being of particular concern for Africa.
> (Medium confidence, Niang *et al.* 2014: 1202)

> The assessment of significant residual impacts in a 2°C world at the end of the 21st century suggests that even under high levels of adaptation, there would be very high levels of risk for Africa. At global mean temperature increase of 4°C, risks for Africa's food security are very high, with limited potential for risk reduction through adaptation.
> (Niang *et al.* 2014: 1204)

What can be gleaned from these scientific calculations is that the adaptation paradigm is predicated upon the fundamental distinction between the climate – which operates as an external variable on the one hand – and society with its alleged internal adaptation logic on the other. This Cartesian dichotomy denies the basic idea that humans (society, culture, language, etc.) are not just *outside* their climates, but rather an integral part of it. Thus, through this separation, as Taylor also argues, climate change is isolated from the ongoing processes of social and ecological transformation that construct our lived environments (Taylor 2015: xiii). What follows from this representation of the climate as an 'intelligible' but complex and technocratic problem are the managerial solutions offered to us by trained experts, predominantly found in the developed, or 'advanced', nations.[1] For instance, according to the IPCC, Africa is expected to face an 'adaptation deficit' that needs to be tackled:[2]

> There is increased evidence of the significant financial resources, technological support, and investment in institutional and capacity development needed to address climate risk, build adaptive capacity, and implement robust adaptation strategies [*high confidence*]. Funding and technology transfer and support is needed to both address Africa's current adaptation deficit and to protect rural and urban livelihoods, societies, and economies from climate change impacts at different local scales.
>
> (Niang *et al.* 2014: 1204)

In other words, expert discourses convey that Africa's future, as far as climate change adaptation is concerned, does not look very bright. These predictions by the natural sciences – which are further translated into policy guidelines, can even be characterised by an *apocalyptic imagery* and *vocabulary* – everything that is being said and visualised about Africa and climate change appears solely in terms of crisis, terror, fear, extinction, doom and decay, deficit, vulnerability, etc. Against this background, I share Kirsten Hastrup's critique, which is directed to both natural and social sciences, that '[…] climate is no longer seen to make places but rather mostly to destroy them' (Hastrup 2015: 146).

The solution that has followed from this supposition of a state of 'deficiency' has been the construction of an 'adaptation imperative' (Ban Ki-Moon 2009; WRI 2010–11; Wisner *et al.* 2012). Common phrases that we hear are '[f]or many in Africa adaptation is not an option but a necessity' (Niang *et al.* 2014). In brief, the only pathway to salvation is by welcoming the expertise, money, and technologies of the developed and technologically more advanced nations. It will be argued that what follows from this all too familiar and repetitive story about Africa's 'crisis' echoes historically produced discourses, which in the context of my research in Tanzania has led to a reproduction of certain questions and scientific misconceptions. It is important to note, however, that on the African continent this vulnerability discourse is not necessarily supported by the

African delegates to the international climate change negotiations. For instance, allow me to share my encounter with Brian, an experienced climate change negotiator for the African Group[3] (to assure anonymity names of informants have been changed). Trained as a climatologist and working for the Botswana Government for 28 years at the Ministry of Environment, he has been part of the negotiations since the very inception of the Kyoto Protocol in 1997:

> Although science tells us that we are the most vulnerable, it is usually because the measure of vulnerability is based on infrastructural development and development at large. But at the same time, we haven't actually talked about how resilient we are to climate variability. I think Africans tend to be very resilient to climate variability! I tell my counterparts in Europe that in a lot of African countries, particularly in the Savannah, people are used to staying six months without rain, eight months without rain. They probably only have about between 40 and 100 days of rain a year. That shows a level of resilience to me, we know a lot of droughts, climate shocks that we go through. And because of all of that I think we should be blowing our trumpet in terms of resilience!
>
> (Interview during the African Ministerial Conference on the Environment (AMCEN) in Arusha, 2013)

Brian's account resonated with many of the NGO representatives in northern Tanzania, speaking in the name of the Maasai communities who live in such semi-arid regions where drought, climate variability, and uncertainty are common. By probing some of the counter voices and narratives that have emerged in northern Tanzania, the following account will give insight into the intricate and contested trajectories of adaptation and the ways in which it is translated by different actors. Whereas the government of Tanzania sees the Maasai both as environmental destroyers as well as the most vulnerable people in the face of climate change, the NGOs representing them argue that they are *masters* of adaptation instead. Finally, an insight into the grassroots voices brings to our attention the fact that adaptation is not serving the interest of all actors in the translation chain. In the following I bring to the fore a few dissenting voices that generally find no resonance on global platforms – and serve as 'tokens', or fulfil a symbolic presence of the subaltern – that often get silenced and 'black-boxed' all along the way. I found it striking to observe that the fiercest opposition to this new discourse on adaptation came from the grassroots. Is it not paradoxical that the greatest resistance to this new paradigm comes from the very people that it seeks to aid? I will explore this paradox by analysing some of the different voices that have emerged in the adaptation community in Tanzania.

On sedimented practices: how adaptation entangles old power struggles

An inherent feature of the structural logic of international development aid is that new or fashionable paradigms inevitably shape and inform the on-the-ground landscape of development organisations. This process by which organisations set, and continuously reframe, their development goals in accordance with international standards – a process of co-optation (Fisher 1997) – has similarly led in northern Tanzania to the emergence of a true 'adaptation community'. Many of the regional NGOs and CSOs that were originally established, for instance, to fight for the rights of indigenous peoples, or for the protection of land rights or sustainability have by now also embraced the adaptation to climate change discourse. In northern Tanzania, where many NGOs can be found, the lexicon of development issues that preceded adaptation comprised issues such as 'livelihood resilience', 'poverty reduction', 'reducing vulnerability', 'adaptive environmental management', 'strengthening customary leadership institutions', 'natural resources management', and 'coping strategies', all of which lend themselves fairly well to a re-labelling of projects in adaptation planning in the drylands. In addition to the structural logic of development aid that informs the translation of adaptation into new projects, there is also something inherently flexible to the idea of adaptation itself. As Ben Orlove concluded in the context of his study in Peru:

> Because of its loose, multifaceted quality, the term 'adaptation' allows the organizations to continue working in areas in which they already have expertise: small-scale technical assistance in one case, disaster relief or water development in others. It also lets them to function in a familiar world of projects, in which they submit and receive proposals, manage budgets and personnel, run and evaluate projects themselves, and produce reports and other briefings.
>
> (Orlove 2009: 158)

The concept of adaptation is, in its broadest sense, thus remarkably open and prone to strategic hijacking by varying actors and serving different purposes. For instance, what I found in Tanzania was that – particularly for political leaders – climate change came in handy as a scapegoat to cast away highly contentious issues such as land grab, and consequently explain the vulnerability of local communities in terms of climate change (de Wit 2014). Moreover, the ways in which adaptation is recast reveals deeply entrenched convictions – that for a long time have been grounded in scientific misconceptions – of government officials that represent the Maasai herders as having an irrational relationship with their cattle, and thus being culpable of degrading the very environment in which they live. Over time these ideas have not only perpetuated processes of 'ethnic othering' but have also provided a theoretical foundation for rangeland management systems that advocated either the reduction of livestock numbers, total abandonment of pastoralism, raising livestock in sedentary settings, commercial ranging, or the privatisation of rangeland resources (Igoe 2002; McCabe 2003). In other words, the history of perceptions of the relationship between the Maasai pastoralists with their cattle and their environment has been fraught with controversy. And currently, while the travelling idea of adaptation is revitalising these very same misconceptions and prejudices of the Maasai as 'backward' and in need of education (from the side of policymakers and the government), it is the same idea that has given way to a counter narrative that will be elaborated on below. In order to understand the translation of adaptation we need a brief socio-political contextualisation of this region, and an insight into the historically produced antagonistic relationship between the national government on the one hand and the agro-pastoral Maasai on the other, to which I will now turn.

The northern part of Tanzania is home to a spectacular abundance of wildlife and biodiversity hotspots. As such, Maasailand and the wider region have been exposed to a range of transnational conservation paradigms, and policies that have travelled to Tanzania before. The most tangible effect of the conservation agenda has been the long history of land grab at the expense of local communities that used to dwell in these areas. As anthropologist Benjamin Gardner recently put it: 'It is not unreasonable to read the history of the Maasai in East Africa as one long land grab in the name of global conservation and national development' (Gardner 2016: 19). It drives too far to elaborate on this complex history in the context of this chapter, but for the moment it will suffice as the background against which we need to understand the emerging dissenting voices that oppose the adaptation to climate change paradigm. Terrat village, where I carried out a large part of my research, has not been exempt from conservation policies. The village is located on the outskirts of Tarangire National Park, which became a game reserve in 1957 and was 'upgraded' to a national park in 1970. The designation of Tarangire as a national park remains a painful memory for people who were evicted (Igoe and Brockington 1999; Igoe 2002). During the wet season Terrat faces a large wildlife influx, which means that cattle must compete for grasses and water with the wild animals (see Figure 2.1). While the wild ungulates graze and give birth in Terrat, the Maasai cannot enter the national park with their herds, which is highly problematic during the dry season, because the most important water sources are found inside the park. Against this background, it is not surprising that many herders in Terrat found climate change an all too easy explanation for the increasing lack of water and pastures in their vicinity; they rather said that it was due to overpopulation and the politics of land use.

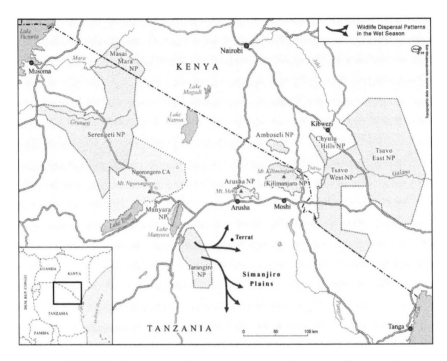

Figure 2.1 Wildlife dispersal in the wet season into Terrat, a village on the outskirts of Tarangire National Park, northern Tanzania.

Source: Monika Feinen, University of Cologne, adapted from openstreetmap.org

Let us now consider a few different voices that have emerged in the
adaptation to climate change community in Tanzania. During one of the
many conferences on climate change that I attended, where stakeholders
from different communities were present, a government official (the leading
climate change negotiator for Tanzania) gave a very clear statement concerning his ideas on the adaptation future for the Maasai:

> I think that due to the current condition we should have a collective
> desire for change. These people [*the Maasai pastoralists*] may not
> change without educating them. This training is so important to them;
> they should get the education so that they can do the productive live-
> stock keeping. Keeping the livestock depending on the availability of
> pastures. And we witness the conflict that occurs between pastoralists
> and farmers when the pastoralists try to get pasture or water for their
> livestock. As I said: I don't think that these people could move from
> one place to another if they could have been given education. I think
> all of that could not have happened if they only could get that educa-
> tion. They should realize that there is no other way for the society to

survive, except by accepting the experts from the private sector and the government's effort.
(Public hearing 'Have you heard us?' November 2011, Dar es Salaam)

We clearly hear the echoes of time in which older scientific paradigms emerged that have been similarly infused with ideas of pastoralists being the main cause of overgrazing, environmental degradation, poaching, overstocking, and poor resource management. Old scientific paradigms and Western misconceptions about the Maasai as destroyers of the environment and about pastoral inefficiency continued to shape range-land policies that advocated for the total abandonment of pastoralism, a sedentary life, reduction in herd sizes, or the privatisation of rangeland resources (Igoe 2002; McCabe 2003; Sachedina 2008). Today the government of Tanzania as well as the media are perpetuating the discourse that the Maasai are causing global warming and have exceeded the 'carrying capacity' of their land. In a basic sense, the notion of carrying capacity denotes the prejudice about the Maasai as having too many cattle and being irresponsible dwellers of their environment – as also became clear during an interview that I had with a senior climate change negotiator that worked at the Vice President's Office (VPO) in Tanzania for the 'adaptation programme'. When I asked him about the adaptation options for the Maasai, he exclaimed:

Do you know the figures of the carrying capacity? The Maasai have really exceeded this number! They think that they can wander around the whole country. You should go to the ministry of livestock and get the numbers, because this is really a great problem that we have in Tanzania.
(Interview with a government official at the VPO, March 2013, Dar es Salaam)

It is remarkable to observe that when speaking about adaptation and pastoralism, instead of pointing to sustainable solutions, the policy vocabulary is regularly cast in terms of 'perpetrators' and highlights the irresponsible ways in which (Maasai) pastoralists relate to their environment. Moreover, the desire to radically change the lifestyle of the Maasai, as expressed by the government official above, is a widely shared opinion among government officials in Tanzania (de Wit 2017). In the National Adaptation Programme of Action, which is the official policy paper that guides long-term adaptation policies in the country, it is stated that the existing number of cattle in Tanzania has already surpassed the normal carrying capacity in most areas (URT 2007: 7). The proposed solutions for the pastoralists include: 'The change of land use patterns, education of farmers and livestock keepers, sustainable range management, control the movement of livestock and advocate zero grazing' (URT 2007: 22).

It is important to point out that for the agro-pastoral Maasai, mobility is their most important adaptation strategy. Therefore, what for the government is translated as solid adaptation strategies – so that they can control the movement of the herders – are for the Maasai rather the *antithesis* of adaptation (see also de Wit 2014). The fact that these paradigms (which were informed by colonial, and later Western range ideas based on 'productivity' and 'efficiency') overlooked complex social relations of production, exchange networks, and reciprocal ties of Maasai systems (Homewood and Rodgers 1991, cited in Bwagalilo and Mwakipesile 2012: 11), attests to widely held prejudices of policymakers that see the Maasai as backward, careless planners. As mentioned earlier, these deep-rooted conceptions reappear over and over again, as they are given new life through the adaptation to climate change paradigm. The irony of conservation discourses is that it is predicated upon the fundamental idea that nature needs to be protected from the irrational Maasai, which ultimately legitimises the creation of national parks and the eviction of Maasai from their traditional grazing lands.

Dissenting voices: the emergence of counter narratives

Largely informed by international discourses, the Maasai agro-pastoralists are perceived to be the most vulnerable community to the effects of climate change (URT 2007). However, many Maasai (from the grassroots, and the NGOs who represent the Maasai) are of a different opinion. In fact, they argue, the Maasai are rather *masters* of adaptation. Pastoralism is a livelihood *system* that should be understood in its full complexity, within which livelihood diversification like crop production and wage labour (Leslie and McCabe 2013), but foremost mobility and a large herd size, are the key coping mechanisms for cattle to survive during severe droughts (see Goldman and Riosmena 2013). In addition to the government official mentioned above, it is interesting to consider the account of an influential Maasai NGO worker who – with more than 25 years of experience in the field of development in the drylands – opposed the statement of the government official as follows:

> Climate change is not new in Africa, especially for pastoralists. They are masters of adaptation; they have key strategies and knowledge. You don't need to tell them about climate change, this is not new to them. They will tell you! The only problem is the laws and policies in our country. Our government is ignorant and there is a big knowledge gap. [...] All we need to have acknowledged is that the livelihoods of pastoralists is a system, and that mobility is part of it. [...] Our leaders are very embarrassed. 52 billion dollars are collected in Ngorongoro Conservation Area and people are dying of hunger! One Maasai man saw that the water in his vicinity was gone, so he followed a pipe and

saw that the water was being used to flush the toilets of tourists. One flush of a toilet is enough to keep a Maasai family alive for two days! Tourists need glittering toilets. Then the Maasai man rightfully complained: 'and then they tell us about conservation.'

In other words, this NGO worker turned the argument around and effectively communicated that it is not the Maasai who need to be educated, but rather those in power who need to understand that pastoralism is a highly complex and strategic system in which mobility forms the lifeblood of adaptation. Considering the historical continuity of the hijacking of scientific misconceptions by those in power – usually at the expense of the pastoralists' interests – I believe that we can understand the newly coined term 'masters of adaptation' as an explicit move to counter the victimisation of pastoral communities. During interviews with development brokers, the term 'masters of adaptation' was frequently mentioned to characterise the agency of pastoral livelihoods, and it also featured in newspaper articles (representing CSO voices), as well as in policy briefs and conference reports. We have to understand this discourse in opposition to the Maasai being portrayed as 'reckless wanderers' in need of education, a concept that emphasises agency and denotes a more sophisticated environmental understanding and sustainable livelihood instead. The emergence of this counter narrative is not to say that we can discard the need for adaptation support altogether, but it rather invites us to take seriously the alternative strategies that are employed to contest hegemonic discourses, and thus should prompt us to 'listen to, rather than speak for' the grassroots communities (see also the work of Hodgson 2011a, 2011b).

Let me conclude by bringing one voice from the grassroots to the fore, which – as became clear throughout my research – represents a larger group of Maasai from the grassroots. The following quote summarises the opinion of Adam, a Maasai herder who participated in one of the climate change workshops. From his account and his tone of voice, it was clear that he was very annoyed with the rhetoric around climate change, and expressed his anger at the government of Tanzania instead:

> The government in this country is using a lot of money to protect animals like giraffe, elephant, but it does not even use a single shilling to protect a person known as the pastoralist. We are in danger of being chased away by the government in our land where we have been living on for several years. So how will this strategy help us so that we are going to have assurance of our land, which we are using for pastoralism? Because for me the big threat to pastoralists is not climate change! The big threat is that the government is going to take away our land and increase vulnerability to pastoralists. To me this is the issue. To me climate change is not the issue.

Adam's account illustrates that vulnerability for people at the grassroots brings highly contested issues to the fore that have more to do with structural issues related to the (global) political economy than with climate change as such. Thus we need to understand what adaptation means for different people, and so gain insight into the politics of land use. Moreover, as I have argued elsewhere, it appears that climate change is increasingly serving as an all-explanatory framework for all societal ills in Africa (de Wit 2017). This tendency has rightfully been criticised by scholars such as Mike Hulme as some sort of neo-environmental determinism in which climate is elevated as the single and predominant determinant of social life, in an otherwise complex matrix of causal relations (Hulme 2011). Against this background, therefore, we need to be increasingly wary of representations that depict Africa's vulnerability or adaptation deficit as being predominantly induced by (anthropogenic) climate change, and instead bring complexity and locally embedded intricacies back into the picture.

Concluding remarks

This chapter began with a critical de-framing of the ways in which global adaptation discourses are advancing, and argued that its current framing sparks an old and repetitive story about Africa being in crisis, which reinforces the dependency relations between developed nations (Global North) and the developing world (Global South). From a critique of the techno-scientific framing of adaptation and the managerial solutions that are consequently proposed, I moved to an exploration of how the idea of adaptation is translated in northern Tanzania. In this brief translation journey I have tried to show how a 'clash of adaptations' can occur in a context where adaptation means different things to different actors, and that for those in power it can be employed as a resource to pursue their own interests. This should remind us that notwithstanding the alarming climate change predictions that are constructed globally, we must keep listening to those voices at the fringes of the world, for whom adaptation might mean something more complex than solely being a matter of a changing climate. Therefore, we should not only pay attention to the question of how people across the globe should adapt to climate change, but also how the ideological underpinnings of this question can be brought to light. In this chapter I have demonstrated that instead of following the common trend that embraces the need for adaptation at face value, critical scrutiny of the emergent politics of adaptation can reveal the truth effects and conflicting interests that the idea of adaptation brings into being. Furthermore, the main problem with treating adaptation as the new and overwhelming determinant of social life inducing vulnerability is that it hides crucial political questions that have produced inequalities in the first place. Giving insight into the translation through which Maasai from the grassroots express their unwillingness to accept climate change as a new hegemonic explanatory framework reveals that – as they argue – it is not the climate they fear, but the politics of land perpetuated by their own government.

Notes

1 It is worth mentioning that in the latest IPCC assessment reports and the UNFCCC there has been an increasing recognition of the importance of the social sciences and the role of indigenous knowledge in understanding adaptation responses (United Nations 2016). Moreover, there is a general growing awareness of the need to incorporate 'alternative epistemologies' that are rooted outside climate science (Jasanoff 2003).
2 The adaptation deficit is defined as: 'The gap between the current state of a system and a state that minimizes adverse impacts from existing climate conditions and variability' (IPCC 2014b).
3 Traditionally, parties to the United Nations are organised into regional groups, but for the climate negotiations other groupings also exist for political purposes, such as the least developed countries (LDCs) and Alliance of Small Island States (AOSIS) etc.

References

Arnall, A., Kothari, U., and Kelman, I., 2015. Introduction to the politics of climate change: Discourses of policy and practice in developing countries. *The Geographical Journal*, 180 (2), 98–101.

Ayers, J.M., and Huq, S., 2009. Supporting adaptation to climate change: What role for official development assistance? *Development Policy Review*, 27, 675–92.

Baldwin, A., 2016. Premediation and white affect: Climate change and migration in critical perspective. *Transactions of the Institute of British Geographers*, 41, 78–90.

Ban Ki-Moon, 2009. Adapting to climate change. *UN Secretary General's Address in Ulaanbaatar* (Mongolia), 27 July.

Bankoff, G., 2001. Rendering the world unsafe: 'Vulnerability' as Western discourse. *Disasters*, 25 (1), 19–35.

Boko, M., *et al.*, 2007. Africa. *Climate Change 2007: Impacts, adaptation and vulnerability. Contribution of Working Group II to the Fourth Assessment Report of the Intergovernmental Panel on Climate Change. In*: M.L. Parry, *et al.*, eds. Cambridge: Cambridge University Press, 433–67.

Burton, I.H., *et al.*, 2002. From impact assessment to adaptation priorities: The shaping of adaptation policy. *Climate Policy*, 2 (2–3), 145–59.

Bwagalilo, F., and Mwakipesile, A., 2012. *Impacts of Climate Change and Land Use Patterns and Livelihoods of Pastoralists and Hunter Gatherers: A case study of Mbulu, Hanang, Kiteto and Simanjiro Districts*, submitted to PINGO's Forum.

Cannon, T., and Müller-Mahn, D., 2010. Vulnerability, resilience, and development discourses in context of climate change. *Natural Hazards*, 55 (3), 621–35.

Czarniawska, B., 2002. *A Tale of Three Cities, or the Glocalization of City Management*. Oxford: Oxford University Press.

Czarniawska, B., and Sevón G., 2005. Introduction to *Global Ideas: How ideas, objects, and practices travel in the global economy*. Malmö: Liber.

de Wit, S., 2014. Denaturalizing adaptation, resocializing the climate: Theoretical and methodological considerations on how to follow a travelling idea of climate change. *In*: F. Gesing, J. Herbeck, and S. Klepp, eds, *Denaturalizing Climate Change: Migration, mobilities and space*, 56–64. Artec-paper 200.

de Wit, S., 2015. *Global Warning: An ethnography of the encounter between global and local climate-change discourses in the Bamenda Grassfields, Cameroon*. Leiden, NL: African Studies Centre.

de Wit, S., 2017. *Love in Times of Climate Change: How an idea of adaptation to climate change travels to northern Tanzania*. Thesis (PhD). University of Cologne.

Escobar, A., 1995. *Encountering Development: The making and unmaking of the third world*. Princeton, NJ: Princeton University Press.

Ferguson, J., 1990. *The Anti-Politics Machine: 'Development,' depoliticization, and bureaucratic power in Lesotho*. Cambridge: Cambridge University Press.

Fisher, W.F., 1997. Doing good? The politics and anti-politics of NGO practices. *Annual Review of Anthropology Annual*, 26 (4), 439–64.

Foucault, M., 1980. Truth and power. *In*: C. Gordon, ed., *Power/Knowledge: Selected interviews and other writings 1972–1977*. Hemel Hempstead: Harvester Wheatsheaf.

Gardner, B., 2016. *Selling the Serengeti: The cultural politics of safari tourism*. Athens, GA: University of Georgia Press.

Gesing, F., Johannes, H., and Klepp, S., 2014. *Denaturalizing Climate Change: Migration, mobilities and space*. Artec-paper 200.

Goldman, M.J., and Riosmena F., 2013. Adaptive capacity in Tanzanian Maasailand: Changing strategies to cope with drought in fragmented landscapes. *Global Environmental Change*, 23 (3), 588–97.

Hastrup, K., 2015. Comparing climate worlds: Theorising across ethnographic fields. *In*: H. Greschke and J. Tischler, eds, *Grounding Global Climate Change*. Dordrecht, NL: Springer.

Hodgson, D.L., 2011a. *Being Maasai, Becoming Indigenous: Postcolonial politics in a neoliberal world*. Bloomington, IN: Indiana University Press.

Hodgson, D.L., 2011b. 'These are not our priorities': Maasai women, human rights, and the problem of culture. *In*: D.L. Hodgson, ed., *Gender and Culture at the Limits of Rights*. Philadelphia, PA: University of Pennsylvania Press, 138–57.

Homewood, K.M., and Rodgers, W.A., 1991. *Maasailand Ecology: Pastoralist development and wildlife conservation in Ngorongoro, Tanzania*. Cambridge: Cambridge University Press.

Hulme, M., 2009. *Why We Disagree about Climate Change: Understanding controversy, inaction and opportunity*. Cambridge: Cambridge University Press.

Hulme, M., 2011. Reducing the future to climate: A story of climate determinism and reductionism. *Osiris*, 26 (1), 245–66.

Igoe, J., 2002. National parks and human ecosystems: The challenge to community conservation: a case study from Simanjiro, Tanzania. *In*: D. Chatty and M. Colchester, eds, *Conservation and Mobile Indigenous Peoples: Displacement, forced resettlement and sustainable development*. New York: Berghahn Books, 77–96.

Igoe, J., and Brockington, D., 1999. Pastoral land tenure and community conservation: A case study from north-east Tanzania. *IIED Drylands Programme: Pastoral Land Tenure Series 11*.

IPCC, 2001. *Climate Change 2001: Impacts, adaptation, and vulnerability: summary for policymakers*. Cambridge: Cambridge University Press.

IPCC, 2014a. *Climate Change 2014: Synthesis report: contribution of Working Groups I, II and III to the Fifth Assessment Report of the Intergovernmental Panel on Climate Change*. Geneva: IPCC.

IPCC, 2014b. Annex II: Glossary. *In*: V.R. Barros, *et al.*, eds, *Climate Change 2014: Impacts, adaptation, and vulnerability: Part B: Regional aspects: contribution of Working Group II to the Fifth Assessment Report of the Intergovernmental Panel on Climate Change*. Cambridge: Cambridge University Press, 1757–76.

Jasanoff, S., 2003. Technologies of humility: Citizen participation in governing science. *Minerva*, 41 (3), 223–44.

Leslie, P.W., and McCabe, T.J., 2013. Response diversity and resilience in social-ecological systems. *Current Anthropology*, 54 (2), 114–29.

McCabe, T.J., 2003. Sustainability and livelihood diversification among the Maasai of northern Tanzania. *Human Organization*, 62 (2), 100–11.

Niang, I., *et al.*, 2014. Africa. *In*: V.R. Barros, *et al.*, eds, *Climate Change 2014: Impacts, adaptation, and vulnerability: Part B: Regional aspects: contribution of Working Group II to the Fifth Assessment Report of the Intergovernmental Panel on Climate Change*. Cambridge: Cambridge University Press, 1199–1265.

Orlove, B., 2009. The past, the present and some possible futures of adaptation. *In*: N.W. Adger, I. Lorenzoni, and K. O'Brien, eds, *Adapting to Climate Change: Thresholds, values, governance*. Cambridge: Cambridge University Press, 129–63.

Roitman, J.L., 2014. *Anti-crisis*. Durham, NC: Duke University Press.

Sachedina, H., 2008. *Wildlife is Our Oil: Conservation, livelihoods and NGOs in the Tarangire ecosystem, Tanzania*. PhD thesis. University of Oxford.

Sherman, M., *et al.*, 2016. Drawing the line between adaptation and development: A systematic literature review of planned adaptation in developing countries. *WIREs, Climate Change*, 7 (5), 707–26.

Tanner, T., and Allouche, J., 2011. Towards a new political economy of climate change and adaptation. *IDS Bulletin*, 42 (3), 1–14.

Taylor, M., 2015. *The Political Ecology of Adaptation: Livelihoods, agrarian change and the conflicts of development*. New York: Routledge.

UNDP, 2007/2008. *Human Development Report 2007/2008: Fighting climate change: human solidarity in a divided world*. United Nations Development Programme (UNDP).

UNFCCC, 1992. United Nations Framework Convention on Climate Change. Available from: http://unfccc.int/essential_background/convention/items/6036.php [Accessed 24 July 2017].

United Nations, 2016. International Day brings recognition of indigenous peoples' contribution to environmental protection, combating climate change. UN Press release 9 August [online]. Available from: www.un.org/esa/socdev/unpfii/documents/int_day_press_release07.pdf [Accessed 24 July 2017].

URT, 2007. National Adaptation Program of Action (NAPA for the UNFCCC). United Republic of Tanzania (URT).

Weisser, F., *et al.*, 2014. Translating the 'adaptation to climate change' paradigm: The politics of a travelling idea in Africa. *The Geographical Journal*, 180 (2), 111–19.

Wisner, B., *et al.*, 2012. *Let Them Eat (Maize) Cake: Climate change discourse, misinformation and land grabbing in Tanzania.* Paper presented at the International Conference on Global Land Grabbing II, New York, 17–19 October.

WRI, 2010–11. *World Resources: Decision making in a changing climate: adaptation challenges and choices.* UNDP, UNEP, World Bank, World Resources Institute (WRI).

3 Rethinking the framing of climate change adaptation

Knowledge, power, and politics

Daniel Morchain

Introduction

Adaptation to climate change has always been part of life on earth. Yet, according to the scientific literature – such as the Fifth Assessment Report of the Intergovernmental Panel on Climate Change (IPCC) – the increased magnitude of global warming the planet is currently experiencing further exacerbates the negative impacts of climate change on people – increasing risk and reducing their capacity to adapt. This is particularly the case for marginalised people in the Global South living in poverty (IPCC 2014). Wide recognition that industrialised countries are overwhelmingly responsible for these changes has, albeit slowly, led to governments of industrialised countries increasingly financing climate change adaptation initiatives in the Global South.

Linking the vulnerability of people and systems to climate change impacts as a basis for designing measures to reduce such impacts is a complex and highly contested socio-political process that creates both winners and losers. Therefore, who participates in adaptation decision-making, how the process is framed, justified, and operationalised has considerable implications for development outcomes. This is never a fortuitous process, but rather one loaded with political agendas. In this chapter, I pay particular attention to which, and the processes by which, knowledge is included or left out of the climate change adaptation debate, because this has implications for the equity and potential for social change that adaptation and development efforts will either promote or hinder.

Against this backdrop, different scholarly and political voices have emerged over the years that foreground the importance of fair, equitable, and ethical adaptation policies (e.g. Paavola and Adger 2006; Shackleton *et al.* 2015) as well as the need to introduce radical changes to adaptation in order to foster social justice (e.g. Eriksen *et al.* 2011; Manuel-Navarrete and Pelling 2015; Pelling *et al.* 2015). Failure to do so risks promoting a paradigm whereby groups with little power in the Global South are constrained to play the role of helpless, while the Global North and Southern enclaves of powerful elites and unrepresentative governments recognise themselves as rightful providers of adaptation solutions. I explore the considerable disconnect between adaptation needs and adaptation focus at different levels of governance, and the significant influence that donors, on the one hand, and climate science and academia, on the other, exert in shaping adaptation agendas. I will claim that this framing of adaptation and development often undermines situated, locally embedded, and practitioner knowledge.

There is also a push in the climate and development communities to gain traction for implementation by promoting climate action as a moral imperative. At the 'Our Common Future under Climate Change' conference in Paris in 2015, Laurence Tubiana, founder of the Institute for Sustainable Development and International Relations (IDDRI), said that global climate talks need to be framed from an ethical perspective, while John Schellnhuber, director of the Potsdam Institute for Climate Impact Research (PIK), believed that decency needs to be the most compelling force in adaptation discussions (Morchain 2015). Adger *et al.* (2017) found evidence that action on climate change is, indeed, most effective when framed it as a moral issue. But this realisation has not, however, managed – or perhaps even intended – to transform the climate action ideology from a natural science framing to a social framing. Furthermore, the idea of framing the adaptation and development discourse around morality begs the question, 'whose morals and whose values?', and demands an examination of how, or indeed whether, indigeneity, power dynamics, and historical legacies such as colonialism contribute to knowledge production.

How adaptation is defined determines to a large extent what and who is and is not addressed by adaptation funding. And while financing commitments, as well as funding released, are currently increasing globally, the very understanding of adaptation remains technocratic – over 40 per cent of all adaptation resources are spent on infrastructure projects (ODI and Heinrich Boell Stiftung 2015). Another 32 per cent is spent on agriculture and includes technocratic adaptation measures as well as capacity-building and empowerment initiatives. (In other words, stating that 40 per cent of adaptation funds are spent on infrastructure does not mean that 60 per cent are spent on non-technocratic adaptation initiatives.) Likewise, adaptation funding remains insufficient and not always targeted at the more vulnerable countries (Rahman and Ahmad 2016).

Based on an analysis of literature, and reflections from ongoing projects, this chapter provides a critical examination of how climate change adaptation has been framed by governments in developed countries and other powerful institutions, such as Southern elites, private sector, and international non-governmental organisations (NGOs). It looks at the effects this is having on the adaptive and developmental potential of people targeted by these efforts.

The chapter concludes that adaptation work has mostly extended the development paradigm, failing to introduce transformational thinking in the sector, or to shift power structures. This is, possibly, an act of self-preservation by the ruling institutions, which has been compounded by their ability to paint an incomplete, biased picture of the climate problem, underplaying the importance of its social dimension, while overemphasising natural sciences as its solution space. The chapter also concludes that making adaptation inclusive, representative, and consultative will require radical changes in the way that adaptation research, knowledge, and narratives are currently formulated. Such changes should aim to build structures that allow knowledge which remains marginalised to become influential.

What's in the word 'adaptation'? Knowledge and politics at play

The IPCC defines adaptation as:

> the process of adjustment to actual or expected climate and its effects. In human systems, adaptation seeks to moderate or avoid harm or exploit beneficial opportunities. In some natural systems, human intervention may facilitate adjustment to expected climate and its effects.
>
> (IPCC 2014, 5)

Translating this concept into practice requires contextualising its meaning by acknowledging different worldviews around what adaptation should be, as well as by examining the historical context that has shaped the way people interact with climate change and other hazards.

It is not naive, I believe, to think that finding a common ground on adaptation and development begins by building trust and empathy between stakeholders. De Vries *et al.* (2017) found that conversations focused on 'connecting', where people openly share their ideas and are receptive to other views, build trust and promote the co-creation of knowledge. In contrast, conversations where the speaker 'sends', 'defends', or 'misunderstands' have the opposite effect. If we accept Dahlberg and Blaikie's (1999) premise that deconstructing adaptation narratives of actors with different values and ways of articulating meaning can lead to surprisingly complementary propositions, then a strategy of 'connecting' can lead to levelling the playing field of 'adaptation framing', which has historically been biased in favour of the Global North and powerful actors.

Furthermore, setting adaptation priorities in a top–down, exclusionary way that prioritises technical solutions and undermines local knowledge results in frustration and distrust of those, ironically, targeted by the adaptation measures (Otto-Banaszak *et al.* 2011). This is partly because adaptation thinking cannot be separated from a holistic understanding of development or well-being; in other words, it cannot reduce the question of vulnerability to issues of climate change impacts. For example, a vulnerability and risk assessment (VRA) exercise conducted in 2016 in Malawi, which included unskilled tea labourers in a discussion with private sector and national-level government actors on the competitiveness of the domestic tea industry, enabled a nuanced exploration of social factors affecting competitiveness, beyond a focus on exclusively economic, climatic, and infrastructural perspectives (Morchain *et al.* 2016).

Bridging this knowledge gap is not easy and should not be oversimplified. In a compelling examination of the role of politics in defining the knowledge that shapes the adaptation discourse in the Canadian Arctic, Cameron (2012) highlighted two key factors: (1) failing to acknowledge the importance of the colonial past in the present debate around vulnerability and adaptation has profound consequences in the way its narrative is produced; and (2) there is a widespread mainstream misuse of the notion of 'indigenous' and 'local' that acts to contain their relevance and influence to indigenous or local practices and knowledge alone. This effectively bars indigenous people and people from rural communities from informing the bigger picture of adaptation and development agendas, which nonetheless have a direct impact on them. Both factors prevent the examination of present-day adaptation and development practices in a way that challenges power structures and their implications. Furthermore, it perpetuates colonial worldviews in development research, policy, and practice, limiting any efforts of stabilisation and 're-organisation of political-economic relations' (Cameron 2012: 104).

De-romanticising indigenous, traditional, and local knowledge is fundamental in making adaptation and development narratives more accurate and in prioritising responses more effectively. To that end, it is important to recognise the strengths and weaknesses both of local knowledge systems and systems based on scientific knowledge – so that a meaningful and constructive hybridisation can result (Lebel 2013).

This hybridisation, nevertheless, should be undertaken with a clear awareness of the existing power disparities and prejudices about the different knowledge sources and the biased arena where ideas are debated. Not only is there a wide recognition of international adaptation fora being tilted toward knowledge from the natural sciences and from the Global North, as this chapter explores, but also of the prevailing discourse embedding and promoting a colonial hierarchy of knowledge (see for example Spiegel 2017).

Having considered the relation between different types of knowledge and the development of an adaptation and development discourse, now look at the present dynamics of the sector and examine their possible implications.

Current framing of climate change adaptation in the development context

Whereas science has succeeded in causally linking human-induced greenhouse gas emissions to global warming and climate change adaptation has increasingly become an element and sometimes a driver of development efforts, what adaptation is and what shapes it takes 'on the ground' remains little explored and understood (Ford *et al.* 2015). People's lives, livelihoods, and, similarly, development pathways are shaped by circumstances and responses to a multitude of hazards and opportunities. As such, it is necessary that adaptation is understood and framed in all its complexity: as a problematic within development that is founded on social concerns, and is supported by the scientific understanding of climate phenomena and their impacts – not the other way around.

There is, of course, no single approach to adapting to climate change impacts because sound adaptation responses vary considerably from one place to another: who lives in a given place, what people and governments value and prioritise, what institutions are in place, who funds the measures, and what is the addition of a climate change response to the overall picture of vulnerability/capacity, etc. Furthermore, political interests and different approaches to development play a determining role in framing climate change adaptation and dictating who is and who is not likely to benefit from adaptation efforts – for example, broadly speaking, some Asian official development assistance tends to focus on physical infrastructure projects, while some Western donors have shown a tendency to combine infrastructure and social development investments, or in some cases emphasise social development.

By the 'framing' of adaptation I mean: what information is sourced and used in decision-making, how and by whom; what data are prioritised or discarded as irrelevant; who is consulted in the process; what questions are asked; who analyses the findings; and how relevant, representative, and inclusive are the findings for a given territory and the different groups of people inhabiting it. Likewise, who, how, and what is *not* consulted/analysed/used is an equally relevant consideration to understand the representativeness of adaptation. The kind of knowledge that forms part of understanding adaptation, and the epistemic practices that are excluded, largely determine the impact that planned climate change adaptation will have on populations and environments.

Furthermore, the climate change sector, having gained global relevance, has the opportunity to present itself as a new way of doing development, thus challenging a long-running model of development that has too often failed to deliver sustainable results. However, its efforts so far have mostly taken a narrow, sectoral focus that have failed to be representative and to address the root causes of vulnerability, and have not challenged the institutions that have shaped development thinking for decades (e.g. Nagoda 2015). Indeed, adaptation efforts have yet to prove their contribution to a new and more equitable approach to development and to people's lives beyond the short and medium term. Hence, there is a strong case for a reorientation and reorganisation of power relations, and for the prioritisation of equitability and redistribution as core elements of the climate agenda.

'It is Northern countries that have set the global climate change policy agenda since the beginning' and in a top–down manner, and in so doing, have swayed the focus of it away from the needs and priorities of lower-income countries (Blicharska *et al.* 2017: 21). For instance, overall climate resources have mostly been allocated to mitigation, while adaptation needs remain underfunded, despite the official position of the United Nations Framework Convention on Climate Change (UNFCCC) being that 'adaptation and mitigation need to be accorded the same level of importance' (UNFCCC 2010). Nexus between mitigation and adaptation have also not materialised sufficiently (Ayers and Huq 2009).

Furthermore, highly influential literature, such as IPCC assessment reports and IPCC special reports, has traditionally overwhelmingly relied on peer-reviewed natural science publications at the expense of other sources of information, such as grey literature (e.g. project reports or publications by multilateral organisations), or local and indigenous knowledge. The concept of vulnerability to climate change is, similarly, often wrongly framed in the sector as something static which can be defined by biophysical impacts more than by socio-economic factors, and which can be understood by technical experts without stakeholder and community engagement (Preston *et al.* 2011). Eriksen *et al.* (2015) further argue that Northern scientific knowledge has been the dominant force in shaping the understanding of adaptation, while the profile of local knowledge has been kept low and has lagged behind (ibid.), making scientific knowledge a steering force for setting adaptation priorities. It also predisposes the framing of adaptation solutions within a 'climate science first' perspective, reducing the influence that social science research on vulnerability can (and should) have on integral adaptation responses.

The emphasis and reliance on external 'expert' knowledge, such as fly-in consultants, reduces local ownership of the adaptation process and the relevance of its findings, limiting the insightfulness of the social analysis conducted (Conway and Mustelin 2014). This predominant practice in adaptation represents a science-centric framing of the subject that undermines the potential that social learning processes can contribute.

But the top–down approach of adaptation practice is not as simple as Global North over/versus Global South. The approach that Southern national and sub-national governments, as well as powerful elites, take vis-à-vis adaptation and development can be an equally important determinant of its outcomes. Spiegel (2017), for instance, described how national policies in the Maldives have in some cases promoted a 'colonial' relationship between the national government and the least powerful groups that the policies intend to benefit.

Several reviews of the adaptation literature have revealed that climate change adaptation initiatives often lack dynamism, innovation, and transformational elements, and that hard infrastructure solutions tend to be the default choice. For instance, Kates *et al.* (2012) showed that 95 per cent of all implemented adaptation measures across seven key sectors in the United States are merely incremental replications of existing measures, whereas much needed transformational and innovative actions remain a rare exception. By contrast, governance structures that recognise the complexity of social contexts and invite the adaptation agenda to be set by a multitude of knowledge have a higher potential to promote both transformational and transformative adaptation actions (Few *et al.* 2017).

In relation to academic research on new ways of thinking and doing adaptation, only 3 per cent of published articles on the adaptation subject 'focus on the social roots of vulnerability and the necessity for political economic change to achieve transformative adaptation' (Bassett and Fogelman 2013: 42). This shows that not only is the nature of existing adaptation measures overwhelmingly incremental, but also that research on the subject fails to acknowledge the climate change problematic as a broader, social, and political problem.

Eriksen *et al.* (2015) understood the crucial role that power dynamics play in framing climate change adaptation, and consequently the need to contest the status quo that restricts the potential for adaptation space to be more representative of a multitude of knowledge. These dynamics can be evidenced in an institution such as the IPCC. According to Corry and Jorgensen (2015), the way the IPCC views adaptation solutions is too narrow: it is based on a 'linear model' that derives vulnerability from scientific evidence and that limits the space for social processes to shape a proper understanding of vulnerability and of adaptation needs.

An international conference organised by the Red Cross Red Crescent Climate Centre in collaboration with the IPCC on climate risk management in April 2017 aimed to address this shortcoming by bringing together the IPCC and adaptation stakeholders who do not normally have an opportunity to engage with the IPCC cycles: practitioners, social scientists, and operational-level government officials (unfortunately no community voices were present). Conversations highlighted the importance of bringing governance, as well as knowledge from grey literature and other non-academic sources, to the fore of discussions on climate risk and vulnerability – a discussion that in the IPCC has traditionally been heavily framed around climate science. The conference report recommended that 'in the coming years, it will be critical for scientists, policy-makers and practitioners to collaborate in developing and co-producing the literature base [...] and [co-develop] research agendas' (RCRCCC 2017: 9). The event served as a warning that unless the ways of working of influential institutions in the climate arena begin to welcome and value presently de-prioritised sources of knowledge, they risk retaining post-colonial undertones and practices that can decimate the social justice element of adaptation.

The next section explores on-the-ground initiatives that have sought to influence the adaptation narrative, such that it understands climate change adaptation as a mainly social construct. They have tried to open up a space for knowledge on the fringe to enter the political spectrum shaping climate change adaptation.

Efforts in re-framing climate change adaptation

Against the backdrop of shortcomings in adaptation and development efforts, the vulnerability and risk assessment (VRA) methodology and the Adaptation at Scale in Semi-Arid Regions (ASSAR) project have sought to increase the representation and relevance of adaptation research and implementation.[1]

The VRA, designed by Oxfam, has focused on opening up spaces for multi-stakeholder interaction and on including marginalised people and those most at risk in these spaces. It has sought to develop a joint under-standing by stakeholders from local to national about the key hazards and issues affecting a landscape, as well as about the characteristics of social groups inhabiting it and the need for their active role in the adaptation debate. Furthermore, the VRA intends to support a joint process of design-ing climate change adaptation measures based on acknowledging the com-plexity of the issues and the capacities of diverse actors to contribute to it, effectively initiating social learning and promoting transformation in plan-ning processes. It is precisely the lack of properly identifying and differen-tiating social groups (partly due to top–down approaches and insufficient engagement with local actors and marginalised groups) that can result in an inaccurate understanding of vulnerability, making climate change adaptation efforts inefficient at best and, at worst, harmful by perpetuating inequality and injustice (Nagoda 2015).

A key challenge for processes such as the VRA is making stakeholder engagement long-lasting and influential. Well-conducted participatory pro-cesses can generate immediate enthusiasm among participants, but main-taining the momentum, as well as getting buy-in from the participating organisations beyond the person who attends, is challenging and requires considerable resource investment. Furthermore, assessing the direct impact that the process has on people and organisations is extremely difficult. However, in the case of Botswana, tangible positive impacts resulted from the implementation of a single VRA in 2015. Principal economist and dis-trict planning officer of the Bobirwa Sub-District, Pelaelo Master Tsayang, indicated at the end of the VRA that 'this exercise will influence and con-tribute to draft our district development plan, particularly the activities related to climate change. Because of the useful outcomes the VRA gener-ated, we will fund workshops like this in other parts of the district'. Both expectations were met: a chapter on climate change adaptation was intro-duced in the district development plan, and nationwide training of district officials from all of the 20 districts in Botswana is planned in 2018, co-funded by the national government.

A key outcome of the VRA, in addition to its more tangible contribution to development and adaptation planning, is behavioural change. This, however, takes time to sink in – if it does – and its effects are hard to pinpoint. Furthermore, social learning processes may result in positive changes in people's lives that are never measured. Until development actors – chiefly donors – become comfortable with the uncertainty and the long timeframe needed for these behavioural changes to come about, and until there is recognition that impacts will be heterogeneous and difficult to measure, progress in climate change adaptation efforts risk remaining largely within the construct of incremental adaptation (e.g. technocratic, infrastructure projects) and falling short of stimulating social transformation.

Some of the main impacts of VRAs conducted between 2013 and 2016 in six countries were cited as: increased awareness and knowledge by communities and government officials of the origin and impacts of hazards; more informed agricultural planning and the development of adaptive agricultural techniques; increased recognition of the need for increased investment in climate change adaptation by the national government (in the Philippines); enhanced involvement of government officials with local stakeholders in planning at district level to include climate change risks, as well as to better understand gender issues and respond. In Pakistan, communities have used this framework, identified adaptive capacities for resilience and newly established relations with stakeholders to set up an advocacy plan for budgetary allocations, in addition to the usual disaster risk reduction/climate change adaptation plan. In Armenia, the design of an agricultural insurance mechanism model and a local risk assessment methodology has resulted from the application of the VRA and from subsequent stakeholder round-table discussions at national level, which are being increasingly implemented nationwide. In Ghana, Oxfam has strengthened its recognition and legitimacy among NGOs and the government as a result of its representative and inclusive participatory processes – being cited frequently by government and invited to discuss its participatory approaches in events. In the Philippines, the VRA has broadened the municipal-level framing of disaster risk reduction and climate change adaptation to include non-climatic stressors – this has enabled including, for example, conflict in a more nuanced discussion about vulnerability and manifested the importance of cross-sectoral planning.[2] In Malawi, the VRA served to shift the focus of the development conversation in the tea industry from an emphasis on climatic and economic issues to one that addressed social elements, such as the harsh treatment and sexual harassment of unskilled workers; a fundamental element of their vulnerability (Morchain *et al.* 2016).

Despite its positive outcomes, the potential for participatory approaches like the VRA to reorganise power structures should be welcomed with caution. Perhaps the VRA's most fundamental contribution in addition to the empowerment of marginalised groups, as Cameron's findings (2012) would suggest, might be to continually challenge multi-stakeholder spaces to acknowledge historical power relations honestly and their implications on present-day knowledge production, policymaking, and practices.

The second brief reference about initiatives aimed at re-framing climate change adaptation is the ASSAR project, led by the University of Cape Town and funded by the UK's Department for International Development and Canada's International Development Research Centre. Arguably, ASSAR's main contribution is to challenge the business-as-usual of climate change research by giving stakeholders an active role in shaping its agenda and making it relevant to their lives. This starts by involving stakeholders at all levels in refining the project's research questions, by encouraging their participation in the assessment of vulnerabilities and risks, by seeking their contribution in designing possible adaptation pathways, and by creating opportunities for stakeholders to interact and discuss adaptation concerns and priorities. Furthermore, ASSAR's so-called research-into-use (RiU) modus operandi embeds the influencing of climate change adaptation policy and practice among its core objectives, ensuring that the social elements of its research drive adaptation and well-being goals. ASSAR's mid-term internal review on RiU confirmed that one key objective of ASSAR's members – most of them are researchers – is to generate behavioural change and changes in social norms, as well as to influence formal policy channels (Morchain and DeMaria-Kinney 2016). The report also concluded that a key outcome of RiU work must be for researchers in fields such as climate change adaptation and development to recognise their duty to engage in the policy and practice debate, effectively as forces to shift the way societies think about and respond to climate change and other challenges. Pushing traditional science beyond its boundaries is perhaps *the* fundamental contribution of ASSAR to climate change adaptation – in addition to its production of new research findings. This approach would, potentially, represent a transformational shift in adaptation research by making it more relevant to people in climate change hotspots, moving away from research agendas driven by Northern institutional interests.

Building this link between research and adaptation needs on the ground is critical. Operationalising adaptation without a thorough understanding and consideration of the complexity of politics and power dynamics of a place risks disempowering the very groups that an adaptation initiative sought to support (Cochrane and Tamiru 2016). Donors and development agencies need to acknowledge the complexity of the task at hand and carefully assess the implications of the initiatives' intended changes. Strategic alliances and coordination at international and national levels is another crucial factor of a rigorous framing of adaptation.

The social learning element of the VRA and ASSAR's ambition to transform adaptation research addresses key gaps that, if left unaddressed, risk jeopardising the relevance and the impacts of adaptation efforts. But what can be learned about good practices; what elements should be incorporated in the framing of adaptation?

By building on an existing framework, the next section proposes a structured way to think about the framing, design, and implementation of climate change adaptation prioritising a joint development of the understanding of adaptation.

Supporting a more equitable framing of climate change adaptation

Eriksen *et al.* (2015: 529) developed a framework that seeks to explain the key interactions framing the politics of adaptation. It is underscored by an understanding that 'climate change adaptation processes have the potential to constitute as well as contest, authority, subjectivity and knowledge, thereby opening up or closing down space for transformational adaptation'. The framework also sees power dynamics and politics as foundational elements needing to shape the climate change adaptation discourse – yet rightly claims that it is precisely politically powerful actors and the set-up of global/multilateral institutions that advance agendas that exclude the least 'established' knowledge (e.g. local knowledge, voices of the marginalised and poorest) and that promote a technocratic understanding of adaptation.

Authority is a major driver of adaptation decisions and outcomes in the framework developed by Eriksen *et al.* (2015). Stakeholders with authority further influence adaptation by claiming the right to legitimise or undermine different types of knowledge. Subjectivity helps explain how power influences the way a person or a group identifies and acts – or is prevented from acting – in social domains. Authority and knowledge produce socially differentiated groups, which can be an empowering or a devaluing exercise for adaptation 'subjects', but which implicitly dictates who is and who is not capable of contributing to adaptation thinking. Figure 3.1 depicts a reworking of the framework developed by Eriksen *et al.* (2015). While the original framework assesses existing power relations, I propose a revision based on promoting empowerment for more equitable adaptation.

Authority and knowledge have a self-reinforcing relationship that will often reaffirm powerful actors and perpetuate the status quo, excluding non-influential yet crucial knowledge from adaptation debates. There is a need to challenge institutions to open up spaces for dialogue that are representative, interdisciplinary, and invite participation from different levels of governance. Beyond the issue of knowledge needing to gain legitimacy from authorities, the interaction between authority and knowledge needs to rely on accountability mechanisms. While NGOs and civil society organisations are often champions of these processes, they cannot always uphold or maintain long-term multi-stakeholder dialogues, or hold governments to account. Donors,

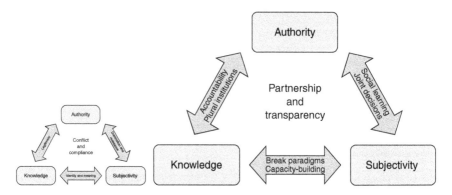

Figure 3.1 A reworking of the framework originally developed by Eriksen *et al.* (2015) describing key interactions framing the politics of adaptation, where empowerment takes on a central role. Left: The original framework by Eriksen *et al.* (2015).

however, could use their leverage to promote and enforce a more open and equitable relationship about what knowledge is and is not legitimised by authority figures at national, regional, and even multilateral levels.

In rethinking adaptation, the relationship between authority and subjectivity needs to be seen as one where subjectivity serves to legitimise marginalised groups, and where they and gender equality are recognised as priority themes in adaptation – which can, in effect, positively influence the attainment of adaptation goals. This implies a process of social learning and joint decision-making by stakeholders across governance scales, and where groups addressed by development and adaptation agendas play a protagonist role. Recent VRAs in Botswana and Malawi, for instance, have enabled the initiation of a collaborative social differentiation exercise that has contributed to deepen the understanding of vulnerabilities and capacities of groups considered vulnerable or marginalised – aiming to transition them from passive to active in the adaptation debate.

These processes require long-term engagement to be meaningful and avoid being 'tokenistic'. In order to foster a long-term engagement, parties need to feel that their participation is beneficial to themselves and that the dialogue space is legitimate and influential. In Honduras, local NGO Asociación Ecológica San Marcos de Ocotepeque (AESMO) has been leading a multi-stakeholder participatory process for the collective management of the Hondo River basin since the 1990s. It has ensured a sufficient and clean water supply to households and to local small-scale farmers, and has established an ongoing dialogue for joint decision-making between landscape stakeholders (communities, private sector, and government), considerably changing the behaviour of the more powerful actors. It shifted, for example, the attitudes of some landowners from an original indifference towards governance processes to submitting to the rule of law and using official channels for requesting permits for water extraction. AESMO considers that some key elements for the successful long-term implementation of this process are: building understanding and 'social conscience' about the importance of water and other natural resources in people's lives; empowering the community to voice concerns and to keep momentum of the process in the face of short lifespans of municipal governments; empowerment of other actors to navigate governance processes (e.g. for large-scale farmers to act less as a strictly business outfit, and more as a landscape steward); accurate knowledge of laws and regulations by all stakeholders engaged in the process; established clear boundaries of the area to be managed; a municipal government that is engaged (in this case, they bought lands within the basin and declared them 'protected'); regular coordination and communication with municipal authorities; inclusion of women in the group and in decision-making roles; and continual participation and co-facilitation by local NGOs or civil society organisations (Saravia and Bustillo 2010).

Underscoring the framework that this chapter proposes is the connection between subjectivity (the way power structures influence people's ability to engage in the adaptation process) and knowledge. Two things are proposed to facilitate the proper inclusion of non-scientific, non-technocratic knowledge, as well as knowledge from disenfranchised persons and non-official institutions. The first refers to the need to break paradigms, such as beliefs, barriers, and prejudices held by multilateral and government bodies, social norms that violate human rights or marginalise minorities, or gender-based inequalities, and explore mechanisms through which these new values can be institutionalised. One example is the ongoing institutional change at the IPCC to make their Sixth Assessment Report (AR6) more inclusive and representative by embedding in its structure a senior social scientist (Dr Debra Roberts) to coach the Working Group II lead and authors. Another example is efforts by NGOs and women's rights organisations to achieve official recognition of unpaid care work in order to facilitate its insertion in budgetary planning and policies.

Capacity-building of climate change adaptation stakeholders across all levels is the second element proposed to ease the connection between subjectivity and knowledge. One aspect that should be covered is the capacity-building of people mostly excluded from formal governance and decision-making processes to better engage with these. Likewise, capacity-building should be targeted at powerful actors to shift their worldviews. In ASSAR, capacity-building of national- and district-level planners is being undertaken to promote bottom–up development planning.

The dynamic interplay described here between authority, knowledge, and subjectivity could thrive in an atmosphere of partnership and transparency, where conflict is addressed openly and fairly, and compliance – understood as submission to an authority set up by inequitable power structures – is ruled out. The changes proposed in the framework, which are aimed at enhancing the positive impact and relevance of adaptation for marginalised groups, require transformation – and not just incremental fixes – in the adaptation and development sector.

Conclusion

As several studies in the field of adaptation have shown, there exists a discrepancy between the conceptual apparatus that has emerged around climate change adaptation, and the adaptation needs of communities on the ground. This chapter has explored the possible reasons for this disconnect and some possible solutions.

Findings of a survey administered by the author to 33 adaptation researchers, practitioners and donors showed that a majority of respondents perceive an existing power imbalance between, at one end, the Global North and Southern elites: dictating the adaptation agenda; and, at the other end, the Global South: mostly lacking power and influence – particularly at local levels. The survey also showed that over half of respondents believe that climate change adaptation is predominantly used by the North as a way to forward its own geopolitical interests in the South; and that climate change adaptation efforts often undermine local values and traditions. Overall, the survey findings suggest that adaptation and development efforts are not focusing on empowering people nor on shaking up the systems that perpetuate their marginalisation.

This chapter looked at two initiatives aimed at shifting the nature of adaptation work. The VRA promotes a constructive dialogue that seeks to legitimise vulnerable people's and Southern institutions' knowledge in front of power-holders. ASSAR contributes to shifting the way climate change research is framed and conducted. But three questions remain as yet unanswered. First, will these types of initiative empower marginalised groups and non-technocrats to play influential roles in adaptation decision-making – and in doing so enable different types and sources of knowledge to contribute fairly to adaptation and development thinking? Second, can they facilitate the hybridisation of knowledge from different disciplines and epistemologies in such a way that they lead to a jointly owned narrative? Third, how effective will – and can – they be in reorganising historical legacies (e.g. resulting from colonialism) and embedded power disparities and injustices in present-day governance structures at all levels?

In terms of translating adaptation thinking into practice, incremental efforts are likely to remain the focus of adaptation funding and are essential to attain risk reduction and food security goals, but transforming the essence of adaptation thinking and doing is what holds most promise in bringing equity to climate governance. Addressing the relation between climate change and social inequalities is more pressing than ever, given that rising temperatures will result in 'a huge redistribution of wealth from the global poor to the wealthy', according to Solomon Hsiang of the University of California, Berkeley (Rotman 2016).

Transformation, nevertheless, entails risk: there will be many unknowns when profound changes are pursued. The implications of initiatives that aim to generate transformation must be analysed carefully. Even so, the need to consider radically different ways to address the climate change challenge is undeniable, particularly as I have argued in this chapter, in relation to reorganising governance and power structures so that they include knowledge that has been restricted from, or hardly influential in, the debate.

Re-politicising the adaptation agenda offers an opportunity to be more inclusive of a wide range of (situated) knowledge and practices, and in so doing reduce the prevailing climate science-centric bias of the field. Fortunately, there is also reason for optimism, as thinking about adaptation is indeed changing. For example, this chapter discussed the shortcomings of the IPCC's position on reporting on climate change and adaptation. For AR6, however, the IPCC has indicated that it intends to incorporate more input from social sciences and grey literature, and to shift its focus from science analytics to supporting decision-making through a more practical exploration of adaptation and mitigation. It has shown openness to having a closer engagement with practitioners and decision-makers (RCRCCC 2017).

Institutional donors also have powerful tools at hand to drive change: money and influence, and with them an opportunity to play equitable politics. There are encouraging signs of development programmes fostering multidisciplinary work and including climate change as a theme, such as the UK government's GBP 1.5 billion Global Challenge Research Fund (GCRF 2017). This implies that adaptation responses are being increasingly understood as not merely sectoral or technical fixes, but as one component of development as a whole.

However, the framing of adaptation remains tied to a system of mostly Northern institutions that cling to power, despite having proved dysfunctional and incapable or unwilling to address the full complexity of the challenge. The gaps are evident especially in failing to address the social component of adaptation in the context of development and in excluding from the debate knowledge that is considered not established by parameters of academia. On the importance of understanding adaptation as a human issue, Weisser *et al.* (2014: 113) suggested that 'the answer to one of the key questions in adaptation research [...] will remain incomplete as long as one talks only about changing climatic conditions'. It is indeed the *so what* about people and the planet that will not only complete the answer, but should also be its foundation. At present, though, solutions to the adaptation challenge remain overly focused on climate and natural sciences. As such, powerful Northern stakeholders and Southern elites continue to hold ownership of the adaptation agenda.

This exclusion of certain voices from adaptation decision-making is used as a reactionary vehicle to sustain power structures. Cochrane (2017), reflecting on the book *Decolonising Methodologies* by Linda Tuhiwai Smith, illustrated it well:

> even when exploitation is not explicit, there is [...] 'a cultural orienta-tion, a set of values, a different conceptualization of such things as time, space and subjectivity, different and competing theories of know-ledge, highly specialized forms of language, and structures of power', which act to reinforce the dominance of one way of knowing over another.

A re-politicisation of adaptation requires transforming the stakeholder landscape to enable an institutional framework that formalises the contri-bution of a wide range of knowledge to the adaptation problematic within development. This will require establishing partnerships that, while seeking consensus-building, do demand a revision of the status quo where it is deemed necessary. Fairness, transparency and participation are pillars of this approach – which does not negate the relevance that 'established' knowledge can bring to adaptation – but which does frame adaptation as inclusive, representative, and consultative.

Acknowledgements

This work was carried out under the Adaptation at Scale in Semi-Arid Regions project (ASSAR). ASSAR is one of four research programmes funded under the Collaborative Adaptation Research Initiative in Africa and Asia (CARIAA), with financial support from the UK Government's Department for International Development (DfID) and the International Development Research Centre (IDRC), Canada. The views expressed in this work are those of the creators and do not necessarily represent those of DfID and IDRC or its board of governors.

Notes

1 The VRA is a methodology designed by Oxfam that develops a holistic, landscape-wide understanding of vulnerability and connects actors across various levels of governance to jointly identify and analyse root causes of vulnerabilities for distinct social groups and later design programmes and strategies to tackle these. For more information visit http://policy-practice.oxfam.org.uk/our-approach/toolkits-and-guidelines/vulnerability-risk-assessment. Using both research and practice to address the present information shortfall on how to minimise vulnerability and promote long-term resilience, the primary aim of the ASSAR project is to produce future-focused and societally relevant knowledge of potential pathways to well-being through adaptation. It is a consortium led by the University of Cape Town, the University of East Anglia, the Indian Institute for Human Settlements, Oxfam, and START, and is funded by DfID and IDRC under the Collaborative Adaptation

Research in Africa and Asia (CARIAA) initiative. I have a direct connection with both the VRA and ASSAR: I led the development of the VRA and I am a collaborative principal investigator, as well as Oxfam's lead, for ASSAR.

2 The examples above are based on emails and conversations with Abdul Latif Walizada (Oxfam in Afghanistan), Vadim Uzunyan (Oxfam in Armenia), Ana Caspe (Oxfam in the Philippines), Asim Saqlain (Oxfam in Pakistan), and Lillian Mwintome Kuutiero (Oxfam in Ghana).

References

Adger, W., Butler, C., and Walker-Springett, K., 2017. Moral reasoning in adaptation to climate change. *Environmental Politics*, 26 (3), 1–20.

Ayers, J., and Huq, S., 2009. The value of linking mitigation and adaptation: A case study of Bangladesh. *Environmental Management*, 43 (5), 753–64.

Bassett, T., and Fogelman, C., 2013. Déjà vu or something new? The adaptation concept in the climate change literature. *Geoforum*, 48, 42–53.

Blicharska, M., *et al.*, 2017. Steps to overcome the North–South divide in research relevant to climate change policy and practice. *Nature Climate Change*, 7 (1), 21–7.

Cameron, E.S., 2012. Securing indigenous politics: A critique of the vulnerability and adaptation approach to the human dimensions of climate change in the Canadian Arctic. *Global Environmental Change*, 22 (1), 103–14.

Cochrane, L., 2017. *Decolonizing Methodologies* [blog]. Available from: www.logancochrane.com/index.php/decolonizing-methodologies [Accessed 21 June 2017].

Cochrane, L., and Tamiru, Y., 2016. Ethiopia's productive safety net program: Power, politics and practice. *Journal of International Development*, 28 (5), 649–65.

Conway, D., and Mustelin, J., 2014. Strategies for improving adaptation practice in developing countries. *Nature Climate Change*, 4 (5), 339–42.

Corry, O., and Jorgensen, D., 2015. Beyond 'deniers' and 'believers': Towards a map of the politics of climate change. *Global Environmental Change*, 32, 165–74.

Dahlberg, A.C., and Blaikie, P., 1999. Changes in landscape or in interpretation? Reflections based on the environmental and socio-economic history of a village in NE Botswana. *Environment and History*, 5 (2), 127–74.

de Vries, J.R., *et al.*, 2017. Where there is no history: How to create trust and connection in learning for transformation in water governance. *Water*, 9 (2), 1–15.

Eriksen, S., *et al.*, 2011. When not every response to climate change is a good one: Identifying principles for sustainable adaptation. *Climate and Development*, 3 (1), 7–20.

Eriksen, S., Nightingale, A., and Eakin, H., 2015. Reframing adaptation: The political nature of climate change adaptation. *Global Environmental Change*, 35, 523–33.

Few, R., *et al.*, 2017. Transformation, adaptation and development: Relating concepts to practice. *Palgrave Communications 3* [online]. Available from: www.nature.com/articles/palcomms201792 [Accessed 8 November 2017].

Ford, J., *et al.*, 2015. Adaptation in climate change hotspots: Analysis from Africa and Asia. *Regional Environmental Change*, 15 (5), 747–850.

GCRF, 2017. Global Challenges Research Fund official website [online]. Available from: www.rcuk.ac.uk/funding/gcrf/ [Accessed 21 June 2017].

IPCC, 2014. *Climate Change 2014: Impacts, adaptation, and vulnerability: Part A: Global and sectoral aspects: contribution of Working Group II to the Fifth Assessment Report of the Intergovernmental Panel on Climate Change: summary for policymakers*. Cambridge: Cambridge University Press.

Kates, R.W., Travis, W.R., and Wilbanks, T.J., 2012. Transformational adaptation when incremental adaptations to climate change are insufficient. *Proceedings of the National Academy of Sciences of the United States of America*, 109 (19), 7156–61.

Lebel, L., 2013. Local knowledge and adaptation to climate change in natural resource-based societies of the Asia-Pacific. *Mitigation and Adaptation Strategies for Global Change*, 18 (7), 1057–76.

Manuel-Navarrete, D., and Pelling, M., 2015. Subjectivity and the politics of transformation in response to development and environmental change. *Global Environmental Change-Human and Policy Dimensions*, 35, 558–69.

Morchain, D., 2015. *Our Common Future under Climate Change: Where science meets social justice* [blog]. Available from: http://policy-practice.oxfam.org.uk/blog/2015/07/our-common-future-under-climate-change [Accessed 21 June 2017].

Morchain, D., and DeMaria-Kinney, J., 2016. *Stocktaking in Researchinto-Use: Progress and thinking to date*. ASSAR project publication. Print.

Morchain, D., *et al.*, 2016. *MALAWI2020: Vulnerability and risk assessment in the tea industry* [online]. Oxford: Oxfam International. Available from: http://policy-practice.oxfam.org.uk/publications/malawi2020-vulnerability-and-risk-assessment-in-the-tea-industry-620101 [Accessed 21 June 2017].

Nagoda, S., 2015. New discourses but same old development approaches? Climate change adaptation policies, chronic food insecurity and development interventions in northwestern Nepal. *Global Environmental Change*, 35, 570–79.

ODI and Heinrich Boell Stiftung, 2015. *10 Things to Know about Climate Finance in 2015* [online]. Available from: www.odi.org/sites/odi.org.uk/files/odi-assets/publications-opinion-files/10093.pdf [Accessed 21 June 2017].

Otto-Banaszak, I., *et al.*, 2011. Different perceptions of adaptation to climate change: A mental model approach applied to the evidence from expert interviews. *Regional Environmental Change*, 11 (2), 217–28.

Paavola, J., and Adger, W., 2006. Fair adaptation to climate change. *Ecological Economics*, 56 (4), 594–609.

Pelling, M., O'Brien, K., and Matyas, D., 2015. Adaptation and transformation. *Climatic Change*, 133 (1), 113–27.

Preston, B., Yuen, E., and Westaway, R. 2011. Putting vulnerability to climate change on the map: A review of approaches, benefits, and risks. *Sustainability Science*, 6 (2), 177–202.

Rahman, S.M., and Ahmad, M.M., 2016. Perception of local experts about accessibility to international climate funds: Case of Bangladesh. *Journal of Developing Areas*, 50 (3), 53–68.

RCRCCC, 2017. *Bridging Science, Policy and Practice: Report of the International Conference on Climate Risk Management*. Red Cross Red Crescent Climate Centre. Print.

Rotman, D., 2016. *Hotter Days Will Drive Global Inequality* [blog]. Available from: www.technologyreview.com/s/603158/hotter-days-will-drive-global-inequality/?utm_content=bufferf7a21&utm_medium=social&utm_source=twitter.com&utm_campaign=buffer [Accessed 21 June 2017].

Saravia, V., and Bustillo, J.A., 2010. *Hallazgos y relexiones sobre gestión compart-ida de los recursos naturales: Microcuenca de Río Hondo*. Print.

Shackleton, S., *et al.*, 2015. Why is socially-just climate change adaptation in sub-Saharan Africa so challenging? A review of barriers identified from empirical cases. *Climate Change*, 6 (3), 312–44.

Spiegel, R.H., 2017. *Drowning in Rising Seas: Navigating multiple knowledge systems and responding to climate change in the Maldives*. BA thesis. Pitzer College.

UNFCCC, 2010. *The Need for Adaptation* [fact sheet]. Available from: http://unfccc.int/press/fact_sheets/items/4985.php [Accessed 21 June 2017].

Weisser, F., *et al.*, 2014. Translating the adaptation to climate change paradigm: The politics of a travelling idea in Africa. *Geographical Journal*, 180 (2), 111–19.

Part III

The political economy of climate change adaptation

4 Climate change economies

Denaturalising adaptation and hydrocarbon economisation

Sophie Webber and Emilia Kennedy

Introduction

In response to the growth of market-based attempts to manage the impacts of climate change, climate scholars have worked up a timely and energised body of scholarship on the contours, nature, and implications of the new carbon economy. Reflecting a shift away from '20th-century carbon-based industry' (Boykoff *et al.* 2009: 2299), the new carbon economy refers to 'the emerging trade in carbon emissions, along with the series of market-based policy instruments designed to reduce carbon emissions' (Brown and Corbera 2003: 41). Rather than denoting an organised, structural shift (Castree 2006), the new carbon economy instead marks the emergence of markets in emissions trading, carbon commodification, voluntary offsets, and other marketised endeavours and actors. In mapping and querying this new carbon economy and its socio-ecological implications, scholars have been quick to 'follow the carbon' (Mitchell 2011, following Marcus 1995) into new circuits, but often conclude that this economy reinforces some rather old social phenomena – uneven capital accumulation, neo-colonialism, and authoritarian state logics. Accordingly, based on his exploration of the geographies of resource extraction, Bridge contends that 'while some contemporary "spaces of carbon" are novel and potentially transformative, others intensify established social and spatial relationships' (Bridge 2011: 10). Yet, the rush to explore the new carbon economy has meant prioritising novelty, at the risk of overlooking the similarities between marketised responses to climate change and other forms of climate governance. This chapter takes its cue from Boyd *et al.*'s (2011) call for a critical and historically situated assessment of novelty, presenting two case studies and theoretical engagements that play within the tensions between what is old, new, borrowed, or hybrid in the evolving world of 'carbon control' (While *et al.* 2010).

Through our exposition of climate services in the Pacific Islands and carbon capture and storage (CCS) in Canada, engaging theoretically with Callon's (2009) work on performativity and Polanyi's (2001 [1944]) writings on embeddedness, we extend research on new carbon economies beyond the somewhat narrow downstream 'carbon optic' (Bridge 2011) that has been the central focus of geographical work in this area. Our argument here is twofold: first, we extend what counts under the purview of the new carbon economy and instead propose the term 'climate change economies'. Using the case of climate services in the Pacific Islands, we move 'backstream' (encapsulating flows from carbon, post-consumption; Bridge and Le Billon 2012: 36) to demonstrate additional forms of economisation not captured by current research on offset markets and emissions trading. Next, using the empirical case of CCS in Canada, we work 'upstream' (where crude oil is 'captured'; Bridge and Le Billon 2012: 36), linking 'new' carbon economies of climate change back to the 'old' fossil fuel-based economies to which they are metabolically and socially joined. Where existing research on the economised governance of climate change overwhelmingly focuses on the production and circulation of bundles of carbon dioxide (CO_2) emissions, we suggest a need to consider the constitution, governance, and effects (following Boyd *et al.* 2011) of economisation as it reaches out to adaptation, and back to old hydrocarbon, worlds.

The second argument is that research on climate change economies should proceed from a theory of economisation rather than marketisation, and should consider the contexts in which these processes unfold. The two climate change economies we explore in this chapter are in-the-making: although they are not yet fully operational markets – not *yet* sites for the exchange and circulation of commodities; both CCS and climate services are institutional thickenings that anticipate linkages, exchanges, or pervasive rationalities of economisation. An examination of these embryonic climate control institutions demonstrates that liberal markets are not sprung independently and fully formed from the private sphere (Polanyi 2001 [1944]) – it is indeed *unnatural* that climate governance operates in this economised manner – but rather emerges, sometimes haltingly, or unpredictably from non-market institutional milieux. Neither of these incipient climate change economies involve the trade of bundles of carbon commodities. Rather, these economies are examples of the variety, creep, and reach of economised responses that have emerged in response to climate change, including, but not limited to, those that strictly exchange carbon. Thinking through climate change economies, particularly as they pertain to 'services' alongside carbon 'goods', brings together the suite of economised attempts to address the risks of climate change.

Our argument proceeds in the following manner. The first section reviews the existing literature on new carbon economies, situating our two expansions – towards climate services and CCS, and towards economisation. Then, the next section introduces climate services in the Pacific Island region in conversation with theories of performativity, and then Alberta's CCS attempts with Polanyian understandings of embedded markets are considered. We conclude this chapter by returning to the idea of climate change economies and the work required to make markets for adaptation and decarbonisation seem the natural response to climate challenges.

Theorising climate change economies

Over the course of the last decade, a new carbon economy has arrived, taking shape in the form of 'several, increasingly interconnected, carbon markets' (Boyd *et al.* 2011: 601). The contours of this economy include an increasing number of regional and national carbon prices and trading schemes, voluntary offset markets, and the United Nations Framework Convention on Climate Change (UNFCCC) enforced compliance mechanisms (Lohmann 2005; Boykoff *et al.* 2009). The novelty of this economy comes more from its reliance on finance capital, globalised market opportunities, and market-oriented governments (Newell and Paterson 2009) – the scale and dominant position of the market in addressing emissions (Lohmann 2010) – rather than from the novelty of these instruments and orientations themselves.

The commodification of greenhouse gas (GHG) carbon-cycling capacity and the creation of carbon markets has been one of the most researched and discussed aspects of the political economy of climate change. Much geographical scholarship has charted the rise of these market mechanisms, and how and why there remains a 'blind' faith (Boyd *et al.* 2011) in their ability to adequately limit GHG emissions (Bailey 2007a, 2007b; Liverman 2008; Boykoff *et al.* 2009; Knox-Hayes 2010; Goodman and Boyd 2011). Despite volatility and patchiness in carbon prices and remaining uncertainty in future international agreements and policies, the market model remains the policy of choice (Lohmann 2010), even if these markets are increasingly subject to state (re)regulation. Geographers have also charted how market approaches to climate governance became the 'politically acceptable' option, the policy choice most satisfactory for its North American proponents and necessary for their agreement to the Kyoto Protocol (Bumpus and Liverman 2008; Liverman 2008; MacKenzie 2009). Concomitant with market approaches and logics has been a rise in participation of non-state actors in carbon control, including business and financial players (Newell and Paterson 2009; Prudham 2009; Ormond 2015), and accountants (Lovell and MacKenzie 2011).

Another major strand of research on the political economies of climate change has sought to expose the uneven production of new carbon economies. This economy assumes a kind of flat earth, where emissions reductions in one corner of the world are made equivalent to emissions in another (Bumpus and Liverman 2008; Knox-Hayes 2010). Yet, the carbon economy is bounded to 'a longer history [and geography] of the development of market-based environmental policies' (Goodman and Boyd 2011: 104). Additionally, although emissions and reductions in different parts of the world are made equal when they enter markets, they link the

Global North and Global South in complex and uneven ways. Thus, Italian verifiers and scientific experts travel to Costa Rica to confront indigenous farmers and land-owners in powerful, but unequal, encounters that seek to maintain a carbon offset (Lansing 2012). The benefits of reducing emissions – financial and otherwise – are also unevenly distributed (Goodman and Boyd 2011).

This chapter expands upon these contributions concerning the political economies of climate governance. In doing so, we build on recent research related to the 'performativity programme' of Michel Callon and his interlocutors who explore the practices required to enact marketisation. In examining the proliferation of marketised forms of carbon control, several authors have paid close attention to how carbon markets come into being, including the forms of commensuration and disentanglement that are necessary for market creation (Callon 2009; MacKenzie 2009; Powell 2009). Market performativity approaches, in Barnes' distillation, suggest that economists with their equations and equipment do not simply describe an external reality of a market, but 'they just do it', helping 'to shape it, to bring it into being' (Barnes 2008: 1433). Markets, continues Barnes, 'do not exist in the abstract … but are produced on the ground' through the aligned efforts of humans and nonhumans alike (Barnes 2008: 1435; Berndt and Boeckler 2009). Accordingly, economic science and technologies are not independent from the realities they describe, but are key in bringing this reality into being. Çaliskan and Callon propose a research programme that devotes attention to processes of economisation, taken to mean 'the processes through which activities, behaviours and spheres or fields are established as being economic' (Çaliskan and Callon 2009: 370). Marketisation is *just one* 'particular form of economisation' (Çaliskan and Callon 2010: 2). As a broader, or more general process, economisation highlights how neoliberal rationalities 'disseminate the model of the market' even where 'monetary wealth generation is not the immediate issue' (Brown 2015: 31). Therefore, the empirical examples we highlight below 'follow the carbon' (Mitchell 2011, following Marcus 1995) to concentrated centres of knowledge production and expertise on climate change which have become 'economic' even when they are not explicitly trading commodified bundles of CO_2.

However, geographers have recently sought to re-politicise and contextualise the performativity programme. Thus, Christophers (2014: 18) argues for 'weak' ('as in less extreme as opposed to less powerful') performativity that recognises the transformative power of economics as an engine of marketisation (MacKenzie 2006), where economics 'contributes to the construction of the reality that it describes' (Callon 2007: 316). However, this weak performativity should also contain a more holistic, explanatory theory of markets that attends to power and political economy. Similarly, Butler brings the political effects of markets to the forefront, looking to 'misfires' – those cases where performativity does not 'work' – and therefore to the 'certain felicitous conditions' (Butler 2010: 147) which enable successful performatives. This is a politicised and situated version of performativity that resists voluntarism, highlights the uneven distribution of abilities to marketise, and illuminates the conditions under which new economisation processes are created and proliferate.

Following this cue, below we draw from Polanyian theories of embeddedness (Muellerleile 2013; Peck 2013) to attend to the institutional 'bedding' that enables actually existing economisation processes, and their interrelations with other coordinating mechanisms. At its simplest, embeddedness[1] 'expresses the idea that the economy is not autonomous, as it must be in economic theory' (Block 2001: xxiii–xiv). The originality in Polanyi's argument is that although classical economists wanted to create economies disembedded from societies, 'they *did not* and *could not* achieve this goal' (Block 2001: xxiv). In arguing that markets are never successfully disembedded from their social bases, Polanyi was not merely 'making the banal point ... that a market economy cannot be coordinated solely by the supply-demand-price mechanism' (Dale 2010: 73). Instead, Polanyi's is an historical argument: that the establishment of markets in land, labour, and money – those three fictitious commodities traded in the market, but not created for the market – in the eighteenth century, produced dramatic negative social consequences that 'push[ed] this tendency to its "utopian" limit' (Dale 2010: 73). Thus, Polanyi posits economic liberalism as a structural impossibility.[2] Therefore, while much attention has been paid to the marketisation of climate of governance, attention to the necessities of state and non-market supports and rationalities is also needed. Moreover, this analytical attention opens up the possibilities of critical analyses of climate change economies as supposed neutral clearinghouses of goods, services, and price signals.

Our empirical claim to broaden what counts in climate change economies examines how and why economic rationalities operate in climate governance. If the performativity thesis helps us understand *how* these market-like mechanisms are created, we turn to Polanyian work on embeddedness to understand outside processes mediating *why* (Muellerleile 2013). We embrace Muellerleile's (2013: 1631) challenge to take 'seriously both the assemblage of market entities emanating outward, and the broader context, whether geographical historical, or institutional that lays the groundwork for the market system to begin with'. In summary, this chapter adds a new dimension to our understanding of political economies of climate change, and the economisation processes and logics involved in climate change governance.

Performativity, economisation, and climate services

Our first empirical investigation of climate change economies looks to the production of climate services, using the case of the Pacific Island Climate

Services Forum (PICSF). Here we draw from participant observation at the PICSF and subsequent interviews concerning climate services throughout the region. The case stems from a larger research project that sought to understand the potentials, limits, and political economies of climate change adaptation in the Pacific region. It involved approximately 120 semi-structured interviews with project managers, consultants, technical experts (including scientists and service providers), aid workers, and government bureaucrats between 2013 and 2015. With respect to the arguments assembled here, these interviews sought to ascertain the processes and practices through which climate services are made, how they circulate in the region, and how they are put to use by consumers.

Climate services[3] are 'easily accessible and timely scientific data and information about climate that helps people make informed decisions in their lives, businesses, and communities' (NOAA 2011, see also Vaughan and Dessai 2014). They can comprise simple information such as historical data sets or more complex 'products' – as they are called by industry insiders – such as climate or weather forecasts intended to encourage smart adaptation decisions. As an example, one climate service is the Island Climate Update, provided by the New Zealand National Institute of Water and Atmospheric Research (NIWA).[4] NIWA emails its subscribers a monthly summary of the climate in the Pacific Islands and an outlook for the upcoming three months. It is accompanied by a monthly teleconference with the national meteorological services to discuss outlooks and issuing forecasts.

According to proponents, transforming climate science into 'actionable information' (Parker *et al.* 2013) is integral to climate change adaptation, especially in vulnerable developing countries. The premise is that precise and timely provision of climate services will aid countries, regions, and communities in coping with the vagaries of climate change, by providing them with projections and predictions to incorporate into planning and decision-making. The need for such services was discussed at the third World Climate Conference in Geneva when thousands of scientists, politicians, and international dignitaries agreed that a framework, institution, and implementation plan must be created in order to supply climate services (Heffernan 2009). The resulting Global Framework for Climate Services (WMO 2011) was prepared as a series of international arrangements and agreements to coordinate efforts to produce and deliver applicable climate services.

There are numerous assumptions underlying the climate services. First, the climate services model replicates a predict-and-adapt model, where climate information is a necessary input to rational and linear adaptation governance (Dessai and Hulme 2004; Mahony and Hulme 2012). Hulme (2011) has called this form of technocratic adaptation 'climate reductionism', as it encourages top–down and narrow strategies for responding to climate impacts. Second, scientists and scientific institutions from the

Global North often produce climate services for application in the Global South, thereby cementing hierarchies of knowledge production and reinforcing uneven geographies of development (Adams *et al.* 2015). Third, the consumers of climate services – those who would use them in their adaptation decisions and investments – are often presumed, rather than investigated or problematised. Common assumed consumers, homogenous in their social categories if not also across them, include small-scale farmers (e.g. Carr and Owusu-Daaku 2016), natural resource managers (e.g. Lemos 2015), and high-level climate policy experts. Within the climate services movement more generally, as in the case here, the production of useful climate information is principally driven from the supply side: scientists construct assumed consumers, and hope to enrol more users into the climate service movement.

The PICSF built on the Global Framework and the US NOAA's climate services work, engaging over 200 'climate experts in a dialogue and information [sharing] with resource and disaster risk managers, community planners … representatives of government ministries and other program managers and policy makers' (PICSF Organizing Committee 2012). The goals of the PICSF included efforts to raise awareness of the 'state of knowledge' and 'available climate and weather service products' (Parker *et al.* 2013: 4). Parker *et al.* (2013: 4) continued: 'The intent … [was to] advance climate services in the Pacific Islands … [and] to strengthen and build new relationships between producers and users of climate information to address issues of critical importance to the region.' Training sessions and a workshop arena provided opportunities for scientists to introduce their climate service products and tools, and how they have been used for adaptation in Pacific Islands. The workshop also provided space for users and providers to identify 'product requirements' through 'iterative dialogue' (PICSF Organizing Committee 2012). Organisers hoped the PICSF would provide decision-makers and planners – the users and clients of climate services – with a 'toolkit of best practices', and that researchers – people designing climate services – would have an indication of product content and format requirements to meet consumers' needs.

At the PICSF, climatologists and proponents of climate service products sought to stimulate demand for their tools. An organiser of the conference exemplifies this:

> If your drinking water comes predominantly from rainwater harvesting, climate services can help ensure that your supply doesn't run out. If you are a farmer wondering what crop to plant, climate services will help you decide which crop will produce the greatest yield. If you are a health practitioner working to eliminate dengue fever, climate services can help identify potential for outbreaks.
>
> (Embassy of the United States Suva Fiji 2013)

The climatologists behind climate service products want to increase uptake as much as possible. Indeed, products depend on their demand: the Island Climate Update recently received additional funding from the New Zealand Government because of the former's enthusiastic usage by, and endorsement and support from, the Pacific Island National Meteorological Services.

Within the PICSF experimental marketplace, climatologists making climate service products sought to ascertain demand for future and current products. Organisers and participants hoped that the different presentations together would create a selection of best practices for using climate services. In reviewing the PICSF, organisers noted that scientists now know key lessons, including the need to tailor products for users in terms of spatial extent, local and regional climatic drivers and issues, specific sectors – services 'keyed to the nature and timing of decision-making' (Parker *et al.* 2013: 5). Scientists continually requested feedback on their products, asking whether simpler or downscaled products were required. For instance, while the Island Climate Update is appreciated for its solid science, it is also considered too 'technical' (Fauchereau *et al.* 2013). This is not to say, necessarily, that it is inconsistent with local knowledge systems,[5] but that in its reporting of seasonal forecasts the Island Climate Update draws too heavily on scientific language. It is, therefore, of limited use in Pacific Islands beyond the meteorological services. The Island Climate Update was urged to use analogues of similar past seasons and the impacts experienced in order to communicate anticipated seasonal trends and therefore to increase usefulness, circulation, and consumption of the product.

According to the language of performativity scholars, we might interpret these efforts as practices of framing and disentangling (Callon 1998) – processes of making service products distinct from one another and perfectly identifiable, and therefore able to be exchanged. The circulation of service products requires 'simplified, uncontroversial owners, products, and modes of ownership, and accounting requires knowing both who is accountable and how and what to count and not to count' (Lohmann 2005: 210). Within the PICSF experimental marketplace, climatologists making climate service products sought to frame and disentangle their products, aiming for maximum usage and demand in adaptation economies. Indeed, the major goals of the workshop were for scientists to gain an understanding of requirements for future and current products. As Robertson (2012: 386) might put it, creating socially necessary abstractions – in the form of service products – 'adequate to bear value in capitalist circulation'.

Yet, these framing and disentangling practices can easily break down. What performativity scholars call 'overflows' – where framing, selecting, severing 'gets out of control and is never completed' because connections and relations 'transgress and can never be contained' (Berndt and Boeckler

2009: 544) – were evident at the PICSF. This was clear as scientists tried to communicate the uncertainties inherent in their climate predictions and services. For climatologists, declaring at once the uncertainties and the robustness of predictions is key (e.g. Fischer-Bruns and Brasseur 2013). The Island Climate Update does this by reporting their 'success' rates – the proportion of time their predictions are realised, recognising that this depends on the definition of success. Another scientist at the PICSF admitted that clients want definitive results; they seek precision over accuracy (Dessai and Hulme 2004; Dessai *et al.* 2009). One way these products respond to uncertainties is by providing 'bandwidths' of results, explaining that uncertainties cannot be overcome even with state-of-the-art simulations and multiple model ensembles. Yet, conversations on communicating uncertainty concluded with calls for more education about such uncertainties and investment in 'no regrets' or 'win-win' developments. Where framing for markets requires that products are severed from their constitutive relations to create a stable and mobile good, the uncertainties of climate prediction reassert themselves.

If the PICSF was a preliminary space from which an experimental marketplace could emerge, this marketplace has distinct non-market characteristics. Despite invocation of commercialised models and performances of supply and demand, these performatives have failed to realise an open market for climate services. Climate uncertainties – and disagreements about trade-offs over precision and accuracy – frustrate processes of framing and disentangling necessary for product circulation in adaptation economies. Moreover, climate services remain publicly funded: one major funder is the Australian Aid Program, which re-allocates Pacific Islands Official Development Assistance to Australian government scientists to fund their service work. In the Pacific Islands at least, there is no effective demand for climate service products to inform adaptation decisions because, among other reasons, they are too technical (Webber 2017).

This is not to say that such economised, but not purely marketised, practices have no effect (Webber and Donner 2017). The hierarchical and technocratic assumptions of the predict-and-adapt model of climate governance are reproduced, and attempts at collaborative, co-produced, even ethical climate services are obscured (Adams *et al.* 2015; Webber and Donner 2017). In terms of economisation, by encouraging a focus on usefulness, creating demand for products, and the circulation of unattached bundles of climate change science, scientists become entrepreneurial figures (see also Robertson 2007). When commenting on competition between different climate service providers in the Pacific, one observer noted that 'the current state of Australian politics, and the budgetary things [i.e. cuts to scientific organisations] that are coming out … [implies that] the whole supply-demand thing is way out of whack'[6] when it comes to provisioning useful information. This observer continued to note that publicly funded scientific organisations 'are being flipped on their heads and they have got to bring in business development people ... because we can't rely on federal funding so we're going to have to promote our services'.[7] Only recently this has further been enforced, as the executive director of the Commonwealth Scientific and Industrial Research Organisation (CSIRO) – where many service providers in the Pacific region work – has implored his employees and organisation to produce according to the competitive and 'high performance culture of Netflix' and other Silicon Valley entrepreneurs (Readfern 2016). Further, the risks of economised enactments such as the PICSF are that climate services become fully commodified, and any benefits that may accrue from them are placed out of reach of the most vulnerable people and communities.

Carbon laissez-faire and carbon capture and storage

Performativity approaches give us the conceptual tools to open up an 'actually existing market', and to see how it comes to operate 'inside'. But these approaches have also been criticised for failing to account for *why* (or why not) markets operate – what ideological, ethical, and cultural 'outside' processes motivate their production, and what larger social outcomes they generate (Muellerleile 2013). Such approaches may fall short of making a 'claim on the *market itself* as a fundamentally political construction' (Peck 2005: 145). The costs of this, echoing Peck, 'are more than semantic, for they imply a continuing naturalisation of some presocial market' (2005: 145). Our second empirical investigation addresses these concerns by looking to preconditions of the economisation of carbon control, through CCS in Alberta, Canada. This research was carried out through interviews and shadowing in the period 2012–13, when the Government of Alberta undertook major policy, regulatory, and financial supports for CCS technology, which was the central tenet of its 2008 climate change plan.

Carbon capture and storage/sequestration technology has emerged over the last two decades as a possible contributor to climate change mitigation efforts. The technology captures CO_2 from hydrocarbon exhaust streams and transports the carbon to temporary storage or permanent sequestration in underground geological formations. While CCS is often referred to as a novel technology, the components – including gas capture and CO_2 injection technology, used for enhanced oil recovery (EOR), which boosts production in mature wells through re-pressurisation with CO_2 – are well established. The novelty of CCS is in using existing technologies to reduce atmospheric GHG concentrations (Pollak *et al.* 2011). Proponents of CCS deem it a necessary 'bridging technology' to reduce atmospheric CO_2 loads while the world energy supply is still dependent on carbon (Unruh 2000).

In Alberta, these rationales for CCS were given added force. Alberta is one of the world's major hydrocarbon-producing regions, known for the large bitumen reserves in the Athabasca oil sands that tend to be more emissions-intensive to extract and process.[8] Yet, these large oil deposits were only actively exploited on a large scale in the last two decades, coinciding with global recognition of, and motivation to act upon, climate change. At the confluence of these two parallel histories, a network of proponents invested in the expansion of Canada's hydrocarbon economy: the locally active fossil fuel energy industry, the Canadian federal government, the Alberta and Saskatchewan provincial governments, and an associated network of researchers and academics all began to work on reorienting existing EOR technologies used for oil production towards the new goal of mitigating GHG emissions. As early as 1992, this 'triple helix' (Etkowitz 2003) of government, academic, and industry actors began to promote EOR techniques as CO_2 mitigation measures (Bailey and McDonald 1993; Padamsay and Railton 1993; Todd and Grand 1993), sometimes explicitly framing the technology as the only solution to the economic–environmental threat posed by climate change to Alberta's hydrocarbon-based economy (Bolger and Isaacs 2003). These concerns intensified in the mid-2000s when production in the bituminous sands took off rapidly. The central role of CCS in the province's climate and energy strategies reached its apex when it was designated as the central theme in the 2008 *Climate Change Strategy* (Government of Alberta 2008), the province's guiding climate policy until late 2015. The strategy targeted an ambitious 200 million tonnes of GHG reductions by 2050, 70 per cent (139 million tonnes) of which were to be achieved by carbon capture. It was bolstered by US$2 billion in funding for four demonstration-scale projects and a formal regulatory review process that aimed to create the most advanced CCS regime in the world.

The GHG reduction target, the direct funding subsidy, the regulatory review process, and other aspects of the government's policy and regulatory actions on CCS were drawn from the recommendations of two (now disbanded) industry–government–academia institutions, the ecoENERGY CCS Task Force (EETF 2008) and the Alberta Carbon Capture and Storage Development Council (ACCSDC 2009). These alliances represented years of discussions and negotiations to develop joint strategies for protecting domestic fossil fuel production in the midst of Kyoto Protocol obligations (Campanella 2011). As described by a provincial bureaucrat: CCS action has 'been driven by the [provincial] government, as they recognise ... the need to maintain our social license to operate ... and continuing to have access to markets to sell our hydrocarbons'.[9] As the GHG-intense oil sands began to attract global scrutiny and infamy, the bitumen export economy and associated 'market access' were threatened, politically and socially. By theoretically enabling both expanded oil sands production and GHG mitigation, proponents hoped CCS would secure a climate-friendly 'social licence' to continue operation, negating the privileging of 'market forces over social forces more generally' (Prudham 2005: 11).

Yet, despite backing from a resource-strong advocate community, and its continuity with the existing dominant political economic pathway, CCS has failed to materialise in any meaningful way.[10] Alberta's CCS aspirations were dashed by a confluence of factors, including the global collapse in oil prices in 2014. Central among them was a crucial disjuncture in the political–economic rationalities deployed by Alberta's CCS proponents: a failure to embed economised carbon governance logics accounts for a significant part of the failed project.

The scenarios and models that formed the basis of Alberta's CCS ambitions assumed a particular marketised milieu for carbon. For example, the scenario work of EETF (2008) and ACCSDC assumed a world price for carbon and a resulting 'carbon constrained' operating environment. Alberta has had its own US$15 per tonne intensity-based price on large industry carbon emissions since 2007,[11] but the 'hypothetical economic profile' justifying CCS in the ACCSDC report assumed a global carbon price of US$30 per tonne, as well as oil prices above US$125 per barrel. The Government of Alberta's *Climate Change Strategy* assumed a price of US$150 per tonne. In describing its 'Guiding Principles to Advance Widespread Adoption of CCS', the ACCSDC recommended that Alberta guide the development of carbon capture within the province using a 'market-based approach where possible' (ACCSDC 2009: 44). The ACCSDC submitted that:

> incentivising the development of CCS in Alberta could be done with greater or lesser degrees of direct government intervention including roles such as market maker, infrastructure owner, project approver and auditor ... [but] where possible, using market-based mechanisms to enable private sector players to bring their ingenuity to the task of CCS may lead to the greatest long-run benefits.
>
> (ACCSDC 2009: 44)

However, while proponents expressed clear preferences for market-based mechanisms and built their business case *assuming* a forthcoming regulatory environment in which stronger carbon prices were in place, proponents avoided actually *advocating* emissions regulations as a means to achieve the business case for CCS.[12] To do so would have explicitly put the government in the critical role of 'market maker', a role that free-market-preferent CCS proponents were unwilling or unable to take. The choice to opt for US$2 billion in subsidies to make up the 'funding gap' belied, however, that the economised logics of carbon governance undergirding the province's CCS strategy were necessarily embedded within the state. Even while the desired targets for CCS assumed both a higher, and more widespread, cost for carbon, the government at the time did little to advocate for a carbon cost at other levels of government or to impose one within its territory.[13] The arguments of CCS proponents that were intended to legitimise a provincial CCS strategy relied on economised rationalities and expectations of integration into carbon markets. In the end, the climate policy and carbon price vacuum meant Alberta's CCS economy could only develop by re-embedding into large, direct state subsidies.

The concept of embeddedness enables us to understand *why* the Alberta CCS alliance struggles to make such a CCS economy. Elaborating on Polanyi's work on embeddedness, as a 'fictitious commodity', any market-like relations concerning carbon are necessarily dependent on continuous regulatory intervention from the state. The case of carbon capture in Alberta shows that the 'felicitous conditions' (Butler 2010) for successful performatives of markets were not met, not least because acting as market-maker and advocating for the higher per tonne prices on carbon necessary to initiate a business case for CCS – truly marketising its climate govern-ance – was not politically aligned with the ruling government's platform. Openly marketising carbon was politically riskier for the party, yet bade worse for CCS, which as an industry has since collapsed.

In the case of Alberta's CCS, state and non-state actors aggressively rolled out the financial and regulatory requisites for the 'new' CCS economy, less as an opportunity to commodify Alberta's CO_2 than as a counter-movement to ensure the continuing legitimacy of 'old' carbon commodities (see also Prudham 2005). That is, the political effects of performing CCS economisa-tion were as important as market effects themselves. While widespread polit-ical movements for enhanced environmental protection and pipeline advocacy have pushed aside carbon capture, many of these dynamics still held (including commitments to hydrocarbon production) with the election of the Alberta New Democrat Party in May 2015, which ended the previous 44-year term of the Progressive Conservative Party that shaped the trajectory of Alberta's carbon economies. Overall, CCS in Alberta was a state-led strategy of market protection, whereby a contingent alliance of hybrid state–market–academic actors coordinated an 'old'-market protective response through a frustrated, but incipient, 'new' carbon market.

Despite careful and sophisticated analyses of the new carbon economy, much geographical literature posits a monolithic retreat of the state and the advance of non-state business and financial players as the key actors in cre-ating and operating carbon governance (Boykoff *et al.* 2009; Newell and Paterson 2009). But the Polanyian perspective we have outlined demon-strates that such social institutions proceed with, not simply following after, climate change economies. In the case of Alberta, rather than a 'wild west' (cf. Boyd *et al.* 2011) of a frontier lawlessness, climate change economies were put into motion by state-sponsored projects. As such, attention to the 'roll back' of state in climate governance must be accompanied by commen-surate attention to 'roll out' carbon control ideological state projects (While *et al.* 2010). Now more than ever, the complex interplays of economisation processes and logics involved in climate change governance in the post-Paris Climate Agreement era deserve scrutiny, where a reinvigoration of political appetite for regulatory intervention for climate goals has reopened the possibilities for expanded marketisation of carbon.

Conclusions

In this chapter, we used our empirical cases to demonstrate the need to extend and complicate recent scholarly literature on the new carbon economy and on climate change adaptation. We looked first to the fledgling adaptation economies of climate services in the Pacific Islands and saw attempts to forge knowledge products in an experimental marketplace. This case revealed insights into how diverse economic actors labour for climate change control and showed that while marketisation in monetary form remains at bay, distinct economised forms of governing science and climate change adaptation flourish. In the case of climate services, a commercialised, rather than explicitly marketised or commodified, governance regime for producing climate information is prioritised, as is a linear predict-and-adapt model of policymaking and planning. As with market-making in climate governance more broadly, there is the risk that the creation of commercialised climate services becomes the principal objective, rather than the tool through which to facilitate adaptation decisions. We also showed that Polanyian-inspired studies of environmental governance help illuminate the necessary continuous regulatory intervention of state and hybrid actors to support economisation practices. The unwillingness of state and regulatory powers to institute market responses through the creation of tradable carbon commodities, which resulted in the failure of CCS to substantively materialise, troubles geographical critiques of spectacular forms of 'accumulation by decarbonisation' (Bumpus and Liverman 2008). Yet, as markets for CCS flounder, the exploitation of Alberta's oil and gas reserves continues unabated through state-sponsored projects of carbon control. We demonstrate the need, therefore, to explore the socio-institutional context necessary in order for any climate-change-related market-performatives to succeed. And although we bring performativity approaches to climate services, and embeddedness to CCS, inverse pairings are also suggestive: one reason for limited uptake of climate services is a lack of regulatory intervention by, and linkage to political authority in, Pacific Island states and decision-making cultures. Conversely, in Alberta, bureaucrats, academics, and trade-insiders labour for subsidised CCS demonstration projects, explicitly for their demonstration impact, and as an 'export opportunity' for the industry.

Thus, we argue for a broadened conception of the new carbon economy – climate change *economies* – which brings configurations of 'new' climate change service-oriented, adaptation economies, as well as 'old' hydrocarbon economies, into conversation with the bundling and making of CO_2- and GHG-equivalents, the emergence and consolidation of which are contingently tied together. These climate change economies spread up and down the carbon commodity chain (Bridge 2011), increasingly connecting economised adaptation responses including financial instruments (Johnson 2015) and information services (Webber and Donner 2017) alongside old fossil fuel and new carbon *qua* CO_2 commodity economies. Much further critical research is required to fully explicate the geographies of climate change economies – research that is both sufficiently expansive to consider the diversity of sites and subjects of economisation, but also suitably analytically precise to diagnose both putative success and failure, and their political effects. Although there is limited explicit marketisation, economisation has political effects on the actions allowed in the name of climate governance. It is not only the exchange of commodities that configures this geography of climate change economies – but economised logics, rationalities, experiments, and equivalencies, hybrid state/markets-in-the making, which pervade ranges of responses to climate change.

The extensions we propose are underpinned by the challenge of theorising two different emerging climate change economies. Rather than seeking a comparison of these cases situated at either end of climate governance, reading CCS and climate services together demands a consideration of the inherent contradictions of economising climate change responses. We bring these ideas together for the questions they demand; following Muellerleile (2013), there is conceptual 'pay-off' in examining the insides/outsides, the hows and whys, of market-making in tandem and in tension. And so, what does this mean about climate change economies? Across the two case studies, we have shown that they are made by a variety of economic and non-economic actors, and that they are 'commanded and controlled' by state and state-like actors equally. Even when explicit market forms remain incomplete, economised logics command expansive reach and power in complex and hybrid/entangled ways: into adaptation sites and back to fossil fuel spaces, even while – perhaps because – the (narrowly construed) new carbon economy has largely not manifest in mature markets. Although Boyd *et al.* (2011: 610) noted that 'pricing and carbon trading mechanisms are … just one small component of a much broader transformation' required to mitigate climate impacts, the capacious economisation that climate services and CCS suggest is perhaps not the shift they envisioned. Rather than redressing the mismatched means and ends of the new carbon economy, economising practices in climate services and CCS indicate a pervasive, if contradictory and faltering, spread in climate change economies. It remains to be seen whether the markets-in-making that we explore here will become sites for calculative exchanges, as they further attach and feed from other, older hybrids. Perhaps there is potential here then that the institutional and intellectual terrain of climate change command and control currently directed to only hybrid-market means might be recuperated towards more socially just ends. What seems more likely, however, is that these climate change economies will continue to fall short of their stated objectives, as their emergence encourages financial resources to flow to, or remain in, elite centres of knowledge production for the putative benefit of 'vulnerable' others.

Notes

1 We largely restrict our discussion of Polanyi's embeddedness concept to the task of understanding how it bolsters a more refined approach to new carbon economies, and we expressly exclude work on Granovetterian embeddedness (Granovetter 1985).

2 Interestingly, Polanyi's (2001 [1944]) *The Great Transformation* demonstrates this argument by examining the work of Smith, Ricardo, and Malthus in shaping what is now experienced as the separation between market and 'interventionist' state activity. By postulating their theories as 'laws', their political economy performed 'free' markets by creating 'laws' which explicated their existence and their naturalness.

3 In some research, a climate service is similar to an ecosystem service, those ecological services that the climate provides to society (see Cooter *et al.* 2013). However, following the pervasive notation throughout the climate service industry and its scholarly literature, we maintain this definition.

4 Most climate services are produced by scientists employed by government agencies, or scientists contracted to work for government agencies and international development assistance agencies. Here, for simplicity, producers of climate services are referred to as scientists.

5 Indeed, in parallel with the PICSF efforts, in Vanuatu many development and climate experts have worked to combine local seasonal forecasting techniques with scientific predictions such as the Island Climate Update to inform coastal management practices (Masale *et al.* 2014). Of course, there are likely to be incompatibilities between these knowledge systems; the assumption of the predict-and-adapt model is common across them.

6 Federal bureaucrat (5 February 2014), Melbourne, Australia.

7 Federal bureaucrat (5 February 2014), Melbourne, Australia.

8 The oil reserves in the bituminous sands are considered the third largest oil reserves in the world, after Saudi Arabia and Venezuela. The province also hosts vast coal reserves, as well as significant volumes of natural gas and conventional oil.

9 Provincial bureaucrat (26 October 2012), Edmonton, Canada.

10 Two of the four projects were cancelled. The Shell Quest deep saline aquifer storage project, the largest of the four projects, began sequestering in autumn 2015, and is expected to sequester 1 million tonnes CO_2 per year. The fourth project as of February 2016 was in the engineering phase, and scheduled to begin operation in 2017.

11 The *Specified Gas Emitters Regulation*, Alta. Reg. 139/2007, as amended, applies to 'large industrial emitters' producing in excess of 100,000 tonnes of carbon per year. This was the first regulation in Canada to enforce a charge on carbon.

12 For instance, in the ACCSDC 'Business Case for CCS', the proposed options for closing the 'funding gap' for CCS were government investment through direct subsidies and capital grants, cost recovery through CO2-EOR, tax and royalty breaks, and double crediting under the *Specified Gas Emitters Regulation* (ACCSDC 2009: 38, 45–8).

13 This has changed, however, with the introduction of an economy-wide price on carbon by Alberta's new government, elected in May 2015. The new price on carbon came into effect 1 January 2017, at US$20 per tonne, rising to US$30 per tonne in 2018. But it is still widely considered to be insufficient to stimulate CCS as a mitigation choice.

References

ACCSDC, 2009. *Accelerating Carbon Capture and Storage Implementation in Alberta*. Alberta Carbon Capture and Storage Development Council (ACCSDC).

Adams, P., *et al.*, WMO Secretariat, 2015. Call for an ethical framework for climate services. *WMO Bulletin*, 64.

Bailey, I., 2007a. Market environmentalism, new environmental policy instruments and climate policy in the United Kingdom and Germany. *Annals of the Association of American Geographers*, 97 (3), 530–50.

Bailey, I., 2007b. Neoliberalism, climate governance and the scalar politics of EU emissions trading. *Area*, 39 (4), 431–42.

Bailey, R., and McDonald, M., 1993. CO2 capture and use for EOR in western Canada: General overview. *Energy Conversion and Management*, 34 (9), 1145–50.

Barnes, T., 2008. Making space for the market: Live performances, dead objects and economic geography. *Geography Compass*, 2 (5), 1432–48.

Berndt, C., and Boeckler, M., 2009. Geographies of circulation and exchange: Constructions of markets. *Progress in Human Geography*, 33 (4), 535–51.

Block, F., 2001. Introduction. *In: The Great Transformation: The political and economic origins of our time*. Boston, MA: Beacon Press.

Bolger, L., and Isaacs, E., 2003. Shaping an integrated energy future, *In*: A. Heinztman, ed., *Fueling the Future: How the battle over energy is changing everything*. Toronto: House of Ananzi Press.

Boyd, E., Boykoff, M., and Newell, P., 2011. The 'new' carbon economy: What's new? *Antipode*, 43 (3), 601–11.

Boykoff, M., Bumpus, A., and Liverman, D., 2009. Theorising the carbon economy: Introduction to the special issue. *Environment and Planning A*, 41, 2299–304.

Bridge, G., 2011. Resource geographies 1: Making carbon economies old and new. *Progress in Human Geography*, 35 (6), 820–34.

Bridge, G., and Le Billon, P., 2012. *Oil*. Cambridge: Polity Press.

Brown, W., 2015. *Undoing the Demos: Neoliberalism's stealth revolution*. Cambridge, MA: MIT Press.

Brown, K., and Corbera, E., 2003. Exploring equity and sustainable development in the new carbon economy. *Climate Policy*, 3, 41–56.

Bumpus, A., and Liverman, D., 2008. Accumulation by decarbonization and the governance of carbon offsets. *Economic Geography*, 84 (2), 127–55.

Butler, J., 2010. Performative agency. *Journal of Cultural Economy*, 3 (2), 147–61.

Çaliskan, K., and Callon, M., 2009. Economization, part 1: Shifting attention from the economy towards processes of economization. *Economy and Society*, 38 (3), 368–98.

Çaliskan, K., and Callon, M., 2010. Economization, part 2: A research programme for the study of markets. *Economy and Society*, 39 (1), 1–32.

Callon, M., 1998. *The Laws of Markets*. Oxford: Blackwell.

Callon, M., 2007. What does it mean to say that economics is performative? *In*: D. MacKenzie, F. Muniesa, and L. Siu, eds, *Do Economists Make Markers? On the performativity of economics*. Princeton, NJ: Princeton University Press, 311–57.

Callon, M., 2009. Civilizing markets: Carbon trading between in vitro and in vivo experiments. *Accounting, Organization and Society*, 34 (3), 440–8.

Campanella, D., 2011. *Fossil Intentions: Carbon capture and storage in Alberta* (Unpublished major paper). York, ON: York University.

Carr, E., and Owusu-Daaku, K., 2016. The shifting epistemologies of vulnerability in climate services for development: The case of Mali's agrometeorological advisory programme. *Area*, 48 (1), 7–17.

Castree, N., 2006. From neoliberalism to neoliberalisation: consolations, confusions and necessary illusions. *Environment and Planning A*, 38 (1), 1–6.

Christophers, B., 2014. From Marx to market and back again: Performing the economy. *Geoforum*, 57, 12–20.

Cooter, E., Rea, A., and Bruins, R., 2013. The role of the atmosphere in the provision of ecosystem services. *Science of the Total Environment*, 448, 197–208.

Dale, G., 2010. *Karl Polanyi: The limits of the market*. Cambridge: Polity Press.

Dessai, S., and Hulme, M., 2004. Does climate adaptation policy need probabilities? *Climate Policy*, 4 (2), 107–28.

Dessai, S., *et al.*, 2009. Do we need better predictions to adapt to a changing climate? *Eos*, 90 (13), 111–12.

EETF, 2008. Canada's fossil energy future: The way forward on carbon capture and storage (Report to the Minister of Alberta Energy and Natural Resources Canada). ecoENERGY Carbon Capture and Storage Task Force (EETF).

Embassy of the United States Suva Fiji, 2013. US Government supports climate services forum for the Pacific. Embassy section [online]. Available from: http://suva.usembassy.gov/regional_environmental_office/u.s.-government-supports-climate-services-forum-for-the-pacific [Accessed 26 October 2017].

Etkowitz, H., 2003. *The Triple Helix: University-industry-government innovation in action*. London: Routledge.

Fauchereau, N., *et al.*, 2013. *The Island Climate Update: A seasonal forecasting platform, forum, and bulletin for the Pacific Islands*. Presented at the Pacific Island Climate Services Forum, the University of the South Pacific Suva.

Fischer-Bruns, I., and Brasseur, G., 2013. *Climate Service Center – Germany: Lessons learned in developing climate services*. Presented at the Pacific Island Climate Services Forum, the University of the South Pacific Suva.

Goodman, M., and Boyd, E., 2011. A social life for carbon? Commodification, markets and care. *The Geographical Journal*, 177 (2), 102–9.

Government of Alberta, 2008. *Alberta's 2008 Climate Change Strategy*. Calgary: Government of Alberta.

Granovetter, M., 1985. Economic action and social structure: The problem of embeddedness. *American Journal of Sociology*, 91 (3), 481–510.

Heffernan, O., 2009. World climate services framework agreed. *Nature*, 461, 158–9.

Hulme, M., 2011. Reducing the future to climate: A story of climate determinism and reductionism. *Osiris*, 26 (1), 245–66.

Johnson, L., 2015. Near futures and perfect hedges in the Gulf of Mexico, *In*: H. Appel, A. Mason, and M. Watts, eds, *Subterranean Estates: Life worlds of oil and gas*. Ithaca, NY: Cornell University Press.

Knox-Hayes, J., 2010. Constructing carbon market spacetime: Climate change and the onset of neo-modernity. *Annals of the Association of American Geographers*, 100 (4), 953–62.

Lansing, D., 2012. Performing carbon's materiality: The production of carbon offsets and the framing of exchange. *Environment and Planning A*, 44 (1), 204–20.

Lemos, M., 2015. Useable climate knowledge for adaptive and co-managed water governance. *Current Opinion in Environmental Sustainability*, 12, 48–52.

Liverman, D., 2008. Conventions of climate change: Constructions of danger and the dispossession of the atmosphere. *Journal of Historical Geography*, 35 (2), 279–96.

Lohmann, L., 2005. Marketing and making carbon dumps: Commodification, calculation and counterfactuals in climate change mitigation. *Science as Culture*, 14 (3), 203–35.

Lohmann, L., 2010. Uncertainty markets and carbon markets: Variations on Polanyian themes. *New Political Economy*, 15 (2), 225–54.

Lovell, H., and MacKenzie, D., 2011. Accounting for carbon: The role of accounting professional organizations in governing climate change. *Antipode*, 43 (3), 612–38.

MacKenzie, D., 2006. *An Engine, Not a Camera: How financial models shape markets*. Cambridge, MA: MIT Press.

MacKenzie, D., 2009. Making things the same: Gases, emission rights and the politics of carbon markets. *Accounting, Organization and Society*, 34 (3), 440–55.

Mahony, M., and Hulme, M., 2012. Model migrations: Mobility and boundary crossings in regional climate prediction. *Transactions of the Institute of British Geographers*, 37 (2), 197–211.

Marcus, G., 1995. Ethnography in/of the world system: The emergence of multi-sited ethnography. *Annual Review of Anthropology*, 24 (1), 95–117.

Masale, P., *et al.*, 2014. *Vanuatu Climate Services Dialogue (Workshop Report)*. VMGD and NOAA, Port Vila Vanuatu.

Mitchell, T., 2011. *Carbon Democracy*. London: Verso.

Muellerleile, C., 2013. Turning financial markets inside out: Polanyi, performativity and disembeddedness. *Environment and Planning A*, 45 (7), 1625–42.

Newell, P., and Paterson, M., 2009. The politics of the carbon economy. *In*: M. Boykoff, ed., *The Politics of Climate Change: A survey*. London: Routledge, 80–99.

NOAA, 2011. *NOAA's Proposed Climate Services (Background)*. National Oceanographic and Atmospheric Administration (NOAA). Washington, DC: United States Department of Commerce.

Ormond, J., 2015. New regimes of responsibilization: Practicing product carbon footprinting in the new carbon economy. *Economic Geography*, 91 (4), 425–8.

Padamsay, R., and Railton, J., 1993. CO2 capture and use for EOR in western Canada: Economic results and conclusions. *Energy Conversion and Management*, 34 (9), 1165–75.

Parker, B., Marra, J., and Muth, M., 2013. *Pacific Islands Climate Services Forum Outcomes and Final Report*. PICSF.

Peck, J., 2005. Economic sociologies in space. *Economic Geography*, 81 (2), 129–75.

Peck, J., 2013. Disembedding Polanyi: Exploring Polanyian economic geographies. *Environment and Planning A*, 45 (7), 1536–44.

PICSF Organizing Committee, 2012. *Pacific Island Climate Services Forum Announcement*. USAID, NOAA, GIZ, AusAID, University of the South Pacific.

Polanyi, K., 2001 [1944]. *The Great Transformation: The political and economic origins of our time*. 2nd edition. Boston, MA: Beacon Press.

Pollak, M., Johnson Phillips, S., and Vajihala, S., 2011. Carbon capture and storage policy in the United States: A new coalition endeavours to change existing policy. *Global Environmental Change*, 21 (2), 313–23.

Powell, G., 2009. Complexity, entanglement, and overflow in the new carbon economy: The case of the UK's energy efficiency commitment. *Environment and Planning A*, 41 (10), 2342–56.

Prudham, S., 2005. *Knock on Wood: Nature as commodity in Douglas fir country*. Toronto: University of Toronto Press.

Prudham, S., 2009. Pimping climate change: Richard Branson, global warming and the performance of green capitalism. *Environment and Planning A*, 41 (7), 1594–613.

Readfern, G., 2016. After climate cuts at CSIRO, who should we ask about global warming impacts on Australia? Netflix? Australia: *Guardian* [online]. Available from: www.theguardian.com/environment/planet-oz/2016/feb/05/after-climate-cuts-at-csiro-who-should-we-ask-about-global-warming-impacts-on-australia-netflix [Accessed 26 October 2017].

Robertson, M., 2007. Discovering price in all the wrong places: The work of commodity definition and price under neoliberal policy. *Antipode*, 39 (3), 500–26.

Robertson, M., 2012. Measurement and alienation: making a world of ecosystem services. *Transactions of the Institute of British Geographers*, 37 (3), 386–401.

Todd, M., and Grand, G., 1993. Enhanced oil recovering using carbon dioxide. *Energy Conversion and Management*, 34 (9), 1157–64.

Unruh, G., 2000. Understanding carbon lock-in. *Energy Policy*, 28 (12), 817–30.

Vaughan, C., and Dessai, S., 2014. Climate services for society: Origins, institutional arrangements, and design elements for an evaluation framework. *WIREs Climate Change*, 5 (5), 587–603.

Webber, S., 2017. Circulating climate services: Commercializing science for climate change adaptation in Pacific Islands. *Geoforum*, 85, 82–91.

Webber, S., and Donner, S., 2017. Climate service warnings: Cautions about commercializing climate science for adaptation in the developing world. *WIREs Climate Change*, 8 (1), 1–8.

While, A., Jonas, A., and Gibbs, D., 2010. From sustainable development to carbon control: Eco-state restructuring and the politics of urban and regional development. *Transactions of the Institute of British Geographers*, 35 (1), 76–93.

WMO, 2011. *Climate Knowledge for Action: A global framework for climate services: empowering the most vulnerable*. Geneva: World Meteorological Organization (WMO).

5 Tourism, environmental damage, and climate policy at the coast of Oaxaca, Mexico

Ignacio Rubio C.

Introduction: tourism and environmental risk

Tourism is a human activity sensitive to climate. In the introduction to the recently published book *Political Ecology of Tourism*, the editors referred to climate change as the key expression of the threats faced by tourism globally (Mostafanezhad *et al.* 2016: 1). Higher air and sea temperatures, rising sea levels, extreme geophysical events, erosion, ocean acidification, and biological effects will all present challenges for tourism (Wong *et al.* 2014: 384–5). A decade ago, an evaluation of the impact of climate change on tourist destinations sponsored by the Intergovernmental Panel on Climate Change (IPCC) concluded that:

> vulnerabilities of industry, infrastructures, settlements and society to climate change are generally greater in certain high-risk locations, particularly coastal and riverine areas, and areas whose economies are closely linked with climate-sensitive resources, such as tourism; these vulnerabilities tend to be localised but are often large and growing.
>
> (Wilbanks *et al.* 2007: 359)

This chapter investigates the situation in one such high-risk location, the small town of Zipolite on the coast of Oaxaca, Mexico (Figure 5.1). My research provides empirical support for the theory that vulnerabilities tend to be localised; however, the aim of this text is to illustrate some problematic aspects of climate change policy in Mexico: namely, the way that climate change is entangled with policy – particularly development policy – and the way that consequences of this interlinkage provide wide space for critical analysis. My discussion focuses on how climate change adaptation policies portray and evaluate the environmental risks that jeopardise tourism development and create environmental fragility and damage.

Since the late 1990s, I have been visiting the coast of Oaxaca regularly – as a tourist and as a researcher, but mostly as both. I have met old and new residents involved in many different activities, from peasants to property investors, and have witnessed the rapid expansion of tourism. Apart

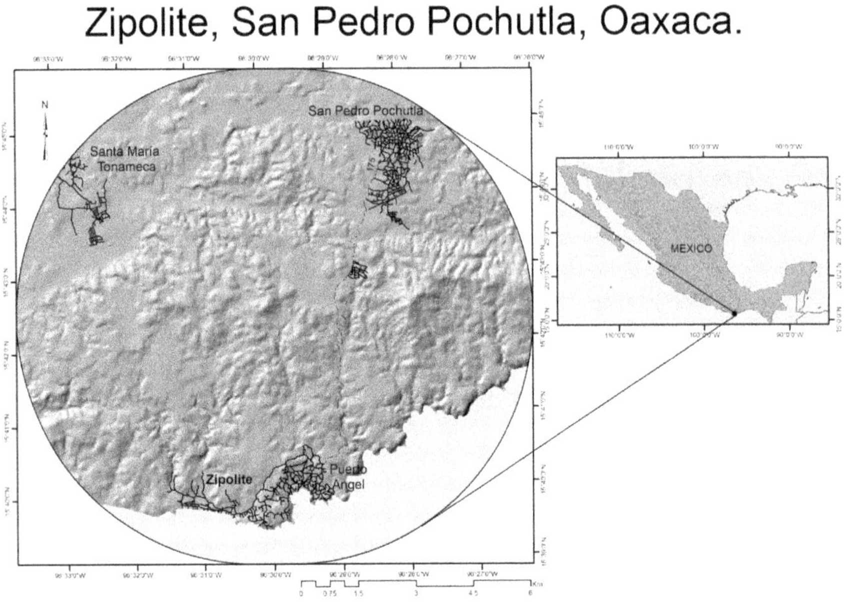

Zipolite, San Pedro Pochutla, Oaxaca.

Figure 5.1 Location map for Zipolite on the coast of Oaxaca, Mexico.

Source: INEGI website: www.inegi.org.mx

from this general experience, the argument I present here draws mainly from a research project on tourism, disaster risk scenarios, and climate change undertaken between 2012 and 2014 with the support of the Research Program on Climate Change (PINCC) at the National Autonomous University of Mexico (UNAM), the Metropolitan Autonomous University, and a small team of research assistants and students. This work involved the collection and organisation of socio-historical and environmental information from official documents, scientific reports, and the press. It also included interviews with hotel and restaurant owners, merchants, workers, fishers, and local authorities. As part of the ethnographic work, I conducted workshops in which the topics of climate change, disasters, and adaptation were discussed with long-standing residents of five coastal settlements, including Zipolite (Rubio 2014).

The next section examines two official documents on disaster risk, adaptation to climate change, and tourism in Mexico to show how policy frames climatic risk and thus drives adaptation strategies. It follows a brief account of an analytical model that provides a critical perspective on risk that helps to understand the problematic nature of risk and adaptation policies. I then go on to substantiate this argument by exploring some critical socio-environmental aspects in the formation of one particular tourist destination at the coast of Oaxaca. This illuminates the critical and contradictory role of the Mexican state in both the expansion of tourism and the creation of environmental damage and fragility and, finally, reiterates the need for socio-political approaches to risk and adaptation that reveal the drivers, agents, and logic that generate the social conditions of vulnerability.

The view of the Mexican Government on climate change adaptation

This study begins from some intertwined *politico-ecological* premises. First, environmental problems (including climate change) are socio-historical constructs. Second, environmental problems in tourist destinations are an intrinsic part of the political economy of tourism – an economy characterised by an uneven distribution of benefits and costs, risks and damage, and opportunities and resources to participate in the benefits of tourism. Thus, it is important to make sense of how such political economy unfolds in specific socio-historical contexts in order to see how environmental fragility and damage are produced. Finally, to understand this, it is necessary to examine how people and governments involved in the production and maintenance of tourist destinations evaluate risks and opportunities and cope with environmental change and damage – both the major and many localised disasters that are common in tourist destinations in coastal Mexico, as is the case in many other recently urbanised areas in Mexico and Latin America (Mansilla 2008).

The political ecology of tourism is an integrative perspective that aims to denaturalise the environment as a discursively constructed category and offer opportunities to examine its myriad forms in tourism contexts (Mostafanezhad *et al.* 2016: 5). Climate change is one of these 'myriad forms'. As anthropogenic climate change escalated to scientific truth, adaptation and risk mitigation became central concepts through which the environment is publicly portrayed as a problem, challenge, threat, or even opportunity for tourist destinations. Among the diverse ways in which climate change helps to frame, make sense of, and act upon the environment, we find risk and adaptation policies.

In the context of increased public anxiety about climate action, the Mexican Ministry of Tourism issued two policy documents addressing disaster risk and adaptation to climate change in tourist destinations.[1] The first is a study of ten 'strategic destinations' (Anid 2014), while the second provides guidance for municipal governments to devise and implement risk mitigation and adaptation actions (Sectur 2014). Both documents (referred to subsequently as the *Study* and the *Local Guide*) provide general information about climate change and propose three broad aims for Mexico's tourism sector: optimise the use of natural resources; respect socio-cultural authenticity; and secure economic operations. The stated objective of these policy documents was to generate a diagnostic method of vulnerability in the face of adverse impacts resulting from climate variability and climate change, and to propose specific recommendations to promote adaptation programmes, including the development of ad hoc early warning systems for the tourism sector (Anid 2014: 3, own translation).

The *Study* (Anid 2014) is a large report on risk, disasters, and climate in ten integrally planned centres (IPC), including Bahías de Huatulco on the coast of Oaxaca in southern Mexico. The IPCs are large complexes comprising resorts, golf courses, marinas, and winter residences, and most are the result of significant public investments in formerly peripheral coastal regions. Despite its title, the document enables a risk–hazard approach that pays attention to the potential impact of single extreme events (heatwaves, tropical storms, coastal erosion, and river flooding). Within a risk–hazard framework, vulnerability is defined as a dose–response relation between an exogenous hazard to a system and its adverse effects (Füssel and Klein 2006: 305; see also Bassett and Fogelman 2013), is concerned with predicting the 'impact' of a given climate event or stress, and estimating the increment of damage caused by an intensification from 'normal' climatic conditions to the conditions expected under climate change scenarios (Ribot 2014: 667). Exemplary of such an understanding of risk, in both the *Study* and the *Local Guide*, the critical aspect of vulnerability is infrastructure's exposure to hazards. From this narrow approach, the *Study* concludes with concise proposals for early warning systems in the ten strategic destinations, while the *Local Guide* lists the legal instruments and programmes that provide the institutional frame within which attention to risk mitigation and adaptation should be procured (such as a risk atlas, early response programmes, ecological and territorial ordinations).

In these policy documents, vulnerability becomes an index comprising socio-cultural factors (information about hazards and safety procedures), socio-demographic and economic indices (including access to education, health, communication and *adequate* income), institutional and political conditions (solid administrative structures, attention strategies, coordination between local authorities and service providers), and geographic and *conjunctural* factors (planning instruments and knowledge of the level of exposure to climatic risks due to location). The fact that location is conceived as a *conjuctural* aspect seems at odds with the decades of intense and planned public intervention to lever tourism in specific regions. It is also an example of what Ribot (2014) called 'additionality' views based on the imaginary (or 'constructed') notion that the effects of climate change are separable from underlying social conditions (Ribot 2014: 667). Consistent with this view, the risk mitigation and adaptation strategy for climate change, as articulated in the two Ministry of Tourism documents, present some critical characteristics:

- Spatially, destinations are seen as 'enclaves', discrete territorial units disconnected from the broader environment.
- Politically, the institutional setting they refer to comprises laws and programmes, but very little attention is paid to the different ways these

crystallise at different levels (state, municipal, local). The political and social problems policy faces are not disclosed.

- Economically, no attention is paid to interactions between tourism and other long-standing productive activities such as agriculture and fisheries.
- Temporally, history is limited to measured rainfall and ocean tides. No information is given concerning the distribution of costs and benefits of past (large) disasters, nor to the social consequences of such distribution.
- Environmental change is reduced to climate variability.

Political ecologists have argued that diverse forms of environmental degradation and risk are often the result of planned interventions promoted by international agencies and nation states, particularly in the Global South (Painter and Durham 1995). Such is the case for tourism on the coast of Oaxaca. The risk–hazard stance is common in climate policy documents, but becomes problematic when attention is brought to the social distribution of costs and damage due to environmental change in local contexts. At this level, vulnerability and marginalisation of local populations and specific groups should receive much higher priority in order to understand the different effects of hazards (including climate change) and the social construction of risk (Blaikie *et al.* 2003).

Political ecology of climate risk: the pressure and release model

Since the mid-1980s, the *pressure and release model* (Blaikie *et al.* 2003: 49–86) has become one of the main schemes for critically analysing environmental risk. In this model, vulnerability results from the progressive articulation of root causes, dynamic pressures, and unsafe conditions. Root causes refer to the political economy that rules the social process of value formation and appropriation. They concern institutions such as property, market, and the state, and the hegemony of a possessive logic that justifies private appropriation of common goods and socialisation of damage. According to Blaikie and colleagues, root causes are materialised in dynamic pressures, namely:

> [...] processes and activities that 'translate' the effects of root causes both temporally and spatially into unsafe conditions [...]. Dynamic pressures channel the root causes into particular forms of unsafe conditions that then have to be considered in relation to the different types of hazards facing people.
>
> (Blaikie *et al.* 2003: 52–3)

Commodification and privatisation of the land, unplanned and/or enforced urbanisation, occupation of fragile sites such as beaches and swamps, change in labour relations and opportunities, public spending, policy, and other forms of governmental intervention are all dynamic pressures that underlie unsafe conditions, namely the vulnerability that compounds the risks individuals, communities, and towns must deal with.

Even though the *pressure and release model* is widely used to describe the importance of social factors in risk analysis, the effort to critically discuss dynamic pressures is less common. In policy documents, such pressures are usually replaced by factors or components that are in turn evaluated through well-being or poverty indices (Cenapred 2006). Replacing dynamic pressures with well-being indices produces a double concealment: it obscures the dynamic, historical nature of the processes it calls upon; and excludes critical analysis of the pressures themselves, of the interests and relations that produce them. Thus, it is an aim of this chapter to provide some insight into these critical issues and to show that the expansion of political economies based on massive investment in infrastructure can involve marginalisation of local communities from development (Peluso 1993; Peet and Watts 2004) – as is the case, I argue, on the coast of Oaxaca. Finally, any political perspective should pay attention to social conflicts and struggles. In these situations, the political character of the state and its class basis, the uses of political positions and state power by the bureaucratic elite and other individuals, cliques and factions, and the advantage to them of bureaucratic 'inefficiency and corruption' becomes visible (Ferguson 1994: 178). Conversely, it is also politically relevant to show that policy does not go unchallenged by local actors, and that the expansion of tourism also conveys struggles in which agency is exerted (see next section).

State, tourism development, and environmental risk in the coast of Oaxaca

David Scowsill, president of the World Travel and Tourism Council, recently declared that tourism grows in Mexico because the government has given it priority status for many years and, that today, there are great investment opportunities as the government continues the expansion of infrastructure, connectivity, and 'sustainable practices' (Puga 2017). The IPC Bahías de Huatulco is a good example of this. It is also a good example of what political ecologists have been documenting worldwide: that nature is the object of contending ideologies and projects, and that powerful agents instrumentalise in many different ways state-led development projects that marginalise local communities and diminish their control over the environmental resources on which those communities depend (Peet and Watts 1993; Stonich 1998; Talledos 2012). A brief description of some of the problems that underlie tourism development in one particular town – Zipolite – will illustrate how the dynamic pressures of risk cannot be simply disconnected from underlying socio-political conditions that should be considered when moving from risk to adaptation.

Settling in Zipolite

Coastline, plateau, and sandy hills covered by deciduous forest shape this settlement that stands 26 metres above sea level. Zipolite's beach – 1,500 metres long and 25 metres wide – is mainly reflective, with strong waves, coarse sediment, and a steep underwater slope, although it also has other sections where the swell breaks onto rocks. In 2010, there were 1,059 permanent residents (INEGI 2010), distributed in eight neighbourhoods or '*colonias*'. According to the local authority, this number could increase to 5,000–7,000 in the peak tourist season (December, Easter week). Between January and May, visitors from Europe, North America, and Canada become a visible group that tends to remain for longer than usual. Some have 'winter homes' and form part of the tourism economy as hotel or restaurant owners or, more recently, as property developers.

Zipolite did not have permanent settlers until the 1950s, a decade when some ten peasant families settled on the east end of the beach, a flat area surrounded by hills that almost split the shore in two. Here, as in many other small coastal towns, occupation of the beach was a difficult socio-environmental process. As described by elders and long-standing residents, the first years usually involved a mix of hardship and joy: hardship associated with the effort of opening up small plots to farm, the total lack of services, communication limited to trails, and poverty:

> We were very poor. There was nothing. My father opened most of this land. It was very difficult because vegetation was too dense. But little by little he succeeded. He was a hard worker and knew how to produce. Few people now understand how it was and how it is to live here.
> (Claudia, age 55 years, restaurant owner, own translation)

Joy is shown in recollections of a resourceful, paradisiac landscape where, cyclically, nature brought relief in the form of turtles, fish, crabs, and shrimps that almost fell into people's hands:

> People used to wait on the beach for the turtles to come, in thousands. Unfortunately, they abused. To catch fish, one just had to go a few meters away from the shore. During the rainy season, as the Zipolite stream carried water from the mountains, kids, women, and youngsters just lay on the mangrove to catch the shrimps that pop up from little holes as the lagoon got filled with fresh water. This was paradise.
> (Urbano, age 66 years, resident)

These recollections illustrate the complexity of the process through which the environment becomes the object of political intervention. The two contrasting visions suggest that for original settlers the environment is not necessarily conceived as unitary and coherent; some used to hold a true knowledge of the place and its hidden treasures. They refer to an ethical dimension that involves issues of rights, limits, endurance, and enjoyment. Finally, they also bring forward the agrarian struggles that accompanied the formation of the village, as well as the collective nature of the damage that has been inflicted on the environment.

Reclaiming the beach front

Two decades after the arrival of the first families, Zipolite's history was definitively bonded to tourism. It all started with a conflict over the ownership of the land. At that time, the national tourism project had been drafted, and had targeted the coast of Oaxaca as one of the isolated, poor, and underexploited regions where an IPC could be developed. But, owing to the agrarian reform that formed the axis of Mexico's development policy in the first half of the twentieth century, much of the coastal region had been granted to various indigenous communities and was subject to a collective form of property, the *agrarian community*. In 1970, the state of Oaxaca expropriated the whole of the sea front of the community of Pochutla, including the old town of Puerto Ángel and the nearby beach of Zipolite, to create a territorial fund for the development of tourism. The expropriation was yet another example of the political nature of state interventions. It not only prepared the institutional conditions for the future development of tourism, but also effectively excluded the communal land owners from the project by rapidly selling the expropriated land to a small number of investors associated with a former state governor who was then to sell it to the federal government for the IPC once the project was ready. However, things turned out differently.

The conflict started in Zipolite in 1976 when the few families that had settled at the eastern end of the beach reclaimed a plot to build a school. The conflict escalated to involve the agrarian community as a whole. The reclaiming peasants gained support from other villages and from economic groups such as coffee producers and merchants of the region. The initial response of the government was violence, but once the conflict reached the national news the federal government backed off. It is not possible to provide a detailed account of the struggle that ended with the restitution of the expropriated land, the distribution of Zipolite's beach among 60 commoners and the relocation (itself not exempt from conflict) of the IPC to the territory of the neighbouring community of Santa María Huatulco. Apart from its exemplary nature regarding the instrumentalisation of development projects by economic elites and political factions, the conflict became part of the local memory and showed that rather than repeal tourism, the families and the community as a whole had to fight exclusion from the tourist project since its inception.

The environmental norms and regulations that began to be issued from the mid-1990s onwards are another form of public intervention that has affected the economy of many families in the region. Of particular relevance is the 1994 ban on the capture and trade of golfina turtles (*Lepidochelys olivacea*), which, by that time, were on the edge of extinction. Helping turtles to reach the sea became a central ecological motif for the attraction of tourists while again restricting local residents from the appropriation of a resource, without once questioning the role of the main agents that caused the crisis: the illegal traders and the private oil industry that for decades had exploited both the chelonians and the fishers without any governmental intervention. None of the economic benefit generated by the industry was invested in the area and so the industry did not bring any social benefits. The resource, and the economic gains, were instead transferred out of the town and the region as a whole. It is also important that the ban and subsequent protection policies – such as the creation of the Bahías de Huatulco National Park – introduced sustainability to mainstream tourism politics and were accompanied by non-governmental organisations that promoted and managed community-based projects for the protection of turtles, other fauna such as alligators or iguanas, or the remnants of mangrove. Under this policy, local communities, rather than active co-investors or partners, found themselves as clients of the government's limited and intermittent funds for protection programmes, framed within the eco-attraction, cast as nature's caregivers, applying norms they did not help to design. Regardless of their ecological appropriateness, it must be noted that environmental protection policies have been fundamental in the commodification of local cultures and landscape for the sake of tourism on the coast of Oaxaca, as in other tourist areas of Mexico (Peluso 1993; Colucci and Mullet 2016).

Building up climatic risk

In the previous section, it was suggested that one of the aspects that undermines the government's climate change risk and adaptation policy in touristic destinations is its lack of attention to the distribution of damage that has accompanied the expansion of tourism, and to the dynamic pressures that create fragile environmental conditions. Climatic threats have long caused damage along the coast of Oaxaca. The region experienced extensive flooding and economic damage in 1974, and then again in 1979, 1981, 1988, and 1990 (Mansilla 2013). This should be enough to corroborate the naïve realism that pervades the official narratives of environmental risk and adaptation: a realism that ignores that some of the scientific facts that compound global warming as a central environmental hazard were available well before the mid-1980s (Lash *et al.* 1996). However, in terms of social conditions, much did indeed change between the 1970s and late-1990s, particularly after the construction of airports in Puerto Escondido (1983) and Huatulco (1988), and once the IPC was built.

Despite Zipolite's small size, the difference between the tourist centre and its residential surrounding is marked. For instance, four new neighbourhoods

(Lomas, Los mangos, Las cascadas, Vistas del mar) spread over the hills that lie across and around the beach, while the old central *colonias* have slowly moved over the mangrove and the two streams that end on the beach (Figure 5.2). In the new *colonias*, there are no paved roads, very limited lighting at night, no running water in some areas, and fragile self-built homes. Meanwhile, wealth concentrates on the beachfront where hotels and local inns attract a wide range of tourists. Concrete buildings, some four-story blocks, have steadily replaced the fragile cabañas or *enramadas*. As the long beach becomes fully occupied, new small hotels and residences are built along the coast in both directions, some occupying cliffs and little bays with difficult access but for which the local authorities have been allocating considerable resources for opening roads and providing electricity. This linear occupation is mainly carried out by foreigners (especially Italians, Americans, and Canadians) and people from other parts of Mexico. Most are ready to help the municipality provide services – to them. It is this new type of enterprise that is expanding and transforming tourism along the entire costal region of Oaxaca

Zipolite, San Pedro Pochutla, Oaxaca

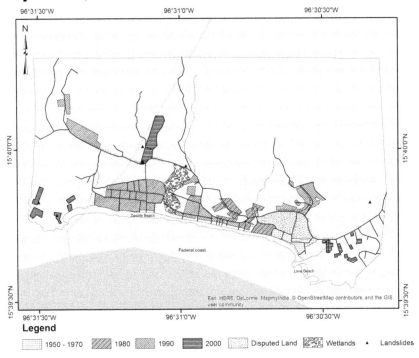

Figure 5.2 Schematic illustration of the coastal development in and around Zipolite, highlighting changes over time and the land under conflict.

Source: INEGI website: www.inegi.org.mx

and placing a major strain on public services, especially sewerage and water provision.

Zipolite's uneven development is both a result and a condition for a model of tourism based on private appropriation of the benefits and socialisation of cost, a model that requires low wages and the exclusion of certain areas in order to be consumed only by those able to pay for them. In three decades, the town grew over a complex network of streams that drain large quantities of water during the rainy season that results in high environmental fragility (Rubio 2014: 32). This was exposed in October 1997, when the town was devastated by Hurricane Pauline. For long-standing residents and hotel owners, the disaster marked a clear before and after:

> We lost three cabañas; the others were seriously damaged. The storm made a swirl and hit us hard. The people in Las cascadas, Lomas, Puerto Ángel … everybody suffered a lot. I cry every time I think of it. After that we started to build with 'material' (concrete), something stronger. The whole place has changed since then.
>
> (Reina, hotel owner, resident since 1987)

Nevertheless, the destruction caused by Hurricane Pauline should not be seen as an isolated event. Coinciding with the growth in tourism, damage linked to climatic conditions has increased from the mid-1980s onwards. Between 1981 and 2013, the national newspapers reported 15 times on negative effects and disasters in Pochutla resulting from rain and heavy seas (Mansilla 2013). Many of those events were small crises that involved *extensive* (versus *intensive*) damage for residents of the poor neighbourhoods along the high road. This type of damage is not considered when adaptation focuses on strategic centres and when climate change is conceptualised as bigger and more frequent storms and hurricanes.

In June 2013, I conducted six workshops with residents of different tourist sites in the coastal region, including Zipolite, where the group comprised seven male long-term residents (a mechanic, a restaurant owner, two workmen, and three fishers). The first activity involved a general presentation on climate change that introduced the climate models used in the Climate Change Atlas of Oaxaca (Fernández *et al.* 2012). The different variables and prognostics considered in the models helped open the discussion on environmental risks and management. Using aerial pictures of the settlement, participants then indicated the hazard-prone areas and zones previously damaged.

According to the models presented in the atlas, mean air temperature in the coastal region is expected to increase by about 1°C between 2015 and 2030, and be about 2°C higher in the period 2030–50. Similarly, for Puerto Ángel the atlas identified annual increases in rainfall of 1.7–11.7mm, which would imply an increase of almost 10cm per decade if this pattern remains consistent. However, for the workshop participants, these average decade-long projections were difficult to grasp. For rainfall in particular, the projections appeared counter-intuitive since it is longer droughts that seem to be happening:

> The problem is that now the drought is longer. It does not rain on time and when it does it pours like hell. There have been fires in the mountain range.... Peasants suffer, but they are partly responsible because they still burn to plant. It is like they do not understand.... My parents used to work the land on the hills just a few minutes from here ... I do not plant anymore. It is hard work, the soil is exhausted, you get very little, and then it is difficult to decide when to do it because of the rain. And then all this burning is no good for the environment; we have to take care of nature.
>
> (Carlos, age 35 years, workman, born in Zipolite)

When damage was discussed, the workshop participants were more forthcoming. At the exact time the workshop was taking place, heavy seas were affecting the beach. A truck had been sent from the municipality to drag part of one hill, to put the sand into sacks and then deposit the sacks on the seafront in an effort to contain the damage that was already threatening the constructions at the east end of the beach. In the view of one participant, this type of effect on the seashore was normal and subject to the rules of chance, 'sometimes it's someone's turn, sometimes it's someone else's'. But when it came to socially produced damage, flooding, fires, and contamination were singled out as threats that mostly affected the *colonias* that surround the beach.

Loss linked to climate is common on the coast of Oaxaca. However, the damage is not always so intense and widespread that disasters are officially declared. Between 2012 and 2016, small disasters were apparent in all periods of fieldwork (from a few weeks to a few months). In Zipolite, at the northwestern end of the beach, a hotel (*Shambala*) on the hillside that encloses the sand was damaged by a landslide. In the opposite direction, groundswell has been eroding the shore front of old establishments (*Lyoban; Lola's*) to the point that the sand has had to be replenished. The Zipolite stream flooded the neighbourhood Roca Blanca twice and small events affected the road connecting the town with Puerto Ángel and San Agustinillo that crosses the many streams that discharge into the sea.

From this perspective, climate change refers to the speeding up of climatic variability, to the displacement of climatic-sensitive activities other than tourism (which attracts the majority of government support) such as agriculture, and to fewer opportunities to adjust, both materially and symbolically, for those that live on the edges of the tourist centres.

Conclusion: dynamic pressures of risk on Oaxaca's coast

This chapter has attempted to provide empirical support for the idea that environmental damage (past and potential) is the result of dynamic pressures linked to Mexico's state-led tourism development. As long as such development remains blind to its own consequences, fragility will be enhanced by climate change. From the perspective of the two policy documents discussed earlier (the *Study* and the *Local Guide*), governmental preoccupations regarding climate change, disasters, and tourism drive the dynamic pressures of risk revealed in the case of Zipolite. The government programme involves an epistemology, a specific means to isolate problems both temporally and spatially. To define objective risk, it considers only big meteorological hazards. The past vanishes, while the future refers only to a small number of variables unrelated to issues that constrain the daily life of local people. Space is split into geographic units isolated from both social life and ecosystems. Thus, the adaptation policy involves a climate and environmental ontology that presents the world as a disjointed multiplicity of dimensions (coastal erosion, increased temperature, governance) and fails to address social re/production as an integrating aspect of reality.

Definitions and analysis styles allow for the technological mystification that characterises the politics of environmental risk. Thus, early warning systems and technical procedures such as hazard maps and top–down zonification become the main 'instruments' for adaptation. In this work, I have attempted to show that given its ahistorical perspective and its lack of critical analysis of the conflicts that underlie the development of tourism, Mexico's climate change adaptation policy for tourist destinations seeks to secure and expand the existing model, instead of addressing the critical dynamic pressures that result in environmental fragility: privatisation of the seashore and marginalisation of local communities from tourist development. I have also attempted to show that this model is intrinsically political and that, because of this, one of the challenging features of Mexico's tourism and climate change adaptation policy is that it excludes a political understanding of environmental risk, and so makes it difficult to imagine an alternative future in which less rather more damage is to be expected.

Acknowledgements

I am thankful to the Research Program on Climate Change (PINCC) at the National Autonomous University of Mexico for founding this project. The majority of the interviews upon which this work is based were undertaken by Giomar Ordóñez and Jonatán Cerros in the period 2012–13. The Laboratory Socio-Spatial Analysis at the Metropolitan Autonomous University – Cuajimalpa, Mexico City, provided help with demographic, geographic, and environmental data collection and analysis.

Note

1 It should be noted that the relevance of climatic or more general environmental factors in the national tourist policy must not be taken for granted. As this chapter was under review, the Mexican Ministry of Tourism published a translated version of a policy study and recommendations produced by the Organisation for Economic Co-operation and Development (OECD), tacitly endorsing it, in which environmental problems are not mentioned.

References

Anid, 2014. *Estudio de la Vulnerabilidad y Programa de Adaptación ante la Variabilidad Climática y el Cambio Climático en Diez Destinos Turísticos Estratégicos, así como Propuesta de un Sistema de Alerta Temprana a Eventos Hidrometeorológicos Extremos. Resumen Ejecutivo.* México: Secretaría de Turismo.

Bassett, T.J., and Fogelman, C., 2013. Déjà vu or something new? The adaptation concept in the climate change literature. *Geoforum*, 48, 42–53.

Blaikie, P., *et al.*, 2003. *At Risk: Natural hazards, people's vulnerability and disasters.* 2nd edition. London: Routledge.

Cenapred, 2006. Estimación de la vulnerabilidad social. *In*: V. Ramos, ed., *Guía básica para elaborar Atlas Estatales y Municipales de riesgo y peligros.* México: Centro Nacional para la Prevención de Desastres, 339–83.

Colucci, A., and Mullet, A., 2016. Maya as a commodity fetish: Accumulation by dispossession and ecotourism in the Yucatan Peninsula. *In*: S. Nepal and J. Saarinen, eds, *Political Ecology and Tourism.* London: Routledge, 149–62.

Ferguson, J., 1994. The anti-politics machine: 'Development' and bureaucratic power in Lesotho. *The Ecologist*, 24 (5), 176–81.

Fernández A., *et al.*, 2012. *Atlas Climático y del Cambio Climático del Estado de Oaxaca, México.* México: Universidad Nacional Autónoma de México.

Füssel, H.-M., and Klein, R.J.T., 2006. Climate change vulnerability assessments: An evolution of conceptual thinking. *Climatic Change*, 75 (3), 301–29.

INEGI, 2010. *Censo Nacional de Población: Datos por localidades.* México: Instituto Nacional de Estadística y Geografía.

Lash, S., Szerszynski, B., and Wynne, B., 1996. *Risk, Environment and Modernity: Towards a new ecology.* London: Sage.

Mansilla, E., 2008. Análisis de riesgo extensivo, urbanización de los riesgos y su expansión territorial en América Latina. Análisis de riesgo extensivo e intensivo en México [online]. *In*: *United Nations: Global Assessment Report on Disaster Risk Reduction (2009) Background Papers.* Available from: www.preventionweb.net/english/hyogo/gar/background-papers/?pid:34&pil:1# [Accessed 8 November 2017].

Mansilla E., 2013. México – Inventario histórico de desastres. *Sistema de Inventario de Efectos de Desastres* [online]. Available from: https://online.desinventar.org [Accessed 8 November 2017].

Mostafanezhad, M., *et al.*, 2016. Introduction. *In*: M. Mostafanezhad, *et al.*, eds, *Political Ecology of Tourism: Community, power and environment.* New York: Routledge, 1–21.

Painter, M., and Durham, W., 1995. *The Social Causes of Environmental Destruction in Latin America.* Ann Arbor, MI: University of Michigan Press.

Peet, R., and Watts, M., 1993. Development theory and environment in an age of market triumphalism. *Economic Geography*, 69, 227–53.

Peet, R., and Watts, M., 2004. *Liberation Ecologies: Environment, development, social movements*. New York: Routledge.

Peluso, N., 1993. Coercing conservation? The politics of state resource control. *Global Environmental Change*, 3 (2), 199–217.

Puga, T., 2017. El turismo en el país vale el doble que la industria automotriz: WTTC. *El Universal* [online], México, 20 June. Available from: www.eluniversal.com.mx/articulo/cartera/negocios/2017/06/20/el-turismo-en-el-pais-vale-el-doble-que-la-industria-automotriz [Accessed 8 November 2017].

Ribot, J., 2014. Cause and response: Vulnerability and climate in the Anthropocene. *Journal of Peasant Studies*, 41 (5), 667–705.

Rubio, I., 2014. *Industrias turísticas y escenarios de desastre asociados al cambio climático en el litoral oaxaqueño*. México: Programa de Investigación en Cambio Climático, UNAM [online]. Available from: www.pincc.unam.mx/INFORMES%20PROYECTOS/23_Informe_final.pdf [Accessed 7 November 2017].

Sectur, 2014. *Guía local de acciones de alto impacto en materia de mitigación y adaptación al cambio climático en destinos turísticos mexicanos*. México: Secretaría de Turismo.

Stonich, S., 1998. Political ecology of tourism. *Annals of Tourism Research*, 25, 25–54.

Talledos, E., 2012. La imposición de un espacio: de La Crucecita a Bahías de Huatulco. *Revista Mexicana de Ciencias Políticas y Sociales*, 57 (216), 119–42.

Wilbanks, T.J., *et al.*, 2007. Industry, settlement and society. *In*: M.L Parry, *et al.*, eds, *Climate Change 2007: Impacts, adaptation and vulnerability*. Cambridge: Cambridge University Press, 357–90.

Wong, P.P., *et al.*, 2014. Coastal systems and low-lying areas. *In*: C.B. Field, *et al.*, eds, *Climate Change 2014: Impacts, adaptation, and vulnerability: Part A: Global and sectoral aspects: contribution of Working Group II to the Fifth Assessment Report of the Intergovernmental Panel on Climate Change*. Cambridge: Cambridge University Press, 361–409.

6 Vulnerability factors among Cocopah fishers

Climate change, fishery policies, and the politics of water in the delta of the Colorado River*

Alejandra Navarro-Smith

Introduction

During spring 2015, Cocopah fishers waited in vain for the gulf corvina (*Cynoscion othonopterus*) to make its annual migration to the Colorado River delta in the Upper Gulf of California, and reach the Cocopah traditional fishing grounds known as *El Zanjón*. Unable to predict that the species they depend on would not arrive in the usual densities as past years, the Cocopah fishers not only incurred a loss in their annual income, but also accrued a hefty debt with the fish buyers who advance loans to the fishers in order that they can buy fishing equipment for the coming season. The fishers had to carry these debts until the beginning of the 2016 fishing season. Although fishing pressure plays an important role in the gulf corvina's population dynamic, changes in oceanographic conditions, some of which are related to climate change, also affect the gulf corvina and the ecosystem on which it depends. From the biological perspective, it is argued that the more stable and resilient an ecosystem, the better it will be at maintaining its component species. Mexican fishing authorities have used this view to establish alliances with environmental non-governmental organisations (NGOs) and some fishermen associations, to monitor the gulf corvina population, fishing activities, and oceanographic conditions in the Upper Gulf of California, which have become increasingly important since 2011.

From a socio-ecological perspective, the debates presented by Gesing *et al.* (2014) aiming to denaturalise climate change, understanding it both as a natural and a social phenomenon, lead me to include the social constructions about climate change itself, and the specific cultural readings that are generated (Gesing *et al.* 2014: 5) at local, regional, and global levels. I will also explore what Gobel *et al.* (2014) pointed out when they argued that the different types of natural resource use promoted by national states, using the discourse of social development, may be working to increase social inequalities.

On this basis, I critically review the consequences of climate change (understanding this as a combination of human action and natural causes) and its effects in the daily lives of the fishing Cocopah families in Baja, California, with a focus on public policy regarding climate change adaptation in northwestern Mexico and the southwestern USA. I argue that climate change, as well as the politics of water, and rigorous fisheries and environmental protection policies, are some of the factors endangering fishers' quality of life that may also be increasing social inequalities in the region.

To provide a better understanding of the complexities involved in this case study, the chapter first introduces the context for planning and observing a sustainable fishery when the reproductive cycle of gulf corvina overlaps with a peak in the demand for fish consumption in Mexico. From the viewpoint of public administration of natural resources, fish should not be overexploited. However, because the authorities do not receive the necessary funding to patrol the delta and so prevent illegal fishing (fuelled by fish buyers), the gulf corvina *are* overfished. This results in tense interactions between fishers (indigenous and non-indigenous), fish buyers, governmental authorities, NGOs, marine biologists, lawyers, anthropologists, human rights defenders, and other actors involved in illegal trades.

These actors help shape the everyday dynamics of the gulf corvina fishing season without consideration to how the politics of water in the Colorado River delta have historically contributed to the environmental degradation of the delta ecosystem, therefore endangering resource availability and indigenous livelihoods. Climate change is not seen as a factor that could make fish scarce, or even absent, thus putting Cocopah and other fishers' livelihoods at serious risk. It might seem that the imaginary of *fish abundance* – which Cocopah fishers clearly recall from their childhood – continues to guide both policymaking and general fishing practices. However, this research shows fish were scarce during 2015, 2016, and 2017. The chapter concludes with some reflections on the possible effects of ecosystem transformations (water management and climate change) on the displacement of local fish populations and the appearance of illegal trades in the region.

Spawning in Easter

In their annual migration to the northern waters of the Gulf of California and the Colorado River delta, the gulf corvina return for spawning to the place where they were born. From late February, they reappear in large groups in the Upper Gulf of California and wait for the high tides which help to carry them into the narrow, shallow, and muddy ancient Colorado River basin. Females enter first and lay thousands of eggs on the river bed. When this is complete they croak to attract the males, who then arrive and fertilise the eggs with their sperm.

The gulf corvina are an easy prey during this period and become overfished as the demand for sea products rises in Mexico. The coincidence of the gulf corvina's spawning period and the peak in seafood consumption for religious beliefs at Easter has not helped efforts to organise fishing cooperatives to develop practices for a sustainable fishery. Just at the very time the Mexican authorities are struggling to apply the regulations for restricting the presence of fishers in the designated fishing areas, the fish buyers who are not regulated are prepared to take as much fish as possible. The fish buyers rely on their networks to produce the legal paperwork needed to transport and sell the catch. An estimated 80 per cent of the annual catch from El Golfo de Santa Clara is fished in the core area of the Reserve, which is a no-take zone (Erisman *et al.* 2012).

This indicates the strong economic interests that shape the gulf corvina fishing dynamics in the Colorado River delta. To give an idea of the relevance of the gulf corvina to the Mexican fish markets: each fully loaded trailer leaves the fishing area with an average of 17 tonnes of gulf corvina. During the 2002 fishing season, 'an historic maximum catch of 5,942 tonnes [of gulf curvina] was recorded' (Ortiz *et al.* 2016). An estimated 39 per cent of the total annual catch travels 3,000 km to *La Viga* in Mexico City, the second biggest fish market in the world after the one in Tokyo. The rest goes to other national markets: Guadalajara, Mazatlán, Mexicali, Tijuana, and Ensenada. With the arrival of such large volumes of gulf corvina, all existing sea produce at the market is reduced in price to remain competitive. The gulf corvina is unique in that regard: there is no other fishery in Mexico that places 2,317,000 kg of a single sea produce in a Mexican fish market during March and April each year (numbers based on the largest catch registered in 2002; Ortiz *et al.* 2016). Speculation, along the laws of supply and demand, make fish buyers powerful players in this scenario.

With such large quantities of gulf corvina in Mexican fish markets, cultural understanding of the gulf corvina is shaped by the social interactions of trade where they are inscribed; thus, they are closely related to issues of income and profit at play in the arena of labour where fishers, buyers, and regulators interact. Scientists and conservationists, on the other hand, struggle to assign gulf corvina other meanings: those connecting this endemic species to its ecosystem, and whose reproductive success relies on controlling overfishing practices and the freshwater balance within the delta. Environmental NGOs are another important player. To date, they have focused on the development of a sustainable fishery. However, NGOs have a tendency to focus on one aspect of a wider issue. For example, the Environmental Defense Fund (EDF), an NGO that entered the delta region in 2010 hired by Sonoran fishing authorities to establish fishing quotas with regional fishers, intended to work with all groups of fishers catching gulf corvina, but was unable to work with Cocopah fishers, arguing that acknowledging their demands for recognition of differentiated rights on their historic territory (Anglés Hernández 2011; Navarro-Smith *et al.*

2013, 2014) 'would distract them from their main objective', as I was told in a meeting where we were exploring ways to collaborate. And although EDF acknowledged the lack of freshwater in the delta, they do not negotiate quotas of water to be returned to the river to maintain a flow of freshwater into *El Zanjón*. Fisheries and environmental authorities all know that a healthy brackish ecosystem is key to maintaining the gulf corvina's spawning environment. But managing water quotas is not within the EDF remit; it falls instead to the Mexican Ministry of Water Management (CONAGUA).

Isolating gulf corvina from the wider ecosystem to which it belongs, to place it as a central 'resource' within the fishing system illustrates how an *economic rationale* works to socially define and justify the use of natural resources to produce profits. The trade-intensive social interactions that shape this cultural understanding of the gulf corvina do not allow for discussions of natural resources extractivism, impacts on the ecosystems, species' lifecycles, or climate change. Impoverished fishers feel that their quality of life is threatened by the restrictions that the paradigm of conservation poses. Illegal trade and greedy fish buyers incentivise fishers to fish for profit. The same economic rationale has been used to justify the extraction of the Colorado River water from its basin (see next section).

These examples of strategic administrative impediments encourage the development of intersectional, interinstitutional, and interdisciplinary approaches to understand fish not as isolated 'natural resources' available for economic gain, but as elements that should be understood in relation to wider ecosystems. Authorities, NGOs, and research efforts to generate knowledge on the intimate relations of every part of the ecosystem have not yet resulted in effective measures and actions to counterbalance the powerful influence of economic rationales to socially justify the extractive model for development.

The politics of water in the Colorado River delta

Translucent 200-litre water tanks hold the water needed in Cocopah homes. Located in *El Mayor Cucapah* (sic) and other settlements dispersed throughout the *Mexicali* Valley,[1] Cocopah households have no regular running water service, or sewage. Peak summer temperatures over 50°C in the shade make bulk water delivery essential for survival in the Colorado River delta.

Desertification is the most visible consequence of the degradation of the local ecosystem. It began at the turn of the twentieth century when Colorado River water was diverted into canals to farm the desert and turn the delta into a profitable agribusiness (Moreno Mena and López Limón 2005). Cocopah testimonies show the radical transformation that their lifestyle experienced, when water stopped flowing in the Colorado and Hardy River basins. The major transformation of the delta ecosystem is rarely discussed in public debates in the Mexicali region. Instead, the discourse of agricultural development is used to guide and justify criteria for water distribution. This example provides us with first-hand material to understand the implications of an ideology of development whereby water, fish, and all natural resources are no longer considered part of larger ecosystems, but as isolated resources available for the production of capital. Following this logic, the cultural understanding of water shifts from being a necessary element to maintain the balance of an ecosystem, to a 'raw resource' that can be extracted and subordinated to the logic of 'development' at any cost used to guide the logic and politics of water in the Colorado River delta since the late 1800s. This use of natural resources has been normalised and positively valued, but has also resulted in the degradation of ecosystems, putting at risk the conservation of endemic species, and thus the well-being of the region's first residents. Cocopah's lifestyle is highly dependent on the presence of water in the rivers (Gómez Estrada 2000: 149–50; Porcayo *et al.* 2016).

Voices remembering the Colorado River delta

When the river water was diverted to farm the desert, the Cocopah were directly affected. Within 70 years, both the ecosystem they relied on and their culture were completely transformed. The accounts of seven Cocopah elders, interviewed in their homes in Baja, California, help us to understand the intimate relationship that 'gathering the desert' has had on their understanding of themselves as Cocopah people. Archaeological, archaeofaunistic, and ethnographic references provide further information that allows us to learn about Cocopah patterns of mobility and use of resources in desert ecosystems in the past 300 years (Porcayo *et al.* 2016).

According to Porcayo *et al.* (2016) a healthy ecosystem was a necessary condition to maintain the lifestyle Cocopah had led until the start of the twentieth century. In his book, he traces the continuities and transformations of settlement, hunting, fishing, and gathering patterns. Based on archaeological and archaeofaunistic evidence, he argued that the disappearance of particular feeding patterns is directly related to the degradation of the delta ecosystem. It could be argued that this process of degradation started as settlers, attracted to the delta region at the turn of the twentieth century, conceptualised the delta territory as a fertile terrain available to develop commercial agriculture. Thereafter, public policies were developed to actively promote the diversion of the Colorado River in order to water agricultural plots.

With the gradual degradation of the ecosystem, Cocopah's subsistence practices were adjusted. They witnessed the diminution of water in the river basins and the disappearance of wetlands, and with these factors, less food was available from hunting, fishing, and gathering. In the following accounts, Cocopah elders recall the changes they experienced in relation to their nourishment habits and availability of foods. Their accounts are organised in terms of three periods that describe abundance, scarcity, and the arrival of welfare. I analysed interviews with seven Cocopah elders living in Baja, California; five between 75 and 95 years old and two between 50 and 75 years old. The interviews took place in 2011.

Abundance. Informants remember a period of abundance during their childhoods. They could eat from gathering, hunting, or fishing. They gathered dry wild fruits; hunted small birds and rodents; and bred goats, cows and chickens. The abundance of fish is especially recalled. In his account, Informant 1 remembered:

> [...] my grandmother had many grandchildren and she always had something to feed each one of them. My aunt Lulú she went fishing and trapped huge carps [*Cyprinus carpio*] in the river. My grandmother had the fire ready, with embers from mezquites [*Prosopis glandulosa and P. pubescens*], she wide opened the carps and placed them over the embers [...]

In the same token, Informant 5 remembered that she started fishing when she was seven years old. Fish was abundant then:

> [...] when we went to fish we caught half sack of fish; I returned loaded with fish when I got back home. We fish to eat every day.

And Informant 7 remembered the occasions when:

> My grandmother would speak to me in Cocopah language only because she barely knew Spanish; and she would ask me to go fishing carps. And off I went to fish just outside where *Prisciliano* lives now. There's where I got the carps from.

In these and other accounts of the interviews, daily life occurs in the presence of abundant fish and water in the river near the Cocopah's homes. Water, fish, landscape, and language were part of what they experienced in their world of life and important elements in their identities. Of course, water was not only related to the abundance of fish and other freshwater creatures, but also to biodiversity and the presence of many other resources in the delta. Wild pumpkins and watermelons were found, as well as edible terrestrial species. Informant 7 remembered:

> [...] from the bush we got many wild animals. We hunted roadrunners, deer, wild pigs. I had my rifle and I could find loads to eat that way.

Scarcity. All interviewees identified a moment in their childhood when water became a scarce resource. They recalled painful memories when they struggled to subsist in an environment marked by scarcity. Informant 7, for example, clearly stated this moment with simple but hard words:

> Water did not enter this far any more. Fish did not get to us and the water that was left did not run and had no oxygen to produce new life. That's how we lost water and fish. We had to move too.

Welfare.   In the interviews, there was also consensus in the way inform-ants interpreted the present. Resources continue to be scarce in their sur-roundings. As Informant 5 stated:

> We used to eat loads of fish, but today we cannot get it. The river has been polluted. The treated sewage from Mexicali is diverged into the Hardy River and that's the reason why we can't eat the fish we could find there. There's people that do eat the fish they catch there, but it tastes as soap, they say.

Along with scarcity of resources to fulfil Cocopah's nourishment needs, other factors affect their well-being in the present: costly processed foods are now available for purchase and these are of low nutritional value. Informant 1 phrased the problem in her own words:

> I call that 'food to feed laziness'. Since that type of products got avail-able things have changed much here. For example, my grandchildren and greatgrandchildren don't want ranch foods. They want packed sausages and ham; pot soups. And we need to buy them, now you have to buy everything, even the water! Before we drank the water from wells and from the river. When we lived in El Mayor, we drank water from the river. And now things have changed. We buy the water we use for cooking, and it wasn't like that before! Whenever we needed water we took some soil off (*escarbábamos un pozo*) and found water near the surface. But it is true that today even the soil is polluted and therefore all water we could find would be contaminated.

The information presented in this section shows how the difficulties in accessing local resources to feed Cocopah's households have not only brought about a reduction in the quantity and quality of the food and water consumed, but also a change in the type of food consumed. Children today expect 'good food' to be bought, and are no longer able to connect the resources and services found in the ecosystem, to a larger cultural Cocopah heritage produced through their grandparents' everyday hunting, fishing, and gathering practices. This phenomenon, framed in the wider context of cultural change and assimilation that Cocopah have experienced since the arrival of new users of the delta ecosystem services, reveals socio-cultural dynamics leading to degradation stigma and inequality; as the ecosystem

Cocopah inhabit is now considerably less productive, agro-industries and fish buyers – to name two external actors – extract what they need, producing economic revenues that are not reinvested in the region. While Cocopah elders draw a close relationship between the use of their territory and a lifestyle they value, their children expect to be fed with *desirable* processed foods that are only found at small local stores and distant supermarkets. Drought increases the scarcity of gathered foods (*comida de rancho*), and pollution affects both water and land, and thus Cocopah's health. For the younger generations, to be raised in such a deeply affected ecosystem teaches them what has been socio-historically naturalised as the stigma to lead an indigenous rural lifestyle. It seems that degradation – impacting ecosystem, health, and the representation of the self as part of a degraded unhealthy place – becomes a cultural norm through which local children learn their place as rural indigenous people, in this case in the northern border region of Mexico and the USA.

Moving south

Fishing in the delta is one of the few subsistence practices still ongoing by the Cocopah. Although gulf corvina has been consumed by Cocopah for at least 300 years, as dated otoliths found in Cocopah camps reveal (Porcayo *et al.* 2016: 56, 67–8), current fishing of gulf corvina is shaped by the demands of an economy-driven world. Cocopah fishers are now equipped with fibreglass boats, outboard motors, and nets, and they hope to keep some of their catch in freezers for consumption after the two-month fishing season ends. But most Cocopah fishers are not able to do so because they feel obliged to deliver their catch to the fish buyer and because they want to keep some cash to pay for expensive ritual celebrations (such as 'sweet sixteen' parties). Social pressures of contemporary life also shape Cocopah's understanding of their fishing practice.

Owing to the lack of water in the Hardy and Colorado Rivers, Cocopah had to move their temporary fishing camps south of their settlements. In the degraded delta ecosystem, gulf corvina is now only found in *El Zanjón*, the last part of the ancient Colorado River basin just a few kilometres before it enters the Upper Gulf of California.

Each year, Cocopah travel south to set their temporary fishing camps by the river, facing the same mountains named in their traditional stories. In this way, they are able to share the meanings of fishing for Cocopah with their descendants, as explained in the following section.

We look forward to *la convivencia*

Among other things, public policy concerning the management of natural resources along the delta river has induced cultural transformation such as a switch from traditional fishing methods to modern practices, or moving south to find new sites to establish temporary fishing camps. Despite such changes, fishing holds a strong shared feeling of what it means to be a contemporary Cocopah. One of the female Cocopah leaders, aged 46, explained: '[f]ishing is part of our culture, like our arts and crafts, our native language, and our ancestral territorial rights.' Another female Cocopah leader stated that '[f]ishing allows us to get together and *convivir* [to live together, to share the same life].' This is perhaps what Cocopah look forward to experiencing while waiting for the fishing season to start, as *convivencia* (sharing together) is a major part of Cocopah families' social world.

During the fishing season, people move to *El Indiviso*, the closest settlement to *El Zanjón*, their point of access to the Colorado River delta and the place where temporary fishing camps are set up. They arrive from at least nine different villages, travelling two to four hours by highway. Since 1993, when laws banned them from fishing in *El Zanjón*, they have had to work together to defend their right to fish. A third female leader stated that '[f]ishing has united us to defend all our ancestral rights.' She asserted that the struggle to continue fishing has also awakened a strong interest in Cocopah cultural revitalisation. For example, they now have a Cocopah teacher providing language classes to the children, helping to retain their mother tongue.

In practical terms, fishing enables the Cocopah to earn enough money to pay their debts and sustain their families for the entire year. The Cocopah goal is to have the freedom to *convivir* in their own social cultural world. Temporary legal jobs available in the region include factory assembly lines, packing plants, crop harvesting, and highway construction or repairs. Illegal and risky jobs tied to the drug trade are also available (Muehlmann 2013: 83–115). This type of work does not provide the community with *convivencia*, which emerges while fishing.

Symbolically and culturally, fishing allows the Cocopah to reconstruct historical ties with their ancestors, to legitimise their fishing rights, and to define their ethnic identity. This identity is represented in history books, ethnographic photographs, and in reminiscences about their ancestors and fishing. The Cocopah are bringing their history and ancestral culture into their present. Thus, the Cocopah are building links between their past and their identity as contemporary Cocopah, as their children grow up in the fishing culture. Paradoxically, transformations of Cocopah social organisation coincide with legal change brought on by public policy regulating land, water, and natural resources. This includes public policy regarding the Colorado River water management and the Upper Gulf of California and Colorado River delta's administration of fishing resources.

Risky business

In the cold mornings of early February, Cocopah fishers repair their fishing nets and boats and turn on their engines to make sure they are ready for the start of the fishing season. For the Cocopah, this fishery represents not only much-needed income, but also (and most importantly) an opportunity for their temporary fishing camps to reappear in the territory that was once occupied by their ancestors. For some families, settling in their temporary fishing camps also means the possibility of getting away from their daily routines in the small and impoverished communities where they reside.

But to continue fishing in the Colorado River delta, Cocopah descendants have had to endure 23 years of legal struggle. Just a few years after they moved their temporary fishing camps to *El Zanjón*, a few miles before the river enters the sea, that same area was decreed the core zone of the Upper Gulf of California and Colorado River Delta Biosphere Reserve (the Biosphere Reserve, onwards). The two other places where they used to fish became polluted or disappeared, forcing the displacement of temporary fishing camps: the Hardy River is now perceived to be polluted after the treated waters from Mexicali were diverted there (see Villarreal-Rosas and Olmos-Aguilera 2017: 7–8, 19); and the *Laguna Salada* dried up after it ceased to receive a regular flow of water (see Figure 6.1). These are the two most recent events of a wider process of environmental degradation that began at the start of the twentieth century as the Colorado River was diverted by canal to irrigate agricultural crops.

The legal struggle endured by the Cocopah also points to two of the most recent structural changes that continue to force the integration of Cocopah people into a wider global economic and political dynamic: their integration into the national fisheries system (Navarro-Smith 2008, 2011) and the creation of the Biosphere Reserve. The latter has resulted in the criminalisation of Cocopah when they question the legitimacy of a law that expels them from their core territory, the only place where they can continue to fish because of the desertification of the region (Navarro-Smith 2017).

The beginning of the fishing season is also problematic economically for Cocopah households. With very low or no regular income during the year, Cocopah fishers rely on loans provided by fish buyers to purchase supplies and repair boats, nets, vehicles, and motors. During 2014 and 2015, every Cocopah household needed to invest MXN 80,500 (US$4,240) on average just to get ready to fish (this value is based on questionnaires supplied by the author to Cocopah fishers in the largest fishing cooperative). In 2014, the catch generated an average profit of MXN48,500 (US$2,553) per household. But in 2015 the gulf corvina did not make it all the way up to *El Zanjón* as expected, and Cocopah fishers were not able to pay back the money they had borrowed. Instead of generating profits, the fishing season meant debt for Cocopah households, who were left owing an average of MXN58,843 (US$3,096) to fish buyers by the end of the season. Buyers added these debts to the 2016 loans they provided to fishers, thus reducing their profits for 2016 as well.

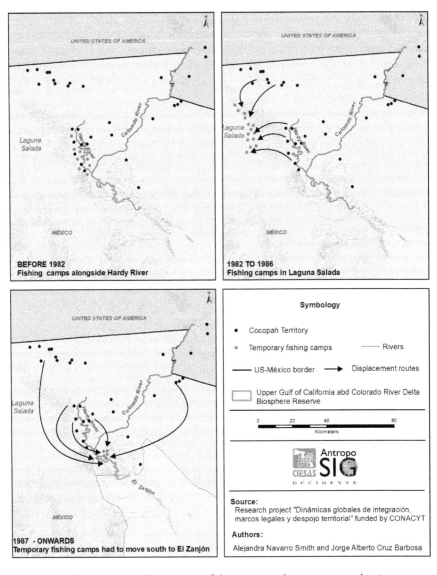

Figure 6.1 Displacement of temporary fishing camps due to water reduction.

Conservation criteria in the Colorado River delta

Fishing pressure over gulf corvina is not just from the Cocopah fishers, as they are not the only group of fishers harvesting this species. There are 109 Cocopah fishing permits. The other three groups of fishers represent 635 permits (see Table 6.1). The Cocopah total catch of gulf corvina in 2002

Table 6.1 Permits per fishing group in the Upper Gulf of California and Colorado River delta

Bajo Río	49 fishing permits
Cucapá	109 fishing permits
San Felipe	151 fishing permits
Golfo de Santa Clara	435 fishing permits

was less than 5 per cent of the total catch in the year with the highest registered catch (Ortiz *et al.* 2016).

Although fishing in the core zone of the Biosphere Reserve is illegal, studies have established that at least 80 per cent of non-Cocopah catch took place there (Erisman *et al.* 2012). This is despite strict laws to protect the Biosphere Reserve as a conservation area and the gulf corvina from being overfished. Conservation goals to achieve a sustainable gulf corvina fishery have not yet been met despite the joint strategies EDF has developed in collaboration with some fish buyers and groups of fishers with respect to the maximum allowed catch per fishing permit. In EDF's view, reducing the volume of fish in the market would raise its price, thus benefiting the fishers' income while reducing catch volume. However, non-reported overfishing has proved difficult to identify and measure. Discarded gulf corvina is just one sign of the difficulty of enforcing the catch limit.

Information spreads quickly among fishers and they claim that those departing from El Golfo de Santa Clara reach their total allowed catch in the first or second day of the fishing season. Because nobody stops them, they continue to fish throughout the season and buyers continue to monetise their catch. So far, no research or NGO has used this or any other factor that would reveal this dynamic and other corrupt practices in the region. Conflicts arising each year in this region make any conservation strategy difficult to implement. Thus, there is an urgent need for serious research that measures the effectiveness of conservation goals in the region and documents the role of authorities, NGOs, market demands, fish buyers, and communities of fishers in the fishery's dynamic. So far, notions of conservation and sustainability strongly frame the local discourse of authorities and NGOs, but in practice market forces and its agents are controlling fishing dynamics in the region.

In 2011, two events developed simultaneously and negatively impacted the efforts to develop a sustainable fishery for gulf corvina: a maximum catch per fishing permit was legally established, and Chinese consumers created a demand for gulf corvina bladder, which caused its price to exceed the value of the rest of the fish. In an unfortunate coincidence of events, the catch limit produced a 'black market' for bladders and gulf corvina was overfished purely to extract the small, highly valued pieces of the fish. As fishers could not obtain the legal paperwork to sell the eviscerated gulf corvina, an unknown quantity of fish was left to rot in clandestine rubbish sites.

Figure 6.2 Gulf corvina clandestine rubbish site, April 2016.
Source: photo: Alejandra Navarro-Smith.

Authorities from the Fisheries and Aquaculture Commission find them-selves needing to apply a legal framework to the most numerous (and eco-nomically powerful) group of fishers from El Golfo de Santa Clara; while at the same time, this is the group whose catch in the core zone of the Biosphere Reserve equals at least 80 per cent (Erisman *et al.* 2012). The same authorities also receive Cocopah's formal requests for the recognition of differentiated rights, and thus access to their historic territory and river to continue fishing. The authorities also face increasing pressure to detect and stop black market trading, not only for gulf corvina bladder, but also other illegal trades.

The Fisheries and Aquaculture Commission authorities do not seem to have sufficient resources, nor the administrative jurisdiction, to address these complex conflicts, and sustainable fisheries become a utopia in the face of increasing social inequalities where economic rationales shape the dynamics of a territory that cannot be legally controlled.

Climate change in the Colorado River delta

To critically review the consequences of climate change in the Colorado River delta ecosystem, it is important to understand its effects on social vulnerability. Therefore, I aim to examine the links between the warming of sea water in Baja, California, and the low catches of gulf corvina reported by Cocopah fishermen in 2015. And all of this is in connection with the lack of local governmental policy regarding climate change and its effects on the sea. I aim to understand the concept of climate change as a process, and as a combination of human action/factors and natural causes. My interest is to analyse its exacerbation of the existing social vulnerability of Cocopah fisher households in Baja, California.

Climate change research is still underdeveloped in the Upper Gulf of California. Regional policy to prevent further effects of climate change in oceans and fisheries is non-existent in the region. Although the 2012 Baja California's Plan of Action to face Climate Change (PEACC-BC) includes an almost premonitory description of the impacts of global warming on the health of marine ecosystems, it does not include any measures to mitigate these impacts. This raises questions as to why there is a lack of strategic actions regarding marine ecosystems and fisheries. Unlike the effects of climate change in land ecosystems, the plan does include a list of mitigating actions to reduce risks for agriculture and tourism (PEACC-BC 2012: 161–6). This indicates how state concerns on climate change and its effects are driven by economic considerations. In spite of the severe risk that climate change poses for marine ecosystems and the livelihoods of rural communities (indigenous and non-indigenous), they do not have sufficient notoriety or political grip as to be regarded worthy of specific public policies. Socially and economically vulnerable groups are left to adapt to climate change using their own solutions.

The warm-water anomaly (WWA) that Cavole *et al.* (2016) identified in 2013 in the northeastern Pacific 'stretched from Alaska to Baja California [at the end of 2015] [...]. The consequences of the WWA were far-reaching, and may presage future ecological shifts as global temperature rise' (Cavole *et al.* 2016: 274). Although this anomaly did not affect the Upper Gulf of California, it pointed to the global interconnections of climate change and its effects on marine ecosystems. In the Upper Gulf of California, 'sea level rise is expected to increase ~0.5–1 m in the next 100 years along the Gulf of California, [being] the most vulnerable areas [...] coastal wetlands which are essential nursery and refugee habitat for many commercial species' (Morzaria-Luna *et al.* 2014: 183). Therefore, gulf corvina spawning habitat is likely to be affected by climate change; in fact, all the linked social and ecological aspects on which fisheries depend would also be put at risk. In their study, Morzaria-Luna *et al.* (2014) concluded that 'susceptibility of fishing communities to the effect of climate change will depend on the importance of fishing relative to other occupations [Cinner *et al.* 2012], changes in economic activity, markets and/or trading patterns [Perry *et al.* 2010]' (Morzaria-Luna *et al.* 2014: 190). For the context described in the previous sections, legal markets and trading patterns offer mostly low-wage and labour-intensive agricultural or assembly line jobs. And illegal trade is becoming increasingly prevalent in the region, possibly due in turn to the lack of employment in the region.

Discussion: vulnerability factors among Cocopah fishers

The cultural rationale used to justify the extraction of natural resources and to define the limited scope and practices of *conservation* and *nature* have had substantial impacts on ecosystems, non-human species, and people living in the region. The concepts of *nature* and the *non-human* have been shaped in a specific socio-historical context of extractive economic practices in the Colorado River delta for the past century. In the acts of imagining, representing, and thinking about nature, societies produce social scripts to guide their relation and treatment of non-human species as muted and malleable materials (Latour 2004; Hinchliffe 2007: 1–2). As previously argued, these social interactions, interweaving nature, and human and non-human species, have increased the pre-existing social vulnerabilities affecting original settlers of the delta region. Through these layers of everyday experience, the extractive cultural rationale has normalised social inequalities brought about by the degradation that industry, intensive agriculture, and fisheries produce in the environment. Paradoxically, Cocopah depend on the wages generated by these profit-oriented extractive practices for their living.

Environmentally, economically, and culturally affected Cocopah find themselves in the crossfire of dispossession,[2] a precarious labour market, stigma, non-legal trades, and weak environmental surveillance of natural resources. In sum, Cocopah face the catastrophe of the environmental degradation of their historic territory due to the commodification of water, lands, and fish in the Colorado River delta. Finally, the correlation of well-produced scientific knowledge on how climate change might impact marine ecosystems versus the absence of public policy aimed at mitigating those impacts, illustrates how climate change mitigation and adaptation policies have been exclusively geared towards profitable ecosystems, via tourism or agro-industries. Artisanal fisheries have not received equal consideration, regardless of their intrinsic importance for the economic subsistence of indigenous and non-indigenous communities.

Notes

* This chapter has benefited greatly from the generous comments of Catalina López-Sagástegui and Gabriela Montaño-Moctezuma.
1 Cocopah residents live in a scattered settlement pattern in rural and urban areas along the ancient Colorado River delta, known as Mexicali Valley (Navarro-Smith 2017: 130; Porcayo *et al.* 2016). Despite this, the Mexican Government recognises only one Baja Californian Cocopah official settlement in *El Mayor Cucapah* [sic], a rural community 48.5 km south of Mexicali. For more information on Cocopah people in Mexico, see Navarro-Smith (2013) and Navarro-Smith and Cruz-Hernández (2015).
2 Cocopah fishers in the Colorado River delta have taken their claim to defend their rights to remain in their historic territory and to be able to use their resources, to Mexican and international legal forums. Since 1992, when the area where their temporary fishing camps are located was declared the core zone of the Biosphere Reserve of the Upper Gulf of California and Colorado River delta, they have started several legal procedures to impeach laws that affect their differentiated rights as indigenous people, as stipulated in the Convention C169 – Indigenous and Tribal Peoples Convention (see online at www.ilo.org/dyn/normlex/en/f?p=NORMLEXPUB:12100:0::NO::P12100_ILO_CODE:C169).

References

Anglés Hernández, M., 2011. La garantía del derecho de acceso, uso y disfrute preferente de los indígenas a los recursos naturales. Caso cucapá. *Publicación Electrónica del Instituto de Investigaciones Jurídicas de la UNAM*, 6, 67–87.

Cavole, L.M., *et al*., 2016. Biological impacts of the 2013–2015 warm-water anomaly in the Northeast Pacific: Winners, losers, and the future. *Oceanography*, 29 (2), 273–85.

Cinner J.E., *et al*., 2012. Vulnerability of coastal communities to key impacts of climate change on coral reef fisheries. *Global Environmental Change*, 22 (1), 12–20.

Erisman, B., *et al*., 2012. Spatio-temporal dynamics of a fish spawning aggregation and its fishery in the Gulf of California. *Scientific Reports*, 2, Article Number 284.

Gesing, F., Herbeck, J., and Klepp, S., 2014. *Denaturalizing Climate Change: Migration, mobilities and space*. Artec-paper Nr. 200. Bremen: Universität Bremen.

Gobel, B., Góngora-Mera, M., and Ulloa, A., eds, 2014. *Desigualdades Socioambientales en América Latina*. Bogotá: Universidad Nacional de Colombia.

Gómez Estrada, J.A., 2000. *La gente del delta del río Colorado*. México: UABC/SEP.

Hinchliffe, S., 2007. *Geographies of Nature: Societies, environments, ecologies*. London: Sage.

Latour, B., 2004. *Politics of Nature: How to bring the sciences into democracy*. Cambridge, MA: Harvard University Press.

Moreno Mena, J., and López Limón, M., 2005. Desarrollo agrícola y uso de agroquímicos en el valle de Mexicali. *Estudios Fronterizos*, 6 (12), 119–53.

Morzaria-Luna, H.N., Turk-Boyer, P., and Moreno-Baez, M., 2014. Social indicators of vulnerability for fishing communities in the Northern Gulf of California, Mexico: Implications for climate change. *Marine Policy*, 45, 182–93.

Muelhmann, S., 2013. *Where the River Ends: Contested indigeneity in the Mexican Colorado delta*. Durham, NC: Duke University Press.

Navarro-Smith, A., 2008. Cucapás, derechos indígenas y pesca. Dilemas del sistema productivo pesquero *vis a vis* las políticas de conservación de las especies en el Golfo de California. *Revista Chilena de Antropología Visual*, 12 (2), 172–96.

Navarro-Smith, A., 2011. De pescadoras libres a pescadoras reguladas. La pesca artesanal ribereña de la curvina golfina entre mujeres indígenas cucapá. *In*: G. Alcalá, coord., *Pescadores en América Latina y el Caribe: espacio, población, producción y política, Volúmen II*. Mérida: UNAM, 219–50.

Navarro-Smith, A., 2013. Los cucapás. *Diccionario Enciclopédico de Baja California*. Mexicali: Instituto de Cultura de Baja California, 160–2.

Navarro-Smith, A., 2016. Dilemmas of sustainability in Cocopah territory: An exercise of applied visual anthropology in the Colorado River delta. *Human Organization*, 75 (2), 129–40.

Navarro-Smith, A., 2017. Antes peleábamos a ciegas: territorio cucapá, etnización y derechos en disputa el delta del río Colorado. *In*: T. Sierra and S. Bastos, eds, *Estado y pueblos indígenas en México. La disputa por la justicia y los derechos*. México: CIESAS.

Navarro-Smith, A., and Cruz-Hernández, S., 2015. Territorio y prácticas culturales amenazadas en pueblos yumanos en Baja California. *Revista EntreDiversidades*, 5, 75–102.

Navarro-Smith, A., Bravo, Y., and López, C., 2013. Legislación de pesca y obstáculos para el reconocimiento de derechos al uso preferencial de recursos naturales del pueblo cucapá. *Revista De Estudos e Pesquisas Sobre as Américas*, 7 (2), 135–73.

Navarro-Smith, A., Bravo, Y., and López, C., 2014. Derechos colectivos, judicialización de derechos y consulta previa: el caso del territorio y recursos pesqueros del pueblo cucapá, en Baja California, México. *Revista Colombiana de Sociología*, 37 (2), 43–64.

Ortiz, R., *et al.*, 2016. Biological and fisheries monitoring of the gulf corvina in the Upper Gulf of California. *DataMares* [online]. Available from: http://datamares. ucsd.edu/stories/biological-and-fisheries-monitoring-of-the-gulf-corvina-in-the-upper-gulf-of-california/ [Accessed 20 September 2017].

PEACC-BC, 2012. *Programa Estatal de acción ante el cambio climático de Baja California (PEACC-BC)*. Secretaría de Protección al Ambiente del Gobierno de Baja California/Secretaría de Medio Ambiente y Recursos Naturales/El Instituto Nacional de Ecología. Mexicali, BC.

Perry, I., *et al.*, 2010. The challenge of adapting marine social–ecological systems to the additional stress of climate change. *Environmental Sustainability*, 2 (5–6), 356–63.

Porcayo, A., *et al.*, 2016. *Cambios y continuidades de la vida ancestral cucapá. Datos arqueológicos, arqueofaunísticos y etnográficos para su comprensión.* México: INAH.

Villarreal-Rosas, J., and Olmos-Aguilera, M., 2017. Ecodegradation and indigenous livelihoods: A case study in northwest México. *Sociedad y Ambiente*, 13, 5–34.

7 Ruling nature and indigenous communities

Renewed senses of community and contending politics of mitigation of climate change in the northern Sierra of Oaxaca, Mexico

Salvador Aquino Centeno

Introduction

While accepting the international agenda of climate change mitigation policy, the Mexican Government has also created a top–down institutional framework of environmental laws and discourses of justification for climate change prevention. It has created a strategy that incorporates both a sense of inclusion of indigenous peoples' institutions and traditions of conservation and strict rules of environmental protection. While creating a sense of inclusion through narratives of respecting indigenous knowledge and traditions of natural resource conservation, the Mexican Government has also enforced strategies of carbon sequestration and prevention of forest degradation in indigenous communities. In this context of what I call multiscale, environmental state formation, indigenous communities have tried to challenge the dominant visions of tradition that feed climate change policy by advancing their own senses of community, autonomy, and identity. This chapter examines how indigenous communities of Oaxaca, Mexico, have entered the politics of climate change and focuses on how they have both incorporated and contested those policies. History, senses of community, and opportunities play a critical role in how indigenous communities have dealt with compulsory new rules of climate change mitigation while creating their own ways of dealing with climate variability. The first section of this chapter discusses how the Mexican Government has become an 'environmental machine' that has created narratives, policies, and laws oriented towards limiting climate change. The next section reflects on how the new climate change policy entered the environmental social memory and social organisation of indigenous communities of the northern Sierra of Oaxaca. The third section discusses how climate policy and community environmental rules have interacted and how indigenous communities have contested climate policy. In the final section, I discuss how indigenous communities have incorporated climate policy while contesting the institutional and official policies of climate change.

Area of study and research methods

I have carried out collaborative research for several years in the Zapotec Sierra of Oaxaca. This has involved cooperation with indigenous authorities of several villages in the sierra, especially those of my home community, Capulálpam. Some of this work provides the basis for this chapter. I have carried out a wide range of tasks: (1) undertaken research on issues of territorial rights and on issues of autonomy and self-determination, systematising information on how communities relate to territorial spaces and how these constructions have changed over time; (2) conducted informal interviews, in-depth interviews with community authorities and with interlocutors of different ages and identities; (3) organised information on concepts of communal organisation and on community rules for access to territorial resources; (4) used a historical approach to investigate how the relationships between communities and their spaces have interacted with wider processes of culture and power over time; (5) focused on how land tenure, community identities, agrarian rules, and environmental policies have changed through time; and (6) compiled data from community archives and data from my own experience as a member of the community of Capulálpam.

Multiscale, environmental state formation in Mexico, 2000–17

Mexico is a small contributor to global greenhouse gas emissions, responsible for just 1.4 per cent of global releases in 2009 (INECC 2013). Nevertheless, the effects of climate change are said to have adversely affected around 68 per cent of the low-income Mexican population (SEMARNAT 2014: 25). As a member of the United Nations Framework Convention on Climate Change (UNFCCC), Mexico has both signed (1998) and ratified (2000) the Kyoto Protocol. This protocol came into effect in Mexico in 2005 (United Nations 2017). From 2000 onwards, Mexico has undertaken major structural transformations in relation to climate change, which has implied the creation of different conceptions and regulations of nature. Law and narratives about nature and multiculturalism have played a significant role in what I call a multiscale, environmental state formation; a totalising process that has meant reconfiguring the institutions, ideologies, and policies that govern nature at all scales of society (Himley 2008). Transforming ecosystems and landscapes into objects to be regulated has suffused the narratives of climate change and policy.

Once Mexico entered the politics of climate change in 2000, the federal government began to develop policies on nature conservation and designed structural actions in preparation for wider policies of mitigation and adaptation to climate change. Indigenous peoples emerged as significant actors during this process, on the basis that they not only hold critical natural resources in Mexico (mainly forests), but are also significantly affected by natural disasters. Most agrarian, forestry indigenous communities of Mexico manage their forests through community forests management. This is largely because local communities and indigenous peoples own around 11.4 per cent of global forest estate and 22 per cent of forest lands in developing countries (Cronkleton *et al.* 2011).

Several structural changes took place during the first few years of the twenty-first century in Mexico. The Mexican Congress approved several legal reforms that highlighted an official narrative of democratic, sustainable development based on the protection of nature and on respecting traditional knowledge of indigenous communities (Bárcenas 2009). In 2001, the Federal Congress approved the General Law for Sustainable Development, which for the first time institutionalised a mandatory, government policy on sustainable development (Cámara de Diputados del H. Congreso de la Unión 2001). This stated that the federal government shall sign contracts or agreements with either individuals or organisations to encourage sustainable development of land and natural resources. The new law sought to diversify agriculture, create jobs, reverse the depletion of natural resources, produce goods and environmental services, protect biodiversity and landscape, respect indigenous peoples' traditions, and prevent natural disasters.

The law advanced a concept of *contract* based on a narrative of protection of nature as well as on respect for indigenous peoples' knowledge and traditions. This concept of contract later became concrete when climate change mitigation policies arrived in the indigenous communities. In the meantime, indigenous communities had access to federal resources and programmes if they complied with the rules of the General Law for Sustainable Development and other environmental regulations.

The regulation of access to nature and legislation on sustainable development continued steadily. In 2003, the Congress approved the General Law of Ecologic Equilibrium and Environmental Protection, a law that had first been enacted in 1988. In 1996, this law introduced the legal concept of natural protected areas and prescribed rules for protecting indigenous peoples' natural resources and biodiversity. It also prescribed that all environmental policy shall observe the law and introduced the right for every person to have access to a healthy environment. It also prescribed several penalties for persons and corporations breaking the environmental laws and ratified the Federal Attorney Office for Environmental Protection to ensure compliance with the laws. In 2011, the General Law of Ecologic Equilibrium and Environmental Protection added rules for prevention of and adaption to climate change, and in 2012 incorporated regulations concerning environmental services as well as rules for investing in such services.

The Mexican Government also modified other laws and programmes related to climate change mitigation. In 2003, Congress enacted the Law for Sustainable Forestry Development, which substantially modified the Forestry Law of 1992. The new law incorporated several regulations concerning environmental services and mitigation and adaptation to climate change as prescribed by international agreements. It also regulated and promoted protection, conservation, management, cultivation, and development of forest in Mexico while endorsing the National Forestry Commission as the institution responsible to carry out and enforce forestry policy. It consolidated indigenous peoples' rights to their forestry resources while prescribing that indigenous forestry communities shall include policies for mitigation and adaptation to climate change in accordance with Article 2 of the Mexican Political Constitution that prescribes indigenous peoples' rights to autonomy and self-determination. Despite this right to autonomy, the new rules required indigenous communities to comply with rules on environmental protection. Although the government had developed several rules and policies on climate change mitigation since 2000, it was not until 2012 that climate change mitigation and adaptation rules became state policy. Article 25 of the Mexican Political Constitution prescribes that the state is responsible for the implementation of democratic and sustainable national development. From this rule, in 2012 the Congress approved the General Law for Climate Change, which cemented climate change policy into a state structure and made it a national priority. Article 1 of the General Law for Climate Change states that:

> The present law is of public order, general interest and observance throughout the national territory and the areas over which the nation exercises its sovereignty and jurisdiction and establishes dispositions to face the adverse effects of climatic change. It regulates the provisions of the Political Constitution of the United States of Mexico on environmental protection, sustainable development, preservation and restoration of ecological balance.
>
> (Cámara de Diputados del H. Congreso de la Unión 2012)

With the enactment of the General Law for Climate Change, the state strengthened its control over environmental protection and sustainable development, and claimed climate change mitigation as a mandatory strategy to prevent and mitigate climate change. This law prescribes that all citizens have the right to a healthy environment while it seeks to regulate greenhouse gas emissions. It also seeks to adopt rules for mitigation and adaptation to climate change and to generate strategies to reduce vulnerability to climate change impacts.

In these legal changes, the federal government advanced the concept of human rights articulated to the effects of climate change to justify climate change policy and to guarantee the observance of human rights protection in the design of climate change policy. In 2012, the National Human Rights Commission incorporated the rights to a dignified life, rights to health, rights to water, rights to a healthy environment, and rights to food and adequate housing that the Federal Congress had incorporated into the Federal Constitution in 2011 to oversee that the National Strategy for Climate Change and the Special Program on Climate Change 2014–2018 supports the protection of human rights (Viveros and Godinez 2015). Thus, the federal government created a legal framework to support climate change policies by linking it to human rights, creating a new legal language or a 'common discursive framework' (Nugent and Gilbert 1994) that created subjectivities and sanctions (Poole 2012) such as *adaptation, greenhouse emission, risk, environmental services, vulnerability, mitigation, economic integration, affordable, fossil fuels*, and so on, through which the state and its subjects would decode and negotiate policies of climate change.

Owing to the new laws, all state institutions incorporated rules and policies aimed at reducing greenhouse gas emissions. As part of its international agreements, the Mexican Government has incorporated several strategies concerning climate change into the National Development Plan 2012–2018. Nevertheless, several challenges still emerged as to how to convince and enforce indigenous communities to adopt the new strategies on climate change mitigation.

I refer to the process by which nature became regulated by law, institutions, and science as 'environmental state formation'. In an era of free market and a presumably state withdrawal from policy, nature became regulated by ideologies, discourses, and regulations to control its destructive potential to human life (Ojeda 2014). To control its potential, governments created ideologies of sustainable development along with institutional legal structures for compulsory climate change mitigation where regulations, penalties, policies, and rules of investment confirmed the state control over nature. Despite this totalising process of legibility (Scott 1998; Das and Poole 2004), there are places at the margins where alternative modes of nature regulation exist that contradict and seek to colonise the dominant institutions and discourses. The state sought to promote sustainable development based on actions for climate change mitigation and on ideologies of multiculturalism (Hale 2002; Novo 2014) while advancing strict rules for controlling nature. An authoritarian state is necessary to carry out legibility. Narratives of compulsory rules and inclusion of knowledge and traditions of indigenous communities permeated climate policy. However, as indigenous communities had to comply with several rules regarding conservation and mitigation policies, the new climate policy entered local communities with strong experiences of political autonomy regarding conservation and administration of local natural resources, as well as with experiences of environmental degradation.

Social memory of environmental impact and communal land possession in the northern Sierra of Oaxaca

By the time climate change policy arrived at the northern Sierra of Oaxaca, indigenous communities had already experienced two contrasting environmental situations: around 25 years of deforestation and around 500 years of managed communal lands. Although forest degradation became the justification for climate policy in the Sierra, narratives of sustainable development and climate policy overlooked these social memories of deforestation and communal forests management. I mention this because it is central to understanding why and how indigenous communities could contribute to climate change mitigation.

Most indigenous communities in the Sierra are aware of who has been responsible for deforestation. In the early 1950s, the Mexican Government constructed a major highway to connect the northern Sierra of Oaxaca to Oaxaca the capital city, and a paper factory began to exploit the Sierra forests. This exploitation was regulated and managed at the national level: private investment was encouraged through government concessions and private companies acquired permits (Fuente and Barkin 2011), usually under political influences (Greenberg and Emanuel 2000; Weaver 2000). Politicians and state officials convinced the Sierra communities of the advantages of selling timber. In 1955, the Mexican Government granted a 25-year permit to a paper factory to exploit the forests of the Sierra and of several other indigenous, agrarian communities of Oaxaca. In exchange for a small amount of logging rights, the Sierra communities received 'benefits' such as jobs, roads, and schools. However, timber extraction had a major environmental impact in the region (Zabin 1989; Perez 2017).

The highway cut through the heart of the Sierra and crossed areas of major biological diversity. It is difficult to calculate the overall damage, but the landscape changed significantly. For example, the paper factory converted zones of high forest density into semi-arid lands. The company built roads everywhere in the Sierra to extract timber, and for the first time many villages had good road communication to the city of Oaxaca and to the state of Veracruz. The paper company extracted thousands of tonnes of timber for cellulose and sawmills (Perez 2017). Although deforestation is now slowing in the Zapotec Sierra, it is still increasing elsewhere in Oaxaca (Ellis *et al.* 2016). The indigenous communities have complained for many years that the paper factory did not pay enough for their wood while demanding higher prices for timber and higher salaries for Indian workers. Once the Sierra communities began to suffer the consequences of deforestation and identified that the paper company was responsible, they decided to stop this practice. However, deforestation is still a challenge because of changes in land use (Gómez-Mendoza *et al.* 2006).

In the late 1970s, several villages began a political movement aimed at avoiding the renewal of permits to exploit the Sierra's forests (Chapela

1999; Bray and Merino-Pérez 2004). Indigenous communities claimed that they had the right to logging, based on the ownership of communal lands they had maintained since pre-colonial times. As a consequence, the federal government refused to grant any new permits to the companies for forest exploitation in the region. By the early 1980s, several villages began to establish their own communal, forest enterprises. In addition, the Forestry Law of 1986 supported the creation of a community forest sector in Mexico, stating that agrarian communities had the right to establish their own communal firms and to have their own technical services (Bray and Merino-Pérez 2002). This transition marked the beginning of a new era of legitimate sustainable development for indigenous communities in the region.

Understanding local history is relevant to discussions of how local communities perceive climate variability and make policy. In my view, to search for alternatives to prevent climate variability is not a matter of creating laws or creating technical solutions but a matter of understanding local populations' understandings and expectations of well-being and climate variability, which are rooted in social relationships, including moral, ethical, and rights issues. Recent patterns of nature commodification through green markets have ignored rights, autonomy, and local needs of indigenous peoples (Ulloa 2013), reinforcing processes of global inequality (Crate 2011). In the Sierra, for example, ways of addressing climate variability are rooted in local, collective institutions and on webs of reciprocity. This social organisation that recent climate change policy encountered in the Sierra is rooted in several years of social and political struggle, social relations that global climate policy wants to profit from. Indigenous communities in the Sierra reworked and transformed several agrarian policies introduced by the state during the latter half of the twentieth century (Bray *et al.* 2006). For example, the Agrarian Law of 1934 regulated the communities' agrarian organisation and granted it several legal roles. It prescribed that agrarian communities with a Presidential Resolution, legal land titles endorsed by the federal government, required two collective bodies: the Communal Assembly and the Commissary of Common Goods, a local authority responsible for the administration of communal lands and resources.

The Communal Assembly already existed within the communities while the agrarian law created the Commissary of Common Goods. Establishing these new levels of local government presented new challenges for indigenous communities (Chance and Taylor 1985). Indigenous commoners whose membership derived from common ancestors became members of the Communal Assembly. This legal body became the highest local authority regarding the management of communal lands and resources. The Communal Assembly elects the commissaries. Most communities incorporated the new authorities into the local system of customary governance (*sistema de cargos*) that came from colonial times (Chance and Taylor

1985). Over time, the Commissary and the Communal Assembly became central elements of the identity of the Sierra communities. For example, commissaries became the executive branch of the Communal Assembly, whereas the Communal Assembly became the highest structure of decision-making with responsibility for electing the commissaries every three years, and monitoring their work. The commissaries became the legal representatives of indigenous villages before the federal government. In fact, the state created these bodies in the communities to have a legal counterpart that allowed it to legalise its interventions in the agrarian communities. Although the laws supposedly granted local autonomy for administration of resources, the communities remained subordinate to the government, a contradiction that recent climate change policy has taken advantage of in several countries (cf. Delgado 2014). Nevertheless, the agrarian communities managed to adapt the agrarian laws to local needs such that the commissaries and the Communal Assembly became vital collective bodies of local decision-making and relative autonomy.

Communal land possession and climate change policy background in the Sierra

Providing legal guaranty to communal land possession became a priority for the federal government because communal land conflicts among indigenous communities would make investment in climate change mitigation difficult. Indigenous communities involved in territorial disputes would not receive federal funds. In addition, each community should have a Communal Statute that ensured compliance with federal agrarian rules and with rules for climate change mitigation and adaptation. In terms of mitigation, the Secretariat of Environment and Natural Resources enforced the creation of land-use plans for all forestry indigenous communities. This model of communal, territorial management would play a critical role in later climate policy: each community should divide its territory into specific areas for conservation, hunting, cultivation, urban planning, forest exploitation, reforestation, and areas for carbon sequestration.

The Sierra indigenous communities thus entered the politics of environment. For example, in 2003 Capulálpam, Ixtepeji, Ixtlan, Comaltepec, Xiacuí, and La Trinidad obtained certification by the Forest Stewardship Council of Rainforest Alliance through their actions to conserve and rehabilitate their forests (Rainforest Alliance 2014). Yet, this involvement in sustainable development also resulted in contradictory processes of controlling nature, as shown in the next section.

The environmental impact that forest extraction caused in the Sierra is linked not only to the Sierra communities' demand for alternatives of sustainable development but also to the emerging international policies of climate change mitigation. Aware of the need to mitigate the impact of around 35 years of forest degradation, the community of Capulálpam adopted various aspects of forest conservation promoted by the Secretariat of Environment and Natural Resources and various non-governmental organisations (NGOs). In 1993, Capulálpam developed its first land-use plan, a programme that incorporated the experience of 25 years of forest exploitation and nearly 15 years of communal forest management. This territorial organisation implied various changes in the ways the community managed its forest. The land-use plan introduced areas for hunting, farming, logging, reforestation, and urban use. The community reorganised its approach to communal land management that had been in place since the early 1980s based on new techniques of reforestation and sustainable forest management. A critical element of the land-use plan was to incorporate the social organisation of the community. According to local rules of governance, the Communal Assembly must approve the principles of the land-use plan, and the Commissary of Communal Goods, the executive branch of the Assembly, must inform the Assembly of progress on the land-use plan at periodic intervals. This ensures that every member of the community participates in the definition and evaluation of the land-use plan. Even though the community struggled to achieve sustainable development, it did help strengthen the community's awareness of the need to protect what they call their ancestors' legacy, that is, their communal lands and natural resources.

The community used the land-use plan to establish four communal enterprises: a bottling water enterprise, a sawmill, a gravel factory, and an ecotourism project. Emerging out of local needs and decision-making, these enterprises generated jobs and income and crucially forged senses of identity and community. The experience proved so successful that the community developed a second land-use plan in 2003 and a third in 2014. The latest land-use plan has benefited from 16 years of communal sustainable management of local resources. It is a nine-year programme that assigns areas for farming, reforestation, wildlife conservation, aquifer protection, ecotourism, and logging. However, once the community entered the politics of land-use plans, it also became subject to environmental laws.

Contradictory climate policy and community responses in the Sierra

Climate policy arrived in the highlands of the northern Sierra of Oaxaca in 2008, as part of the ongoing legal and institutional changes to mitigate climate change. Indigenous communities will play a critical role in these changes given that they hold the right to 100 per cent of the area's natural resources through communal property in the Sierra. Climate policy exploited collective property by using a strategy of co-opting indigenous organisations' leaders and representatives of indigenous communities. Ways of local government, historic marginalisation, and the new mandatory rules of regulating ecosystems facilitated the implementation of climate policy.

The Mexican Government drew upon the institutional arrangement that the federal government had consolidated during the twentieth century to establish and legitimise climate change mitigation policies among indigenous communities of the Sierra. As previously mentioned, the National Forestry Commission, a branch of the Secretariat of the Environment and Natural Resources, became responsible for climate change policy. Because climate policy required the involvement of civil society, the National Forestry Commission called for key representatives of organisations directly involved with climate consequences. It joined PRONATURA, an NGO long involved in issues of natural resource protection, and promoted the formation of Environmental Services of Oaxaca, an NGO comprising several indigenous communities in Oaxaca. The purpose of Environmental Services of Oaxaca was to use already established indigenous communities' organisations to implement climate change policy. NGOs play a significant role in this process because they link diverse actors across the climate policy spectrum, mobilising ideologies and resources (McCarthy 2005; Himley 2008; Göbel *et al.* 2014). Once this institutional structure had been created, the National Forestry Commission, PRONATURA, and Environmental Services of Oaxaca called for a programme of voluntary marketing of forestry carbon assets to encourage indigenous communities to obtain carbon assets (Bray 2012). This programme aimed at supporting low-income, indigenous communities to encourage protection and conservation of local ecosystems. Nine indigenous communities of the northern Sierra of Oaxaca entered the programme. For the communities to be included, the National Forestry Commission required them to be free of communal land tenure conflicts, to have an authorised land-use plan, and to have a Communal Statute. That is, the programme had to secure investment in carbon assets by guaranteeing that indigenous communities observed the environmental laws. The programme also ruled that federal courts shall resolve any dispute emerging during the programme execution.

Climate change policy and its multiple links to rural sustainable development have undermined core indigenous peoples' rights to autonomy and self-determination. For example, patterns of cultivation of corn, beans, and several other farming techniques have changed following the prioritisation of forest conservation. In addition, laws and regulations have made illegal various traditional practices of forest use and local hunting and gathering, what environmental discourses term 'biodiversity conservation'. The new rules have caused conflict within communities because local, traditional authorities must apply these mandatory new rules of environmental protection. Marginalisation has increased because the survival of most communities relies on local ecosystems for food. Moreover, land conflicts between indigenous communities could increase because contentious forestry areas (i.e. those involved in conflicts/dispute) have now entered the business of climate change.

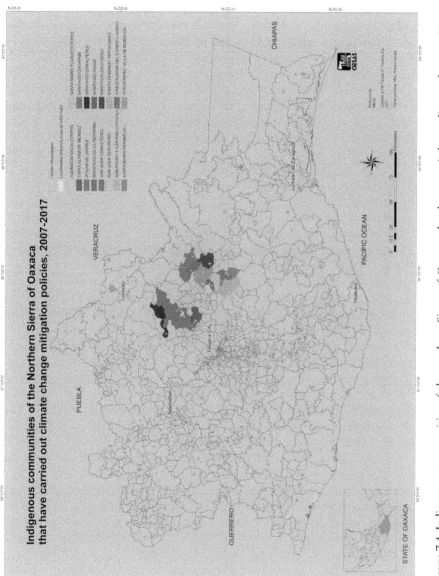

Figure 7.1 Indigenous communities of the northern Sierra of Oaxaca that have carried out climate change mitigation policies, 2007–17.

The community of Capulálpam began a carbon capture programme in 2008 when it designated around 700 hectares of forest for carbon capture. In 2012, the community signed an extra five-year contract and in September 2017 local authorities prepared to renew an additional contract for carbon sequestration. I have asked the authorities whether the income generated by these programmes is enough to make them profitable. They assert that carbon capture payments are not fair because the community invests a lot of resources in conservation programmes. Indeed, in most of the indigenous communities of Oaxaca, *tequio* – unpaid work that community members provide to maintain common property (including reforestation work, forest maintenance, and management of land resources) – constitutes the main way of sustaining communal property. This labour source is part of the system of customary governance in the communities of Mesoamerica and Oaxaca (Newling 2001; Robson and Wiest 2014). *Tequio* allows communities to maintain a wide range of autonomy in their local decision-making and allows them to supply labour for the conservation of territorial resources. This mechanism of wealth production has been generational, which explains the long-term maintenance of biological diversity in the Sierra communities (Bray 2010). However, this community labour mechanism has been exploited by institutions promoting climate change mitigation because it lowers the costs of so-called environmental services.

In the case of Capulálpam, around 250 commoners maintain the areas allocated to carbon capture through *tequio* workforce. However, the income that the institutions and companies provide is used for shared facilities such as running water and road maintenance. In this respect, the conservation and maintenance of biodiversity, thanks to *tequio* and the cargo system, are mechanisms that climate change policies have exploited. At 18 years of age, a *comunero* must provide *tequio*. For example, on 8 July 2017, I joined 249 other community members to clean up a reforestation area destined for carbon sequestration. We worked using machetes and axes for about seven hours in *El Cajón* on the mountains, cutting weeds and vegetation that can compete with the pines that capture carbon. The community receives US$25,000 per year for an area of 2,000 hectares for carbon sequestration. This carbon capture is effective because the community has conserved these areas for centuries. Currently, for example, the commoners supply six *tequios* in different months of the year to conserve these areas. The minimum wage in Capulálpam is around US$12.50 per day, which means that through six *tequios* the community invests around US$18,750 in conservation per year, not including the 12 people that make an ongoing unpaid contribution to the work of the Commissariat responsible for the administration of communal forests. As a result, climate change programmes extract wealth from indigenous communities and transfer this to the global economy through low-cost environmental services subsidised by the indigenous communities, thereby taking advantage of communities such as Capulálpam.

Climate change policies usually aggrandise indigenous traditions and knowledge, yet in practice they discriminate and dismiss historical indigenous knowledge. Documents presented at UNFCCC COP13, when referring to indigenous peoples' traditional knowledge, defined this as follows:

> Developed from experience gained through centuries and adapted to local culture and environment, it is transmitted orally from generation to generation. It tends to be collectively owned and takes the form of stories, songs, folklore, proverbs, cultural values, beliefs, rituals, community laws, local language and agricultural practices including the production of plant and animal species. It is sometimes referred to as oral tradition since it is practiced, sung, danced, painted, carved, recited and acted over thousands of years.
>
> (SEMARNAT *et al.* 2016: 32)

This depiction of indigenous traditions and knowledge obscures historical struggles and experiences and places them in a binary, traditional versus modern culture thereby denying indigenous peoples political power and agency. Thus, discrimination and racial profiles suffuse climate change policy. Traditional knowledge, in my view, is the one that indigenous communities have constructed over time through dialogue: a local knowledge produced in relation to wider politics of the dominant society. Experience of forest extraction during the latter half of the twentieth century, for example, constitutes traditional knowledge in the Sierra communities.

State institutions respect indigenous traditions as long as they do not contradict the laws and government policies. In practice, indigenous communities must comply with climate change rules in order to receive funding for conservation activities. For example, as part of the National Strategy for Reducing Emissions from Deforestation and Forest Degradation (ENAREDD+) and as part of the dissemination of the Strategy, in 2007 the Mexican Government promoted the creation of CORENAMICH (Regional Committee on Natural Resources Mixe-Choapam), an indigenous NGO of the Sierra *Ayuuk*. According to REDD+, CORENAMICH emerged with the aim of undertaking activities to conserve and benefit natural resources (CORENAMICH 2015). However, it emerged from the ENAREDD+ initiative, which has co-opted communities to carry out its strategy to reduce emissions from deforestation. Although CORENAMICH comprises 22 Mixe communities with principles of autonomy without affiliation to political and religious parties, and while the strategy promotes respect for traditional knowledge and rights of indigenous peoples, CORENAMICH must comply with international obligations regarding climate change (see CORENAMICH 2015). Thus, indigenous traditions of conservation remain subordinate to global objectives, while locally produced wealth is transferred to companies generating carbon emissions. This multicultural discourse marginalises indigenous experiences, approving of those considered suitable (such as living in a community – which supports climate change policy) and ignoring others (such as traditions that work against conserving biodiversity).

Indeed, climate policy has introduced significant, contradictory ways of viewing communal lands because rules concerning mitigation of climate change contradict the ways in which communities have traditionally interacted with their territories. For centuries, indigenous communities had used the slash and burn technique for cultivating corn, beans, and cucumber. They had also combined cultivation of corn in forest lands and had collected various plants, insects, and animals for food. Dedicating forests for carbon sequestration has had an enormous impact: the availability of areas for maize cultivation has been significantly reduced owing to forest conservation and biodiversity protection rules that prohibit the conversion of forest lands into arable lands, a practice that communities had used for centuries to produce food (González 2001). Such changes have also meant a structural change among indigenous communities who must now deal with a labyrinth of rules regarding environmental protection from diverse state institutions.

Rationalisation of nature has displaced cultivation of corn and has also impacted local beliefs. For instance, corn is used not only for food but also for rituals associated with the earth and for various religious celebrations during the year. Rituals conceiving the earth as a living being have been displaced since nature's conceptions now belong to the realm of law and policies, although some indigenous communities do still perform rituals to the earth to protect aquifers and forests from depletion. For example, in 2011 the community of Capulálpam declared a communal protected area for recharge of aquifers and for protecting wildlife and forests; moreover, the community also decided not to register the area at the National Commission for Protected Areas as prescribed by environmental laws. This decision shows the failure of climate change policies because they are not designed to meet local needs and local identities. The recent emergence of a labyrinth of laws ruling the environment and natural resources has undermined the rights of indigenous peoples to their historical resources and has led to the view that local communities are backward because they do not know the law (Navarro 2016). When the legislature enacted the General Law of Ecologic Equilibrium and Environmental Protection, it prohibited domestic hunting and cultivation in forestry areas, and the cutting down of trees for domestic use. Any community activity involving the environment required supervision and approval by the Federal Attorney Office for Environmental Protection. While the state enacted and enforced rules for climate change, indigenous communities lost autonomy in their management of local ecosystems because they remained subordinate to the policies of the Secretariat of Environment and Natural Resources, the National Forestry Commission, and the Federal Attorney Office for Environmental Protection.

Although the Sierra communities have joined the realm of climate policy and environmental laws, they have also struggled for autonomy. For example, in 2011 the community of Capulálpam reopened an old road that had previously linked the village with neighbouring communities. The road had been unused for decades until the community decided to reopen and widen it. The Federal Attorney Office for Environmental Protection imposed a fine on the community because it did not, as required by law, undertake an environmental impact assessment. The community argued that reopening the road had no impact other than to reconnect the communities, so they had decided to rehabilitate it and keep it operational. In 2016, the Secretariat of Environment and Natural Resources and Federal Attorney Office for Environmental Protection closed the communal sawmill because of a potential land conflict with a neighbouring community. The community of Capulálpam argued that it had run the sawmill for years observing the environmental laws and that it did not have any conflict with communities that affected its communal enterprise. Despite the official closure, the community decided to keep the sawmill running because it had not broken any law. This case is now under consideration by a federal court. Capulálpam has thus entered the global pattern of judicialising politics (Sieder *et al.* 2016) and, I would say, has joined a global trend of judicialising nature – a process whereby courts resolve conflicts arising from strict regulation of ecosystems. The community has thus faced the tough laws associated with climate policy. When the community decided to establish its own area for protecting aquifers in 2011, it contributed to hydrological services but the community decided not to register the reserved area at the National Commission for Natural Protected Areas and not to involve REDD+ in managing the reserve, to keep community control of the aquifers and so avoid environmental laws. Indigenous communities must *take risk* by challenging and redirecting environmental rules and ideologies (Poole 2012). This very effective way of climate change mitigation is consistent with the *travelling idea of climate change* (de Wit 2014) in the sense that local communities create diverse stances and identities when confronting hegemonic climate change policies (Coombe 2016) and the commodification of nature (Comaroff and Comaroff 2009).

The community of Capulálpam has a vast amount of expertise in terms of community forest management and has built a strong political position to recover from the environmental impact caused by the paper company. Dominant narratives and policies, however, dismiss this historical knowledge by detaching traditions from their historical roots. Capulálpam's traditions of conservation are rooted in experiences of exploitation encouraged by the federal government and the paper company. In this tradition, land tenure is crucial in the community identity. Pre-colonial, colonial, and contemporary traditions of land tenure feed its senses of land possession. However, when global policies of climate change define traditional knowledge, they often refer to it as a knowledge aside from local histories of land tenure and of environmental impacts that suffuse local identities. As has already been described, the communities of the Sierra have had devastating experiences of environmental impact as well as significant experiences of dealing with federal government rules and policies of forests and land management. These experiences constitute traditional knowledge and local identities, which climate change policies often ignore.

As one example of the dismissing of historical indigenous knowledge, one of the main goals of the *Summit Muuch' tambal on Indigenous Experience: Traditional Knowledge and Biological and Cultural Biodiversity* that took place in Cancun, Mexico, in 2016 was to respect, preserve, and safeguard indigenous peoples' knowledge and innovations. Yet, in apparent contradiction, the Summit focused on identifying *successful* indigenous projects of biodiversity conservation, based on the criteria of the United Nations Convention on Biological Diversity.

When national and international organisations promote conservation projects, those idyllic hegemonic visions of tradition collapse because they do not recognise the structural sources of natural resource depletion and climate variability. Although the National Strategy provides a sense of inclusion of Ayuuk (Mixe) communities by assuring respect for Ayuuk traditions of organisation and conservation, it also emphasises that the communities must observe the aims of the National Plan for Sustainable Development and the environmental laws when undertaking actions associated with climate change mitigation. Crucially, this strategy promotes and takes advantage of indigenous communities and the collectives, a strategy that even some scholars support (see Klooster and Masera 2000). The strategy assumes that climate change is happening because of unlimited and inefficient use of forests, lack of investment in forestry enterprises, low income from forest management, government subsidies for agriculture, illegal logging, lack of rights to land property, poverty, and a lack of public policy for sustainable rural development (CORENAMICH 2015: 32–3). Reversing these drivers of climate change has become a priority for CORENAMICH, the Mexican Government, and REDD+. As the National Strategy depicts indigenous communities as being responsible for climate change, Mexico gets ready to reverse the loss of forestry areas and environmental services via sustainable forest management, and to counteract carbon emission by reversing deforestation and ecosystems degradation. The strategy projects that potential carbon dioxide absorption by forests is around 58 million tonnes in 2020 and 96 million tonnes in 2030. Thus, by 2022 carbon sequestration should be enough to compensate for carbon emitted from other sectors of the economy. To achieve this, the Mixe will have to stop using ancestral patterns of dealing with their territory because the National Strategy states that these are now obsolete. Although their patterns of territorial management of ecosystems have proved successful (Lipp 1991; Greenberg 2012), the Mixe are required to observe environmental laws and global climate policy.

While the Mexican institutions responsible for implementing climate change mitigation policies have sought to incorporate traditional knowledge of indigenous communities as a key pathway to biological conservation, the indigenous communities have understood those policies in different, contentious ways. The official definition of tradition is a repetitive behaviour that has been maintained, without change, over time – an accumulation of techniques and ways of being. In this view, tradition has thrived in parallel to scientific knowledge and must be valued because of its persistence. Moreover, the official narrative of traditional knowledge is based on ideologies that communities have kept their knowledge intact from time immemorial and away from the politics of past exploitation, biases that deny indigenous communities political resistance and agency. Thus, policy on climate change mitigation frequently ignores the fact that past politics of exploitation have impacted local communities' ecosystems. This mainstream view of tradition defines indigenous communities as if they had lived in a vacuum. However, indigenous communities have not forgotten memories of resource depletion; in fact, these memories of the past suffuse the way in which communities have contested the official narratives of climate change prevention and biodiversity protection. Traditional knowledge and scientific knowledge have interacted and have fed each other over time to produce *new* traditional knowledge (González 2001). Ecosystems in the Sierra are well preserved because of a dialogical traditional knowledge, and thus indigenous experiences are essential for policies of conservation. History, identity, and power play a crucial role in how indigenous communities have challenged and redirected the dominant views of environmental conservation, mitigation of, and adaptation to climate change.

Whereas state institutions insist on defining traditional knowledge as a knowledge not touched by time, indigenous societies argue that experiences of the past feed their proposals for protecting the environment. Environmental conflicts arise because climate policy encounters various historical ways of living in local territories (Escobar 2014) where relational natures based on demands for autonomy and self-determination thrive (Ulloa 2012, 2014: 164). Cruikshank (2005), for example, illustrated the way in which scientists, colonisers, and local populations have developed different conceptions of nature in the Yukon region. While scientists and colonisers saw glaciers as a source of extraction and commodification, local indigenous communities incorporated glaciers and their experiences of exploitation into their human interactions and constructed glaciers as animated, sentient subjects. I suggest that the forgetfulness of histories is still a powerful ideology when governments and institutions define the policies of environmental protection. The construction of indigenous ontologies about nature has incorporated a diverse interpretation of environmental impact. While modern narratives about the environment seek to obscure these historical relations, and thus this divide and forgetfulness of history, indigenous communities such as Capulálpam have used their memories to construct their land-use plan for the defence and protection of communal lands. By denying historical relationships, climate change mitigation policy focuses on conservation and productivity, overlooking the critical processes of dispossession (Composto and Navarro 2014) and wealth extraction from indigenous communities. Although this institutional arrangement took advantage of the historic organisational practices of indigenous communities that have ensured their subordination to the Mexican state, indigenous communities are now bringing their own political agendas to deal with the politics of climate change.

Conclusions

The indigenous communities of the northern Sierra of Oaxaca became involved in the politics of climate change mitigation following the lessons learned from several years of environmental impact due to forest extraction. They did this because of structural changes carried out by the Mexican Government to meet the global agendas of climate change mitigation and adaptation. The new rules associated with climate change arrived in a region historically impacted by the policies of forest extraction and in communities with long-standing experience in forest conservation and administration. In a period of around 14 years, the indigenous communities of the Sierra changed dramatically their local understandings of territory and natural resources because they were required to incorporate a set of rules and measures relating to climate change policy. In this process, the government incorporated the communities through the narrative of respecting indigenous organisational practices and traditions of conservation, highlighting a sense of including indigenous communities in climate change policies. Through the model of territorial corporate control that the state had introduced to the region in previous years, the government in alliance with NGOs promoting conservation (such as PRONATURA) introduced the programme of carbon sequestration and several measures to prevent forest degradation. The communities had to comply with the new rules or they would not receive government resources through programmes for forest extraction. The communities were required to stop cultivating corn and beans in the forests because of new rules banning these practices, while indigenous communities had to make their Communal Statutes available, observing rules and actions to mitigate climate change. A new language of environmental protection and conservation inundated everyday life. A multiscale, environmental state formation took place in the Sierra, not only emerging in the narratives and rules of government institutions but also in the practices of group organisation of the indigenous communities. A narrative of including indigenous communities' traditions of conservation emerged while the government advanced and enforced the climate change policy. As the communities incorporated those policies they also challenged the new conservation rules.

Struggle for autonomy is an enduring process and has enriched indigenous communities' knowledge of environmental issues. Forest conservation is a political issue among the Sierra communities that implies moral issues with the environment. For centuries, the communities have interacted with diverse governmental policies while providing unpaid communal labour for the maintenance of their communal lands, such as labour for reforestation, for preventing fires, for preventing illegal logging by outsiders, and crucially for asserting rights to communal lands. In so doing, the communities have invested in environmental services, services that the communities provide at a non-remunerated, excessive cost. Indigenous communities provide wealth to the global society, a way of dispossession that sustains a chronic marginalisation. Climate change politics have overlooked this historical relationship with nature while it has profited the social infrastructure of corporate indigenous communities. In my view, effective climate change policy will depend on whether it involves the multiple voices and experiences emerging in those collective, indigenous institutions of political representation. It remains to be seen if Mexican state climate policy will survive in an era of indigenous rights to lands and in the context of changing patterns of land use causing growing marginalisation among indigenous communities.

References

Bárcenas, F.L., 2009. *Legislación y derechos indígenas en México*. Cámara de Diputados, Centro de Estudios para el Desarrollo Rural Sustentable y la Soberanía Alimentaria. Ciudad de Mexico.

Bray, D. 2010. Capitalism meets common property. *Americas Quarterly*, 4 (1), 30–5.

Bray, D., 2012. *Environmental Services of Oaxaca: A Mexican success story* [online]. Available from: www.ecosystemmarketplace.com/articles/environmental-services-of-oaxaca-br-a-mexican-success-story/ [Accessed 3 May 2017].

Bray, D., and Merino-Pérez, L., 2002. *The Rise of Community Forestry in Mexico: History, concepts, and lessons learned from twenty-five years of community timber production*. Miami, FL: Report for the Ford Foundation.

Bray, D., and Merino-Pérez, L., 2004. La experiencia de las comunidades forestales en México. México: Semarnat, INE, CCMSS.

Bray, D.B., Antinori, C., and Torres-Rojo, J.M., 2006. The Mexican model of community forest management: The role of agrarian policy, forest policy and entrepreneurial organization. *Forest Policy and Economics*, 8 (4), 470–84.

Cámara de Diputados del H. Congreso de la Unión, 2001. *Ley de desarrollo rural sustentable* [online]. Available from: www.diputados.gob.mx/LeyesBiblio/pdf/235.pdf. [Accessed 30 May 2017].

Cámara de Diputados del H. Congreso de la Unión, 2012. *Ley general de cambio climático* [online]. Available from: www.diputados.gob.mx/LeyesBiblio/pdf/LGCC_010616.pdf [Accessed 25 May 2017].

Chance, J., and Taylor, W., 1985. Cofradias and cargos: An historical perspective on the MesoAmerican civil-religious hierarchy. *American Ethnologists*, 12 (1), 1–26.

Chapela, F., 1999. Emergencia de las organizaciones sociales de Oaxaca: la lucha por los recursos forestales. *Alteridades*, 9 (17), 105–12.

Comaroff, J.L., and Comaroff, J., 2009. *Ethnicity, Inc.* Chicago: University of Chicago Press.

Composto, C., and Navarro, M.L., 2014. Claves de lectura para comprender el despojo y las luchas por los bienes comunes naturales en América Latina. *In*: C. Composto and M.L. Navarro, eds, *Territorios en disputa. Despojo capitalista, luchas en defensa de los bienes comunes naturales y alternativas emancipatorias en America Latina*. México: Bajo Tierra Ediciones, 33–75.

Coombe, R.J., 2016. The knowledge economy and its cultures: Neoliberal technologies and Latin American reterritorializations. *HAU: Journal of Ethnographic Theory*, 6 (3), 247–75.

CORENAMICH, 2015. *Dissemination and Socialization Program of REDD+: National strategy for forestry communities with high biodiversity of the Mixe and Choapam region*. Oaxaca, MX: National Forestry Commission, REDD+, CORENAMICH.

Crate, S.A., 2011. Climate and culture: Anthropology in the era of contemporary climate change. *Annual Review of Anthropology*, 40 (1), 175–94.

Cronkleton, P., Bray, D., and Medina, G., 2011. Community forest management and the emergence of multi-scale governance institutions: Lessons for REDD+ development from Mexico, Brazil and Bolivia. *Forests*, 2 (2), 451–73.

Cruikshank, J., 2005. *Do Glaciers Listen? Local knowledge, colonial encounters, and social imagination*. Vancouver: University of British Columbia Press.

Das, V., and Poole, D., 2004. Introduction: State and its margins: comparative ethnographies. *In*: V. Das and D. Poole, eds, *Anthropology in the Margins of the State: Comparative ethnographies*. Santa Fe, NM: New Mexico School of American Research Press, 3–33.

de Wit, S., 2014. Denaturalizing adaptation, resocializing the climate: Theoretical and methodological reflections on how to follow a travelling idea of climate change. *In*: F. Gesing, J. Herbeck, and S. Klepp, eds, *Denaturalizing Climate Change: Migration, mobilities and space*. Bremen: artec, 56–64.

Delgado, P.D., 2014. ¿Cómo se afectan los derechos de los pueblos indígenas con las reformas para facilitar la integración económica y la conservación de la Amazonia? *In*: B. Göbel, M. Góngora-Mera, and A. Ulloa, eds, *Desigualdades socio-ambientales en América Latina*. Bogotá: Universidad Nacional de Colombia, Facultad de Ciencias Humanas, 459–86.

Ellis, E.A., *et al.*, 2016. Determinantes de deforestación en el estado de Oaxaca. Agencia de los Estados Unidos para el Desarrollo Internacional (USAID), The Nature Conservancy (TNC), Alianza México REDD+, Mexico, Distrito Federal [online]. Available from: www.researchgate.net/profile/Edward_Ellis/publication/312653088_Determinantes_de_la_deforestacion_en_el_estado_de_Oaxaca/links/58877517a6fdcc6b791ea211/Determinantes-de-la-deforestacion-en-el-estado-de-Oaxaca.pdf [Accessed 14 September 2017].

Escobar, A., 2014. *Sentipensar con la tierra. Nuevas lecturas sobre desarrollo, territorio y diferencia*. Medellín, CO: Ediciones UNAULA.

Fuente, M., and Barkin, D., 2011. *Desacatos*, 37, 93–110.

Göbel, B., Góngora, M., and Ulloa, A., 2014. Las interdependencias entre la valorización global de la naturaleza y las desigualdades sociales: abordajes multidisciplinarios. *In*: B. Göbel, M. Góngora-Mera, and A. Ulloa, eds, *Las interdependencias entre la valorización global de la naturaleza y las desigualdades sociales: abordajes multidisciplinarios en Desigualdades socio ambientales en América Latina*. Bogotá: Facultad de Ciencias Humanas, Universidad Nacional de Colombia, 13–59.

Gómez-Mendoza, L., *et al.*, 2006. Projecting land-use change processes in the Sierra Norte of Oaxaca, Mexico. *Applied Geography*, 26 (3), 276–90.

González, R.J., 2001. *Zapotec Science: Farming and food in the northern Sierra of Oaxaca*. Austin, TX: University of Texas Press.

Greenberg, J.B., 2012. The impact of neoliberal policies on rural producers in Oaxaca, Mexico. *In*: J.B. Greenberg, *et al.*, eds, *Neoliberalism and Commodity Production in Mexico*. Boulder, CO: University Press of Colorado, 225–39.

Greenberg, J., and Emanuel, M.R., 2000. Lluvia Enojada-Tyoo Kuasi': The political ecology of forest extraction in the Sierra Chatina, Oaxaca, Mexico. *Journal of Political Ecology*, 7, 43–64.

Hale, C.R., 2002. Does multiculturalism menace? Governance, cultural rights and the politics of identity in Guatemala. *Journal of Latin American Studies*, 34 (3), 485–524.

Himley, M., 2008. Geographies of environmental governance: The nexus of nature and neoliberalism. *Geography Compass*, 2 (2), 433–51.

INECC, 2013. *Inventario Nacional de Emisiones de Gases de Efecto Invernadero 1990–2010* [online]. Available from: www.inecc.gob.mx/descargas/cclimatico/inf_inegei_public_2010.pdf [Accessed 23 May 2017].

Klooster, D., and Masera, O., 2000. Community forest management in Mexico: Carbon mitigation and biodiversity conservation through rural development. *Global Environmental Change*, 10 (4), 259–72.

Lipp, F.J., 1991. *The Mixe of Oaxaca: Religion, ritual, and healing*. Austin, TX: University of Texas Press.

McCarthy, J., 2005. Scale, sovereignty, and strategy in environmental governance. *Antipode*, 37 (4), 731–53.

Navarro, S.A., 2016. Dilemmas of sustainability in Cocopah territory: An exercise of applied visual anthropology in the Colorado River delta. *Human Organization*, 75 (2), 129–40.

Newling, E., 2001. *The Mixe of Oaxaca and the Cultural Meanings of Indigenous Autonomy in Mexico: An ethnographic portrait of a social movement*. PhD thesis. University of Pennsylvania.

Novo, C.M., 2014. Managing diversity in postneoliberal Ecuador. *Journal of Latin American and Caribbean Anthropology*, 19 (1), 103–25.

Nugent, D., and Gilbert J., 1994. *Formas cotidianas de la formación del Estado*. México: Ediciones ERA.

Ojeda, D., 2014. Descarbonización y despojo: desigualdades socioambientales y las geografías del cambio climático. *In*: B. Göbel, M. Góngora-Mera, and A. Ulloa, eds, *Desigualdades socioambientales en America Latina*. Bogotá: Universidad Nacional de Colombia, 256–89.

Perez, J. 2017. *La ODRENASIJ 'educación en nuestras manos' y procesos de educación y fortalecimiento de la identidad a partir de la lucha forestal en la sierra Juárez de Oaxaca*. Master's thesis. Oaxaca, MX: CIESAS Pacifico Sur.

Poole, D. 2012. Corriendo riesgos: Normas, Ley y Participación en el Estado Neoliberal. *Antropológica*, 30 (30), 83–100.

Rainforest Alliance, 2014. *Indigenous Communities in Southern Mexico Protect Their Forest Heritage* [online]. Available from: www.rainforest-alliance.org/articles/indigenous-communities-in-southern-mexico-protect-their-forest-heritage [Accessed 30 May 2017].

Robson, J., and Wiest, R., 2014. Transnational migration, customary governance, and the future of community: A case study from Oaxaca, Mexico. *Latin American Perspectives*, 41 (3), 103–17.

Scott, J.C., 1998. *Seeing Like a State: How certain schemes to improve the human condition have failed*. New Haven, CT: Yale University Press.

SEMARNAT, 2014. Versión de Difusión del Programa Especial de Cambio Climático 2014–2018 (PECC 2014–2018). Gobierno de la República, México [online]. Available from: www.sagarpa.gob.mx/desarrolloRural/Programa%20 Especial%20de%20Cambio%20Clim%C3%A1tico%202014-2018%20 (PECC)/Documents/Programa%20Especial%20de%20Cambio%20 Clim%C3%A1tico%202014-2018_Versi%C3%B3n%20de%20 Difusi%C3%B3n_.pdf [Accessed 30 May 2017].

SEMARNAT, CDI, RITA, PNUD, GIZ, 2016. Decimotercera Conferencia de las Partes del Convenio Sobre la Diversidad Biológica. Integrando la biodiversidad para el bienestar. Foro Regional Indígena Rumbo a la COP13 Cuaderno de Trabajo. Ciudad de México.

Sieder, R., Schjolden, L., and Angell, A., 2016. Introduction. *In*: R. Sieder, L. Schjolden, and A. Angell, eds, *The Judicialization of Politics in Latin America*. New York: Palgrave Macmillan, 17–38.

Ulloa, A., 2012. Los territorios indígenas en Colombia: de escenarios de apropiación transnacional a territorialidades alternativas. *Scripta Nova. Revista Electrónica de Geografía y Ciencias Sociales*, 16 (418), 65.

Ulloa, A., 2013. Controlando la naturaleza: ambientalismo transnacional y negociaciones locales en torno al cambio climático en territorios indígenas en Colombia. *IberoAmericana*, 13 (49), 117–33.

Ulloa, A., 2014. Escenarios de creación, extracción, apropiación y globalización de las naturalezas: emergencia de desigualdades socio ambientales. *In*: B. Göbel, M. Góngora-Mera, and A. Ulloa, eds, *Desigualdades socioambientales en América Latina*. Bogotá: Universidad Nacional de Colombia, 136–66.

United Nations 2017. *Framework Convention on Climate Change* [online]. Available from: http://unfccc.int/tools_xml/country_MX.html [Accessed 15 September 2017].

Viveros, T., and Godinez, R., 2015. *Cambio climático y derechos humanos*. México: Comisión Nacional de Derechos Humanos.

Weaver, T., 2000. Changes in forestry policy, production, and the environment in northern Mexico: 1960–2000. *Journal of Political Ecology*, 7 (1), 1–18.

Zabin, A., 1989. *Grassroots Development in Indigenous Communities: A case study from the Sierra Juarez in Oaxaca*. PhD thesis. University of California Berkeley.

8 Adapting in a carbon pool?

Politicising climate change at Sumatra's oil palm frontier

Jonas Hein and Yvonne Kunz

Introduction

When visiting villages in Jambi province on the island of Sumatra in 2013, peasants told us that the Indonesian Government had recently proclaimed their forests to be 'lungs of the earth'. This phrase is the local interpretation of a recent concept developed by economists and conservationists within the context of international climate policy – specifically the REDD+ mechanism (Reducing Emissions from Deforestation and Forest Degradation). The Indonesian Government declared Jambi province as one of its official provinces for piloting the UN-backed REDD+ mechanism. Since about 2010, Jambi province has sought to position itself as a frontrunner in low-carbon development illustrated by a number of low-carbon development, greenhouse gas reduction, and forest conservation strategies and new public and private forest conservation initiatives. However, many peasants and indigenous communities have not welcomed new protected areas and the expansion of corporate oil palm concessions for global mitigation objectives. Peasants are engaging in open and hidden resistance against oil palm companies and conservation authorities in the area. This has led to violent clashes with private and public security agencies (see Colchester *et al.* 2011; Steinebach 2013; Beckert *et al.* 2014; Hein and Faust 2014; Hein 2016; Hein *et al.* 2016).

The expansion of conservation areas and oil palm plantations – at a first glance two contradictory developments – was at least partially driven by the same global climate policy objective articulated within Jambi's low-carbon development strategy: mitigating climate change. The reasoning is that oil palms would capture atmospheric carbon and provide a source of apparently carbon-neutral fuel while forest conservation would result in the capture and long-term storage of atmospheric carbon. However, mitigation policies in rural Jambi involve significant trade-offs, indicated by violent conflicts, water scarcity, and biodiversity loss (Hein 2016; Klasen *et al.* 2016; Merten *et al.* 2016; Teuscher *et al.* 2016). Violent conflicts and water scarcity, in particular, undermine the second objective of climate policy, namely adaptation to the impacts of climate change. Adaptation and mitigation are often framed as a binary opposition which originates in these topics having been discussed separately under the United Nations Framework Convention on Climate Change (UNFCCC) and the Intergovernmental Panel on Climate Change (IPCC) (Swart and Raes 2007: 289; Görg 2011: 413; Watts 2015: 37). Mitigation policies focus on reducing greenhouse gas emissions and thus limiting global warming, while adaptation policies focus on reducing vulnerability to the effects of global warming. However, this does not take account of the interdependent relationship between society and nature (e.g. atmosphere) (Görg 2011: 415). Nature and inherent biophysical processes of the atmosphere can be shaped by society (as anthropogenic climate change illustrates), while the material condition of the natural environment at the same time influences society (ibid.). Climate policy, and adaptation and mitigation as its component parts, reshapes societal relationships with nature in multiple ways (Görg 2011: 413). Forest conservation, forest carbon offsetting, and oil palm cultivation challenge pre-existing modes of production such as shifting cultivation. Conservation, oil palm cultivation, and shifting cultivation are characterised by different and competing societal relationships with nature. Oil palms indeed capture greenhouse gases if the plantations are not replacing forests. However, in addition to a number of land tenure conflicts involving palm oil companies in Jambi, oil palm cultivation might also compete with the cultivation of food crops and increase water scarcity (Merten *et al.* 2016).

This chapter seeks to contextualise and contribute to the politicisation of climate change policy. Emphasis is given to trade-offs between different policy objectives formulated and realised at different political scales. Impacts of mitigation policies on the ability of societal actors to adapt to climate change and climate variability are highlighted. We consider adaptation and mitigation as embedded in existing power asymmetries and political ecologies. First, we focus on climate change policy in Jambi province. We argue that a sole focus on mitigation and the lack of a provincial adaptation policy reflects the interests of international donors, conservation organisations, and national government rather than societal actors in Jambi. Second, based on two case studies we show how climate policy changes geographies of resource access and control and how certain actors may become marginalised, making them more vulnerable to environmental change (Zimmerer and Bassett 2003; Watts 2015: 34). The first case study shows how the expansion of oil palm cultivation, which is at least partially driven by low-carbon fuel policies in Indonesia and the European Union (Bourguignon 2015: 2), has caused water pollution and freshwater scarcity and as a result has reduced the adaptive capacity of rural households. The second case study illustrates how the expansion of a privatised biodiversity and carbon conservation area, financed by the German International Climate Initiative (IKI), challenges peasant agriculture. The expansion of this conservation area has fostered land conflicts by restricting access to natural resources to local actors, hence challenging pre-existing modes of production. As a consequence, this has reduced the adaptive capacity of peasant migrants while protecting watersheds and providing alternative income sources for parts of the indigenous population.

To investigate the climate politics in Jambi province and the ability of societal actors impacted by environmental change and climate policies to adapt to climate shifts, this research follows a multi-sited qualitative approach. Semi-structured interviews with actors, most of them directly involved in different forest conservation and climate mitigation projects or impacted by the projects as well as by oil palm expansion, were conducted on different political scales between May 2012 and August 2016. Field trips to Jambi province took place between July and December 2012, between August and September 2013, and in August 2016. Interviews were used to unravel provincial climate policies, environmental change, access relations, land-use trajectories, and land-use conflicts. Interviews were recorded, transcribed (in part by Indonesian and German research assistants), and coded using Atlas Ti and MaxQDA data analysis software. This chapter also builds on a review of Indonesian laws and regulations, as well as reports and policy documents from non-governmental organisations (NGOs) and state agencies.

Beyond mitigation and adaptation: towards a political ecology of climate change

The causes and consequences of climate change and related climate policy have material and spatial implications (Liverman 2015: 303). Political ecologists focus on the 'constantly shifting dialectic between society and land-based resources and also within classes and groups within society itself' (Blaikie and Brookfield 1987: 17). The starting point for our endeavour to investigate climate policy and its impacts on Sumatra's peasant communities is the assumption that power differentials and social identity are important explanations for socially differentiated impacts of climate, forest, and conservation policies and for the ability of actors to shape these policies. We build on a dual understanding of nature based on the societal relationships with nature concept (e.g. Görg 1999). Nature has a material dimension and a symbolic dimension. Although the meanings of nature are socially constructed, we acknowledge that nature has a material basis (Escobar 1999: 3; Görg 2011: 416). The material properties of the very same nature (Görg 2011: 416), for example a forest, can be socially constructed in many different ways and depend on the social position of actors (Escobar 1999: 5). A forest can serve either as a carbon pool and sink or as a space used by shifting cultivators. The ability to define nature is inseparably linked with power relations and so affects the way different actors interact with nature, and thus affects their ability to adapt to a changing climate.

We argue that trade-offs between different actors, different types of natural resource use, and different policy objectives (such as reducing greenhouse gas emissions from deforestation, expanding agro-fuel production, and adaptation to climate change) characterise the political ecologies of climate change (Gezon and Paulson 2004: 2; Görg 2011: 419–20; McShane *et al*. 2011: 966; Bustamante *et al*. 2014: 3275). Drawing on the 'double exposure' framework developed by Leichenko *et al*. (2010), we argue that marginalised actors face *triple exposure*. They are not only affected by climate change and neoliberal globalisation, but are also increasingly negatively affected by attempts to reduce greenhouse gas emissions (Osborne 2011; Aggarwal 2014; Hein and Faust 2014; Schade and Obergassel 2014; Smits and Middleton 2014; Horstmann and Hein 2017). We therefore situate the vulnerability of actors to climate and environmental change within the context of the wider political economy (Bassett and Fogelman 2013: 45).

National and provincial climate policy

The Indonesian Government has formulated a number of policies on climate change since the UN climate change conference in Bali in 2007. Most focus on reducing greenhouse gas emissions. In 2011, the Indonesian Government committed to reduce its carbon emissions until 2020 by 26 per cent compared with business-as-usual (41 per cent with international support) (DNPI 2010; Hein 2013; RoI 2016). A National Plan for Greenhouse Gas Emissions Reductions (*Rencana Aksi Nasional penuruan Gas Rumah Kaca*, RAN-GRK) based on the Presidential Regulation of the Republic of Indonesia No 61 Year 2011 outlined a number of different policies. The regulation requires each of the 34[1] provinces of Indonesia to set out a Local Action Plan for Greenhouse Gas Emissions Reduction (*Rencana Aksi Daerah Pengurangan Emisi Gas Rumah Kaca*, RAD-GRK). RAN-GRK and RAD-GRK both include policies that promote oil palm cultivation (RoI 2011: 3; Pemerintah Provinsi Jambi 2012).

More recently, the Indonesian Government has formulated its nationally determined contribution (NDC) as required under the Paris Agreement. The first NDC of the Republic of Indonesia states the national commitment 'towards a low carbon and climate change-resilient development' (RoI 2016: 1). The document mainly repeats pre-existing policies such as RAN-GRK but also includes adaptation objectives. In the NDC, it is further explained that Indonesia plans to achieve, by 2020, an 'archipelagic climate resilience as a result of comprehensive adaptation and mitigation programs and disaster risk reduction strategies' (RoI 2016: 2). Under its mitigation initiatives, the document mentions Indonesia's role in the international REDD+ process. In 2011, Jambi province was appointed as one of 11 provinces in Indonesia to be designated a REDD+ pilot province. The REDD+ Strategy and Action Plan for Jambi province from 2013 refers to adaptation only as a co-benefit of policies reducing deforestation. For further adaptation efforts, the NDC refers to the National Action Plan on Climate Change Adaptation (*Rencana Aksi Nasional – Adaptasi Perubahan Iklim*, RAN-API). Under this plan, risks shall be reduced in various sectors including agriculture, water, and forestry. Compared with the National Action Plan for Greenhouse Gas Emission Reduction (i.e. RAD-GRK), this document is at an early stage of development. To date, it only provides preliminary thoughts on ways to achieve increased resilience to the effects of climate change. Although the important role of local government is stressed, provincial action plans are yet to be compiled (RoI 2013: 16). 'To date there is no climate change adaptation funding policy specifically developed to support the implementation of adaptation action plans in Indonesia' (ibid.: 17). Priority pilot locations have been recommended, but Jambi province is not among them (ibid.: 20). Also mentioned in the NDC is the joint adaptation and mitigation programme PROKLIM, an initiative implemented at the village level. Although 12 villages in Jambi province have been proposed as potential PROKLIM villages, only one has so far been accepted.

At the provincial level, the *Creating Low Carbon Prosperity in Jambi* strategy is worth mentioning here (DNPI 2010), as well as the *Singaporean-Indonesian collaboration to deal with the land and forest fires in Jambi province* (NEA 2009).

Examining what these strategies entail for Jambi province is sobering. Even though mitigation and adaptation appear as a couple in national-level documentation, this is not the case for provincial-level documents. The low-carbon prosperity strategy has a sole focus on mitigation. There is no reference to adaptation, not even as a co-benefit of mitigation efforts such as forest conservation and low-carbon agriculture.

How to adapt in a carbon pool: contextualising Jambi's climate policies

Jambi province covers over 5.3 million hectares. Oil palm and rubber are the predominant crops, with 1.2 million hectares under rubber cultivation and 1.3 million hectares under oil palm cultivation in 2015. Of the 3.3 million people living in Jambi, around 54 per cent earn a living through agricultural activities (for 2014) (BPS Provinsi Jambi 2014). In 2016, 7.3 per cent of Jambi's rural population lived below the national poverty line. This is significantly lower than the national rural average of 13.96 per cent (BPS 2017).

The case study area in southeastern Jambi addressed here is located in the hilly lowlands or peneplain zone that makes up two-thirds of the province (Hein 2016). The lowlands are classified as wet tropical climate, typically with one short dry season (only one month having less than 60 mm average rainfall) (Perbatakusuma *et al.* 2012: 38). Nevertheless, droughts

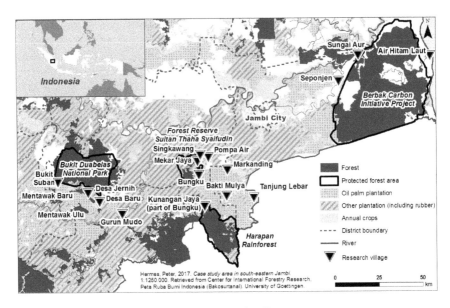

Figure 8.1 Southeast Jambi including research villages.

associated with the El Niño Southern Oscillation (ENSO) phenomenon occur regularly in Jambi. Severe ENSO droughts took place in 1983, 1998, and 2015 (Merten *et al.* 2016).

To investigate the triple exposure of societal actors to climate variability (such as periodic ENSO events), climate policy, and neoliberal globalisation, it is necessary to understand the historical political economy context. This helps to explain the root causes of structural inequality in southeastern Jambi. In pre-colonial times, Jambi was one of several Sultanates along the Strait of Malacca. In the eighteenth and nineteenth centuries the Sultanate was a prosperous trading centre for forest products (beeswax, resin, gum, rattan, timber), and for pepper and gold (Locher-Scholten 2004: 37). At the time of the Dutch conquest over Jambi province in the early twentieth century, shifting cultivation, hunting, and forest gardens were important livelihood strategies for the different semi-nomadic ethnic groups that lived in Jambi's lowlands (Andaya 2008: 205; Hein 2016: 118). The Batin Sembilan groups that constitute the indigenous population in southeastern Jambi trace their origins back to these groups (Steinebach 2013: 71; Hein 2016: 125). The Dutch introduced rubber cultivation, established the first protected areas, initiated sedentarisation of the Batin Sembilan, and challenged customary land tenure (Hein 2016: 120; Hein *et al.* 2016: 384).

Even more profound and disruptive changes occurred after independence and in particular during President Suharto's autocratic rule (1967–98)

(Hein *et al.* 2016). The post-colonial government declared large parts of Jambi's lowlands as state forest and allocated this land to logging companies and later to oil palm companies and transmigrants from Java, ignoring the presence of indigenous groups and displacing them from their ancestral lands. From the 1980s onward, land increasingly became a commodity, and the expansion of corporate logging concessions, oil palm concessions, and smallholder oil palm and rubber cultivation challenged pre-existing modes of production and access and property relations (Hein 2016: 118–24). The most recent change has been driven by global climate policy and by the idea of 'governing through markets' (Peet *et al.* 2011: 7). Environmental issues such as deforestation and climate change are now subject to commodity markets, land, carbon, and ecosystem service markets. In Indonesia, ideas of market environmentalism and market-oriented spatial planning (Radjawali *et al.* 2017) have resulted in regulations that permit companies to bid for ecosystem restoration concessions, again neglecting the presence of peasant and indigenous settlements in the forests (Hein 2016: 139).

Southeastern Jambi is currently experiencing violent land conflicts involving different state agencies, peasant activists, indigenous communities, and oil palm, conservation, and timber companies (Steinebach 2013; Beckert *et al.* 2014; Hein *et al.* 2016; Merten *et al.* 2016). These conflicts set the scene for climate policies in Jambi. At the same time, attempts to reduce greenhouse gas emissions intensify the conflicts and the impacts of conflicts, such as the dispossession of agricultural land, destruction of houses, evictions, and environmental change owing to oil palm expansion (ibid.). These impacts in turn influence the ability of peasants to adapt to climate change and climate variability which, as outlined above, is the second goal of the UNFCCC.

Case study 1: agro-fuel,[2] water scarcity, and land conflicts

Rapid land-use and land-cover change has shaped the socio-ecological transformation in Indonesia over recent decades. Between 1985 and 1997, 22.5 million hectares of Indonesia's tropical rainforest were cleared at an average rate of 1.9 million hectares per year, a process which has been slowed but is far from having been halted (Forest Watch Indonesia 2014: 4). The area under oil palm cultivation in Indonesia, one of the reasons why forest is cleared, reached 11.3 million hectares in 2015 (Direktorat Jenderal Perkebunan 2015: 3). Indonesia is the biggest palm oil producer, followed by Malaysia. India, China, and the EU are the largest net importers of palm oil (FAPRI 2014). More palm oil will be needed to serve the growing agro-fuel demands. In 2010, 57 per cent of the European palm oil imports were used for food production, with only 8 per cent used for the production of agro-diesel. Four years later, the numbers had reversed, with 45 per cent used for biodiesel and 34 per cent for food production (and 16 per cent for electricity and heating) (Valin *et al.* 2015). The aim of increased use of biofuels, for which palm oil is also used, is to decarbonise the transport sector (Bourguignon 2015: 2). The EU's biofuel policy, which sets the reduction of carbon dioxide (CO_2) emissions as its primary goal, has been the subject of much debate (ibid.: 3). Nevertheless, a blending target in the EU Biofuels Directive remains. In short, oil palm is also grown for international mitigation purposes. In many parts of Jambi, we observed negative adaptation trade-offs related to this mitigation objective.

Oil palm cultivation is less labour-intensive than rubber cultivation, results in a higher gross per labour unit than other crops (Schwarze *et al.* 2015; Clough *et al.* 2016), and so provides the opportunity to invest additional labour in off-farm activities. However, villagers also report a number of trade-offs of oil palm cultivation. These include water scarcity, lower food production and thus lower food availability, and land-use conflicts.

Bakti Mulya, for instance, is a transmigration village located in a district where 22 transmigration villages were set up in the 1980s, all in cooperation with oil palm companies. The transmigration programme is the world's largest government-sponsored voluntary resettlement programme (World Bank 1988: iii). Participants received a house and in many cases 2.5 hectares of oil palm plantation ready for cultivation. For Jambi province, 70,000 households were moved to the province under the transmigration programme between 1967 and 1995, many in cooperation with oil palm companies.

In Bakti Mulya, the doctor of the local health station is a young woman from Jakarta. She reported that the oil palm plantation affects water quality as well as water quantity and would not shower her children in the water from the wells without first cleaning it with a filter. Her household is the only one in the village equipped with a filter. She also reported that the wells periodically run dry, which had not happened in the past.[3] Merten *et al.* (2016: 9) confirmed this observation as a correlation of water scarcity and oil palm plantations by stating that oil palm is 'largely responsible for decreasing local water tables and water supplies'.

As oil palm plantations take up an increasing amount of land, less is available for other crops. In all villages visited, there were reports of a strong decrease in food production in the area. None of the villages visited produced food for local markets. The food in the markets is brought in from other areas of Sumatra. The villages west of Desa Baru are all aligned along a dirt road (see Figure 8.1). In times of heavy rain the road becomes virtually unpassable, periodically preventing local markets from taking place and resulting in higher food prices when they resume.[4] Moreover, the sole focus on oil palm makes peasants highly vulnerable to the market price of palm oil. At the time of fieldwork in 2012, palm oil prices were relatively low. One interviewee reported that he usually employs 20 people; in November 2011 he had to dismiss ten of them. The woman hosting us during the fieldwork told us that she was pleased to have visitors because they meant a distraction from the worries she was experiencing caused by the low palm oil price. Decreasing prices during an economic crisis put those households that do not produce food crops at particular risk.

Another direct trade-off from policies supporting the expansion of corporate oil palm plantations is the increasing amount of land-use and land-tenure conflicts (Beckert 2017; Steinebach and Kunz 2017). Local smallholders without *de jure* land titles struggle to maintain access to increasingly contested land (Kunz *et al.* 2016). In particular, the rapid expansion of smallholders and corporate oil palm plantations and the simultaneous expansion of protected areas have been conflictive and contradictory (Hein *et al.* 2016). A Batin Sembilan elder explained: 'Originally this was all community land. We had rubber, durian, and jernang [dragon blood]. It was land of the people but the oil palm company destroyed it with bulldozers' (cited in Hein 2016: 143). In many cases, the Batin Sembilan do not accept being expelled from their ancestral land and so occupy the oil palm plantations established on these grounds (Beckert and Keck 2015). At the end of 2013, one such conflict escalated into violence when 1,500 soldiers pulled down 300 houses allegedly built on land under concession to an oil palm company (Parker 2013).

Case study 2: conflicts in the 'Forest of Hope'

The Harapan Rainforest[5] is a private forest conservation project (see Figure 8.1) established by the conservation company Restorasi Ekosistem Indonesia (PT REKI)[6] in an ecosystem restoration concession. PT REKI won the bid for the concession in 2010. The project has received financial support from the Environmental Support Program of Danida, the German International Climate Initiative (IKI), the European Commission, and Singapore Airlines (Hein 2016). The project aims to restore and protect dry lowland rainforest and to store up to 15 million tonnes of CO_2 over 30 years (IKI 2016). At the same time, it aims to maintain the provision of other ecosystem services such as water regulation and protection against extreme weather events (BirdLife International 2007). In addition to the forest conservation and climate change mitigation objectives, PT REKI aims to develop ecotourism, offer 'green jobs' (IKI 2016), and support peasants and indigenous communities in developing low-carbon and biodiversity-friendly land-use practices. Some of the indigenous peasants that agreed to cooperate with the conservation company received conditional land tenure, access to health care, clean water, agricultural extension services, and have been employed as forest rangers or as labourers in the community nurseries (Hein 2016: 174). The main idea behind these 'community benefits' is to decouple the livelihood strategies of local communities from the exploitation of local natural resources or at least to transform them in ways that PT REKI considers 'environmentally friendly'. Moreover, PT

REKI argues that conserving forests reduces the vulnerability of the poorest local communities that depend on forest resources (European Commission 2006; BirdLife International 2007).

However, not all actors agree with PT REKI's objectives. Some peasant migrants and indigenous communities supported by village and district governments and by peasant organisations such as Serikat Petani Indonesia (SPI, Indonesian Peasant Union) engage in open resistance and claim large parts of the project area. In the course of the still ongoing conflict between peasants and the conservation company, a number of peasants reported that they had lost access to their agricultural land, that their plantations had been destroyed, that they had had to stop swidden rice cultivation, and that they had been evicted from their land within the conservation concession (Hein 2016). Some peasants criticised the objectives of the conservation project and argued in reference to the European engagement that the rich countries should reduce greenhouse gas emissions at home. Others reminded us that their 'home is not the carbon toilet for the rich countries' (ibid.).

The ability of the conservation company to manage almost 100,000 hectares of land for conservation and climate mitigation purposes and its impacts on the local peasants can only be explained when considering the political economy context. PT REKI's success in obtaining its concession indicates that the company is well positioned with regard to different power dimensions. PT REKI's material resources, such as the ability to pay taxes in advance, were necessary to obtain the concession. Furthermore, active lobbying of the founders of the conservation company led to the Ministry of Forestry reforming the forest management, which included the introduction of the earlier not yet existing ecosystem restoration concessions that permit access to land in the first place (Hein 2016: 188). In contrast, peasants and indigenous communities were unable to access *de jure* land titles. As a result, they are highly vulnerable to being evicted by *de jure* rights-holders – in this case PT REKI.

All these conflicts reflect controversial ontological assumptions about nature. Despite PT REKI's argument to support the poorest local communities, the project mainly aims to protect 'nature' and the atmosphere from humankind. PT REKI claims to protect indigenous communities, forests, and other non-human species from the influence of peasant migrants. For instance, one of PT REKI's shareholders argues that 'the establishment of the Harapan Rainforest Initiative provides them [the Batin Sembilan] with the option of continuing to reside in a forest environment' (BirdLife International 2008: 5). A field officer of PT REKI referred to the Harapan Rainforest as 'a last resort for the Batin Sembilan'.[7] The German NABU (Naturschutzbund Deutschland), who is a member of BirdLife International, argues that the survival of the Batin Sembilan depends on the protection of the Harapan Rainforest (NABU 2010: 1). In contrast, another field officer of PT REKI considers migrants 'as a major challenge for conservation'. A representative of one of PT REKI's donors argued that peasants and landowners operating in the project are a challenge for the Batin Sembilan. These statements show that conservationists associated with PT REKI distinguish between peasant migrants (which are seen as external to nature) and indigenous groups (which are seen as part of a nature that should be preserved). However, the construction of simple dichotomies – indigenous groups versus peasant migrants and nature versus humankind – does not reflect the complex and dynamic social-ecological relations at Jambi's oil palm frontier. Rather it reflects the strategic interests of PT REKI, using the presence of the Batin Sembilan and their alleged role as 'forest-dependent people' (BirdLife International 2008: 5) for legitimising forest conservation (Hein 2016: 202). Peasant migrants and indigenous groups are cooperating and have formed strategic alliances through inter-ethnic marriages and joint activism. Since pre-colonial times, both groups have actively transformed societal relationships with nature and have co-produced lowland rainforests, complex rubber and fruit tree agro-forestry systems, and more recently oil palm plantations (see Steinebach 2013; Hein *et al.* 2016).

Conclusion

The conflicts surrounding expanding oil palm plantations and the Forest of Hope indicate that peasants are exposed to climate change, climate change policy, and neoliberal globalisation. The conflicts centre on several often-neglected aspects of climate politics. First, they illustrate trade-offs between different objectives of the UNFCCC, namely between mitigation and adaptation. For example, forest conservation might reduce greenhouse gas emissions but in so doing might also restrict access to forests, and prohibiting agriculture and displacing peasants has a negative impact on the ability of actors to adapt to climate shifts. EU biofuel policies may also have negative indirect and direct land-use change impacts. For example, even if oil palm plantations do not directly replace forests, they may be indirectly responsible for forest clearance if they are grown on agricultural land that was previously used to grow other crops, and where the demand for the original crops remains and such crops are planted on land formerly under forest (Gerasimchuk and Koh 2013: 3).

In the Jambi province research area, livelihood strategies and peasants are not only challenged by climate variability; they are also challenged by climate policy interventions such as forest conservation and oil palm cultivation for biofuel production. This is not surprising given that avoiding emissions from deforestation is not a politically neutral intervention. Forest conservation and oil palm expansion are highly political processes that redefine societal relationships with nature. Forest conservation transforms forests that have been used for swidden rice farming since pre-colonial times into areas designated for interventions that maintain forest carbon. The two case studies show that adaptation and mitigation are not a binary opposition; they influence each other in positive and negative ways (Görg 2011: 415). Indeed, forests could also support adaptation, for instance by maintaining water provision during droughts or by providing forest products. The emerging literature on ecosystem-based adaptation (e.g. Munang *et al.* 2013) builds on the assumption that the protection of biodiversity and ecosystem services supports the ability of actors to adapt to the impacts of climate change (ibid.: 2). However, more important than the aggregated contribution of ecosystem services to well-being (Lele 2013) and adaptation is whether actors in need can actually benefit from them. This leads to questions of access to resources and ecosystems. For the Forest of Hope, the project restricts access to resources (e.g. to land) for peasants. Thus, how far actors will directly benefit from climate policy – whether labelled as adaptation, ecosystem-based adaptation, or mitigation – ultimately depends on the social position of actors and not only on the intervention as such.

Second and closely related to the first argument, the conflicts that have occurred in the Forest of Hope and conflicts between peasants and oil palm companies are embedded in power asymmetries between North and South and between different national actors. From a Northern perspective, forest conservation and oil palm expansion for agro-fuel production to mitigate climate change is an interesting approach for maintaining the current carbon-intense accumulation regime. It permits business as usual and avoids expensive mitigation activities in the global centres. Forest conservation in the Global South has lower opportunity costs than transforming fossil-fuel-dependent economies of the Global North. Consequently, the attractiveness of carbon conservation depends fundamentally on uneven development, and could thus contribute to its perseverance; and could even increase the vulnerability of actors to climate risks (McAfee 2012a, 2012b; Hein 2014). At the national level, allocating land to conservation and oil palm companies is a spatial planning decision that reflects power asymmetries. Losing access to land, which is the most important asset in rural landscapes, makes actors highly vulnerable to any kind of shock, including climate shocks.

Reports from other parts of the world indicate parallels with the situation in Jambi province. It is not only in Jambi that actors suffer from losing access to land (De Schutter 2011; Fairhead *et al.* 2012; Osborne 2013) and, as is the case in Jambi, this could result in a higher vulnerability to climate shocks in these areas.

This chapter has shown that the causes for these increased vulnerabilities are also to be found in the way societal–nature relationships are conceptualised and how mitigation and adaptation policies are developed. We therefore urge a change in perspective. We need to accept that society and nature, as well as mitigation and adaptation, are entangled on a discursive as well as practical level. These terms need to be considered as coupled concepts. Hence, the system of thinking about these terms needs to be changed in order to avoid negative impacts of climate change. In short: system change, not climate change.

Notes

1 Actually only 33 provinces have developed a provincial action plan. At the time of enactment, North Kalimantan was not yet a province and is included in the provincial plan of East Kalimantan.
2 This chapter avoids using the terms 'biofuel' and 'biodiesel' as the prefix 'bio' implies a sustainability component. For the reasons outlined in this text the term is, to a certain extent, a mismatch, which is why the more neutral term 'agro-fuel' or 'agro-diesel' is preferred for referring to fuel from vegetable oils through trans-esterification.
3 Personal interview, Bakti Mulya, 11 November 2012.
4 Own observations from October to December 2012, and July to November 2013.
5 English: forest of hope.
6 A transnational non-governmental (NGO) consortium comprising BirdLife International, Burung Indonesia, and the Royal Society for the Protection of Birds.
7 Personal interview, Jambi, 2 September 2012.

References

Aggarwal, A., 2014. How sustainable are forestry clean development mechanism projects? A review of the selected projects from India. *Mitigation and Adaptation Strategies for Global Change*, 19 (1), 73–91.

Andaya, L.Y., 2008. *Leaves of the Same Tree: Trade and ethnicity in the Straits of Melaka*. Honolulu, HI: University of Hawaii Press.

Bassett, T.J., and Fogelman, C., 2013. Déjà vu or something new? The adaptation concept in the climate change literature. *Geoforum*, 48, 42–53.

Beckert, B., 2017. *A Post-frontier in Transformation: Land relations between access, exclusion and resistance in Jambi province, Indonesia*. PhD thesis. Georg August Universität Göttingen.

Beckert, B., and Keck, M., 2015. Palmöl für den Weltmarkt: Landkonflikte in Sumatras Post-Frontier. *Geographische Rundschau*, 67 (12), 12–17.

Beckert, B., Dittrich, C., and Soeryo, A., 2014. Contested land: An analysis of multi-layered conflicts in Jambi province, Sumatra, Indonesia. *ASEAS*, 7 (1), 75.

BirdLife International, 2007. *Long Term Conservation of the Harapan Rainforest in Sumatra: An innovative partnership for the conservation and restoration of the most threatened and valuable rainforests in Indonesia*. 2nd interim report to the Nando Peretti Foundation. Cambridge: BirdLife International.

BirdLife International, 2008. *Long term Conservation of the Harapan Rainforest in Sumatra: Final report to the Nando Peretti Foundation*. Cambridge: BirdLife International.

Blaikie, P., and Brookfield, H.C., 1987. *Land Degradation and Society*. London: Routledge.

Bourguignon, D., 2015. *EU Biofuels Policy: Dealing with indirect land use change* [online]. European Parliamentary Research Service. Available from: www.europarl.europa.eu/RegData/etudes/BRIE/2015/548993/EPRS_BRI(2015)548993_REV1_EN.pdf [Accessed 29 March 2017].

BPS, 2017. *Persentase Penduduk Miskin Menurut Provinsi 2013–2016* [online]. Badan Pusat Statistik Indonesia (BPS), Jakarta. Available from: www.bps.go.id/linkTableDinamis/view/id/1219 [Accessed 20 July 2017].

BPS Provinsi Jambi, 2014. *Jambi dalam Angka 2014 [Jambi in Figures 2014]*. Badan Pusat Statistik (BPS), Provinsi Jambi.

Bustamante, M., *et al.*, 2014. Co-benefits, trade-offs, barriers and policies for greenhouse gas mitigation in the agriculture, forestry and other land use (AFOLU) sector. *Global Change Biology*, 20 (10), 3270–90.

Clough, Y., *et al.*, 2016. Land-use choices follow profitability at the expense of ecological functions in Indonesian smallholder landscapes. *Nature Communications*, 7, 1–12.

Colchester, M., *et al.*, 2011. *Human Rights Abuses and Land Conflicts in the PT Asiatic Persada Concession in Jambi: Report of an independent investigation into land disputes and forced evictions in a palm oil estate: independent investigation of PT AP*. Moreton-in-Marsh, UK/Bogor/Jakarta, Indonesia: HuMa/Sawit Watch/Forest Peoples Programme.

De Schutter, O., 2011. How not to think of land-grabbing: Three critiques of large-scale investments in farmland. *Journal of Peasant Studies*, 38 (2), 249–79.

Direktorat Jenderal Perkebunan, 2015. *Statistik Perkebunan Indonesia: The crop estate statistics of Indonesia. 2013–2015 Kelapa Sawit – Palm Oil* [online]. Available from: http://ditjenbun.pertanian.go.id/tinymcpuk/gambar/file/statistik/2015/SAWIT%202013%20-2015.pdf [Accessed 20 July 2017].

DNPI, 2010. *Creating Low Carbon Prosperity in Jambi*. Dewan Nasional Perubahan Iklim (DNPI).

Escobar, A., 1999. After nature: Steps to an antiessentialist political ecology. *Current Anthropology*, 40 (1), 1–30.

European Commission, 2006. *Natural Resources: Pioneering a new way to conserve Indonesian rainforest: from illegal logging to good governance* [online]. Available from: http://ec.europa.eu/europeaid/documents/case-studies/indonesia_natural-resources_illegal-logging_en.pdf [Accessed 29 March 2017].

Fairhead, J., Leach, M., and Scoones, I., 2012. Green grabbing: A new appropriation of nature? *Journal of Peasant Studies*, 39 (2), 237–61.

FAPRI, 2014. *U.S. and World Agricultural Outlook*. Ames, IA: Food and Agriculture Policy Research Institute (FAPRI).

Forest Watch Indonesia, 2014. *The Unending Disintegration of Indonesia's Forests* [online]. Available from: http://fwi.or.id/english/publikasi/the-unending-disintegration-of-indonesias-forests/ [Accessed 10 March 2017].

Gerasimchuk, I., and Koh, Y.P., 2013. *The EU Biofuel Policy and Palm Oil: Cutting subsidies or cutting rainforest?* Geneva, Switzerland: International Institute for Sustainable Development [online]. Available from: www.iisd.org/gsi/sites/default/files/bf_eupalmoil.pdf [Accessed 29 March 2017].

Gezon, L.L., and Paulson, S., 2004. Place, power, difference: Multiscale research at the dawn of the twenty-first century. *In*: L.L. Gezon and S. Paulson, eds, *Political Ecology across Spaces, Scales, and Social Groups*. New Brunswick, NJ: Rutgers University Press, 1–16.

Görg, C., 1999. *Gesellschaftliche Naturverhältnisse*. Münster, DE: Westfälisches Dampfboot.

Görg, C., 2011. Shaping relationships with nature: Adaptation to climate change as a challenge for society. *DIE ERDE–Journal of the Geographical Society of Berlin*, 142 (4), 411–28.

Hein, J., 2013. *Reducing Emissions from Deforestation and Forest Degradation (REDD+), Transnational Conservation and Access to Land in Jambi, Indonesia.* EFForTS Discussion Paper Series 2 [online]. Available from: www.die-gdi.de/uploads/media/Hein_Reducing_emissions.pdf [Accessed 29 March 2017].

Hein, J., 2014. Politiken zur Reduktion von Emissionen aus Entwaldung und Schädigung von Wäldern (REDD+). *PERIPHERIE*, 136 (34), 508–11.

Hein, J., 2016. *Rescaling Conflictive Access and Property Relations in the Context of REDD+ in Jambi, Indonesia.* PhD thesis. Georg August Universität Göttingen.

Hein, J., and Faust, H., 2014. Conservation, REDD+ and the struggle for land in Jambi, Indonesia. *Pacific Geographies*, 41, 20–5.

Hein, J., et al., 2016. Rescaling of access and property relations in a frontier landscape: Insights from Jambi, Indonesia. *The Professional Geographer*, 68 (3), 380–9.

Horstmann, B., and Hein, J., 2017. *Does the UNFCCC Regime Align Climate Mitigation with Sustainable Development? Governance approaches under the CDM, REDD+ and the GCF* (Studies 96). Bonn, DE: Deutsches Institut für Entwicklungspolitik.

IKI, 2016. *Harapan Rainforest: Pilot restoration of a degraded forest ecosystem on Sumatra.* Berlin: German Federal Ministry for the Environment, Nature Conservation, Building and Nuclear Safety. International Climate Initiative (IKI).

Klasen, S., et al., 2016. Economic and ecological trade-offs of agricultural specialization at different spatial scales. *Ecological Economics*, 122, 111–20.

Kunz, Y., et al., 2016. Mimicry of the legal: Translating de jure land formalization processes into de facto local action in Jambi province, Sumatra. *Austrian Journal of South-East Asian Studies*, 9 (1), 127–39.

Leichenko, R.M., O'Brien, K.L., and Solecki, W.D., 2010. Climate change and the global financial crisis: A case of double exposure. *Annals of the Association of American Geographers*, 100 (4), 963–72.

Lele, S., 2013. Environmentalisms, justices and the limits of ecosystem services frameworks. *In*: T. Sikor, ed., *The Justices and Injustices of Ecosystem Services.* New York: Routledge, 119–39.

Liverman, D., 2015. Reading climate change and climate governance as political ecologies. *In*: T. Perreault, G. Bridge, and J. McCarthy, eds, *The Routledge Handbook of Political Ecology.* London: Routledge, 303–19.

Locher-Scholten, E., 2004. *Sumatran Sultanate and Colonial State: Jambi and the rise of Dutch imperialism, 1830–1907* (37). Ithaca, NY: Cornell South East Asia Program Publications.

McAfee, K., 2012a. Nature in the market-world: Ecosystem services and inequality. *Development*, 55 (1), 25–33.

McAfee, K., 2012b. The contradictory logic of global ecosystem services markets. *Development and Change*, 43 (1), 105–31.

McShane, T.O., et al., 2011. Hard choices: Making trade-offs between biodiversity conservation and human well-being. *Biological Conservation*, 144 (3), 966–72.

Merten, J., et al., 2016. Water scarcity and oil palm expansion: Social views and environmental processes. *Ecology and Society* [online], 21 (2). Available from: www.ecologyandsociety.org/vol. 21/iss2/art5/ [Accessed 10 March 2017].

Munang, R., et al., 2013. Climate change and ecosystem-based adaptation: A new pragmatic approach to buffering climate change impacts. *Current Opinion in Environmental Sustainability*, 5 (1), 67–71.

NABU, 2010. Harapan – Hoffnung für Tiger & Co. *NABU-INFO* 3/2010, Berlin: Naturschutzbund Deutschland Bundesverband.

NEA, 2009. *Indonesia–Singapore Collaboration to Deal with the Land and Forest Fires in Jambi Province*. NEA-Singapore National Environment Agency.

Osborne, T.M., 2011. Carbon forestry and agrarian change: Access and land control in a Mexican rainforest. *Journal of Peasant Studies*, 38 (4), 859–83.

Osborne, T.M., 2013. Fixing carbon, losing ground: Payments for environmental services and land (in) security in Mexico. *Human Geography*, 6 (1), 119–33.

Parker, D., 2013. *Indonesian Palm Oil Company Demolishes Homes and Evicts Villagers in Week-long Raid* [online]. Available from: https://news.mongabay.com/2013/12/indonesian-palm-oil-company-demolishes-homes-and-evicts-villagers-in-week-long-raid/ [Accessed 29 March 2017].

Peet, R., Robbins, P., and Watts, M., 2011. Global nature. *In*: R. Peet, P. Robbins, and M. Watts, eds, *Global Political Ecology*. Milton Park: Routledge, 1–47.

Pemerintah Provinsi Jambi, 2012. Rencana Aksi Daerah Penurunan Emisi Gas Rumah Kaca (RAD GRK) Provinsi Jambi Jambi, Indonesia Pemerintah Provinsi Jambi.

Perbatakusuma, E.A., *et al.*, 2012. *Strategi dan Rencana Aksi Provinsi Jambi 2012–2030. Dokumen Risalah Eksekutif*. Jambi, IDN: Komisi Daerah REDD+ Jambi.

Radjawali, I., Pye, O., and Flitner, M., 2017. Recognition through reconnaissance? Using drones for counter-mapping in Indonesia. *Journal of Peasant Studies*, 44 (4), 817–33.

RoI, 2011. *Presidential Regulation of the Republic of Indonesia No. 61 Year 2011 on the National Action Plan for Greenhouse Gas Emissions Reductions*. Jakarta: Republic of Indonesia (RoI), 61.

RoI, 2013. *National Action Plan for Climate Change Adaptation (RAN-API) Synthesis Report* [online]. Jakarta: Republic of Indonesia (RoI). Available from: https://gc21.giz.de/ibt/var/app/wp342deP/1443/wp-content/uploads/filebase/programme-info/RAN-API_Synthesis_Report_2013.pdf [Accessed 29 March 2017].

RoI, 2016. *First Nationally Determined Contribution* [online]. Jakarta: Republic of Indonesia (RoI). Available from: www4.unfccc.int/ndcregistry/PublishedDocuments/Indonesia%20First/First%20NDC%20Indonesia_submitted%20to%20UNFCCC%20Set_November%20%202016.pdf [Accessed 29 March 2017].

Schade, J., and Obergassel, W., 2014. Human rights and the clean development mechanism. *Cambridge Review of International Affairs*, 27 (4), 717–35.

Schwarze, S., *et al.*, 2015. *Rubber vs. Oil Palm: An analysis of factors influencing smallholders' crop choice in Jambi, Indonesia*. EFForTS Discussion Paper Series 11 [online]. Available from: www.die-gdi.de/uploads/media/2015_goedoc_jonas_hein_rubber_vs_oilpalm_02.pdf [Accessed 29 March 2017].

Smits, M., and Middleton, C., 2014. New arenas of engagement at the water governance-climate finance nexus? An analysis of the boom and bust of hydropower CDM projects in Vietnam. *Water Alternatives*, 7 (3), 561–83.

Steinebach, S., 2013. 'Today we occupy the plantation–tomorrow Jakarta': Indigeneity, land and oil palm plantations in Jambi. *Adat and Indigeneity in Indonesia*, (7), 63–79.

Steinebach, S., and Kunz, Y., 2017. Separating sisters from brothers: Ethnic relations and identity politics in the context of indigenous land titling. *Austrian Journal of South-East Asian Studies*, 10 (1), 47–64.

Swart, R., and Raes, F., 2007. Making integration of adaptation and mitigation work: Mainstreaming into sustainable development policies? *Climate Policy*, 7 (4), 288–303.

Teuscher, M., *et al.*, 2016. Experimental biodiversity enrichment in oil-palm-dominated landscapes in Indonesia. *Frontiers in Plant Science*, 7, 1–15.

Valin, H., *et al.*, 2015. *The Land Use Change Impact of Biofuels Consumed in the EU: Quantification of area and greenhouse gas impacts*. Utrecht, NL: ECOFYS.

Watts, M., 2015. Introductory overview: The origins of political ecology. *In*: T. Perreault, G. Bridge, and J. McCarthy, eds, *The Routledge Handbook of Political Ecology*. London: Routledge, 19–50.

World Bank, 1988. *Indonesia: The transmigration program in perspective*. Washington, DC: World Bank.

Zimmerer, K.S., and Bassett, T.J., 2003. *Political Ecology: An integrative approach to geography and environment-development studies*. New York: Guilford Press.

Part IV

Local vs national vs global understandings of climate change adaptation

9 Adapting in the borderlands

The legacy of neoliberal conservation on the Mexican–Guatemalan border

Celia Ruiz de Oña Plaza

Adaptation to climate change in a neoliberal world: a critical stance

The view of mitigation and adaptation measures as separate – and some-times competing – approaches was of little use in achieving a more integrated climate policy. Since the fourth assessment report of the Intergovernmental Panel on Climate Change (IPPC) in 2007, searching for measures with which to simultaneously mitigate and adapt to climate change – the so-called synergies between mitigation and adaptation – has become the main focus of action in recent conservation projects (see Biesbroek *et al.* 2009).

For years, mitigation strategies have been the focus of international climate change policies. Built relying on principles and assumptions of mainstream economic thought, mitigation was promoted as an apolitical and technocratic issue, where carbon commodification was the key topic around which international politics revolved, and where conflictive interests and power imbalances were unseen (Urry 2011; Büscher *et al.* 2012). The foundations of such an approach are to be found in the belief in free-market ideology as the principal means to address the climate crisis (Lohmann 2010; Newell and Paterson 2010: 20), in the form of *ecosystem services* commodification and monetisation (Robertson 2012: 387). However, as well as no internationally established targets of carbon control having been achieved, mitigation has also failed to bring about meaningful policies for people in the Global South (see Lohman 2010).

While mitigation strategies to address climate change could be designed under the technocratic and managerial trends of neoliberal management to create carbon markets (Urry 2011; Büscher *et al.* 2012: 2ff.), adaptation strategies are not as readily predisposed to commodifying processes to suit the dynamics of a capitalist green market.

Nevertheless, as critics point out, mainstream adaptation proposals retain this apolitical and naturalised climate change conception (Felli and Castree 2012), being mainly conceptualised in biophysical and technical terms (Dietz 2013). The resulting adaptation projects ignore local notions of climate and historical specificities (Taylor 2015), and conceive the practice of adaptation as an environmental management issue, ignoring its transformative dimension (Eriksen *et al.* 2015).

From this perspective, adaptation operates as an unquestionable, universal, and natural political device, applied to a range of socio-ecological scenarios regardless of local particularities (Taylor 2015: 49ff.). For Taylor, the suppression of historical specificities as well as the simplification of local socio-ecological dynamics to a set of predefined categories underlies the failure of many adaptation policies (Taylor 2015: 54). The end result is a lack of innovative approaches to adapt to climate change effects in the long and medium term; repetition of the same trends of action, now under the banner of adaptation (Barnes *et al.* 2013); and local submission to national and international political guidelines in order to secure finance for local conservation tasks.

This chapter examines the implications of this situation for the Tacaná Volcano Biosphere Reserve, located in the borderland of the Mexican state of Chiapas with Guatemala. This is a high-mountain bi-national ecosystem, where environmental conservation is closely intertwined with agroforestry coffee systems, with a long trajectory of colonial history and international economic globalisation.

The discussion presented here highlights first the historical specificities that built a territory marked by an early entry into globalised agroeconomic processes. Second, it argues that conservation and forestry projects based on carbon capture for mitigation purposes via payments for environmental services have left a legacy on the communities where this has been implemented that influences more recent adaptation projects. With a narrative that promotes a synergistic relationship between mitigation and adaptation, those projects maintain a strong focus on the first aspect, to the detriment of the second.

The final aim of this chapter is to highlight the historical and socioeconomic conditions under which adaptation practice will play out. It will examine the fundamental contradiction that emerges between the proposed adaptation practices (recovery of landscape biodiversity) while simultaneously retaining a strong focus on carbon capture for mitigation purposes (Programa Mexicano del Carbono 2016), and the ongoing historical processes of capitalist accumulation that caused the loss of its original biodiversity richness in order to increase coffee productivity. Paradoxically, under the current coffee leaf rust crisis, biodiversity turns out to be crucial for the success of adaptation strategies based on agro-ecological control (McCook and Vandermeer 2015).

Insights presented here are drawn from fieldwork conducted on the Mexican side of the study area between October 2014 and September 2015, and in September 2017. This field research involved interviews and conversations with local conservation officers, professionals from the international development sector (from Mexico and Guatemala), leaders from

Mexican small-farmer organisations, and coffee farmers from the Mexican side of the border in the communities of Talquián and Cordova Matasanos, in the Unión Juárez Municipality, around 1,300 m above sea level. Policy briefings and project documentation have been analysed to identify the climate change adaptation conception and the policies arising from that conception.

In summary, emerging from the ashes of mitigation, the technocratic reading of adaptation has recently become the core paradigm within the field of international development and its main source of legitimacy (Taylor 2015). Confronting such a view, Taylor highlights the notion of lived environments co-produced between humans and meteorological forces, immersed in a historical flow and subject to ongoing transformation triggered by the forces of capitalism and its resistances (Taylor 2015: 62ff.). The next sections try to make evident such criticisms by outlining the history of coffee production and conservation management in the borderlands of the Tacaná Volcano.

The Tacaná Volcano: a vulnerable territory deemed to adapt

The historical construction of social marginality and the environmental transformation of a coffee-producing region

In the southwestern extreme of the border between Chiapas and Guatemala, at the end of its 1,000-km extension, the Tacaná volcanic complex rises to an altitude of 4,000 m above sea level. It is the highest peak in Chiapas State and the second highest of the Central American Isthmus, after the Tajomulco Volcano. The Mexican–Guatemalan border crosses just over its summit, fragmenting an area that is biologically and culturally a unity (Damián 1988: 69). The descendants of the *Mame* ethnic group,[1] the indigenous inhabitants of the volcano, are settled along its middle and higher slopes, between the remnants of the cloud forest and the high mountain plateaus, now preceded by undulating hills covered by *Arabica* (*Coffea arabica*) and *Robusta* (*Coffea canephora*) shaded coffee plantations. The introduction of intensive coffee production during the final decades of the nineteenth century initiated unprecedented socio-ecological changes and also the entry of the area into the capitalist agro-exporting plantation economy (Damián 1988: 70; Hernández and Nigh 1998).

Deeply marked by a cross-border identity, the Tacaná Volcano belongs to the borderland region of the Soconusco, a territorial entity of natural wealth that remained disputed between Mexico and Guatemala throughout much of the nineteenth century. The border, as we know it today, was finally agreed upon by the two nations in 1892, with Mexico incorporating the Soconusco to the nation as part of the State of Chiapas and as key geopolitical territory to control the southern Mexican border (Damián

1988: 68; Nolan-Ferrell 2010: 582). Two decades earlier, around 1874, and amid struggles caused by an undefined political border, the Mexican liberal governments first, and the autocratic regime of Porfirio Diaz, afterwards, fostered the establishment of coffee plantations on what were considered to be unproductive and unpopulated wastelands (*tierras baldías*) as a driver for economic development while at the same time reinforcing Mexican national identity of this rather independent region (Tovar González 2000; Nolan-Ferrell 2005: 302, 306).

Therefore, and in the context of liberal reforms aimed at modernising Mexico with a colonisation policy based on white supremacy (Nolan-Ferrell 2005; Marañón-Pimental 2012), European settlers, primarily, were offered extensive portions of these supposedly empty lands under extremely favourable economic conditions (Nolan-Ferrell 2005). Incomers came from Germany, England, Spain, and the United States, but the German immigrant community was key to the establishment of the coffee export economy (Tovar González 2000). Most of the German immigrants arrived from the Pacific coastland of Guatemala, where they owned big coffee plantations. However, land restrictions and the prohibition of forced labour in Guatemala prompted the expansion of their coffee industries into the Soconusco, taking advantage of the Mexican policies to attract foreign investment and an elite of colonisers (Damián 1988: 69; Tovar González 2000: 30). The first coffee plantations owned by Germans were established on the slopes of the Tacaná Volcano around 1890 (Tovar González 2000: 34). They were already experienced coffee planters and by 1900, three-quarters of the coffee plantations in the Soconusco were under the property and management of the Germans (Lewis 2005: 38) in big land extensions (*fincas*) with names such as 'Hamburgo', 'Bremen' or 'Nueva Alemania' (Tovar González 2000: 30).

A socio-ecological landscape of inequality was forged by this process of colonisation based on a racist ideology that sought to modernise the country not only by the amelioration of its technocratic level, but also by the 'social regeneration of the indigenous Mexico' (Nolan-Ferrell 2005: 301; Marañón-Pimental 2012). Although the Europeans, North Americans, and Japanese mixed to some degree with the Mexican elite, they never abandoned their foreign national identities and kept their private interests unconnected to those of the Mexican state (Nolan-Ferrell 2005).

Coffee became the first economic agro-industry in the Soconusco and in Chiapas, and this has remained the case to the present day, albeit with different social relations of production. Agrarian reform prompted by the 1910 Mexican revolution barely occurred in Chiapas, where conservationist forces strongly opposed it and retained land and political power for the big landowners, cattle ranchers, and coffee planters (Damián 1988: 74; Marañón-Pimental 2012). By 1936, none of the coffee plantations in the Soconusco had been expropriated (Lewis 2005: 56).

Guatemalan and Mexican indigenous peoples and their lands were reduced to *resources* for capitalist accumulation of this new elite of foreign owners (Nolan-Ferrell 2005). *Mame* indigenous peoples from the borderlands of Tacaná first, and indigenous groups from the Highlands of Chiapas later, became the workforce for the coffee plantations throughout much of the twentieth century in hard conditions of exploitation (Marañón-Pimental 2012).

Eventually, by the 1940s, land expropriation took place to some extent in the Mexican lands of Tacaná, and some of the big coffee plantations were fragmented and redistributed among farmers, and turned into *ejidos* – social communal property – under the President Cárdenas mandate (Marañón-Pimental 2012). However, agrarian land distribution was very limited over the following decades, mainly because of the counter-revolution measures taken up by Chiapas local elites (Marañón-Pimental 2012). In the Soconusco region as in many cases, the collective lands of the *ejidos* lacked infrastructure and productive capacity, which remained in the Germans landowners' hands, and who refused to process in their plants the coffee grown on the *ejido* lands (Marañón-Pimental 2012: 227). So, from their onset, the *ejidos* constituted underfinanced and underproductive economic units and, in the words of Marañón-Pimental (2012), 'monuments of poverty'.

However, *ejidos* of the Unión Juárez Municipality, with the help of the federal government, could retain not only the previously owned lands by *finqueros*, but also the coffee processing plants or *beneficios*. In the years that followed, this enabled them to sell their coffee at a higher price, right up until the 1990s international coffee price crisis. Then, the four coffee processing plants in the municipality were abandoned and today lie in ruins.

In the Tacaná area, a few of the big private coffee plantations are still operating and still receive Guatemalan seasonal workforces.[2] However, they have not been immune to the capitalist coffee crisis, nor to attack by coffee leaf rust. As a result, some of the big coffee-growing properties have diversified into agro-ecotourism luxury resorts, combining tourism with organic coffee production and other crops such as flowers (fieldwork of the author, October 2014, face-to-face communication with Bruno Gliesseman, owner of Argovia Finca Resort).

As for the *ejidos* in the Tacaná area, they became part of the economic dynamism of what became the first organic coffee-producing region in the state of Chiapas, due in part to the richness of its soils and to the high rainfall of the region, the highest in the country.

Conservation and poverty: the effects of globalisation today

However, the combination of these historical processes with recent globalisation dynamics has forged a borderland characterised by a highly polarised social differentiation, a concentration of land and wealth, and a strong dependence on international agro-business markets (Damián 1988; Eakin *et al.* 2006), under which landscape biodiversity is reduced to meet international demand for agricultural products. Today, the natural wealth of this borderland region and its conservation continue to be in dispute, together with the marginality and poverty of most of the Tacaná inhabitants whose lives are characterised by an intense cultural coexistence across the border (Fábregas Puig and González Ponciano 2014).

At the onset of the twenty-first century, an entirely new process of land management emerged, encompassing new perspectives on how to conceive nature and land and interacting with the coffee economic activity: the environmental conservation realm. In 2003, the territory of the Tacaná Volcano was decreed a Natural Protected Area by the Mexican Federal Government in the category of Biosphere Reserve, with an extension of just over 6,000 hectares, located in the municipalities of Unión Juárez, Cacahoatán and Tapachula, Chiapas (SEMARNAT and CONANP 2013). Twenty-nine farming communities are within the Reserve's area of influence on the Mexican side of the border, accounting for about 15,000 inhabitants with a high degree of socio-economic marginalisation (ibid.). Regulations of the Reserve set a limit to coffee expansion and resource extraction in the higher parts of the buffer zone, where some of the coffee farmers of Unión Juárez have their lands.

Conservation policies and coffee agro-forestry systems became closely intertwined in a landscape where, nevertheless, market influences, climatic change, and local political conditions play a critical role in shaping people's lives. The low international price of coffee – a drop of over 65 per cent since the end of the 1990s (Eakin *et al.* 2005; Goodman 2008) – put an end to a time of economic prosperity in the Tacaná *ejidos*. In addition, fragmentation of coffee cooperatives following the retirement of government technical and economic support began a period of high dependency on *coyotes* or intermediaries to access markets. Today, coffee producers have lost power and autonomy to impose profitable commercial conditions. The impact of the last coffee leaf rust outbreak has deepened a sentiment of uncertainty and despair regarding which is the best course of action to follow. Nevertheless, coffee remains the main economic activity within the buffer area of the Reserve, but is no longer the principal source of income: immigrant remittances and government assistance programmes now provide more than 65 per cent of household income (Ruiz Meza 2012).

In other parts of Chiapas, coffee farmers have started to sell their coffee beans directly to the export companies, such as Nestlé, in an effort to avoid low prices set up by *coyotes*. Those companies are filling the void left by the withdrawal of public assistance by providing technical and agricultural inputs, and by guaranteeing higher prices (Henderson 2017). In the Tacaná coffee sector, these agreements are about to start (fieldwork observations on 6 September 2017 in a Unión Juárez Ejido meeting). However, for Henderson, despite economic advantages, those arrangements do not increase market autonomy for Chiapas coffee growers: unequal power relations imply a limited bargaining capacity to renegotiate contracts and a submission to production criteria defined exclusively to fit export companies' needs (Henderson 2017: 139).

Old coffee, new pests: impact of climate variability amid changing political contexts

As well as economic and local environmental vulnerability, this territory suffers the effects of global environmental change in the form of current and future climate change impacts. In southeast Mexico, changing rainfall and temperature patterns are modifying traditional agricultural production cycles (Eakin *et al.* 2006). At medium and higher mountain altitudes, such as those of the Tacaná Volcano area, these changes seem more intense because of the orographic complexity of the mountain ecosystems (see Carrasco *et al.* no date).

Since 2012, unusually strong rainfall from August to October has facilitated the spread of one of the most aggressive and atypical coffee leaf rust (fungus *Hemileia vastatrix*) outbreaks throughout the Central American region (Avelino *et al.* 2015), not only through its intensity but also because it affected areas over 800 m above sea level, which had previously been coffee rust-free (Henríquez 2013). The coffee plantations of the Tacaná Volcano were seriously affected, especially in the Mexican municipalities of Cacahoatán and Unión Juárez, both located in the buffer zone of the Biosphere Reserve, where agro-forestry systems of coffee are considered to play an important role in halting deforestation. In Cacahoatán, the fungus attacked an extension of about 10,000 hectares, where 70 per cent of arable land is occupied by coffee plants. Another 6,000 hectares of coffee plantations in Unión Juárez were also seriously affected (SEMARNAT and CONANP 2013).

The Mexican local and national press have echoed the production disaster that the coffee leaf rust outbreak brought about. As the disease spread, demands for the federal government to issue an emergency declaration in this and other coffee-producing zones gained momentum (López 2013). The extent of the outbreak initiated a restoration process for the coffee plants and reinforced sanitation practices on the agricultural land, promoted by diverse state and federal programmes. However, they were unable to eradicate the fungus. By mid-2015, even the recently planted coffee plants were affected by coffee leaf rust (Trinidad 2016).

The latest wave of coffee leaf rust has placed climate change at the centre of attention (Landeros Martínez 2013). Local, national, and even international mass media have had a significant role in pointing to climate change as the main driver of the current coffee crisis. Headlines in the main Mexican newspapers abound in alarming news of 50 per cent, 60 per cent and even 70 per cent losses in the coffee crops in Chiapas (Martínez and Torres 2016). Such messages contributed to the promotion of coffee leaf rust as a natural disaster derived from a seemingly naturalised climate change, marginalising other crucial factors, such as economic and historical factors that interact with climatic variability (Barnes *et al.* 2013: 534).

The argument of climate change as a disruption force and as an external environmental threat takes on special relevance in the area of influence of the Reserve. In Tacaná, coffee under shade is considered a sustainable agro-forestry system (and not a monoculture), which contributes to the conservation of biodiversity, soil and water, by virtue of its tree cover (Altieri and Nicholls 2013).

Owing to their qualities as sustainable agricultural systems, agro-forestry systems in Mexico and Central America are under intense scientific research in relation to the effects of climate change and adaptation options (see Schroth *et al.* 2009; Läderach *et al.* 2011). The changes in temperature and rainfall could be affecting flowering and growth of the coffee crop and could lead to a displacement of the optimum areas of cultivation to higher altitudes (Villers *et al.* 2009). In fact, climate models for Mexico project a significant reduction in the optimal area for coffee cultivation, as well as decreased productivity and grain quality (Gay *et al.* 2006).

For the coffee farmers of the Tacaná highlands, this has particular consequences, since the options for moving crops to higher altitudes are constrained by the limits on coffee production imposed by the regulations of the Biosphere Reserve of the Tacaná Volcano, where coffee cultivation is only permitted in the area of influence and as long as it does not imply a change in land use (SEMARNAT and CONANP 2013).

However, climate scenarios do not take into account that coffee leaf rust takes place in a territory with a history of coffee management practices that can exacerbate climate variability affectations, spurring unexpected consequences in other agricultural systems and in natural spaces without productive use. During the 1970s, the increasing technification and intensification of coffee systems involved a reduction in the variety of native forest species (Grajales *et al.* 2008). Priority was given to those species that allowed easy shade management to increase grain yield. However, the reduction of tree diversity coupled with shade-opening techniques restricted food availability for wildlife, which began to forage on the *milpa*, the traditional cropping system of maize crops, the most staple food. As a *Mame* farmer from the borderland village of Cordova Matasanos remembers:

> Before the arrival of the Mexican Coffee Institute [INMECAFE], the shade [of the coffee] was different, it was not like now. There were more trees, *chicharro, jobio*…. But, in the 1970s and 1980s, INMECAFE introduced new techniques brought from other countries, I do not know, like Colombia perhaps, Costa Rica maybe, but I do not know, techniques [that are] not typical of the region. INMECAFE told us that we must regulate the shade; now it is cut short and what is

flourishing is removed, they cut it down; then the birds and little animals cannot find food and now they are going to eat corn. There is hardly any corn planted because of little animals and birds eating it. We are to blame because we take their food away.

(H.G., *Mame* farmer of Cordova Matasanos, October 2014)

Standardisation of coffee techniques through different landscapes and cultural conditions in order to increase yield resulted in a homogenisation and simplification of the mountain ecosystem (Grajales *et al.* 2008). It shows different conceptions of how to understand coffee systems immersed in a broader cultural landscape, revealing a contradiction between the narrow productivist view of the technicians and a more holistic conception of what it meant to farm coffee and what it involved. Another *Mame* farmer recalls and reflects on the clash between technical knowledge and local experiences that modernising pathways at that time uncovered:

I do not want to say that we know more than technicians; however, or they did not take into account the climate, or did not consider the type of land, or did not consider the wildlife that existed here, because you can't have the same kind of wildlife in all countries, right?

(F.B., *Mame* farmer of Cordova Matasanos, October 2014)

After more than a century of intensive coffee production, the mountain biome shows significant signs of exhaustion, such as the destruction of natural habitats and the extinction of animal species (Grajales *et al.* 2008: 41). Similar degradation is also occurring within the coffee systems of the area, where ageing plantations on eroded soils of low fertility generate low yields of coffee, and the presence of pests and diseases, particularly coffee leaf rust, which spread over a land without natural enemies (Grajales *et al.* 2008).

Environmental explanations alone do not account for the complexity of this degradation process, rooted as much in history as it is in the global economy. But historical processes are subject to rather different interpretations depending on knowledge, life experience, and professional interests. Readings of local history and its present consequences by the environmental authorities of the Biosphere Reserve entrench a negative view on the way people have been dealing with their coffee plantations since they regained them from big landowners in the past:

The problem of coffee rust is due to coffee plantations that are very poor, old, and malnourished. So, this is a result of 30 years without any renovation of coffee plantations; they have not been given maintenance. [Before] many farmers were day labourers on the big plantations and it was the manager and the owner who knew what to do, 'you do this, that and the other'. Then, when they became independent farmers owning a plot of land, they were only engaged in picking the coffee, right? Because it was what they knew how to do.

(O.C.B., deputy of Tacaná Volcano Reserve, October 2014)

From conservationist approaches to climate change policies: the legacy of mitigation

As the coffee leaf rust spread, the risk of substituting agro-forestry systems by other more profitable land uses, or even by simply abandoning the coffee plots, began to concern environmental authorities.

Arabica varieties were dominant in the Tacaná highlands throughout much of the twentieth century. Because of its high quality, *Arabica* beans enabled higher prices in the international coffee market. For several decades, the region experienced a period of economic prosperity, in fact up until the crash in international coffee prices in the 1990s. However, *Arabica* varieties are highly sensitive to coffee leaf rust attack. One of the first consequences of this epidemic was the substitution of high-quality coffee varieties of *Arabica* for *Robusta* species, resistant to the fungus, but of lower yields and price, and considered lower quality. But for some coffee growers in the highlands of Tacaná, *Robusta* coffee is an option for maintaining their coffee plots without investing much labour and inputs.

> [With the coffee leaf rust] unfortunately, our people have been chang-ing more to the cultivation of *Robusta*, which is the worst coffee. The *Arabica* is more tedious to work with but has a better price. Thus, coffee is still a way of life, it is our tradition.
>
> (H.G., leader of Democratic Peasant Union, Unión Juárez
> Municipality, July 2015)

Other coffee varieties (natural hybrids as well as artificially modified hybrids, the so-called F1 hybrids) resistant to the rust are slowly being incorporated, such as *Catimore* or *Costa Rica 95*. The spread of such vari-eties is subject to local political struggles and corruption. Coffee plants offered by federal state agencies to renew coffee plots are being used to gain local political support for new municipal candidates with the help of local state officers. Only those coffee farmers who pledge loyalty to those controlling plant distribution are securing enough plants to restore their plots. This local dynamic raises consequences, connected to migration and food security, important to consider in terms of potential adaptation projects:

> The government promised 300 new plants plus tools, chemicals and a pump but, you know, corrupt officers retained the plants, they gave us

only 100. So, if you look down towards the Suchiate River, you will see many abandoned coffee plantations. People is going out to the United States. But coffee is my life, I am now trying this *Catimore* variety, and the Costa Rica one. I am also planting other crops such as rambutan (*Nephelium lappaceum*) and Persian lemon. Unfortunately, because hardly anybody is cultivating, people steal my fruits, so who knows if it's worth it.

(J.G., coffee grower of Unión Juárez Municipality, September 2017)

It is too early to see how these changes in the coffee systems could affect landscape transformation. Newly introduced varieties are typical sun varieties that require low levels of shade and different cultivation practices. The transition from coffee systems grown under shade to coffee-under-sun systems could reduce tree biodiversity and accelerate the loss of forest cover. The transformation of agro-forestry systems into monocultures could also increase dependency on agribusiness inputs.

This trend towards a more homogenous landscape (less biodiverse but with higher yields) makes evident a fundamental contradiction: the need to protect biodiversity to increase environmental resilience and adaptation capacity versus the need to reduce it in order to increase coffee yield. While agricultural production options are pressing towards a reduction in the variety of native species, the recent conservation and adaptation strategies together with programmes to combat the coffee leaf crisis are aiming at increasing local biodiversity as a means to limit the impact of coffee leaf rust (Programa Mexicano del Carbono 2016).

It is at this point that environmental policies meet climate mitigation and adaptation lines of action. At present, in the territories of Chiapas, official environmental policy places strong emphasis on climate change abatement rather than on climate justice issues, such as the possibility for communities to set their own carbon prices rather than submit to international conditions. Forest conservation is strongly linked to the struggle against climate change as it is understood in the international political arena. Following this line of reasoning, many of the environmental projects in Chiapas are now implemented as part of mitigation schemes, or the removal of carbon from the atmosphere. Environmental projects, dealing with mitigation through carbon capture, such as programmes of payments for environmental services (PES), first under the voluntary carbon market and later as subsidies issued by the National Forestry Commission (CONAFOR, for its acronym in Spanish), have been popular in the Chiapas conservation sphere since the 1990s and have received significant international recognition (McAfee and Shapiro 2010). The later, despite being developed from a neoliberal mindset, will in Mexico retain the idiosyncratic political culture based on a powerful central state (McAfee and Shapiro 2010).

PES projects are one of the main examples of a neoliberal approach to conservation, relying on market environmentalism (Büscher *et al.* 2012). The logic of these was initially based on the conceptualisation of ecological flows and functions as economic assets under the idea of them being services ecosystems provide to society, such as water or carbon. Economic valuation and carbon quantification methodologies became a central part of conservation strategies whose final aim was to internalise environmental *free benefits* into the economic system that currently does not contemplate the cost of consuming them.

Despite being considered the leading strategy of commodification of nature, in Mexico, PES programmes were promoted as a state policy aimed at halting deforestation. Since 2003, the federal government through CONAFOR implemented the Program of Payments of Environmental and Hydrological Services (PSAH); and since 2005, another PES scheme aimed at developing carbon markets and promoting agro-forestry systems (PSA-CABSA, for its acronym in Spanish) was issued throughout many forestry regions in the country, with Chiapas the state with most communities participating. By issuing a regular payment subject to certain conditions on forest management, communities were compensated for refraining from using their forest resources (COLPOS-CONAFOR 2008).

The Mexican PES version configured a mixed and contradictory strategy, where neoliberal conservation principles conflated with a powerful centralist state. In fact, Chiapas has been a laboratory to test those projects, and at present is one of the territories selected to host early actions for the REDD+ National Strategy,[3] which has several pilot projects in Chiapas state (see CONAFOR 2016). REDD+ is the last generation of international mitigation strategies based on issuing money to Third World communities in order to avoid deforestation. It is presented as a strategy that creates synergies between mitigation and adaptation by stating that payments received from future REDD+ projects will help to achieve mitigation objectives by conserving forest carbon and avoiding its emission to the atmosphere. At the same time, it will also meet adaptation targets, visualised as soil and water conservation. Carbon retention is aligned in this way to biodiversity conservation and forest protection.

The Mexican state has played a key role in legitimising a certain level of monetisation of nature. The alliance with international organisations has helped the federal government to secure funding to operationalise PES projects. This has been the case for those communities receiving PES in the buffer area of the Tacaná Volcano Reserve, where an alliance between the International Union for Nature Conservation (IUCN) and CONAFOR operated the national PES programme for hydrological services in the bi-national river basins. The effect of these programmes seems to be reduced to the receipt of the payment for a short and discontinued work that does not generate long-term change either in forest conservation or in the way people relate to institutions.

Well, I made an evaluation of payments for environmental services, from the payment made by CONAFOR. [...] payment is simply used to make a forest protection. There is no management, there is no valuation of the bird, of the tree. It is nothing more than protection. In other words, people come, receive the money, they give it away and it's over, all year long. And you go and ask him what a payment for environmental services is, and they do not know it.

(A.L.R., biologist working for the environmental federal agency, Cacahoatán, September 2015)

As in other PES experiences throughout the world, monetisation and marketisation of ecosystem services encounter different degrees of resistance to economic valuation and a limited integration into global capital flows (Dempsey and Suarez 2016). But in the Tacaná area, expectations raised in many rural communities of receiving a payment for extended periods are stirring unexpected consequences, the main one being the monetisation of communal activities that previously took place on a collaborative basis – be it handouts from the federal government or from international environmental organisations. Following Dempsey and Suarez (2016: 1), the main effects of PES programmes concern 'how it reaffirms narrow, antipolitical explanations of biodiversity loss, instils neoliberal political rationalities among conservationists'. As evidenced in the Tacaná case, neoliberal rationalities extend well beyond conservationists, into the social and communal life of peoples in rural communities.

On the Mexican side of the border, it seems that PES programmes have contributed towards the reinforcement of a monetised approach to conservation that extends to adaptation practices. This hinders the possibility of involving people in actions aimed at reducing local vulnerability unless they receive a payment to implement those actions and reveals a contrasting attitude on the Guatemalan side where the commodification of environmental systems has not been as intense and regular as on the Mexican side. As explained by a Mexican farmer participating at a bi-national exchange experience of soil conservation techniques lead by CONANP, in charge of managing the Biosphere Reserve:

[In Guatemala] what they [environmental projects and authorities] give to communities is technical assistance. They do not give money. They send their technicians. And when they [Guatemalan farmers] come here [on the Mexican side of the border] and see that people have the capital and everything, and do not do the work [...] Guatemalan get angry, and they think 'if we had this money, we would do wonders'.

(J.M., coffee farmer, Cordova Matasanos, September 2015)

The emergence of adaptation: what sort of adaptation is being promoted?

Adaptation to climate change in the Tacaná Volcano Biosphere Reserve constitutes the latest generation of policies defined under the threat of climate change. For some time, local communities on both sides of the border have been drawing the attention of international cooperation agencies and international environmental non-governmental organisations (NGOs)[4] to the urgency of adapting to climate change and the future risks associated with global warming.

Named as the 'multinationals of conservation', these international environmental NGOs from the Global North, with a worldwide structure and massive budgets (Dumoulin-Kervran 2007: 60), have a strong presence in the borderlands of the Tacaná Reserve, particularly on the Guatemalan side of the border because of its status as a developing country. In the Tacaná, as in other regions of Central America, these organisations implement bi-national and transnational projects,[5] thus fostering a transborder environmental cooperation that operates through public–private partnerships, with different arrangements with national state actors, but with an important influence in defining the national environmental agenda.

Through these organisations, the same model of conservation – and adaptation – is reproduced in a highly coherent and standardised way, over a wide array of territories and with a clear apolitical stand, not free from certain local/regional political elitism (Dumoulin-Kervran 2007: 61ff.), and as a universal framework that 'transcends political, economic, ecological and cultural settings' (Taylor 2015: 54).

Some projects explicitly place adaptation as the central component (such as the IUCN project PROVE 'Adaptation, Vulnerability, and Ecosystems'), while others refer to climate change adaptation, vulnerability, or impacts of climate change in general as one of their operative lines (such as Pro-Bosques of Helvetas Swiss Intercooperation). Despite differences in the projects, they all share similar *modus operandi* and strong standardised institutional arrangements that have disseminated a similar conception of adaptation, one that revolves principally around the ecosystem-based adaptation model (EbA), whose emphasis is on ecological restoration.

International adaptation programmes and the considerable financial resources attached to them are arriving with already defined objectives and ecological targets, such as conserving biodiversity, river basin management, or deforestation. Economic and political factors underlying environmental degradation are not considered. Local communities are consulted over a proposal that has already been finalised, seeking legitimation and the collaboration of the people, but without altering the underlying assumptions over what needs to be addressed and how. As admitted by professionals working for the international cooperation sector in the region:

Often the context of the communities is unknown and the projects are not aimed at where they should go. They are aimed at certain areas where the needs are not really as latent as in other areas. Environmental agencies often arrive with a proposal, however, which is not the most appropriate and does not fit the context. So that's a weakness, I think.

(C.L., independent consultant working for a bi-national project in Tacaná, Sibinal, Guatemala, September 2015)

On the Mexican side of the border, the environmental federal agency in charge of managing the Reserve, CONANP, is channelling the adaptation mainstream conception issued from the international environmental organisations. Adaptation planning follows the guidelines specified in the document 'Guide for the elaboration of programs of adaptation to climate change in Natural Protected Areas' (CONANP, FMCN, and TNC 2011). Financed by different international cooperation agencies and international environmental organisations, such as the Nature Conservancy, the document offers an example of a collaborative outcome among different types of actors, from universities to federal agencies and international NGOs. However, they all belong to the biological and scientific domains. The inclusion of different types of knowledge, particularly that derived from people living in the territories subject to conservation, does not occur. The concerns addressed in these guidelines to be used in future adaptation plans are those exclusively linked to conservation and ecological management. As put by an ex-official of the CONANP in charge of the climate change programmes for the natural protected areas for several years:

[...] We have focused a lot in the biologist part, right? We think adaptation as an adaptation of species, of animal species [...]. At least from the environmental sector, the idea of adaptation is not human [...]. It responds to a policy already established and hierarchised from the international level and CONANP tries to adapt to that structure; I must fit [my tasks] into those guidelines [if not] I cannot mobilise resources.

(M.T., ex-CONANP officer, 4 October 2017, San Cristóbal de Las Casas, Chiapas)

As a result, environmental conservation actions and outcomes are prioritised over agricultural production. The link between production, income generation, and conservation remains broken.

As for the coffee sector, international agencies – for example the Center for International Forestry Research (CIFOR) and the Consortium Group for International Agricultural Research (CGIAR) – have focused on programmes aimed at reducing the impacts of climate change on coffee plantations by promoting synergies between mitigation through carbon capture and adaptation based on coffee sanitisation and regeneration (see Locatelli 2014). Promoting this synergy aims at reducing environmental vulnerability while at the same time mitigating emissions, by conserving soil fertility and water, and maintaining soil carbon. However, these international proposals place greater weight on carbon capture through REDD+ to serve international commitments rather than on other options more directly connected with local needs that could open new economic possibilities for people to make a living.

Adaptation plays only a secondary role to complement and lessen unwanted social outcomes of mitigation strategies. The social, economic, and political dimensions remain ignored, despite their crucial role as drivers of local environmental degradation. From this perspective, the construction of ecologically sustainable territories depends exclusively on adjustments made to farmers' management practices and their capacity to capture carbon, but without touching the political and historical processes that have led to the current state of environmental devastation.

In Chiapas, and for the area of the Tacaná Volcano, a proposal that follows some of those guidelines has been designed to specifically reduce the impact of coffee leaf rust in the context of climate change. Financed by Conservation International, the 'Strategy for the coffee sector for adaptation, mitigation, and reduction of vulnerability to climate change in the Sierra Madre of Chiapas' (Schroth *et al.* 2009), aims to develop a synergy between the early actions of REDD+ and an agro-ecological approach that increases environmental resilience of small coffee farmers to coffee leaf rust. This proposal represents a serious effort to combine different actors' perspectives, from different sectors, such as academia, international NGOs, government agencies, and the Ecological Indigenous Federation of Chiapas (a regional association of 18 indigenous cooperatives of organic coffee). But the final (consented) document keeps prioritising the REDD+ mitigation approach with an adaptation component. The latter is comparatively less well represented and discussed than the mitigation case. Reflections on social aspects are absent, again conceiving adaptation as a set of agro-ecological practices and not as an interweaving of socio-environmental factors.

Conclusions

Apolitical and naturalised conceptions of adaptation are key features of the international adaptation paradigm. This conception does not pay attention to historical and current patterns of capitalist accumulation, which play an important role in landscape homogenisation and deepen social, economic, and environmental vulnerability over the long term. Interactions between national and local political cultures of paternalism and clientelism with these global economic patterns epitomise a complex substrate for the incipient adaptation practice.

In the Tacaná Volcano Biosphere Reserve, coffee production under shade and forest conservation become entangled in the context of unstable precipitation patterns and unusual coffee leaf rust outbreaks. From this situation, official adaptation strategies are starting to emerge, but these are strictly conceived as an environmental issue, and exclude consideration of local and global factors, which are the sources of socio-environmental vulnerability. Strongly aligned with the international development's understanding of adaptation, these projects have focused on recovering landscape resilience, ignoring the political struggles and market volatility that underlie this lack of resilience.

Over this complex picture, adaptation planning and practice in the Tacaná exhibit two paradoxical features that compromise the future effectiveness of adaptation projects. First, in the coffee systems, adaptation proposals based on an increase in biodiversity and resilience, work in opposition to the political economy of coffee, which pushes towards a reduction in biodiversity in order to increase harvests. Second, the predominance of mitigation projects, with a strong focus on carbon sequestration and nature commodification, are obscuring alternative pathways of adaptation more attuned with local realities.

The aim of this chapter has been to highlight how the complexity of these local–global interactions could permeate the practices of climate change adaptation in contexts where previous mitigation pathways have been at the centre of conservation strategies. Adaptation projects are unfolding within these conditions, retaining much of the mitigation logic that still prevails in the conservation policies of the area. Hardly questioned international policy designs characterised by a strong focus on carbon continue to play a major role in climate change adaptation strategies. Fuelled now by mitigation–adaption synergy rhetoric, reducing carbon emissions to achieve international commitments (and receive finance) seems to downplay adaptation pathways at the local scale.

To achieve true synergy, mainstream mitigation and adaptation conceptions must be reformulated, transcending the technocratic and monetised approach typical of mitigation. Knowledge of local politics could add to a reformulated adaptation conception beyond the apolitical and naturalised limited approach. In the Tacaná scenario of local political struggles and coffee–conservation tensions, adaptation proposals could place strong emphasis on rebuilding organisational ties, integrating the landscape knowledge of local inhabitants, and redefining adaptation objectives through truly consultative processes.

Notes

1 The *Mame* ethnic group constitutes 70 per cent of the population of the Coatán River basin in Guatemala and 50 per cent of the population of the Suchiate River basin in Mexico (60 per cent in the Biosphere Reserve area), the two main basins

of the Tacaná Volcano. On the Mexican side of the border, the *Mame* are present mainly in the municipal councils of Tapachula, Cacahoatán, and Unión Juárez, where the Tacaná Volcano Biosphere Reserve has been established.

2 During the coffee harvest, an average of 20,000 Guatemalan workers migrate to pick coffee on the Mexican side of the border. But during the 2016 season this migration flow was up to 70 per cent lower. Year by year, Guatemalan workers are preferring to stay and work on poppy crops in communities bordering Mexico rather than migrating to work on the coffee plantations (Escenario. Periodismo Actual 2017).

3 Reducing Emissions from Deforestation and Forest Degradation, conservation of carbon stocks, sustainable management of forests and rise in carbon reserves.

4 The International Union of Conservation for Nature (IUCN), the Nature Conservancy (TNC), and Conservation International (CI) are present in the Tacaná Reserve, forming alliances with Mexican environmental NGOs, both local and regional, such as PRONATURA-SUR, or the Sociedad de Historia Natural del Soconusco, with academic institutions and with Mexican environmental authorities. In Guatemala, those organisations have a strong political influence in a context of limited presence of the nation state and lack of finance and political support for the environmental sector.

5 For example, the Water and Nature Initiative of the IUCN, with projects such as Governance and Adaptation to Climate Change, Governance of Watersheds or Tacaná I and II Projects, associated with the Tacaná Volcano Tacaná Reserve, between 2007 and 2012; or the Swiss Intercooperation Agency, Helvetas, with the bi-national project 'Pro-Bosques'.

References

Altieri, M.A., and Nicholls, C.I., 2013. Agroecología y resiliencia al cambio climático: principios y consideraciones metodológicas. *Agroecología*, 8 (1), 7–20.

Avelino, J., *et al.*, 2015. The coffee rust crises in Colombia and Central America (2008–2013): Impacts, plausible causes and proposed solutions. *Food Security*, 7 (2), 303–21.

Barnes, J., *et al.*, 2013. Contribution of anthropology to the study of climate change. *Nature Climate Change*, 3 (6), 541–4.

Biesbroek, G.R., Swart, R.J., and van der Knaap, W.G.M., 2009. The mitigation–adaptation dichotomy and the role of spatial planning. *Habitat International*, 33 (3), 230–7.

Büscher, B., *et al.*, 2012. Towards a synthesized critique of neoliberal biodiversity conservation. *Capitalism Nature Socialism*, 23 (2), 4–30.

Carrasco, J., *et al.*, no date. *Impactos del Cambio Climático, Adaptación y Desarrollo en las Regiones Montañosas de América Latina*. FAO, Banco Mundial, Gobierno de chile, Alianza para las Montañas.

COLPOS-CONAFOR, 2008. *Evaluación externa de los apoyos de los servicios ambientales. Ejercicio fiscal, 2007*. México: CONAFOR.

CONAFOR, 2016. *Conservación, restauración y aprovechamiento sustentable en el Estado de Chiapas* [online]. Available from: www.conafor.gob.mx/web/temas-forestales/bycc/redd-en-mexico/acciones-tempranas-redd/conservacion-restauracion-y-aprovechamiento-sustentable-en-el-estado-de-chiapas/ [Accessed 23 October 2017].

CONANP, FMCN, and TNC, 2011. *Guía para la elaboración de programas de adaptación al cambio climático en áreas naturales protegidas*. México. Comisión

Nacional de Áreas Naturales Protegidas (CONANP)-Fondo Mexicano para la Conservación de la Naturalesa A.C (FMCN), and the Nature Conservancy (TNC).

Damián, A., 1988. Conformación histórica de la región del Soconusco, Chiapas. *Estudios Fronterizos*, 17, 61–80.

Dempsey, J., and Suarez, D.C., 2016. Arrested development? The promises and paradoxes of 'selling nature to save it'. *Annals of the American Association of Geographers*, 106 (3), 653–71.

Dietz, K., 2013. Hacia una teoría crítica de vulnerabilidad y adaptación: aportes para una reconceptualización desde la ecología política. *In*: A. Ulloa and A.I. Prieto-Rozo, eds, *Culturas, conocimientos, políticas y ciudadanías en torno al cambio climático*. Bogotá, COL: Universidad Nacional de Colombia, Sede Bogotá, Facultad de Ciencias Humanas, 19–46.

Dumoulin-Kervran, D., 2007. Las políticas de las ANP (Areas Naturales Protegidas) como laboratorio para los esquemas público-privado. Una interpretación a partir del Fondo Mexicano para la Conservación de la Naturaleza. *In*: G. van Vliet and G. Fontaine, eds, *Viajes en los terruños de la gobernabilidad en las políticas ambientales en América Latina*. Quito, ECU: Flacso-Sede Ecuador, 57–78.

Eakin, H., Tucker, C.M., and Castellanos, E., 2005. Market shocks and climate variability: The coffee crisis in Mexico, Guatemala, and Honduras. *Mountain Research and Development*, 25 (4), 304–9.

Eakin, H., Tucker, C., and Castellanos, E., 2006. Responding to the coffee crisis: A pilot study of farmers' adaptations in Mexico, Guatemala and Honduras. *The Geographical Journal*, 172 (2), 156–71.

Eriksen, S.H., Nightingale, A.J., and Eakin, H., 2015. Reframing adaptation: The political nature of climate change adaptation. *Global Environmental Change*, 35, 523–33.

Escenario. Periodismo Actual, 2017. Jornaleros guatemaltecos no vienen a cortar café a Chiapas. *Escenario. Periodismo Actual*, 9 (171), 11. Tapachula: Chiapas.

Fábregas Puig, A., and González Ponciano, R., 2014. La frontera México-Guatemala, Guatemala-México: 1983–2013. *Frontera norte*, 26 (SPE3), 7–35.

Felli, R., and Castree, N., 2012. Neoliberalising adaptation to environmental change: Foresight or foreclosure? *Environment and Planning A*, 44 (1), 1–4.

Gay, C., *et al.*, 2006. Potential impacts of climate change on agriculture: A case of study of coffee production in Veracruz, Mexico. *Climatic Change*, 79 (3–4), 259–88.

Goodman, D., 2008. The international coffee crisis: A review of the issues. *In*: C.M. Bacon, *et al.*, eds, *Confronting the Coffee Crisis: Fair trade, sustainable livelihoods and ecosystem in Mexico and Central America*. Cambridge, MA: MIT Press, 18–42.

Grajales, M., De la Piedra, R., and López, J., 2008. Diagnóstico biofísico y socioeconómico de la parte media y alta de la subcuenca Cohatan, Chiapas. *Avances en Investigación Agropecuaria*, 12 (1), 28–44.

Henderson, T.P., 2017. La reestructuración de los sectores del café y el cacao en México y Ecuador. Control agroempresarial de la tierra y trabajo campesino. *LiminaR. Estudios Sociales y Humanísticos*, 15 (1), 128–41.

Henríquez, E., 2013. Cosechas de café en Chiapas podrían caer 60% por la plaga de la roya. *La Jornada*, 14 July, 26.

Hernández, R.A., and Nigh, R., 1998. Global processes and local identity among Mayan coffee growers in Chiapas, Mexico. *American Anthropologist*, 100 (1), 136–47.

Läderach, P., *et al.*, 2011. Café MesoAmericano: Desarrollo de una estrategia de adaptación al cambio climático. *CIAT. Políticas en síntesis*, 2, 1–4.

Landeros Martínez, E.I., 2013. Las rutas del café mexicano: Zona de desastre. *FronteraD Revista Digital* [online]. Available from: www.fronterad.com/?q= rutas-cafe-mexicano-zonas-desastre [Accessed 23 January 2017].

Lewis, S.E., 2005. *The Ambivalent Revolution: Forging state and nation in Chiapas, 1910–1945*. Albuquerque, NM: University of New Mexico Press.

Locatelli, B., 2014. Sinergias de adaptación-mitigación. *HAL. Center for International Forestry Research (CIFOR)*, (18 August), 4.

Lohmann, L., 2010. Uncertainty markets and carbon markets: Variations on Polanyian themes. *New Political Economy*, 15 (2), 225–54.

López, I., 2013. Aplicarán 8 millones de pesos para combatir la roya en cafetales. *El Heraldo de Chiapas*.

Marañón-Pimental, B., 2012. Forced labor and coloniality of power in Chiapas, Mexico, in the nineteenth and twentieth centuries. *Review (Fernand Braudel Center)*, 35 (3/4), 211–38.

Martínez, T., and Torres, Y., 2016. Producción de café al menor nivel en cuatro décadas. *Observatorio Económico LatinoAmericano, OBELA* [online]. Available from: www.obela.org/palabras-clave/caf%C3%A9-baja-producci%C3%B3n-m% C3%A9xico [Accessed 23 January 2017].

McAfee, K., and Shapiro, E.N., 2010. Payments for ecosystem services in Mexico: Nature, neoliberalism, social movements, and the state. *Annals of the Association of American Geographers*, 100 (3), 579–99.

McCook, S., and Vandermeer, J., 2015. The big rust and the red queen: Long-term perspectives on coffee rust research. *Phytopathology*, 105 (9), 1164–73.

Newell, P., and Paterson, M., 2010. *Climate Capitalism: Global warming and the transformation of the global economy*. Cambridge: Cambridge University Press.

Nolan-Ferrell, C.A., 2005. El desarrollo de una región sin una identidad nacional: La zona del Soconusco, Chiapas, 1880–1920. *In*: M.D. Palomo-Infante and M. Olivera-Bustamante, eds, *Chiapas: de la Independencia a la Revolución*. México, D.F: Publicaciones de la Casa Cata, 301–12.

Nolan-Ferrell, C., 2010. Agrarian reform and revolutionary justice in Soconusco, Chiapas: Campesinos and the Mexican state, 1934–1940. *Journal of Latin American Studies*, 42 (3), 551–85.

Programa Mexicano del Carbono, 2016. Una REDD para Salvar la Sombra de la Sierra Madre de Chiapas: la Roya del Cafeto. *Breves de Políticas Públicas*, June 2016, 4.

Robertson, M., 2012. Measurement and alienation: Making a world of ecosystem services. *Transactions of the Institute of British Geographers*, 37 (3), 386–401.

Ruiz Meza, L.E., 2012. Cambio climático y migraciones laborales en la Frontera Sur de México. *Revista Luna Azul*, 35, 301–20.

Schroth, G., *et al.*, 2009. Towards a climate change adaptation strategy for coffee communities and ecosystems in the Sierra Madre de Chiapas, Mexico. *Mitigation and Adaptation Strategies for Global Change*, 14 (7), 605–25.

SEMARNAT and CONANP, 2013. *Programa de Manejo Reserva de la Biosfera Volcán Tacaná*. México D.F.: SEMARNAT y CONANP.

Taylor, M., 2015. *The Political Ecology of Climate Change Adaptation: Livelihoods, agrarian change and the conflicts of development*. New York: Routledge.

Tovar González, M.E, 2000. Extranjeros en el Soconusco. *Revista de humanidades: Tecnológico de Monterrey*, 8.

Trinidad, J.M., 2016. Afecta plaga de roya naranja por el rebrote a 20 mil hectáreas de café en Chiapas. *Tapachula Hoy*, 7 March, 15.

Urry, J., 2011. *Climate Change and Society*. Cambridge: Polity Press.

Villers, L., *et al.*, 2009. Impactos del cambio climático en la floración y desarrollo del fruto del café en Veracruz, México. *Interciencia: Revista de ciencia y tecnología de América*, 34 (5), 322–9.

10 Climate change adaptation narratives in the Gulf of Mexico

Luz María Vázquez

Introduction

Climate change first entered the Mexican government agenda in 1992 when the country became a signatory to the United Nations Framework Convention on Climate Change, prompting the development of institutional structures and initiatives. However, climate change was not incorporated into the government planning agenda until 2007, when it formed part of the National Development Plan 2007–2012 (Presidencia de la República 2007). Mexican government narratives echo broad framings circulating at the international level based on the global climate change regime (Okereke *et al.* 2009), which emphasise adaptation as a new paradigm to improve the quality of life as well as a key strategy to protect natural ecosystems (CICC 2012a: 147). These framings emphasise the need to mainstream adaptation within development projects, with the final aim of promoting sustainable development in the country (CICC 2012a: 146).

Government climate change narratives state that the integration of adaptation objectives with development planning is a challenge since they need to address poverty and inequality, which implicitly 'question[s] the development model' (CICC 2012a: 82). These ideas are seconded by the Mexican state of Tabasco Plan, which states that climate change policies are an important step towards the reconsideration of 'human–environment relationships' (SERNAPAM 2011: 9). These narratives state that adaptation is a process that 'will lead to better resource management (water and land), conservation of ecological processes and biodiversity, more sustainable human activities, [and to the] reduction in vulnerability to extreme weather events' (Buenfil 2009: 30).

This chapter analyses Mexican government climate change adaptation narratives. It discusses some of the potential challenges government officials may face when they implement climate change adaptation measures in fishing communities in the Gulf of Mexico, taking into account historical local struggles for territories and their resources. I argue that climate change adaptation interventions are highly political on the ground. This argument emerged following a close analysis of local socio-environmental processes in coastal lagoon communities. Climate change adaptation initiatives become highly political to the extent that they define the nature of local environmental changes and involve solutions that require resource control, access, or management. Government initiatives that are presented as neutral strategies to help communities to be better equipped to address climate change impacts are contentious, and their implementation may encounter different political, economic, and environmental challenges, which are not currently considered when governments define the climate change problem.

Analysis of this argument draws on two interrelated issues. The first is a broad discussion of vulnerability and adaptation. I discuss how government climate change adaptation narratives focus on promoting people's abilities to adapt, leaving aside the set of policies and initiatives that would address structural factors that may determine communities' vulnerabilities in the first place (e.g. poverty). Governmental climate change initiatives are based on the Intergovernmental Panel on Climate Change (IPCC) scenario-driven approach that evaluates the impacts of climate change and assesses potential adaptation and mitigation measures aimed at reducing climate change vulnerabilities (Beck 2011: 299). In this framework adaptation 'refers only to actions taken in response to climatic changes attributed to green-house gas emissions' (Beck 2011: 302). Although the government narratives discuss climatic and non-climatic causes in the construction of coastal communities' vulnerabilities, the purpose of these analysed government interventions is to propose adaptation measures that aim to deal with climate impacts. Government narratives omit issues related to what governments may do to address the sources of people's vulnerability; instead, they focus on how people may be able to cope with impacts through adaptation practices. And in so doing, I argue, some contentious political issues are rendered technical (Li 2007).

The second issue I discuss is an analysis of two adaptation measures that the federal government has included in its climate change plans – communities' relocation and the creation of natural protected areas (CICC 2007) – but has not yet implemented. I discuss these measures in light of fishers' perceptions and views about local environmental changes as well as the socio-economic issues they face. I identify a discrepancy between what government initiatives propose as potential strategies to promote adaptation to climate change, and the views of fishers about interrelated local issues. An analysis of this contextual setting allows us to understand better the viability of these adaptation plans.

It is important to highlight that fishers' views are shaped by their historic conflict-driven relations with the state-owned oil company that has impacted fishers' natural ecosystems, their social relations, politics, and economy (Velázquez 1982; Botello *et al.* 1983; Rosas *et al.* 1983; Negrete 1984; Allub 1985; Lezama 1987; Tudela 1989; Rodríguez *et al.* 1995; Town and Hanson 2001; Vázquez and Pérez 2002; Ponce and Botello

2005). It is beyond the aim of this chapter to analyse these conflicts. However, the issues discussed should be understood in the context of the structural negative impacts that the oil industry has had in the region.

In this chapter I apply a narrative analysis approach (Roe 1991, 1995). In particular, I draw on political ecology approaches to environmental change narratives (Fairhead and Leach 1995, 2000; Batterbury *et al.* 1997; Forsyth 2003; Forsyth and Walker 2008) and critical perspectives on climate change (Bravo 2009; Hartmann 2010; Cameron 2012; Farbotko and Lazrus 2012; Felli and Castree 2012). Analysis of narratives highlights how particular actors understand and frame problems. It allows us to scrutinise what and who are included or excluded (Gasper and Apthorpe 1996: 8) or what aspects are being distinguished or avoided in the storylines of such frameworks (Dreher and Voyer 2014). It helps us to analyse how problems get defined and the sort of political consequences these definitions convey (Hajer and Versteeg 2005: 2). This approach critically examines the way in which evidence is gathered and the types of solutions actors propose to solve problems (Scoones 1997). In my case study, government narratives have a dominant voice in terms of designing, implementing, and mobilising resources in climate change projects and initiatives in Mexico. Therefore, the relevance of integrating into the discussion other, less visible perspectives from fishers allows us to identify how dominant frameworks on climate change adaptation convey ideas and assumptions that are problematic for local inhabitants actually experiencing local environmental changes. I argue that accounts of environmental change should be more inclusive and should consider the existence of multiple sources of knowledge and understanding about them – specifically local environmental knowledge and the political economic context in which it emerges.

The chapter is based on broader qualitative research (Vázquez 2014). The study includes five coastal communities located in the Gulf of Mexico, in the southern Mexican state of Tabasco (Figure 10.1). I conducted face-to-face semi-structured interviews with 98 fishers from the five study communities, 13 interviews with scientists working in the Gulf of Mexico, and 14 interviews with government officials. I also analysed government archival materials and planning documents (CICC 2007, 2012a, 2012b; Buenfil 2009).

The fishing communities

The fishing communities that form part of this study are located in a lacunar system that includes three coastal lagoons (the Carmen–Pajonal–Machona), in the Mexican state of Tabasco, in the Gulf of Mexico (Figure 10.1). They are part of a marginal region; Tabasco is characterised as one of the poorest states in Mexico (CONEVAL 2012). The state of Tabasco is rated below the national average in terms of access to social security,

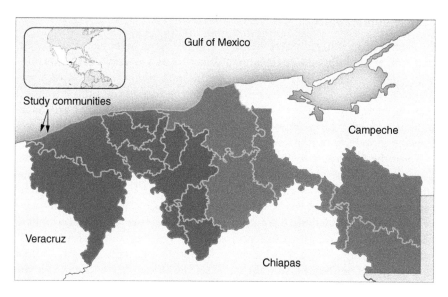

Figure 10.1 Study site: The Carmen–Pajonal–Machona lacunar system in Tabasco, Mexico.

Source: Regiones_de_Tabasco.png: The original uploader was Celay at Spanish Wikipedia https://commons.wikimedia.org/wiki/File:Regions_of_tabasco-Es.png

housing, social services, and food (ibid.: 51). In 2010, over half of the population was classified as living in poverty (ibid.: 12). The study villages have between 374 and 1,600 inhabitants (INEGI 2010).

Fishing is the most important income-generating activity in the lacunar system, and according to the interviews, is the only source of livelihood for the majority of the fishers living in the region (Pérez-Sánchez and Muir 2003; Pérez *et al.* 2012). This lacunar system is one of the most important oyster-producing areas in Mexico. Fishers who are members of the oyster-producing cooperatives exploit this resource with legal permits that are allocated by the federal government. These communities also include private fishers with permits to exploit some sea species. Independent free-lance fishers also exploit these resources; however, they do not have permits issued by fishing authorities, and represent the most vulnerable fishing group within these communities. Their main demand is to get per-mission from the government to create more cooperatives. However, fishing authorities are no longer issuing fishing licences; as a result, inde-pendent fishers must work 'illegally' with the many risks this implies. Lack of fishing permits, illegal fishing and use of illegal nets, lack of law enforcement, overexploitation of lagoons and sea resources, oil pollution, and waste water pollution are among some of the problems fishers dis-cussed in interviews.

Dealing with complexity? Underlying causes of climate change vulnerability

Government narratives point to the existence of a wide range of social, political, economic, and environmental factors as key drivers in determining vulnerability to climate change. But despite this recognition, government climate change initiatives are not designed to address the structural factors, such as poverty or lack of environmental planning, that are determining people's vulnerabilities to climate change. Instead, such initiatives focus on how to face impacts.

I use the *Climate Change Adaptation in Mexico: Vision, Elements and Criteria for Decision-making* report (CICC 2012a), which integrates case studies carried out by Mexican scholars, to indicate how government narratives integrate vulnerability into their analyses. One such case study concerned coffee producers from two marginal regions of Mexico, where peasants 'need to adapt to different sources of vulnerability, not only climatic variability' (CICC 2012a: 30). The author of this case study argued that coffee trade liberalisation during the 1980s was a key event in increasing the vulnerability of coffee producers, who as a result experienced price drops and variability. According to this analysis, the insecurity in coffee prices was part of a long chain of impacts that included a reduction in investment, technology, inputs, and training, and a lack of access to credit. The researcher also argued that it is under this scenario that climate change effects – such as an increase in rainfall and temperature variability and the associated impacts on coffee plants through an increase in pests and diseases, or more frequent and stronger storms and frosts – exacerbate the already severe social and economic vulnerability of coffee producers.

The *Climate Change Adaptation in Mexico* report, however, does not integrate this wide array of factors determining vulnerability into its analysis. Instead, the case study is brought into the narrative by highlighting that social participation and organisation are important factors that strengthen peasants' capacities to adapt. From a government perspective, vulnerability will only be reduced if the country develops 'adaptive capacities', defined as the development of a system's social and institutional capacities to adjust to climate change (CICC 2012a: 81). By this logic, local peasants should develop adaptive capacities to adjust to the different challenges they may face, while macro-structural economic transformations or other structural changes fall outside the scope of these government framings. Government narratives therefore 're-pose' (Ferguson 1994; Li 2007) political questions (the structural political, economic, social, and environmental sources of vulnerability) as 'technical problems' with a focus on impacts that can be addressed through adaptation initiatives such as irrigation schemes, drought-tolerant seed varieties, or infrastructure.

Adaptation measures in Mexican government plans

In this section, I discuss two adaptation measures proposed for coastal communities by the federal government: community relocation and the establishment of protected areas. These are analysed in light of the views expressed by local fishers about local issues. The testimonies indicate the type of challenges governments may encounter when trying to implement adaptation initiatives.

Community relocation

Community relocation has received increased attention worldwide as a strategic response to the impacts of climate change, especially in regions that are projected to be impacted by sea-level rise (e.g. Pacific Island countries) (Campbell *et al.* 2005). In the context of Mexico, planning documents from the federal government propose the relocation of settlements currently located in vulnerable areas (CICC 2007). These narratives recommend the relocation of infrastructure and populations that are less than ten metres from rivers and lagoons (Gama 2008: 73). Examining this adaptation option in various places worldwide, climate change researchers have concluded that relocation is a complex process that can often only be achieved at vast economic, environmental, emotional, and social cost (Campbell *et al.* 2005: 5). Land tenure, land availability, and infrastructure are some of the issues that need to be taken into account in elaborating relocation initiatives. According to some perspectives, in certain contexts community relocation reflects a managerial and technocratic approach to adaptation that draws on physical, technological, economic, and managerial frameworks, values, and narratives to explain the problem of adaptation to climate change and its possible solutions (Smit *et al.* 2000; Heyd and Brooks 2009; Leach *et al.* 2010; Nelson *et al.* 2010). This type of approach overlooks and neglects cultural, social, and political issues; as Nelson *et al.* (2010: 272) argued, it 'leave[s] aside the important role that individuals, cultures, and societies play in constructing and living out an adaptation dynamic'.

In my study area one of the most visible phenomena that has impacted these communities is coastal erosion. Coastal erosion impacts on the study communities are startling. During the period 1995–2003, scientists reported retreat rates in some of the study communities of 60–87 m (Hernández *et al.* 2008). Erosion has destroyed houses, public buildings, and the only road that connects the villages to other places. In interviews, authorities admitted that they did not know the number of people affected. Affected local inhabitants moved to other places without government or community support.

According to government narratives, coastal erosion in these communities is one of the climate change impacts already affecting coastal regions (SERNAPAM 2011). As I discuss elsewhere, these narratives are challenged by fishers' understanding of coastal erosion (Vázquez 2014). Fishers commented that some government officials have mentioned the possibility of relocating their village. When I asked the fishers about their thoughts on relocation, they expressed concern, explaining that 'the only occupation we have learnt since we were born has been fishing, what are we going to do in another place with no job waiting for us and without any other skill?' The majority of the fishers stated clearly that they would reject moving to another place; there are many concerns preventing them from moving, among which lack of jobs and means to make a living are the most important.

Fishers' subjective risk perception is also an important factor in this rejection of relocation. Specifically, fishers from two of these communities where erosion rates are not as high as in other towns do not think that erosion in their villages will get any worse than it is now. From their perspective, they can live as they are, with the water just beside their houses. They understand coastline changes as part of a natural dynamic. They explained that this condition is part of their life and recalled their ancestors' accounts about different positions of the shoreline over time – sometimes closer to their homes, sometimes further. The consultation and negotiation process that must be undertaken by government officials in considering this adaptation option must consider the relevance of local environmental knowledge in shaping local perceptions of risk, and in allowing fishers to manage to live with this type of environmental change. This example illustrates the importance of integrating local knowledge into climate change adaptation initiatives.

Natural protected areas

Another type of adaptation measure proposed by the federal government is the establishment of natural protected areas in coastal regions (CICC 2007). In the context of global climate change governance, these areas constitute part of the policy and management response to face climate change. Strategies include guidelines to select new protected areas, pre-emptive actions such as the development of connective corridors between protected areas, and management interventions (Halpin 1997: 828). According to experts, these areas are established because they 'contribute significantly to reducing impacts of climate change' (Dudley *et al.* 2010: 6). In Mexico, the establishment of protected areas was promoted during the 1980s and 1990s as part of the sustainable development policy framework. Natural protected areas were envisioned as strategies to combat environmental degradation and resource overexploitation. Their establishment aimed at addressing natural resource restoration, conservation, and management on the one hand, and poverty reduction on the other. As I discuss next, natural protected areas cross-cut issues of resource exploitation and social inequality.

In Mexico, problems generated by the creation of natural protected areas are numerous – for example, displacement of people from their lands (Paz 2002; Paz and Vázquez 2002). In many cases, local inhabitants are not informed that their legal land has been expropriated by the government, and so they continue to use the resources and are then penalised for doing this (Paz 2002). Governments lack the capacity to enhance the law that prohibits access to some protected resources, owing to a lack of human and financial resources or because officials engage in practices such as corruption, allowing the illegal exploitation of resources. Other studies have shown that this type of conservation initiative can also enhance the economic power of a few local and extra-local actors that benefit from these illegal practices (Paz and Vázquez 2002).

In my case study, key challenges to the establishment of natural protected areas include lack of compliance and enforcement of resource exploitation and conservation regulations to protect the lacunar system, the closed seasons, and lack of communities' recognition of territorial borders.

Lack of compliance and lack of enforcement of regulations

Local fishing authorities explained in interviews that population growth and resource scarcity are the key factors explaining overexploitation of local fishing resources. In the interviews, fishers and authorities mentioned corruption as a major factor preventing law enforcement and accountability. As the fishing authorities explained, fishers must comply with certain fishing regulations. In the case of oysters, for example, fishers are required to fish specimens that have a minimum length of 7cm. They must also return the shells to the lagoons, in order to restock oyster banks. However, in interviews fishers and authorities complained that poaching, 'illegal' fishing by fishers, and corruption are factors preventing law enforcement.

Fishers explained that everyone can fish – legally or 'illegally' – there is an informal agreement among fishers. Fishers can fish any species without a permit. There is also a lack of enforcement and oversight concerning the nets fishers are able to use. One of the fishers' leaders referred to a new fishing law. On the one hand he complained about the law, because for fishers it would mean more regulations, more surveillance, and the fulfilment of more health rules and requirements, while on the other, he commented that through this new law fishers would be regulated to use appropriate nets to fish in the lagoon and at sea. He mentioned the environmental impacts of using nets that should not be allowed in the lagoons.

Sometimes members of the cooperatives pass on to freelance fishers a ticket that allows them to fish legally. Independent fishers get the tickets by buying them directly from the cooperative's representatives, or from the people who buy their fish. They are called *fayuqueros* – people who buy something illegally. The *fayuqueros* buy the tickets from the cooperative's representatives. They allocate these tickets to the independent fishers so that the latter can get oysters and sell them to the *fayuqueros* directly, without drawing up a formal invoice including taxes. Some fishers recognised their close dependency on these dealers, who buy their product and give them tickets for free. There is also a social stigma against independent fishers, who are blamed for many of the problems the communities face; some fishers felt they were considered responsible for polluting the lagoon or for doing nothing to protect their resources; as one fisher explained, 'they are illegal, therefore they don't care.'

Other fishers' narratives portray the existence of an ideal past that was more or less perfect: fishing cooperatives were well managed, there was no corruption, and the state funded them with many subsidies and projects. It was a time when only two large cooperatives existed; however, everything has changed since the 1990s after the government provided more permits and around nine new cooperatives were formed. In the past, fishers said, community members complied better with their social commitments. Before, every family used to restock the lagoons with shells, unlike now when only very few do that. In the past they used to restock because they were conscious about the need to protect their resources, they said. Unfortunately, they explained, the government started to spoil their communities because public funds were used to pay people to restock: before it was for free, now people do not do it unless they get paid. Before, fishers only fished mature species, and now they devastate everything: they fish small sizes, interrupt the reproductive cycle of many species, and use nets that are not appropriate or that are illegal for fishing.

Closed seasons

Considering that the only way to meet their livelihood needs is fishing, having two closed seasons per year each lasting for three months is a key problem. If fishing is their only means to survive, all types of fisher will risk fishing and selling their product on the black market. At the time of the interviews, fishers explained that some freelancers were still in jail. This is because during the fishing season they can negotiate with the authorities but during the closed season they cannot, and during this period the authorities follow the legal norms. Freelancers explained that when they are caught during the fishing season, they immediately gather together in the lagoon and 'negotiate' with the authority: 'We tell them [the authorities], either you take all of us or you don't take any of us.' The fact that they need to pay a bribe in exchange for being freed was implied in the interviews. As Pérez *et al.* (2012: 141) explained, a closed season is not exactly a threat, for it has the objective of regulating oyster reproduction, but the lack of clear policies around it, in order to respond to the needs of the poorest population, generates this perception. This is so because the population is highly dependent on oyster capture and shelling to generate earnings, yet without viable and clear options to substitute it, their food security is affected.

As other studies recognise, the two closed seasons are very difficult for the fishers since fishing is their main source of income (Pérez-Sánchez and Muir 2003; Pérez *et al.* 2012). Fishers' alternatives are constrained: they either need to put their lives at risk by violating the law and fish, or they need to exploit other species. During one of the closed seasons one fisher interviewed told me that the night before he and his family had gone to what they call the 'crab's race', the time when the crustacean lays eggs. As Pérez *et al.* (2012: 142) explained:

> the blue crab (*Cardisoma guanhumi*) exits the mangroves towards the sea, and at night, women and children go out to capture crabs; in a few hours, up to thirty specimens can be captured, which are sold to people in nearby communities or taken to the municipal township, where they can sell them.

Their study showed this to be one of the alternative economic activities families engage in to generate income. It is not clear how in an already difficult situation for fishers and their families, establishing natural protected areas will help their communities survive in both the short and medium term. Law enforcement in a context where fishers have no other economic options may become a daunting task for the local fishing authorities, who, according to the interviews with officials, lack human and material resources to enforce the law.

Lack of recognition for territorial borders

A critical challenge in planning a conservation project in this area is the history of struggles local communities have experienced over their resources: there is a lack of consensus among communities about their territorial boundaries. In the interviews, fishers explained that rivalries have resulted in murders and permanent tensions among local inhabitants. From the fishers' perspective, any conservation measure to protect their resources is a waste of effort, since the authorities are not preventing resource over-exploitation and degradation by fishers from other communities. They argued: 'Why would I protect the resources if the government is protecting – through corruption – other fishermen who come to our communities to use our resources without any limit, using illegal nets?' But most importantly, even if they do want to help to protect these resources, to do so they must put their personal security at risk – including the risk of physical confrontation.

Summary comments

Discussion of these two adaptation measures – community relocation and the establishment of protected areas – illustrates how government climate change adaptation initiatives may fail to protect coastal communities if they are not designed to address local socio-economic, environmental, and governance conflicts related to natural resource access and management, which are at the core of these communities' vulnerabilities to climate change and other environmental changes. By ignoring these issues, government adaptation initiatives could potentially exacerbate existing conflicts, or reinforce inequalities in an already precarious region.

Conclusion

Government climate change narratives illustrate the process of oversimplification that states undertake in their task to make societies legible (Scott 1998). Reducing the complexity of climate change vulnerability and its transition into specific managerial adaptation measures forms part of the process of making climate problems legible for government agencies. As I have discussed in this chapter, government narratives recognise some of the underlying factors causing climate change vulnerability; however, they do not explain how to address them. This simplification of the problem focuses on how to promote adaptation instead of how to address the root causes of social and environmental vulnerability (Ribot 2011).

Marston (2004: 5) argued that in analysing public policies, 'we need to pay due attention to the everyday struggles over policy meanings and deeply held convictions – stories of conflict and contestation that are often missing from textbooks on how policy development "should" happen'. In my study, fishers disclosed competing problems that are the product of past state interventions in the region, especially the imposition of an oil exploitation strategy which has given rise to struggles over people's lands and their marine and coastal resources. In Tabasco, and in light of past 'failed' state interventions (Tudela 1989), it is important to closely analyse the potential implications that new adaptation to climate change interventions may have for local communities. As I have discussed, adaptation measures that aim at promoting better socio-ecological conditions to face climate change impacts need to take into account the socio-environmental history of the region. These initiatives should consider the contextual political economic processes, and also fishers' expertise and relationships with their environment. State agencies and non-governmental organisations designing climate change initiatives would also benefit from acknowledging the existence of competing views about environmental issues, and their effectiveness may improve to the extent that these initiatives recognise and address local struggles and concerns.

References

Allub, L., 1985. Polarización de clases y conflicto social en regiones petroleras. *Estudios Sociológicos*, 3 (8), 351–70.

Batterbury, S., Timothy, F., and Thomson, K., 1997. Environmental transformations in developing countries: Hybrid research and democratic policy. *The Geographic Journal*, 163 (2), 126–32.

Beck, S., 2011. Moving beyond the linear model of expertise? IPCC and the test of adaptation. *Regional Environmental Change*, 11 (2), 297–306.

Botello, A., Goñi, J., and Castro, S., 1983. Levels of organic pollution in coastal lagoons of Tabasco State, Mexico; I: Petroleum hydrocarbons. *Bulletin of Environmental Contamination and Toxicology*, 31, 271–7.

Bravo, M.T., 2009. Voices from the sea ice: The reception of climate impact narratives. *Journal of Historical Geography*, 35 (2), 256–78.

Buenfil, J., 2009. Executive summary. *In*: J. Buenfil, ed., *Adaptación a los impactos del cambio climático en los humedales costeros del Golfo de México*. México: SEMARNAT, 25–34.

Cameron, E.S., 2012. Securing indigenous politics: A critique of the vulnerability and adaptation approach to the human dimensions of climate change in the Canadian Arctic. *Global Environmental Change*, 22 (1), 103–14.

Campbell, J., Goldsmith, M., and Koshy, K., 2005. *Community Relocation as an Option for Adaptation to the Effects of Climate Change and Climate Variability in Pacific Island Countries (PICs)*. Asia-Pacific Network for Global Change Research.

CICC, 2007. *Estrategia nacional de cambio climático*. Comisión Intersecretarial de Cambio Climático. México: SEMARNAT.

CICC, 2012a. *Adaptación al cambio climático en México: Visión, elementos y criterios para la toma de decisiones*. Comisión Intersecretarial de Cambio Climático. México: SEMARNAT.

CICC, 2012b. *Quinta comunicación nacional ante la convención marco de las Naciones Unidas sobre el cambio climático*. Comisión Intersecretarial de Cambio Climático. México: SEMARNAT.

CONEVAL, 2012. *Informe de pobreza y evaluación en el estado de Tabasco 2012*. México: Consejo Nacional de Evaluación de la Política de Desarrollo Social.

Dreher, T., and Voyer, M., 2014. Climate refugees or migrants? Contesting media frames on climate justice in the Pacific. *Environmental Communication*.

Dudley, N., *et al.*, 2010. *Natural Solutions: Protected areas helping people cope with climate change*. Slovenia: IUCN/WCPA 'Parks for Life' Coordination Office.

Fairhead, J., and Leach, M., 1995. False forest history, complicit social analysis rethinking some West African environmental narratives. *World Development*, 23 (6), 1023–35.

Fairhead, J., and Leach, M., 2000. Desiccation and domination: Science and struggles over environment and development. *Journal of African History*, 41 (1), 35–54.

Farbotko, C., and Lazrus, H., 2012. The first climate refugees? Contesting global narratives of climate change in Tuvalu. *Global Environmental Change*, 22 (2), 382–90.

Felli, R., and Castree, N., 2012. Commentary. *Environment and Planning A*, 44, 1–4.

Ferguson, J., 1994. *The Anti-politics Machine: Development, depoliticization, and bureaucratic power*. Cambridge: Cambridge University Press.

Forsyth, T., 2003. *Critical Political Ecology: The politics of environmental science.* New York: Routledge.

Forsyth, T., and Walker, A., 2008. *Forest Guardians, Forest Destroyers: The politics of environmental knowledge in northern Thailand.* Seattle, WA: University of Washington Press.

Gama, L., 2008. *Evaluación de la vulnerabilidad de los estados del sureste de México ante lluvias extremas debidas a la variabilidad y el cambio climático: Tabasco, estudio de caso. Final report.* Tabasco: SEMARNAT.

Gasper, D., and Apthorpe, R., 1996. Introduction: Discourse analysis and policy discourse. *European Journal of Development Research,* 8 (1), 1–15.

Hajer, M.A., and Versteeg, W., 2005. A decade of discourse analysis of environmental politics: Achievements, challenges, perspectives. *Journal of Environmental Policy and Planning,* 7 (3), 175–84.

Halpin, P.N., 1997. Global climate change and natural-area protection: Management responses and research directions. *Ecological Applications,* 7 (3), 828–43.

Hartmann, B., 2010. Rethinking climate refugees and climate conflict: Rhetoric, reality and the politics of policy discourse. *Journal of International Development,* 22 (2), 233–46.

Hernández, J.R., *et al.,* 2008. Morfodinámica de la línea de costa del estado de Tabasco, México: Tendencias desde la segunda mitad del siglo XX hasta el presente. *Boletín Del Instituto De Geografía,* 65, 7–21.

Heyd, T., and Brooks, N., 2009. Exploring cultural dimensions of adaptation to climate change. *In*: W.N. Adger, I. Lorenzoni, and K. O'Brien, eds, *Adapting to Climate Change: Thresholds, values, governance.* Cambridge: Cambridge University Press, 269–82.

INEGI, 2010. *Censo de población y vivienda 2010* [online]. Instituto Nacional de Estadística y Geografía. Available from: www3.inegi.org.mx/sistemas/iter/consultar_info.aspx [Accessed 20 December 2011].

INEGI, 2014. *Mapa digital de Mexico* [online]. Instituto Nacional de Estadística y Geografía (INEGI). Available from: www.inegi.org.mx/geo/contenidos/mapadigital/ [Accessed 8 June 2014].

Leach, M., Scoones, I., and Stirling, A., 2010. Governing epidemics in an age of complexity: Narratives, politics and pathways to sustainability. *Global Environmental Change,* 20 (3), 369–77.

Lezama, J.L., 1987. Migración y petróleo en Tabasco. *Estudios Demográficos y Urbanos,* 2 (5), 231–56.

Li, T., 2007. *The Will to Improve: Governmentality, development and the practice of politics.* Durham, NC: Duke University Press.

Marston, G., 2004. *Social Policy and Discourse Analysis: Policy change in public housing.* Farnham: Ashgate.

Negrete, M.E., 1984. Petróleo y desarrollo regional: El caso de Tabasco. *Demografía y Economía,* 18 (1), 86–109.

Nelson, D.R., West, C.T., and Finan, T.J., 2010. In focus: Global change and adaptation in local places. *American Anthropologist,* 111 (3), 271–4.

Okereke, C., Bulkeley, H., and Schroeder, H., 2009. Conceptualizing climate governance beyond the international regime. *Global Environmental Politics,* 9 (1), 58–78.

Paz, M.F., 2002. *Entre el interés público y los intereses colectivos: Obstáculos y oportunidades para la participación ciudadana en el Corredor Biológico Chichinautzin, Morelos.* PhD thesis. Universidad Autónoma Metropolitana.

Paz, M.F., and Vázquez, L.M., 2002. Control de los recursos naturales y conflictos territoriales en la zona de bosque templado del norte de Morelos: Un recorrido entre lo local y lo regional. *In*: J. Delgadillo, ed. *Actualidad de la investigación regional en el México central*. México: UNAM, 309–28.

Pérez, E., *et al*., 2012. Contexto de vulnerabilidad de las mujeres desconchadoras de ostión (crassostrea virginica), del Ejido Sinaloa, Primera Sección, de Cárdenas, Tabasco. *Agricultura, Sociedad y Desarrollo*, 9 (2), 123–48.

Pérez-Sánchez, E., and Muir, J.F., 2003. Fishermen perception on resource management and aquaculture development in the Mecoacan estuary, Tabasco, Mexico. *Ocean and Coastal Management*, 46 (6), 681–700.

Ponce, G., and Botello, A.V., 2005. Niveles de hidrocarburos en el Golfo de Mexico. *In*: A. Botello, *et al*., eds, *Golfo de México. Contaminación e impacto ambiental: Diagnostico y tendencias*. México: Instituto Nacional de Ecología, 681–95.

Presidencia de la República. 2007. *Plan Nacional de Desarrollo* [online]. Available from: http://pnd.calderon.presidencia.gob.mx/pdf/PND_2007-2012.pdf [Accessed 16 September 2017].

Ribot, J., 2011. Vulnerability before Adaptation: Toward transformative climate action. *Global Environmental Change*, 21, 1160–2.

Rodríguez, E., Jiménez, I.S., and Valenzuela, M., 1995. *Contaminación acuática generada por la producción de hidrocarburos en Tabasco*. Tabasco, MX: Universidad Juárez Autónoma de Tabasco.

Roe, E., 1991. Development narratives, or making the best of blueprint development. *World Development*, 19 (4), 287–300.

Roe, E., 1995. Except Africa: Postscritp to a special section on development narratives. *World Development*, 23 (6), 1065–9.

Rosas, I., Báez, A., and Belmont, R., 1983. Oyster (*Crassostrea virginica*) as indicator of heavy metal pollution in some lagoons of the Gulf of Mexico. *Water, Air, and Soil Pollution*, 20 (2), 127–35.

Scoones, I., 1997. The dynamics of soil fertility change: Historical perspectives on environmental transformation from Zimbabwe. *The Geographical Journal*, 163 (2), 161–9.

Scott, J.C., 1998. *Seeing Like a State: How certain schemes to improve the human condition have failed*. New Haven, CT: Yale University Press.

SERNAPAM, 2011. *Programa estatal de acción ante el cambio climático*. Tabasco, MX: Secretaría de Recursos Naturales y Protección Ambiental.

Smit, B., *et al*., 2000. An anatomy of adaptation to climate change and variability. *Climatic Change*, 45 (1), 223–51.

Town, S., and Hanson, H., 2001. Oil at the grassroots: Report from Tabasco. *NACLA Report on the Americas*, 34 (4), 34–5.

Tudela, F., 1989. *La modernización forzada del trópico: El caso de Tabasco*. México: El Colegio de México.

Vázquez, L.M., 2014. *Adaptation Narratives: Climate change and environmental politics in Mexican coastal communities*. PhD thesis. York University.

Vázquez, F., and Pérez, L., 2002. Concentrations of elements and metals in sediments of the southeastern Gulf of Mexico. *Environmental Geology*, 42 (1), 41–6.

Velázquez, M.G., 1982. Afectaciones petroleras en Tabasco: El movimiento del Pacto Ribereño. *Revista Mexicana de Sociología*, 44 (1), 167–87.

11 Leaving the comfort zone

Regional governance in a German climate adaptation project

Heiko Garrelts, Johannes Herbeck, and Michael Flitner

Introduction

Adaptation to climate change in Germany takes place in the context of complex federal structures, with the participation of a range of actors from all policymaking levels. At the federal level, adaptation to climate change has been discussed since the early 2000s and is, to some extent, addressed in the federal government's Climate Protection Programme of 2005. The issue is given greater prominence in the German Adaptation Strategy (Bundesregierung 2008) and Adaptation Action Plan (Bundesregierung 2011), adopted in 2008 and 2011 respectively. At the same time, these early policy initiatives – and others – assigned a special role to the regions in climate change adaptation. As a result, the regional governance approach has recently attracted considerable attention as a framework both for policymaking and for the design of specific measures. In 2007, the German Federal Ministry of Education and Research (BMBF) included elements of the debate in the programme Managing Climate Change in the Regions for the Future (KLIMZUG), in which it sought to strengthen regional cooperation networks beyond pre-fixed administrative boundaries (such as the German *Länder*) and harness the 'endogenous potential' of the regions to contribute to climate change adaptation (see Knieling and Roßnagel 2015). Seven regions were selected by competition to serve as model regions. To different degrees, the seven German KLIMZUG projects all incorporated elements of a regional governance approach. This is an approach based on voluntary action that lacks or has at best only rudimentary political or juridical grounding and transcends the traditional boundaries of social subsystems (politics, public administration, economy, civil society). Correspondingly, the self-organised networks in the KLIMZUG regions (that had formed during the application phase) operated outside formal hierarchies, relying mainly on horizontal forms of interaction to disseminate information, discussion, and negotiation (see Fürst 2004).

This chapter looks more closely at one of the projects in the KLIMZUG framework programme. The project 'nordwest2050' was carried out in the Bremen–Oldenburg Metropolitan Region in Northwest Germany[1] from

2009 to 2014. It was a transdisciplinary project in which scientists from different universities – including the authors of this paper – were involved in the formal research process (such as a vulnerability analysis, elaboration of adaptation options in the different clusters, etc.), and also in the organisation of stakeholder meetings, networking activities, and the facilitation of decision-making. This chapter focuses on how progress made in the course of the project can be understood in the context of debates on regional governance. In particular, we consider the extent to which the project fulfilled the expectations commonly associated with the new forms of regional governance. Was there an increase in the effectiveness and legitimacy of political processes? How did forms of cooperation develop and to what extent did these give rise to new integration and innovation processes? What conflicts and obstacles arose and how can these be explained from a theoretical perspective?

We begin by briefly outlining the concept of *regional governance*, focusing on key characteristics that are relevant to the topic of climate change adaptation, as set out above. We then address two central issues in debates on regional governance: stakeholder participation and cooperation. This is followed by a brief summary and preliminary assessment of the results achieved. This leads us to conclude that the mechanisms of regional governance, as they unfolded in the context of the case study project, were hampered by (partly inherent) weaknesses and, overall, were not successful in reducing conflict. By examining widely differing ideas about what adaptation should look like and in which institutional frames it should be managed, the project demonstrated the contested and politicised nature of adaptation projects. Yet in our view, the 'broadening of the field of struggle' that we experienced constitutes a necessary starting point for future climate change adaptation in the region – and maybe in other regions, too.

The concept of regional governance and what it promises

The concept of regional governance is tied up with the search for regulatory structures that can complement or partially replace traditional ways of functioning of state hierarchies. The debate on regional governance in the German-speaking world, which serves as the basis for the following discussion, is not only concerned with purely theoretical issues. It also addresses the requirement for clear design principles and has had a notable influence on policy processes. Some defining characteristics of regional governance have already been mentioned. Other characteristics, which in part follow directly from them, include: the interaction among (individual) actors who follow different action logics (e.g. local politicians, business people, and members of civil society organisations); overlaps in areas of responsibility assigned to different parts of the system; the emergence of self-organised networks with non-hierarchical forms of interaction; and links to self-determined or negotiated control systems that formally canalise these interactions (Fürst 2004: 50). Further elements of regional governance include, for example, those identified by Giessen (2010b: 6f.): the emphasis on functional connectivity (for example in special-purpose associations); the development of linkages between content-related and financial dimensions of regional development; and the emergence of new forms of higher-level management such as performance-based competition among the regions.

According to the literature, regional governance is expected to provide a number of benefits, of which two are of particular interest in the context of climate change adaptation, namely greater efficiency in harnessing 'endogenous' development potential through increased participation (which also enhances input legitimacy), and improved cooperation across sectoral and political boundaries.

These expectations can also be found in policy documents relating to climate change adaptation. For example, regional mechanisms figure prominently in descriptions of KLIMZUG, the BMBF funding priority that is the focus of the present study:

> The aim is to adequately integrate [future] expected climate change into regional planning and development processes [...] and in this way both to enhance future regional competitiveness and to promote the development and application of new technologies, processes and strategies for regional climate change adaptation.
>
> (BMBF n.d.)

In the context of the nordwest2050 project that we examine in more detail below, similar assumptions and expectations can be found. Above all, the expectation of informal, network-based, regional management structures is clearly evident; implicitly, these are viewed as prerequisites for the project and its different areas of activity. In the two following sections, we discuss the extent to which regional governance fulfilled its 'promises' in northwest Germany, in terms of increased efficiency and improved cooperation.

Participation: problems of access and commitment

Broad-based participation by actors is understood to be a factor in the success of regional governance (Böcher and Tränkner 2008: 117). For empirical investigation, this raises the question of who actually participates (Fürst 2004: 57): Who is allowed to take part? And how are the participants chosen?

At the start of nordwest2050, participants were chosen by 'self-recruitment' (cf. Fürst 2004: 57); that is, a group of interested people in the region came together to discuss the proposal. This group included representatives of academic institutions, that is, the Universities of Bremen and

Oldenburg, two environmental consulting firms, and an important regional association, the Bremen-Oldenburg Metropolitan Region in northwest Germany (hereafter MPR),[2] whose members include regional industries, chambers of commerce, municipalities, and the federal states of Bremen and Lower Saxony. The selection of participants therefore owed much to practical and micro-political circumstances, including existing contacts and relationships. Initial meetings were mainly organised by a single consulting firm.

The frame of reference for nordwest2050 was, in this early phase, set by the sphere of action of the MPR. Thus, nordwest2050 was a self-referential initiative that – with full intention – served to strengthen an important actor in regional governance. Consequently, the agenda of the MPR also substantially determined the scope of the project proposal, giving weight to economic development of the metropolitan region. For the subsequent formulation of the project proposal, and specific proposals for three fields of action (known as 'clusters': energy, ports and logistics, and the food industry), invitations were extended to 'practice partners', that is, expert practitioners in the respective fields. The selection of stakeholders therefore primarily took place through co-option, and this remained the case throughout the duration of the project.

To get these and other regional actors to participate, nordwest2050 adopted a variety of different approaches. As in the KLIMZUG initiative as a whole, this meant that different levels of participation were achieved at different stages of the project. The spectrum of levels of participation encompassed communication, consultation, co-production, and co-decision. The last of these came to the fore in the innovation phase of the three priority clusters. Practice partners, predominantly from commercial enterprises, worked together with academics to get climate change adaptation projects off the ground. A total of 15 innovation projects were implemented, with titles such as *Resilient Port Structures: Building a best practice database* (ports cluster), *Summer Ventilation in the Turkey Shed* (energy cluster) and *Revitalization of Old Varieties and Breeds* (food cluster).

Other initiatives carried out with the participation and involvement of regional actors included the following:

- establishment of a prize competition for businesses: 'Fit for climate change';
- launch of a project homepage and production of information material in a variety of formats (scientific studies, short films, printed material);
- conduct of surveys, interviews, and focus groups relating to perceptions of climate change in the region and in particular to vulnerability assessment;
- organisation of six regional conferences focusing on various topics (e.g. vulnerability, business development);
- establishment of a working group to advise the project comprising well-known personalities from the region;

- carrying out consultations and, for this purpose, establishment of the working group 'Roadmap of change' with a membership representative of a wide spectrum of actors from the region (a full list of members can be found on the project homepage.)

Among key outcomes of the consultations was the formulation of a vision statement, entitled *Vision 2050 for a Climate-adapted and Resilient Bremen–Oldenburg Metropolitan Region in the Northwest* (see nordwest2050 2013a) as well as ten 'sectoral roadmaps' (also listed on the project homepage). 'Vision 2050' was intended to serve as a kind of compass and orientation framework for climate adaptation strategies in the metropolitan region. The sectoral roadmaps focused on a variety of fields of action (such as the energy industry, coastal protection, and the natural environment) and contained recommendations for meeting the challenges of climate change. Vision 2050 and the sectoral roadmaps were drawn up in 2012 and 2013, in a process involving many regional actors, especially members of the working group and those involved in work of the priority clusters. Special focus group workshops were also held.

Turning now to the participatory *structures* that evolved over the course of the project as a whole, the highly unequal representation of actor *types* is clearly evident. Market actors (companies and commercial associations) were strongly represented and a large proportion of the federal funds was allocated for their support, especially for the 'practice partners' in so-called *Leuchtturmprojekten* (flagship projects). This programmatic imbalance was to an extent embedded in the KLIMZUG programme, which is oriented towards the development of new products and strengthening 'regional competitiveness' – a concept which is not further defined. However, since KLIMZUG's remit also includes regional planning and development processes and their alignment with requirements for climate change adaptation, the participation of *other* regional actors is an issue of particular importance. Over the course of the project, the underrepresentation of other actor types was evident, as in other KLIMZUG projects: legislative actors have been poorly represented in KLIMZUG as a whole. According to Rotter *et al.* (2013: 48), this is because climate change adaptation is still accorded relatively low priority on the political agenda or is not seen as a sufficiently controversial topic. Some studies have shown that political actors only become interested in environmental change when the changes that occur are highly visible, tangible, and can easily be measured – in the northwest, these are mainly issues related to coastal protection (Garrelts *et al.* 2013: 145ff.). Nevertheless, the nordwest2050 project helped establish 'contacts' between members of MPR and representatives from state parliaments of the federal states of Bremen and Lower Saxony.

Civil society was also represented rather poorly in nordwest2050. It is true that the project succeeded, for example, in involving a number of political environmental groupings, and a few other groups in specific regional policy processes. Examples of the latter include BUND (Bund für Umwelt und Naturschutz Deutschland; a German section of Friends of the Earth, one of the leading environmental non-governmental organisations in Germany) and Energiewende Osterholz (regional association dedicated to the local implementation of the German 'energy transition', short *Energiewende*, see www.energiewende-osterholz.de).

In addition, some organisations with no previous involvement in climate policy (employee associations, consumer protection organisations) agreed to take part in the consultation process. However, as in many participatory processes of this kind, from the perspective of participating actors the requirements were inequitable and prohibitive. Non-governmental organisations did not have the resources, especially personnel, for continual engagement in this kind of regional governance – moreover, their available resources are already committed to high-profile regional controversies such as the proposed dredging of the River Weser. The low level of participation by 'critical' actors was therefore not primarily due to their exclusion by project managers; it was also a reflection of these actors' priorities and their limited resources. As became evident over the course of the project, the capacities of many civil society actors and organisations are (of necessity) already fully committed. While some degree of engagement with projects like nordwest2050 is possible, this is often short-lived and in an individual capacity (not as organisations). Moreover, symptoms of 'stakeholder burnout' – an all too common phenomenon in the KLIMZUG programme as a whole – quickly became apparent (Rotter *et al.* 2013: 48) and led to a decreasing level of engagement in the course of the project phase. This arose when stakeholders were consulted in a way that exceeded their capacities (such as too frequent meetings).

A further reason for the low level of participation is that the current and expected impacts of climate change are either highly uncertain or affect segments of the population who, as interest groups, have little organisational capacity and even less capacity to engage in conflicts. However, the problem is not only due to the weakness of particular interest groups (Winter and Willems 2000). In fact, it proves difficult even to determine in advance which actors are to be targeted by activities of adaptation projects. For example, this depends on which approach to social vulnerability is adopted. Should vulnerability already be apparent or should actors who are likely to be affected by a possible intensification of climate change also be considered (cf. O'Brien *et al.* 2007)?

If it is recommended that all actors considered relevant for regional development processes should participate in the network, this would require in our case that climate change is a common reference framework for observed environmental changes. Findings of social science research by the nordwest2050 project do in fact demonstrate that climate change is to a certain extent a topic of everyday conversation and public discourse. However, perceptions of climate change and their influence on, for example, consumer behaviour and attributions of responsibility – and therefore also on attitudes towards participatory processes – are markedly different among different social groups (Weller *et al.* 2010). Thus, for some social groups, fears about increasing social disparities as a consequence of climate change are at least as great as fears of climate change impacts themselves (Weller *et al.* 2010: 59). Consequently, the distinction between adaptation to climate change and climate protection is not as clear in the public perception as it is in expert circles (e.g. the KLIMZUG programme). In addition, there is now little support for the idea that consumers alone are responsible for climate protection and adaptation. On the one hand, despite considerable scepticism about the commitment of political decision-makers, it is generally agreed that the state has a decisive role to play. On the other hand, respondents to questionnaires say that economic actors also have a duty to promote climate change adaptation and support climate-friendly innovation (Weller *et al.* 2010: 52).

This implies that it is not enough to ask whether implementation of measures contained in the National Adaptation Strategy can be 'improved' through increased participation. It is clear, first, that the extent to which the aim of increased effectiveness of regional policy can be achieved is dependent on the specific issue concerned and objectives of the actors involved (e.g. business development and the reduction of social vulnerability). Second, as became clear in focus group interviews, effectiveness is not the only criterion by which climate policy should be judged; for example, distributional effects of climate policy measures are also considered important.

The experiences of the nordwest2050 project with respect to participation are in accordance with findings from other cases reported, for example, by Giessen (2010a, 2010b). These studies draw particular attention to the growing importance of non-state actors in regional governance, including civil society and private sector actors. Since the latter possess effective organisational structures and ample resources, they are able to shape regional governance to their advantage and, if necessary, dominate weaker interest groups (Giessen 2010a: 15). Thus, governance processes can work strongly in favour of already existing interest group constellations (Giessen 2010a). This inevitably raises further questions regarding the legitimacy of the process. However, this can also be viewed in a positive light, in that it at least gives new voices and interests access to programmatic processes and – as the next section shows – has considerable resonance.

Cooperation: leaving the comfort zone of ignorance

The core of the concept of regional governance, per se, is the requirement for collective solutions that are achieved through 'collaboration of actors, without the existence of formal structures' (Fürst 2004: 353); in particular, win–win coalitions are expected to lead to success in this regard (Böcher and Tränkner 2008: 114). Networks are conceptualised as key coordinating mechanisms in research on the topic. Empirically, the nordwest2050 project was characterised by a complex juxtaposition of cooperative and conflictive constellations, which can best be understood from this perspective.

With respect to cooperation, it is first necessary to distinguish between instances of cooperation that are permanent, or at least persist for long periods, and those that, from the start, are conceived of as temporary. An example of the former is the Intercommunal Coordination Office for Climate Adaptation, supported by the Federal Ministry for the Environment, Nature Conservation, Building and Nuclear Safety (BMU), which is tasked with further raising awareness of the importance of climate change adaptation at the level of administrative districts and local authorities.

An example of temporary cooperation from the project nordwest2050 is that which occurred between 'practice partners' from the key business clusters and actors from the consortium. This came to the fore particularly in the vulnerability assessment and in the design and implementation of the innovation projects. The practice partners had various motives for cooperation, ranging from anticipated access to financial resources and (free) expertise, to a better public image, entry into the network, and the possibility of influencing discourse on a regional level. All this is *the* field of win–win coalitions: since actors from the project consortium (including some of the researchers) were also winners, gaining financial resources, new contacts, job prospects at the practice partners, and enhanced reputations.

The innovation projects are, as indicated by the examples already given, predominantly technical in nature. They react to climate change by responding to disruptive climatic events, such as heavy rainfall. An exception among the innovation projects that deserves to be examined more closely is the 'Aurich Declaration' (nordwest2050 2013b). This document returns to *integrative questions* that were the original focus of work of the research association, and the concern that adaptation to climate change could lead to intensification for existing competition for land – specifically: competition for valuable soils – and thereby to increasing pressure on, for example, water resources (Karlstetter and Pfriem 2010). A symposium on this topic, organised by Oldenburg University in Aurich in East Friesland in February 2013, gave rise to a remarkable declaration. The declaration draws attention to the 'land acquisition, in large measure on a global level by nation states and international corporations' – and, in Germany, also regional ones. According to the declaration, this constitutes 'an almost unchecked consumption of available space, that is used [not only for agriculture but] also in particular for construction of settlements and transport infrastructure' (nordwest2050 2013b: 5, 7). The underlying causes are seen, for example, as competition among communal regional authorities, related to environmental problems arising from the 'accelerated concentration' of agriculture and 'the increasing presence of investors from outside [the agricultural sector]' (nordwest2050 2013b: 9). Key elements of a solution to this problem include that 'different organizations, institutions and associations should find forums [for communication] and forms of agreement' (nordwest2050 2013b: 12); and 'there must be an increased readiness to cooperate and coordinate closely' (nordwest2050 2013b: 12) at a regional level and among the 'diversity of actors that are able to support the transformation towards sustainable agriculture' (nordwest2050 2013b: 12). The options for action identified at a regional level – above all dialogue-oriented communication – represent an optimistic response to the problem situation. The key feature of the Aurich Declaration is that it considers climate change in its wider *social and above all economic context.* Thus, it stands in contrast to mainstream approaches to climate change which are more technically and scientifically oriented.

Broadening out the policy context in this way led elsewhere in the project to intractable conflicts among members of the consortium and between the consortium and other economic policy actors in the region. In this regard, the MPR played a pivotal role as a partner in the consortium. The conflicts became apparent during the process of drawing up the Vision 2050 and the sectoral roadmaps. Some of the economic actors strongly objected to points brought up by different stakeholders and the subsequent feedback from researchers in the consultation rounds. These conflicts concerned, for example, a section in Vision 2050 dealing with gender equity and reduced working hours, issues that have not been considered of major importance by some of the involved actors. Other contentious issues included the focus on regulatory options (such as construction bans) in urban land-use planning, and the strong emphasis placed on the connection between economic growth, climate change through greenhouse gas emissions, and the need for adaptation measures. Equally controversial was the idea of coordinated action across state boundaries – in cases where this seems functionally necessary and is to a certain extent already being practised, such as for coastal protection. This was mainly because of a potential change in mandates of some of the involved actors.

Finally, action options in the framework of what was referred to by stakeholders as 'plans for the Northern State[3]' were (falsely) interpreted by influential actors in the region as a call to dissolve the federal state of Bremen. In summer 2013, the conflict came to a head. Some partners in the consortium felt threatened and blackmailed; false information was published about the sources of finance for the project; and agreements already taken on the location for the project's closing conference were rescinded. Plans for a stakeholder consultation by the MPR were put on hold. From this point onwards, leaders of the MPR distanced themselves from the contents of previous project documents. There was intense debate over the role and mandate of scholarly research which, it was claimed,

aimed at 'changing reality' (see Gleich 2009). In these debates, however, it was repeatedly overlooked that the controversial declarations of the project that we have summarised briefly above were the result of *transdisciplinary research* – and were by no means the product of academic discussion or fantasies dreamed up by researchers. Thus, nordwest2050 evoked a political resonance in the region to an extent unusual for a research project. This effect was encapsulated in the words of one stakeholder, who stated that the project had gone 'outside the comfort zone of ignorance'.

These disputes not only reduced the degree of trust between key actors – which, according to theory, is a fundamental precondition for the success of regional governance (or for it to have an effect of any kind). Other factors discussed in the literature also came into play. These include the finding that regional governance processes can be interest-led from the start and are not necessarily oriented towards the collective good (cf. Giessen 2010a: 15). What Fürst (2004: 57ff) has called the 'fundamental problem of regional governance' was also clearly in evidence, namely that outcomes are largely context-dependent.

First, context includes institutional frameworks, which in this case were strongly influenced by the MPR. In general terms, it can be affirmed that participants in regional governance initiatives (in this case, for example, economic actors or the state minister of the environment) are representatives of organisations (e.g. chambers of commerce, state governments, or political parties) and therefore have limited freedom with respect to their behaviour in collaborative processes. Each participant must seek consensus on several levels: in the cooperation process as such (in this case in both nordwest2050 and MPR), and within the organisation they represent – taking account of the different levels of interaction that exist within the organisation itself and interactions and obligations with respect to other organisations. To sum up: cooperation – and likewise conflict – are complex multi-level processes of interaction (Benz 2000). This, naturally, also means that the interpretation of regional governance as a 'state organized mechanism to reduce the burden on the state' based on 'the principle of activation and increased individual responsibility' (Offe 2008: 69) can easily turn out to be unrealistic. The conflictual phase of nordwest2050 is at the same time an example of the fact that the general distinction that is often made between governance and government is empirically unsustainable (cf. Pütz 2004: 165), since in practice actors act and form coalitions more often along the lines of sectoral interests (e.g. transport) than institutional structures.

Second, context of regional governance is determined through situational influences and, importantly, by personal factors (cf. Fürst 2004: 57). Thus, in this case, some actors were convinced that the policy priorities of directors of the MPR had shifted following personnel changes, towards giving primacy to economic interests in response to climate change issues, as elsewhere. In any case, it seems clear that the issue of whether a more precise analysis of actors in the context of regional governance and climate change adaptation should include not only 'entrepreneurs' but also the explicit category of 'laggards' that slow the processes of climate change adaptation or mitigation is one that should be explored in more depth in the future.

Third, context is determined by the power of veto held by some of the participating actors (Offe 2008: 72). The influence of these actors with de facto power to block decisions may even be stronger in the context of weak institutionality than when there is a stronger institutional framework (Giessen 2010a, 2010b); at the very least – as the experience of nord-west2050 demonstrates – it gives them 'exit options'. This exit option is not only not available to other partners, but also, in conflict situations, highlights their dependency on resource flows *from within the region*. This dependency is another topic that is rarely discussed in regional governance literature.

Therefore, as long as the status quo of regional economic structures in the MPR's field of operations was not questioned, and innovation focused (mainly) on technical project-based solutions, cooperation flourished and the famous win–win constellations were attainable. With the emergence of ideas for change in regional power structures, even over the long term, this unity quickly broke down. The process of change that the project had set in motion, at least in part intentionally, shifted participation by the private sector from the level of individual enterprises to that of economic lobbying organisations. From this point onwards, the idea of supporting competitiveness alongside structural change on a regional level, conceived of by KLIMZUG as a synergetic and intrinsically converging process, was shown to be oversimplified. Similarly to KLIMZUG's idea of participation (uneasily balanced between the poles of emancipation and effectiveness), which at least requires further clarification, the whole idea of affirmative networks needs to be scrutinised more closely. Are these conceived primarily as policy networks or as more or less familiar interest group alliances? How do informally organised actor networks operate in the wider context of public action (cf. Prittwitz 2007: 212ff.)?

Conclusion

In a general sense, the term *governance* addresses a 'problematic basic experience' of actors in public life: in some problem situations, hierarchical forms of action will 'fail' just as surely as market- or quasi-market-based incentives (Offe 2008: 67), for example as a result of the veto power held by some of the actors involved. By contrast, the concept of governance promises compensatory effects: it appears suited to fill a gap by providing a 'paradigmatically new and somehow more advanced, frictionless, voluntarist-mutualist and liberal form of socio-political regulation' (Jordan *et al.* 2005: 478, cited in Offe 2008: 63). However, it is notable that the discussion of regional governance hardly touches upon *what* it can or should be expected to achieve. The approach, including the discussion of 'success factors', is predominantly process-oriented.

This chapter has outlined what regional governance projects focused on climate change adaptation are likely to achieve. Alongside general awareness-raising and provision of information to actors and citizens in the region on a comparatively new topic, such projects are broad-based participatory and innovation processes. At the same time, these positive effects are limited, for example through the veto power held by some actors, and it is precisely this that is difficult for informal regional govern-ance projects to deal with. Here the decisive effects of the unequal distribu-tion of power showed themselves clearly in the designated climate change adaptation regions. In this respect, we can also draw on newer approaches from the emerging field of critical studies on climate change adaptation, for example those of Dietz and Brunnengräber (2016), who called for taking local power relations more fully into account, as they have decisive influence on adaptation measures. As the literature shows, these observa-tions do not apply solely to climate change adaptation (and adaptation policy). Specific to the field of climate change adaptation is, however, the unwillingness of powerful actors to envision alternative social relations or even to consider different approaches to the problem. This shortcoming is neither only apparent in a temporal dimension nor exclusive to powerful actors (although in this case it is interest-led). The emphasis on uncertainty is a common feature of most public debate on climate change, but this typically refers to the inherent uncertainty of climate models. There has been much less discussion about the uncertainty regarding the drivers of development in the societies that will need to adapt to climate change. Huge differences can be expected in this respect between societies that are evolving in a post-democratic direction and others characterised by a strong state and a well-developed civil society (Flitner and Garrelts 2012).

This observation leads once more to the idea of the 'gap-filling function' of regional governance that threatens to divert attention away from other key evaluation criteria. More so than in other policy fields, the normative implica-tions of climate policy will remain controversial. This applies above all to its distributive effects in a variety of contexts (e.g. sectors, regions). One conclu-sion to be drawn from this is therefore that regional governance as a concept cannot be discussed independently of its contextual frame of reference, that is, general socio-economic development and its societal valuation. What should regional development look like? How should society be organised? These questions are a reminder of the conceptual fuzziness inherent in the promises of regional governance. For example, does participation serve to achieve effectiveness, emancipation, and transformation – or is it simply a means of *control* (for the latter view, see Maasen and Lieven 2006)?

Was nordwest2050 effective? To the extent that the aim of the project was to adopt a roadmap of change *in consensus* with all regional actors, it was a failure. However, there is another reading. The conflicts that we have described broke out precisely because the project was able to raise the possibility of new approaches towards climate change in unpredictable forums. In so doing, it also called into question customary practices and political narratives. In particular, coastal protection had previously been considered as a consensual climate change adaptation project that, in northwest Germany, hardly needed to be explained. In fact, there was a lack of clarity about a wide range of matters concerning the scope of the issue and those affected by it. Many assumptions regarding common interests, values, and political views had never clearly been articulated (Flitner and Garrelts 2012: 73) – as it is also the case at the global level, for example, in discussions on keeping global temperature rise below 2°C above pre-industrial levels (Swyngedouw 2010). Now, however, new conflicts have become apparent and this has allowed the issue to become politicised. Substantial differences have been made visible, in relation to both the project and more fundamental societal issues (such as the roles of distribution, innovation, and technology); these raise questions of political priority and participation. Precisely because of the conflicts that emerged in the course of its implementation, the experience of nordwest2050 helped to clarify why and in what sense, in an artificially constructed 'northwest region', people are not 'all in the same boat'. The project showed both the possibility and the necessity of adopting transformatory approaches, but also the huge difficulties and obstacles to get there. In this sense, we see 'leaving the comfort zone of ignorance' as something positive, and 'broadening the field of struggle' as a necessary point of departure for a future climate change adaptation policy.

Acknowledgements

This chapter is a substantially revised version of a German-language paper published as Garrelts *et al.* (2015). Work on the paper was undertaken under the BMBF project 'nordwest2050', grant number 01LR0813C, at the Sustainability Research Center (artec), University of Bremen (among other institutions).

Notes

1 The Bremen–Oldenburg Metropolitan Region in northwest Germany comprises, geographically, the federal state of Bremen and administrative districts and towns of the neighbouring state Lower Saxony. It covers an area of 13,750 km^2 and has a population of 2.73 million inhabitants. Despite the description 'metropolitan', the region contains both densely populated urban areas and rural areas. With regard to climate change, drier and warmer summers, as well as wetter and warmer winters are expected during the period 2071–2100. Scientific experts project that the region will be affected by a sea-level rise of between 18 and 140 cm (cf. Winges *et al.* 2015: 199f.). This will

create climate challenges, especially concerning coastal and tidal protection and water management. Warmer, drier summers will affect agriculture, while the logistics and energy sectors will be impacted by extreme weather events and through changing consumption patterns (Schuchardt *et al.* 2011). Land-use conflicts are already widespread in the region, and these could intensify because of the demands on land for climate change adaptation measures, such as the construction of polders or secondary dikes for coastal protection (Winges *et al.* 2015: 200). The metropolitan region is represented politically by the association Bremen–Oldenburg Metropolitan Region in the Northwest.

2 The aims of the association include the:

> improvement of the structure and development of the common cooperation area through networking and interaction among local authorities and the Federal States of Lower Saxony and Bremen, as well as business, science and other sectors; profiling the Metropolitan Region as a national and European economic region [… and] support for and initiation of measures to maintain and enhance the competitiveness of the local economy and scientific landscape […].
>
> (MPR 2013)

3 The term 'Northern State' is used to describe a proposal for a union of the federal states of Lower Saxony and Schleswig-Holstein with each of the federal city states Bremen and Hamburg. This proposal has sometimes met fierce opposition from local political actors.

References

Benz, A., 2000. Politische Steuerung in lose gekoppelten Mehrebenensystemen. *In*: R. Werle and U. Schimank, eds, *Gesellschaftliche Komplexität und kollektive Handlungsfähigkeit*. Frankfurt am Main: Campus, 125–54.

BMBF (Bundesministerium für Bildung und Forschung), no date. *Über KLIMZUG* [online]. Berlin: BMBF. Available from: www.klimzug.de/160.php [Accessed 1 October 2013].

Böcher, M., and Tränkner, S., 2008. Erfolgsfaktoren integrierter ländlicher Entwicklung. *In*: M. Böcher, M. Krott, and S. Tränkner, eds, *Regional Governance und integrierte ländliche Entwicklung. Ergebnisse der Begleitforschung zum Modell- und Demonstrationsvorhaben „Regionen Aktiv"*. Wiesbaden, DE: VS-Verlag, 109–49.

Bundesregierung, 2008. *Deutsche Anpassungsstrategie an den Klimawandel* [online]. Berlin: Bundesregierung. Available from: www.bmub.bund.de/fileadmin/bmu-import/files/pdfs/allgemein/application/pdf/das_gesamt_bf.pdf [Accessed 7 November 2017].

Bundesregierung, 2011. *Aktionsplan Anpassung der Deutschen Anpassungsstrategie an den Klimawandel* [online]. Berlin: Bundesregierung. Available from: www.bmub.bund.de/fileadmin/bmu-import/files/pdfs/allgemein/application/pdf/aktionsplan_anpassung_klimawandel_bf.pdf [Accessed 7 November 2017].

Dietz, K., and Brunnengräber, A., 2016. Klimaanpassung. *In*: S. Bauriedl, ed., *Wörterbuch Klimadebatte*. Bielefeld: transcript, 127–31.

Flitner, M., and Garrelts, H., 2012. Postdemokratie und Kälte auf Rädern: Ein Dialog über Politik und Klimawandel in der Metropolregion Bremen-Oldenburg im Jahre 2037. *Hannoversche Geographische Arbeiten*, 61 *(Nordwestdeutschland 2037)*, 66–73.

Fürst, D., 2004. Regional governance. *In*: A. Benz, ed., *Governance: Regieren in komplexen Regelsystemen. Eine Einführung*. Opladen, DE: VS-Verlag, 45–64.

Garrelts, H., et al., 2013. *Vulnerabilität und Klimaanpassung. Herausforderungen adaptiver Governance im Nordwesten Deutschlands*. Retrieved from Nordwest2050 Database (23. Werkstattbericht 2013).

Garrelts, H., Herbeck, J., and Flitner, M., 2015. 'Raus aus der Komfortzone': Regional Governance im Kontext des Projekts nordwest2050. *In*: J. Knieling and A. Roßnagel, eds, *Governance der Klimaanpassung. Akteure, Organisation und Instrumente für Stadt und Region*. München: oekom, 267–82.

Giessen, L., 2010a. *Regional Forest Governance: Forstliche Potentiale und politische Kräfte in der integrierten ländlichen Entwicklung*. Cumulative thesis (PhD). Universitätsverlag Göttingen.

Giessen, L., 2010b. Regional Governance für ländliche Räume – innovativer Ansatz, politischer Gegenwind und der Weg vorwärts. *Raumforschung und Raumordnung*, 68 (1), 3–14.

Gleich, A. v. 2009. *nordwest2050. Auf dem Weg zu einer klimaangepassten Region*. Lecture by Prof. Dr Arnim von Gleich (Universität Bremen) at the kickoff meeting for the nordwest2050 project at Bremen City Hall.

Jordan, A., Wurzel, R.K.W., and Zito, A., 2005. The rise of 'new' policy instruments in comparative perspective: Has governance eclipsed government? *Political Studies*, 53 (3), 477–96.

Karlstetter, N., and Pfriem, R. 2010. *Bestandsaufnahme: Kriterien zur Regulierung von Flächennutzungskonflikten zur Sicherung der Ernährungsversorgung*. Retrieved from Nordwest2050 Database. (4. Werkstattbericht 2010).

Knieling, J., and Roßnagel, A., 2015. Welche Governance brauchen Städte und Regionen für die Anpassung an den Klimawandel? Fragestellungen und Zugänge aus der Forschungsinitiative, Klimzug – Klimawandel in Regionen zukunftsfähig gestalten'. *In*: J. Knieling and A. Roßnagel, eds, *Governance der Klimaanpassung. Akteure, Organisation und Instrumente für Stadt und Region*. München: Oekom, 9–25.

Maasen, S., and Lieven, O. 2006. Transdisciplinarity: A new mode of governing science? *Science and Public Policy*, 33 (6), 399–410.

MPR, 2013. *Ziele und Aufgaben* [online]. Metropolregion Bremen/Oldenburg im Nordwesten e.V. (MPR). Available from: www.frischkoepfe.de/internet/page.ph p?naviID=901000013&site=901000061&brotID=901000013&typ=2&rubri k=901000011 [Accessed 1 October 2013].

Nordwest2050, 2013a. *Vision 2050 für einen klimaangepassten und resilienten Raum der Metropolregion Bremen-Oldenburg im Nordwesten*. Retrieved from Nordwest2050 Database.

Nordwest2050, 2013b *Auricher Erklärung. Outcome of the conference „Klimaangepasste Landnutzung im Nordwesten – Lösungsansätze rund um die Ernährungswirtschaft"*. Retrieved from Nordwest2050 Database.

O'Brien, K., et al., 2007. Why different interpretations of vulnerability matter in climate discourses. *Climate Policy*, 7 (1), 73–88.

Offe, C., 2008. Governance: 'Empy signifier' oder sozialwissenschaftliches Forschungsprogramm? *Politische Vierteljahresschrift*, Special Issue 41, 61–76.

Prittwitz, V.v., 2007. *Vergleichende Politikanalyse*. Stuttgart: Lucius & Lucius.

Pütz, M., 2004. *Regional Governance: Theoretisch-konzeptionelle Grundlagen und eine Analyse nachhaltiger Siedlungsentwicklung in der Metropolregion München*. München: oekom.

Rotter, M., *et al.*, 2013. *Stakeholder Participation in Adaptation to Climate Change: Lessons and experience from Germany* [online]. Dessau, DE: Umwelt-bundesamt. Available from: www.uba.de/uba-info-medien-e/4558.html [Accessed 1 October 2013].

Schuchardt, B., Wittig, S., and Spiekermann, J., 2011. *Klimawandel in der Metropolregion Bremen-Oldenburg. Regionale Analyse der Vulnerabilität ausgewählter Sektoren und Handlungsbereiche.* Retrieved from Nordwest2050 Database (11. Werkstattbericht 2011).

Swyngedouw, E., 2010. Apocalypse forever? Post-political populism and the spectre of climate change. *Theory, Culture and Society*, 27 (2–3), 213–32.

Weller, I., *et al.*, 2010. Untersuchung der Wahrnehmung des Klimawandels und seiner Folgen für Konsumverhalten und Vulnerabilität in der Nordwest-Region. Ergebnisse einer explorativen Studie. Retrieved from Nordwest2050 Database (6. Werkstattbericht 2010).

Winges, M., *et al.*, 2015. Die Anpassungskapazität der Regionalplanung in der Metropolregion Bremen-Oldenburg. *In:* J. Knieling and A. Roßnagel, eds, *Governance der Klimaanpassung. Akteure, Organisation und Instrumente für Stadt und Region*. München: oekom, 195–212.

Winter, T.v., and Willems, U., 2000. Die politische Repräsentation schwacher Interessen. Anmerkungen zum Stand und zu den Perspektiven der Forschung. T.v. Winter and U. Willems, eds, *Politische Repräsentation schwacher Interessen. Anmerkungen zum Stand und den Perspektiven der Forschung*. Wiesbaden, DE: VS Verlag für Sozialwissenschaften, 9–36.

12 Reconfiguring climate change adaptation policy

Indigenous peoples' strategies and policies for managing environmental transformations in Colombia[1]

Astrid Ulloa

Introduction

Conceptual discussions on the notion of 'adaptation' as a strategy to face climate transformations around the world have highlighted the wide range of interpretations about its meaning and scope. Debate on this concept is important given the far-reaching implications of 'adaptation' for public policy, and for plans and programmes institutionalised at the local level. On the one hand, both academic and political arenas (national and international) recognise the broad diversity of worldviews and practices around climate variability in specific contexts. On the other, given the lack of detailed cartographic information, and climatological and other types of data, the challenge to develop climate scenarios for specific and localised scales highlights the difficulty of generalising adaptation proposals for the particular cultural and geographic conditions of a given region. The political dimension to adaptation strategies is also important given the inequalities they create in terms of access and implementation at the local level. Thus, detailed analyses of the political and cultural dimensions of adaptation policies and dialogue with institutions become ever more necessary in order to generate adaptation strategies that take into account cultural and historical contexts.

This chapter addresses the need to incorporate cultural perspectives about weather and climate into global–national–local climate change policy. It starts with the premise that cultural perceptions of the causes of climate change as well as the local responses to it, are based on conceptions of the non-human. However, decisions around climate change policies do not consider cultural differences. Moreover, global–national policies and decisions around climate change have unequal implications in local contexts. Therefore, I argue that it is necessary to generate cultural strategies of climate 'adaptation' that fully account for the historical, cultural, and political contexts of specific places and territories. I also argue that national proposals that exclude cultural differences will not generate answers appropriate to local contexts. For these reasons, it is necessary to include the political and cultural dimensions of climate change in global–national–local climate change adaptation policy.

This analysis is based on research and fieldwork that I led with a team of indigenous and non-indigenous researchers. It was developed in urban, peasant, and indigenous contexts in Colombia, between 2008 and 2013. However, I focus on indigenous peoples' perspectives, which arose from collaborative research with indigenous researchers in their territories. Their perspectives are presented in the second part of this chapter in order to show their voices (based on ethnographic fieldwork, interviews, and representations) and the complexity of cultural perspectives and practices in relation to notions of weather and climate in specific settings.

The material presented in this chapter is divided into three parts. The first highlights discussions around the concept of adaptation, in order to highlight how this concept is political and cannot be used in the same way in different contexts (i.e. different regions or locations). The second part focuses on indigenous peoples' cultural perspectives and strategies related to the weather and climate change, in order to bring into discussion how historical context and in particular cultural dynamics do not fit with global perspectives of climate change policy. Finally, I offer some reflections on the relevance of including cultural perspectives on climate change within the realm of climate change policy: global–national–local.

Discussions around the concept of adaptation and its political dimensions

The definition of adaptation adopted by the Intergovernmental Panel on Climate Change (IPCC) is used in most texts or programmes on adaptation to climate change. For example, in Colombia, the National Plan for Adaptation (DNP 2012) assumes the global perspective and follows the IPCC definition such that it is defined as:

> those initiatives and measures aimed at reducing the vulnerability of natural and human systems to the actual or expected effects of climate change. There are different types of adaptation. For example: preventive and reactive, private and public, and autonomous and planned [adaptation].
>
> (DNP 2012: 63)

However, several actors see a need to define adaptation differently and, linked to this, are proposing an alternative approach in terms of its implementation in different contexts (Head 2010; Liverman 2015; Watts 2015).

Following Head (2010), the term adaptation may have various interpretations and implications, ranging from deterministic ideas (in which humans adapt to the environment in a functional way) to proposals that consider adaptation to be linked to cultural and environmental alterations and dynamics, while articulated to concepts of risk, vulnerability, and resilience. However, Head (2010) indicated that current discussions on adaptation to climate change have some emerging features: (1) the duality mitigation/adaptation has become institutionalised through the reproduction of short- and long-term binary categories; (2) adaptation is viewed as a deliberate and conscious process that requires specific policies; and (3) the need to focus not just on climate change but on an assemblage of various elements (scientific knowledge, political practices, means of communication, and ideas of fear). These features highlight the complexity of associations and interpretations around the concept of adaptation. As a result, Head (2010) saw a need to further complicate the concept of adaptation by highlighting the social and cultural dimensions related to the change in social practices through educational processes, while simultaneously taking a critical stance regarding use of the notion of adaptation itself. He also saw a need to take into account indigenous knowledge of climate and climate change as seen at a global level, focusing on day-to-day practices, while going beyond the idea that 'developing' countries are not well adapted to climate transformations – but also taking into account how developed countries become adapted to climate change, for instance, within households. Head (2010) also suggested a need to focus on cultural beliefs about climate change. In this way, it is possible to confront presumptions around adaptation, while analysing cultural constructions of risk and vulnerability, analysing the diversity of scales and times that involve the processes of adaptation, as well as including a non-anthropocentric view of this issue – one that involves other environmental, historical, and scalar aspects.

In a similar way, Liverman (2015) highlighted the need to analyse the human dimensions of climate change that consider not only nature but also human agency and economic, cultural, and political contexts. She asked that consideration be given to the economic linkage between adaptation programmes and their effects on local processes, and the interactions that occur on different scales.

Several researchers have analysed the political implications of IPCC-led mitigation/adaptation proposals (Watts 2015), and the implications they have for generating global policies that are implemented in national and regional contexts, without consideration for local-cultural perspectives and practices (Ulloa 2011a, 2017; Dietz 2013). Likewise, there is misrecognition of indigenous knowledge and their sense of place, given that knowledge, subjectivities, identities, and practices around nature and its specific changes occur in particular places. The notions of climate change and cultural responses are thought about in a different way within local and cultural contexts. In this sense, it is becoming increasingly necessary to analyse the political and cultural dimensions of climate change policy, giving consideration to indigenous perspectives, and thus generating culture-specific strategies to address current climate and environmental transformations.

Political and cultural dimensions are therefore necessary in order to rethink the strategies around adaptation from the institutional point of view.

The political dimension

As expressed by Dietz (2013), the political dimension has been little considered in discussions around adaptation strategies. However, the political dimension is highly relevant given that both individual and collective decision-making around environmental issues are fully embedded in political processes. As Eriksen and Lind (2009) argued: 'Adaptation is a political process. This is because the adjustments that people make to their livelihoods in the face of multiple shocks and changes have uneven outcomes. Individuals and groups interact and compete to promote their own discrete interests' (Eriksen and Lind 2009: 817).

While global policies on climate change have entailed actions centred on mitigation and adaptation proposals, with important political implications given in part to their origin in IPCC-led mitigation/adaptation proposals and their specific ways of generating knowledge about nature (Ulloa 2011a, 2011b; Dietz 2013), such policies have also garnered attention around indigenous participation in scenarios of transnationalisation and globalisation of nature, as well as the incorporation of green markets and environmental services (e.g. carbon sequestration, forestry projects, and Reducing Emissions from Deforestation and forest Degradation (REDD)), through commodification of the global climate. However, indigenous knowledge is not part of the global proposals on adaptation. In this context, indigenous relationships with non-humans are not included. This is because global policies are based on notions of a 'carbonised nature' and 'zero-carbon citizens' (Ulloa 2017). The first concept, carbonised nature, refers to the fragmentation of nature into smaller parts, while granting value to it on the basis of carbon markets. The second articulates a new subjectivity and identity associated with the idea of a zero-carbon citizen. That is, a de-territorialised, homogeneous, and gender- and ethnicity-free global citizen. On this basis, a zero-carbon citizen manipulates a carbonised nature through a new valuation of nature within global carbon markets (Ulloa 2017). And indigenous knowledge does not fit with these notions.

This requires a rethinking of discussions on climate change. In fact, power relations are a major element of the implementation of adaptation programmes. As Dietz (2013: 31) put it:

> Assuming that social relations of power structure society-nature relations in a constitutive manner, an approach to the concepts of vulnerability and adaptation that privileges the political has to focus on the

configuration of relations and political processes historically and currently determined by such relations between society and nature, as well as the political management of the climate. The term society-nature relationship emphasises all social practices including the institutional and organisational forms (formal and informal) through which societies regulate and transform their relationships with nature (Görg 1998, 2003, 2004). Capitalist relations between society and nature predominate today around the world, which does not mean that there are no other non-capitalist forms.

The cultural dimension

In addition to the political dimension, it is also necessary to consider cultural aspects, including non-capitalist practices and relations with nature, in order to account for other ways of producing knowledge. Discussions around climate have so far relied heavily on expert knowledge at the expense of local knowledge. Processes and politics connected to climate change transform and reconfigure indigenous peoples' territorial, cultural, identity, and relationships with non-humans, as well as economic dynamics. Thus, the conceptual, political, and territorial borders are undergoing constant change and affect the autonomy of indigenous peoples. For these reasons, indigenous peoples demand the recognition of their rights in the new context of territorial and environmental changes, and call for a cultural vision of climate justice, including humans and the non-humans, under their conceptions of ancestral law and justice.

For these reasons, indigenous peoples demand recognition of their own ways of thinking about climate and environmental change in the face of these new articulations. Indigenous ways of thinking and acting are based on concepts of the territory, non-humans as relatives, autonomy, environmental self-determination, as well as on their own life practices. In brief, indigenous populations demand the recognition of indigenous-based environmental, territorial, and cultural politics. Thus, it is necessary to analyse alternative knowledge, practices, perceptions, and representations associated with climate change in order to create proposals capable of reconfiguring current adaptation strategies.

Indigenous peoples' cultural perspectives and strategies related to the weather and climate change

Culturally speaking there are various ways of approaching the relationship between knowledge and climate. In brief, we can say that knowledge related to climate responds to the perspectives that each culture has of the human and the non-human, beings or entities that make up the non-human world, characteristics of entities, related places, associated practices, ways of knowing, and conceptions about the causes of environmental change.

Indigenous peoples consider territory/nature as a central component of any political proposal. In the current trend for the globalisation of nature, indigenous communities propose local control of nature. This includes a mode of control over indigenous territories following alternative notions and visions of nature, knowledge, and politics – for example, an indigenous territoriality that includes concepts and territorial scales both horizontally and vertically.

These processes involve local, territorially based politics that conceptualise the territory as a process of cultural and political relationality, where it is considered a living entity with agentive and social capacities in its own right (see also de Sousa Santos 2010; Escobar 2015). Such conceptions of territoriality arise from an idea of relational nature that supersedes the relationship with the territory and the soil, while involving other dimensions (spatial, physical, symbolic, and daily life). These perspectives of territoriality also consider notions of the fixed and the mobile (extensions, discontinuities, continuities) projected upon several scales (body–territory–nationality). Moreover, they establish a relationship between the body and the territory involving cultural dimensions of specific places, such as a sense of belonging, identity-making, and the experience of emotions. In other words, the making of the territory expresses local constructions of a geographical self (the imbrication of being, doing, feeling in/with the territory), as well as local decision-making, political organisation, and mobilisation associated with places and/or sites of symbolic, political, and cultural relevance. Furthermore, these local constructs of the geographic self include dimensions and relations of horizontal and vertical territoriality bringing about the territorial control of several aspects of life: spiritual, symbolic, material, cultural, environmental, and political. Thus, indigenous peoples propose a cultural and territorial politics based upon notions and practices of autonomy and territorial self-determination.

To develop these aspects, I will focus on the Colombian context, taking indigenous perspectives as a point of reference. However, because not all such aspects are homogeneously given in all cultures, I provide specific examples of different cultures in each of the following sections.

For Kogui, Arhuacos, Wiwa, and Kankuamo peoples of the Sierra Nevada de Santa Marta in Colombia, territorial autonomy and self-determination is the better way to face environmental transformations, including climate change. From this perspective, territory is seen and felt as an experience of the sacred in daily life, as an adherence to sacred laws, as an interaction with other beings who may be human or non-human, and as the management of the relations that are involved therein (Ulloa 2011c).

These dimensions of the political, the territorial, and the environmental also involve cultural notions of the non-human and environmental change from the point of view of local processes and situated knowledge practices – all of which give rise to the recognition of differential identities demanding autonomy and self-determination, as well as a new way of imbricating global, national, and local environmental policies, that is, climate change. These new dimensions express themselves in specific processes and relations with the non-human based on cultural views about humans and non-humans and the beings or entities that form part of their universe, and inhabit specific places. These relationships also imply ways of knowing these entities and transformations.

Cultural conceptions of the human and the non-human and their relationship with climate

Such a multiplicity of associations and perceptions of climate leads us to ask how the non-human world is conceived in each culture. There are certainly several theoretical approaches when it comes to the relationship between the human and the non-human (including, but not limited to, the environment, nature, and ecosystem). Thus, there are multiple cultural understandings regarding climate change.

For example, some indigenous cultures in Colombia focus on the very idea of variation in the weather, and interpret it as 'bad weather' (*mal tiempo*), 'change of weather' (*cambio del tiempo*), 'it is no longer as it used to be' (*ya no es como antes*), 'the weather is confused' (*el tiempo está confundido*), or they simply refer to an 'out of time' event or series of events (*destiempo*). Others highlighted specific transformations in the environment, such as the increase or decrease in river flow, the length of certain periods of time, and the increase or decrease in species considered as plagues. They also consider that the lack of regularity in rain cycles, frost events, and harvest periods, among others, are all cultural ways of knowing the alterations of climate change.

For indigenous people, there is a great diversity of conceptions. However, broadly speaking, they arise from the idea of reciprocity with the non-human world that considers all elements in the universe to be in relation with one another. For example, for Amazonian peoples:

> the climate manifests itself through relationships between tangible and intangible beings of the territory, for example, the divine, the human, and the natural. They are all mediated by the traditional norm (*la norma tradicional*) dictated by the creator and transmitted to the people by traditional leaders (the *yetarafue*) both through knowledge and life practices. Such relationship grants order to the territory from the innermost of the earth to the world of stars above. All this is made possible thanks to the tobacco, the coca, and the sweet cassava, as expressed both in ethnic and environmental calendars.
>
> (Henao and Farekatde 2013: 324)

These perspectives show how cultural views of climate change require a differentiated national and global policy that includes not only ideas but also strategies to deal with variability and environmental changes, or in other words cultural strategies of adaptation.

Beings or entities making up the non-human

Conceptions as to what the climate is or might become involve a multiplicity of beings or entities that compose it. Each culture offers different explanations about those beings that integrate different worlds, and especially those related to the climate. For instance, the Pasto people in Cumbal narrate how, in ancestral times, some humans became meteorological phenomena in their own right. In the *Tale of children who became wind, frost, summer and hail*, the Pastos narrate this transformation:

> The day came when the children no longer brought the food back home. The situation was complicated because the grandmother felt very sick, and she died a few days later. The children, liars and lazy, were punished by the spirits of Nature who then turned them into wind, frost, summer, and hail.
>
> (Puenayan 2013: 302)

In this perspective, adaptation must include not only human relation with nature, but also cultural conceptions of all non-human beings, because they are entities that play an important role in the whole interrelations with the weather and climate transformations. These perspectives therefore imply a change for adaptation programmes.

Features of non-human entities

Beings that inhabit the places that make up the universe have special characteristics and responsibilities depending on the place they occupy. For example, for the Kamëntsá Biyá people, who live in the Putumayo department, words such as sun, wind, rain, and thunder articulate not only graphic, sonic, and tactile representations associated with these concepts, but also power-laden notions with material effects in the world. Hence, these concepts generate concrete actions in the territories impacted by climate change. It is similar for the Amazonian peoples, for whom beings that can be related to weather such as sun, rain, or wind are entities that have their own place and act in some specific manners (Henao and Farekatde 2013).

Places related to climate

Each human and non-human being occupies a specific place where they establish different types of relationship and sense of belonging. For the Pasto people, for instance, climate–nature–humans and the territory are all related:

> In the territory, you find the natural being (the indigenous person) and the *chagras* (small plots), where there are mythical plants, plants of power, plants that allow for a harmonious relationship between the climate, the Mother Earth, and the natural beings. The territory and their natural components are all filled with ancestral wisdom; the mythical paths and places intertwine with the oral Word of the elder through the *mingas de pensamiento* (collective thinking), *mingas de trabajo* (collective work), and most especially, through storytelling around the family galley (*fogón*).
>
> (Puenayan 2013: 290)

That means that for indigenous peoples their territories are interrelated with all the beings and entities; for these reasons, any programme or plan of adaptation must involve consultation and must include their cultural perspectives.

The relationship between climate phenomena, natural beings, and places requires ritual practices as well as daily activities that foster reciprocity or change. These practices are related to knowledge and the ways in which indigenous people know the variability of seasons.

Ways to know the climate

Once relationships with climate-related entities become established, there are culturally legible ways to indicate their stability or change. These processes are linked to local indicators of climate change that allow the development of activities and practices consistent with what is happening in the surrounding environment. Such local indicators also provide helpful elements to act at different times. For example, the indigenous Pasto consider that each being is protected by spirits of nature. There is a spirit of water, which can communicate with humans in their dreams and ask for protection and care of water (Puenayan 2013).

Local worldviews, perceptions, and representations about the weather and climate are based on indigenous knowledge. This knowledge refers to the relationships between, on the one hand, meteorological factors and atmospheric and climatic conditions, and on the other, flora, fauna, and cultural aspects. In turn, such life relations reflect local knowledge systems that are based on experiences and perceptions about the climate and weather. In fact, local knowledge is related to specific places whereby relationships with the non-human allow for a cultural dialogue between memories of previous experiences, and everyday practices and processes. Within these approaches, local indicators of climate change are considered basic to understanding the relationship between climate and culture.

Types of local indicators of climate change

Knowledge about nature and climate is expressed through the management of indicators, that is, through the reading of signals present in the surrounding environment. Among others, these indicators vary in terms of size, colour, and changes over time.

Moreover, cultural knowledge around climate is based upon practices and experiences expressed through several cultural indicators, which are centred on some aspects of human and non-human beings in entangled relations. Therefore, I suggest to consider the following types of indicator: meteorological, biological, physical-geographical, corporal, cognitive, symbolic, sensorial, and the specific characteristics of different objects. These cultural indicators are not considered in global or national ways of knowing and registering climate change. For these reasons, I propose that it is important to include indigenous knowledge and cultural indicators in order to develop adaptation strategies based on situated knowledge, instead of general policies that do not correspond to specific environmental and cultural features.

Predictions of changes in climate

Local indicators enable the prediction of dry and rainy seasons, sowing cycles, and the selection of plants or animals for breeding purposes. Such events can be predicted through time categories: short term (i.e. days, such as swallows flying low announce rain), medium term (i.e. years, such as germination and the first fly of birds), or long term (i.e. generations, such as the position of the stars in the sky). Rudnev (1997) argued that local knowledge and observation practices concerning relationships between meteorological factors (observation of stars, constellations, flora, fauna, etc.), as well as climatic conditions and cultural aspects allow for observations around short- and long-term predictions. Some examples of short-term predictions are based on the observation of specific features at particular moments in time, for instance hygroscopic substances and atmospheric phenomena (rainbows), the behaviour of animals (small crabs in the water or near the sand announce a sunny day), the behaviour of plants (dandelions that do not open their flowers in the morning suggest rain), and bodily sensations (bone ache indicates rain). Similarly, long-term predictions can be based on the observation of periodic cycles of natural phenomena (high temperatures, storms), for instance if it rains at the beginning of the season this implies it will rain from then on. Furthermore, the relationship between calendars and indicators (the time between the end of winter, and the first spring tree, or the colour of birds' feathers) shows changes in climate variability (Rudnev 1997).

The direct outcome of reading indicators leads to the planning or change of sowing plots or hunting patterns. Indicators are directly related to predictions. Here, I highlight one of the most common prediction mechanisms – the *cabañuelas* – which involves analysing daily changes in the atmosphere throughout January to predict what will happen at particular times in the rest of the year.

All these ways of knowing are historically a better way to deal with climate variability in specific places, and in this way such knowledge claims a political space within global policy and within national programmes related to climate change. Indigenous practices and knowledge are based on cultural principles around five axes:

1. The relationships with the non-human as kin (relational natures) are essential because they allow understanding of the entangled human relationships with the non-human.
2. Horizontal and vertical territorial politics, in which conceptions of indigenous peoples of territory and their territorial politics are conceived as processes of cultural and political relations, in which the territory is a living being; a social actor, capable of agency.
3. Political autonomy and cultural governability are the centre of proposals. They comprise being and exercising power through territoriality, governability, and self-determination.
4. Relationships between men and women under other categories of gender in the processes of access, use, control, rights, and decision-making on territorial and environmental practices. They also consider that there are specific places related to gender according to cultural representations and classifications.
5. Life practices based on indigenous knowledge.

Final remarks: rethinking adaptation from a cultural standpoint

Considering the multiplicity of cultural understandings of climate change yields different responses to such change. Many of those responses are grounded in socio-cultural proposals that consider the relationship between humans, non-humans, and territories. These proposals also invite us to imagine ways of consolidating local environmental knowledge, but also to recognise indigenous ancestral practices, places of knowledge-making, situated ways of knowing, and, more broadly, life practices that include the non-human world.

Among the most common socio-cultural causes are changes in social relations, that is, when social practices change it also translates into a change in natural processes. Similarly, the loss of rituals associated with climate variation is considered to involve a rupture or imbalance, and thus also alterations in climate. Therefore, 'bad social behaviours' lead to an imbalance in the relationship between humans and non-humans. Nevertheless, some cultures consider that such alterations are a form of divine punishment – that a divine entity is angry given the rupture of social relations, or the lack of action to harmonise the communication between humans and these divine entities. Finally, there are explanations that are related to the increase in global population. Another axis of explanations involves the relationship with (i.e. respect for) nature, or even the lack of knowledge regarding traditional ways to interpret climate variations.

When thinking about the causes of climate change from different cultural points of view, we also learn about cultural responses including social and economic strategies. Several socio-cultural strategies include strengthening and consolidating local knowledge practices, the restoration of rituals and *rogativas* (prayers) that are related to weather and, more generally, collective practices related to a harmonious relationship with nature. Proposals also span from the recovery of local seeds and food, to traditional breeding and sowing practices; from agrarian practices that take advantage of thermal floors (*pisos térmicos*), to the enhancement of cultivation areas; from the generation of soils and 'trial plots', to the control and management of water sources, and irrigation systems. However, local responses also include the establishment of new economic strategies: traditional barter, silos and food reserves for future exchange, local trade circuits, and production without contamination. Such is the case for Pasto and Kamëntsa peoples and some local peasants near Bogota, who farm organically and who have networks of interchange with urban people.

Among cultural proposals, we have the systematising of indigenous relationships with the climate as well as the strategies they propose in the face of climate change. This analysis considered the following aspects:

1. worldviews and the relationship between the human and non-human – in particular, conceptions about weather and climate change and elements related to climate, for example the relationship that humans have about climate variability and cultural behaviours in order to prevent environmental change;
2. perceptions of changes in local climatic conditions;
3. local management strategies, and the articulation with regional, national, and global processes in relation to adaptation policies.

These examples demonstrate that, to be effective, national policy on climate change adaptation must include both the political and cultural dimensions. However, as it is clear that each culture has a particular understanding of what they consider to be the causes of climate change, and then act accordingly, the responses undertaken at the local level are not always consistent with those agreed at the national and international level. Thus, in developing climate change adaptation strategies, there is a need to articulate both the political dimension and cultural knowledge and strategies related to the direct experience of climate variability.

The first process is the political dimension of climate change and, thus, the issue of adaptation. On this Dietz (2013: 38) suggested:

> Vulnerability is a political phenomenon in the same way in which adaptation is a political process. The first refers to the political production of vulnerability through mechanisms of exclusion, the denegation of citizen's rights, and the lack of public channels and spaces where contradictions and antagonisms can be properly articulated. Both nationally and internationally, climate change politics is characterised by a high degree of depoliticisation of the crisis, and also by an apolitical interpretation of the causes and effects. Instead of political debates, what gains center stage is expert knowledge, the mediation of interests, and the management of change.

Under this dimension it becomes necessary to account for the historic and social processes of exclusion of indigenous knowledge in relation to environmental decision-making. Moreover, it is important to realise situated analysis of the causes and effects of climate variability in specific contexts where there are parallel economic agendas (such as mining and deforestation) with incidence in climate change. These causes and effects are disregarded in institutional adaptation proposals.

This leads us to the second process/dimension, namely culture. The aim here is to account for other ways of producing environmental knowledge in the case of indigenous peoples. Drawing on previous work (Ulloa 2011a, 2011b), it is clear that indigenous communities want to be recognised as political and cultural actors within global discussions concerning climate change – a fact that would allow for the emergence of new local proposals in relation to climate change. These proposals are mobilised from the culture and knowledge practices of social actors that claim more pluralistic and democratic rules of the game – including climate justice. From this vantage point, social movements comprising the local population – including their interrelation with their territory – are proposing forms of relation nature management that would allow for alternatives to dominant climate globalisation while challenging modern notions of control over nature (Ulloa 2011a: 489–90). All these processes imply reconfiguring climate change adaptation policy, as I have stated:

> With this rethinking must come a willingness to reimagine contemporary climate change discourse, to allow for the emergence of other knowledges – what Mignolo (2003) calls *pensamiento fronterizo* (border thinking) – based on alternative ecological conceptions and logics. A new, inclusive constellation of knowledges, temporalities, and recognitions is needed to confront and present alternatives to facing climate change, following de Sousa Santos (2006), in which indigenous knowledge is recognised and other nonhuman ontologies are included.
> (Ulloa 2017: 117)

The articulation of these two processes (political and cultural) suggests a new way of understanding adaptation, which requires both conceptual and practical rethinking and re-elaboration. Conceptually, mitigation and adaptation should be re-thought for the Colombian context (perhaps other contexts too), in order to create new concepts capable of integrating political and social complexities. However, at the level of action, it would be necessary to generate proposals at different scales – local, regional, and national – that include the practices and strategies already implemented locally. Clearly, generating cultural and political strategies to manage environmental and climate transformations will require starting from cultural (local) strategies of climate management and control.

The proposals of indigenous peoples are based on self-determination, autonomy, cultural, and political governability. These are also tied to particular knowledge and environmental management strategies and territorial control, as well as to as their own economic production. All this helps to position local knowledge and legitimise indigenous peoples as environmental authorities in collective territories. Thus, their demands and proposals are related to territories and localised knowledge concerning specific locations and historical process. These alternatives to adaptation are based on cultural principles around five axes: the positioning of other relationships with the non-human as kin (relational natures); horizontal and vertical territorial politics; relations between men and women under other categories of gender; life practices based on their knowledge; and environmental autonomy and self-determination.

In this way, indigenous peoples confront the approaches to climate change adaptation based on 'carbonised nature' and the 'zero-carbon citizen' in order to relocate territories as alive, relational natures, and humans and non-humans as political beings and as relatives, and to propose alternatives to face climate change based on local knowledge and cultural practices.

Note

1 Translation from Spanish by Ivan Vargas, Duke University.

References

de Sousa Santos, B., 2006. La sociología de las ausencias y la sociología de las emergencias: Para una ecología de saberes. *In*: B. de Sousa Santos, *Renovar la teoría crítica y reinventar la emancipación social (Encuentros en Buenos Aires)*. Buenos Aires: CLASCO, 13–41.
de Sousa Santos, B., 2010. *Descolonizar el saber, reinventar el poder*. Montevideo: Trilce.
Dietz, K., 2013. Hacia una teoría crítica de vulnerabilidad y adaptación: aportes para una reconceptualización desde la ecología política. *In*: A. Ulloa and A. Prieto-Rozo, eds, *Culturas, conocimientos, políticas y ciudadanías en torno al cambio climático*. Bogotá: Universidad Nacional de Colombia, 19–46.

DNP, 2012. *Plan nacional de Adaptación al Cambio Climático*. ABC: Adaptación bases conceptuales. Marco Conceptual y lineamientos. Bogotá: Departamento Nacional de Planeación (DNP).

Escobar, A., 2015. Territorios de diferencia: la ontología política de los 'derechos al territorio'. *Desenvolv Meio Ambiente*, 35, 89–100.

Eriksen, S., and Lind, J., 2009. Adaptation as a political process: Adjusting to drought and conflict in Kenya's drylands. *Environmental Management*, 43 (5), 817–35.

Görg, C., 1998. Die Regulation der biologischen Vielfalt und die Krise gesellschaftlicher Naturverhältnisse. *In*: M. Flitner, *et al.*, eds, *Konfliktfeld Natur. Biologische Ressourcen und globale Politik*. Opladen, DE: Leske + Budrich, 39–61.

Görg, C. 2003. Gesellschaftstheorie und Naturverhältnisse. Von den Grenzen der Regulationstheorie. *In*: U. Brand and W. Raza, eds, *Fit für den Postfordismus?* Münster, DE: Westfälisches Dampfboot, 175–94.

Görg, C., 2004. Postfordistische Transformation der Naturverhältnisse. *In*: J. Beerhorst, *et al.*, eds, *Kritische Theorie im gesellschaftlichen Strukturwandel*. Frankfurt am Main: Suhrkamp, 199–226.

Head, L., 2010. Cultural ecology: Adaptation – retrofitting a concept? *Progress in Human Geography*, 34 (2), 234–42.

Henao, C., and Farekatde, G., 2013. Concepción y control del clima entre los hijos del tabaco, la coca y la yuca dulce del resguardo Predio Putumayo, La Chorrera, (Amazonas, Colombia). *In*: A. Ulloa and A. Prieto-Rozo, eds, *Culturas, conocimientos, políticas y ciudadanías en torno al cambio climático*. Bogotá: Universidad Nacional de Colombia, 317–49.

Liverman, D., 2015. Reading climate change and climate governance as political ecologies. *In*: T. Perreault, G. Bridge, and J. McCarthy, eds, *The Routledge Handbook of Political Ecology*. London: Routledge, 303–19.

Mignolo, W., 2003. *Historias locales/diseños globales: Colonialidad, conocimientos subalternos y pensamiento fronterizo*. Madrid: Ediciones Akal.

Puenayan, Z., 2013. Mingambis: minga de percepciones y concepciones propias de los indígenas pastos, sobre tiempo y clima, resguardo Panan, Cumbal (Nariño, Colombia). *In*: A. Ulloa and A. Prieto-Rozo, eds, *Culturas, conocimientos, políticas y ciudadanías en torno al cambio climático*. Bogotá: Universidad Nacional de Colombia, 273–316.

Rudnev, V., 1997. Ethno-meteorology: A modern view about folk signs. *In*: M. Goloubinoi, E. Katz, and L. Annamaria, eds, *Antropología del clima en el mundo hispanoAmericano*. Quito: Abya-Yala, 27–47.

Ulloa, A., 2011a. Políticas globales del cambio climático: nuevas geopolíticas del conocimiento y sus efectos en territorios indígenas. *In*: A. Ulloa, ed., *Perspectivas culturales del clima*. Bogotá: Universidad Nacional de Colombia-ILSA, 477–93.

Ulloa, A., 2011b. Autonomie indigène et politiques globales du changement climatique: repenser la relation avec la nature dans la Sierra Nevada de Santa Marta, Colombie. *In*: C. Gros and D. Dumoulin Kervran, eds, *Le multiculturalisme 'au concret': Un modèle latino-américain?* Paris: Presses Sorbonne Nouvelle, 361–75.

Ulloa, A., 2011c. The politics of autonomy of indigenous peoples of the Sierra Nevada de Santa Marta, Colombia: A process of relational indigenous autonomy. *LACES*, 6 (1), 79–107.

Ulloa, A. 2017. Geopolitics of carbonized nature and the zero carbon citizen. *South Atlantic Quarterly*, 116 (1), 111–20.

Watts, M., 2015. Now and then: The origins of political ecology and the rebirth of adaptation as a form of thought. *In*: T. Perreault, G. Bridge, and J. McCarthy, eds, *The Routledge Handbook of Political Ecology*. London: Routledge, 19–50.

Part V

Beyond critical adaptation research

Innovative understandings of climate change adaptation

13 Atlases of community change

Community collaborative–interactive projects in Russia and Canada

Susan A. Crate

Introduction

In the research context of local adaptation to climate change, one methodological approach – ethnography – has played a central role (Crate 2011; Marino 2015). Using ethnographic methods, anthropologists have documented the diversity of ways of knowing that communities and individuals use to perceive, understand, and respond to unprecedented change (Crate and Nuttall 2009, 2016). These same investigations have also clarified that for many communities, although scientists can project that climate change is clearly occurring and challenging their daily survival, it is often not their most immediate concern. Local issues due to the effects of economic globalisation and the demographic shift that draws their youth out of rural regions and to the urban centres appear to consume more of their adaptive attention – issues such as how to adjust household production to keep up with the vagaries of the changing market; how to afford basic necessities when prices fluctuate daily; how to plan for labour needs when their main workforce, their youth, are drawn to urban areas to join their peers (Crate 2014). Not that these more immediate effects diminish the effects of climate change, but rather that it is important for anthropological investigations to recognise, identify, and integrate them into their analysis of climate change research. And, it is perhaps more critical for researchers to facilitate understanding within affected communities about how various drivers of change are bringing about environmental, sociocultural, economic, and other change. Lastly, once that understanding exists, it is critical to facilitate ways and means towards community-based monitoring, assessment, and action.

To these ends, this chapter discusses a research effort to do just that: a community collaborative effort to develop intranet (within the communities) atlases of community change in order to empower local communities to monitor that change, including unprecedented local change due to climate perturbations, and move forward with appropriate responses. I begin with an introduction to the larger research field and our specific case studies. I then explain the atlas collaborative process by discussing the commonalities and differences in facilitating the projects in two different Arctic contexts: a post-Soviet Viliui Sakha community of northeastern Russia, and a coastal community of Nunatisavut, Labrador, Canada. The chapter explores important questions:

1. How can sharing local knowledge (observations, memories, ideas, thoughts, recollections, archival documents of a qualitative nature) and scientific knowledge (past and present instrumental readings, proxy data, and archival documents of a quantitative nature) foster knowledge about those changes within local community contexts?
2. How can social scientists and community members, bringing ecological, socio-cultural, and economic information into a preliminary theoretical frame, empower communities with integrated, comprehensive knowledge of change?
3. Does this, in turn, affect community perceptions, understandings, and responses?
4. Finally, can the facilitation of such atlas projects for community self-monitoring of change, in all its forms, work to improve local adaptations to climate change?

The larger research context

Rural communities represent *complex adaptive systems*, a dynamic interplay of 'biophysical systems' (e.g. mechanisms of change and communication) and compatible key features of social systems: the holistic nature of culture, knowledge-sharing through the senses, and the formative power of traditions, structures/materials, strategies, and 'habits of mind' (Crumley 2012).

Diversity is a generative feature of complex adaptive systems (Gregory 2006). Through the continued use of local plant, animal, and natural resources, rural community inhabitants manage and steward biological diversity. In addition, by maintaining a diversity of languages and dialects, basing use and management of local resources on situated local knowledge, utilising a variety of effective and robust institutional arrangements for community-based resource management (Ostrom 1990, 2009), and practising historically founded and place-based cultural and spiritual practices, rural community inhabitants support biocultural diversity (Maffi and Woodley 2010). In this way, many researchers argue that rural areas are 'biocultural refugia' that safeguard not only biodiversity towards global food security but also the culture-specific practices that maintain that biodiversity (Barthel *et al.* 2013).

The Arctic represents one world region where these rural community characteristics are readily apparent and where the complexity of change is clear: '[f]or the Arctic, social, political and economic drivers of change may be of equal or greater importance, bringing about thresholds whether or not there are changes in the climate' (Arctic Council 2013: 56). Rural Arctic communities continue, to a greater or lesser extent, to rely on community/extended kin networks of interdependence, labour and resource reciprocation, and on informal economies and barter. While all societies are vulnerable to significant perturbations in the equilibrium of their socio-ecological systems (Smith and Wishnie 2000), rural Arctic inhabitants have long utilised biocultural diversity to ensure their adaptability and resilience to a changing world (Berkes *et al.* 2007; Sveiby 2011). However, the larger mix of changes present in contemporary rural Arctic communities increasingly threatens diversity and necessitates approaches that have the analytical power to discern between root causes. The local and regional effects of climate change result in a 'cascade' of other ecological change within the ecosystem. Once identified, the cascading ecosystem effects need to be considered within the context of other change, not climate related. For example, O'Brien and Leichenko (2000) demonstrated how the synergisms between two global processes, climate change and globalisation, need to be reconsidered. They named this synergism 'double exposure', and showed how their joint impact in analysis created different results than each taken alone. Other researchers term the host of impacts 'multiple-stressors' in determining the vulnerability of Arctic peoples and ecosystems to potentially harmful impacts (McCarthy and Martello 2005). Interdisciplinary climate science often engages ecologists, climatologists, modellers, and social scientists to discern multi-stressors (Stenseth *et al.* 2002). Using the frameworks of adaptation and resilience, interdisciplinary groups working in the Arctic have emphasised the need to investigate this larger mix, from the Arctic Climate Impact Assessment, which argued that understanding the impact of climate change could only be accomplished 'by considering an ensemble of relevant, concurrent changes in the system' (McCarthy and Martello 2005), to the Arctic Resilience Interim Report, which states, 'The need for "integrative concepts and models" that can aid systemic understanding of the Arctic, including the cumulative impacts of a diverse suite of interconnected changes, is critical in the current period of rapid ecological, social, and economic change' (Arctic Council 2013: 4).

Attempts to account for the complexity of change using modelling (Pielke *et al.* 2012) often fall short at integrating human aspects, even though 'development and testing of interactive models that can simulate the evolving nature of interactions among social and environmental states is a major research priority' (Dearing *et al.* 2010). One critical step is to take an inter-epistemological approach, contemplating the 'upstream' questions related to understanding the foundations of the knowledge system(s) being considered and focusing on *how* things are known rather than *what* is known (Murphy 2011: 492). This, along with other approaches to bringing in human parameters, are key components of the holistic approach needed to bring climate science and other socio-ecological analyses to full realisation.

Efforts to integrate a 'human dimension' in climate science remain lacking (Houghton *et al.* 2001; IPCC 2007; Field *et al.* 2012; AHDR 2004; ACIA 2005; Krupnik *et al.* 2005; Hovelsrud *et al.* 2011). There is a need for a systematic understanding via social science methods because 'studies of the functioning of social systems generally take more diverse perspectives, recognize the contingency of social change, and seek to respect and reflect the specificity of local concerns' (Arctic Council 2013: 56). What is needed is a holistic approach, an appreciation and accommodation for how indigenous/local knowledge is synthetic and holistic (Agrawal 1995, 2002; Sillitoe 1998; Cajete 1999; Berkes 2008; Aporta 2010).

Arctic research is one arena that increasingly uses such a holistic and human-inclusive approach to understanding change by downscaling to the community level and engaging communities in the documentation and monitoring process (Berkes *et al.* 2007; Pearce *et al.* 2009). The last decade has seen a significant increase in community engagement in and ownership of communicating local change (Hovelsrud *et al.* 2011). Such efforts in Arctic climate change research began with community-based research discerning how the global phenomenon of climate change was affecting long-standing human adaptive strategies (Krupnik and Jolly 2002). These types of investigations led increasingly towards efforts to substantiate local knowledge, to corroborate it with scientific data, and to integrate the two knowledge systems towards new knowledge (Danielsen *et al.* 2009; Crate and Fedorov 2013a) and also to build community capacity towards these ends (Krupnik *et al.* 2010; Gearheard *et al.* 2011).

One major hurdle to holistic approaches that comprehensively integrate qualitative and quantitative data and that are scaled down to the local level where effects on humans and ecosystems are occurring (Arctic Council 2013: 4) is that both require significant time and resources. Qualitative approaches require in-depth and often multiple local studies, fulfilment of proper ethical considerations, additional time to gain entry, learning local protocols, accommodation of community expectations, and sensitivity to political alliances, among others (Heikkilä and Fondahl 2012: 62). Despite these constraints, there are multiple levels of society that benefit when researchers use such a holistic approach. Most obvious are the immediate benefits to the affected communities and the researchers collaborating with them. Less obvious are the latent benefits as such approaches work to transform ways of thinking among the larger group of stakeholders associated with the project and, eventually, to 'the dominant society that suffers a shortage of wisdom' (Herman 2008: 77).

Adolescents and youth are poised to play a pivotal role in rural contexts, despite finding themselves at the centre of major transformations, observed indistinctively throughout the world, including depopulation, deagrarisation, and loss of the previous generations' knowledge (Bryceson 1996; Steward 2007; Virtanen 2012). Concomitantly, the older generations' limited acceptance of youth's abilities and interests leads to high unemployment and an overall lack of future perspectives within rural communities (Hamilton and Seyfrit 1993; Garcia and Gonzalez 2004; Lundholm and Malmberg 2006; Rasmussen 2009). The severity of this situation is further exacerbated by youth's lack of skills and qualifications and the lack of adequate educational resources to respond to new demands in rural areas (Rasmussen *et al.* 2010; Carson *et al.* 2011; Virtanen 2012). Promoting opportunities for the upcoming generations to actively participate in their culture and livelihood while at the same time guaranteeing access to high-quality educational and training opportunities and also strengthening research are key to the development of rural area human resources (NORDBUK 2006). Although youth out-migration from rural areas is highly variable, the global trend is an overall decrease of youth populations (Stockdale 2006; Argent and Walmsley 2008; McGranahan *et al.* 2010). The phenomenon is highly variable: in some areas it is one-way (rural to urban) and others show patterns of rural–urban circulation (Hansen *et al.* 2012). There are also wide divergences in local, regional, and state efforts to retain youth, with a tendency for more-developed countries to have retention programmes and less developed countries to not (Glendinning *et al.* 2003; Wyn and Harris 2004). Because youth play a pivotal role in shaping the future of rural communities, understanding and enacting rural youth's values, aspirations, and future perspectives towards addressing the short- and long-term effects of change is key to the global transformation to sustainability.

The project context

In the process of tracking the local effects of climate/seasonal change in the project, *Climate-Driven Phenological Change: Observations, Adaptations and Cultural Implications in Northeastern Siberia and Labrador/Nunatsiavut* (PHENARC),[1] and also with communities in several other rural sites where Principal Investigator Crate had the opportunity to collaborate and consult (including Kiribati, Peru, Wales, Chesapeake Bay), local changes – including socio-cultural, economic, demographic, historical, and geopolitical changes – were more immediate and urgent to the affected communities than changes in climate and seasonality (Crate 2014, 2015). Indeed, although climate and phenological change are clearly affecting these contexts, most noted by the absence of important resources for major parts of the year and the 'wrong timings' of the seasons, communities perceive the other drivers of change to have a more immediate and urgent impact on daily life. One needs only to consider the quantum changes that many of the local residents have seen in their lifetimes to appreciate this:

> I have seen a lot of change – when I came here first – no TV, we had dances – had our own band with Gary Mitchell – he was the band leader – played every weekend and the dance floor was always full –

no running water till '79 – got it from a well – had to haul it or go to the brook – had a rink here and they flooded it with barrels of water from the brook – then came phone – radio telephone for long distance – quite a few changes....

(Makkovik resident 2011)

Their main concerns, above and beyond the effect of climate, were the effects of economic globalisation, which interacts with the local subsistence economy to generate imbalances and defer economic stability; and the out-migration of youth to regional and urban centres for education and employment, most of whom do not return to their communities, impeding the generational rural process.

Furthermore, similar to how ice dependence was generalisable across Arctic communities (Crate 2012), these changes have broad similarities, but the socio-cultural responses – the way the communities perceive, interpret, and respond – is highly variable, and much of that variation is due to geopolitical, ethno-historical, socio-cultural, economic, and other relevant differences. In other words, climate and its accompanying phenological change acts as one of several main drivers of change affecting and interacting with local communities.

Comparison of these contrasting contexts works to illuminate the drivers specific to local change and their effects. It can also show the bio-cultural particularities that shape how communities perceive, understand, and respond, which, in turn, shows how knowledge exchanges can be used to engage all relevant stakeholders, the best 'tools' to promote communication and information exchange, and the ways cross-generational interaction can proceed.

The PHENARC project worked in two contrasting Arctic contexts. One is in northeastern Siberia, in former state farm villages of post-Soviet Russia with Viliui Sakha, horse and cattle-breeding agro-pastoralists. I have conducted research in the Viliui regions of the Sakha Republic, located in northeastern Siberia, Russia, since 1991. Viliui Sakha are a Turkic-speaking people whose ancestors migrated from central Asia to southern Siberia around 900, then migrated northward, along the Lena River, to their present homeland, beginning in the 1200s. This is an Arctic/sub-Arctic region, characterised by continuous permafrost and average winter temperatures of –50°C. Viliui Sakha represent an exemplary case of adaptation, adapting to an extreme climate, Russian colonisation, the last 100 years of Sovietisation, and contemporary post-Soviet decentralisation (Crate 2002, 2006a, 2006b). The latest challenge, and perhaps the most difficult for local communities to perceive ways to adapt to, is climate change.

The other field site was in the Nunatsiavut territorial government area of Labrador, Canada, with most inhabitants either Inuit, Kablunângajuit (Metis), or settlers of European descent. Historically inhabitants are involved in coastal activities, including marine mammal harvest, fishing, trapping, and hunting. These settlements boomed during the abundant cod fishery period then experienced economic distress before transitioning to commercial salmon, char, and snow crabbing. After the 1991 moratorium on salmon catch, most residents continue fishing commercial char and snow crab, although with an increasingly disinterested youth, there has been a declining frequency in fishing of late. Voisey's Bay, one of the richest nickel–copper–cobalt finds in the world, is also a source of employment. Local economies are also depending increasingly on a growing tourism trade, attracting tourists with the quality and purity of its natural landscapes. A recent plan for economic development, the mining of uranium deposits, will work against that objective and is presently a strongly debated issue in the communities.

One of the key challenges of retaining the next generation and reversing the trends of young people's out-migration is countering the external forces – including economic globalisation and the impacts of consumer culture – that work to disrupt local economies and increase unemployment, setting youth sights away from home prospects. Internal forces are also at work. Most prominent is the failing of knowledge transmission from elders to youth because knowledge is not being transmitted in pace with social change in rural areas. This is further complicated by the fact that knowledge has moved from being local and activities-based to being global and virtually based.

Considering these issues and having worked in both locations on the issues of climate and other changes, I decided towards the end of the PHENARC project to hire ELOKA (Exchange of Local Observations and Knowledge in the Arctic), which is a project housed in the University of Colorado that is a network and a service that facilitates the collection, preservation, exchange, and use of local observations and knowledge of the Arctic. I had known of their work in other Arctic contexts and requested them to develop two pilot atlas interfaces that the communities could use to continue to monitor change long after the PHENARC project ended. The atlas projects described here worked to address these issues and forefronted the place of youth with questions such as: how can knowledge systems be best integrated? What (and where) are the disconnects between youth and elders' contrasting ways of knowing, understanding, and communicating, and their varied understandings of the usefulness of knowledge?

The projects worked with a variety of tools to share and integrate knowledge (such as booklets, SMS messaging, web-based interfaces) within and between the communities and their relevant stakeholders. Like the variation found across the two Arctic contexts, the combination of such tools also varied and was a factor in each community's integration and representation of relevant knowledge systems that bolster agency. Furthermore, the array of potential tools must first be introduced in each community then integrated so that communities can facilitate and use them independently of outside input and resources beyond the project.

I collaborated with Alexander Fedorov, permafrost scientist with the Melnikov Institute in Yakutsk, in summer 2010 to develop a knowledge exchange methodology in Sakha communities that engaged affected communities with regional scientists to be able to integrate knowledge systems (Crate and Fedorov 2013a). In order to share the knowledge more widely following the eight exchanges that summer, we engaged a multi-year community collaborative writing process to develop a booklet that was later distributed throughout the regions via the participation of the Sakha Ministry of Ecology (Crate and Fedorov 2013b). The atlas projects described here were the next step to further the knowledge exchange process.

This section explores the two prototype online atlases, developed as part of PHENARC. It is important to understand that I had significant support from the ELOKA team, who trained me in the process of developing the interactive atlas with each community. In the Viliui Sakha context, I chose to work with the community of Kutana (population 975), based on the enthusiasm of several village teachers during the 2010 knowledge exchange process (Crate and Fedorov 2013a) and also our follow-up work with the school to develop a permafrost observation station for students to monitor, under the guidance of Alexander Fedorov. I also knew I needed a computer specialist and that there was a technology staff member in the school who was extremely interested in the atlas project. In summer 2012, I facilitated a hands-on workshop in the school's computer lab with ten students, three teachers and the computer specialist. I chose to work with students who were in the seventh to twelfth grades (aged 12–18) because they would have enough computer skills to potentially take leadership. I began by sharing the Google Earth map of the Kutana village on the projected screen and describing how the interactive atlas process worked. I explained that they could choose various layers of knowledge to bring into the interface, depending on what they as a community were interested in monitoring and having access to. To get them engaged, I created a sample layer and asked each student to come and put a point in the layer where their home was. Then I showed how they could bring a picture in by finding a few of them who had pictures on their phone that we could easily bring into the interface. I explained that in addition to pictures, they could bring in audio, video, and other documents to a specific point.

Once they had each had a turn to put their house into the layer, we moved to brainstorming what layers they wanted. I was trained beforehand by ELOKA to introduce the community to the interface without suggesting exactly what they should do in terms of deciding on the layers. It took some time to get ideas flowing, but finally they did. The first idea was to make a layer for the permafrost monitoring, which another student supplemented by suggesting that they could also bring in other environmental observations to this layer. For example, they knew that many community elders recorded daily temperatures, which could be put into that layer. One of the teachers then commented on how their local museum had all kinds of materials that could be brought into a layer. This began a discussion of creating a layer focused on cultural heritage, including locating toponyms and sacred sites on the landscape adjacent to the village. This quickly moved to discussion of a third layer that would show settlement patterns over time. Kutana, like other contemporary post-Soviet villages, was established as a compact village based on the collective processes in the twentieth century. Prior to that, inhabitants lived dispersed across the landscape in order to take best advantage of the sparse resources of the sub-Arctic environment. However, most older inhabitants, to this day, know their ancestral homeplace and return to feed the spirits annually. In an effort to document this settlement change, the group wanted to create a layer of those patterns with a historical timeline so that whoever was using the atlas could move the timeline and see how settlement patterns had changed over time. The Kutana community gravitated towards representing Alaas, an ecosystem complex historically used for subsistence in pre-Soviet times. A Sakha-specific atlas was developed based on the fields defined by the community.

In the Labrador/Nunatsiavut field site, I worked with the community of Makkovik (population 380). I followed a similar process to introduce the interactive atlas project to a group of students, one teacher and the school's computer specialist. Once most participating students had brought a point to represent their home into the sample layer and some pictures to show how photos and other materials could be brought in, we opened to discussion of what layers they wanted. Like in Kutana, Makkovik has a very rich village museum that also works with the school to teach about local heritage and to work with students on cultural heritage projects. As a result, students quickly volunteered the idea to make a layer showing how their ancestors did subsistence prior to the amalgamation of the community for the cod fishing industry. They also said it would be good to make a layer that showed how their water would be affected by the proposed uranium mining project. Lastly, they wanted to have a layer where they could monitor changes in the land due to climate perturbations. In Makkovik, I also met with the village head, the director of the museum, and the computer specialist to understand how they could associate each fishing stage with audio and video interviews, images and performances to capture information about their heritage/culture, including information about people, important events, and artefacts both from the local museum and found locally. In both contexts, the community nominated a local school teacher to facilitate and demonstrate for community use, especially students. Both demonstration atlases remain available today and both communities have expressed a strong interest in developing them further.

Discussion

There exist critiques of using technology for cultural heritage and other ways of preserving and perpetuating local culture, mainly identifying it as breaking the oral tradition or other 'in situ' mechanisms, or the risk of situating indigenous knowledge within a framework driven by the dominant culture (Leclair and Warren 2007). *However*, many researchers and practitioners argue for the use of information and communications technology (ICT) by indigenous people who share common knowledge and resources as a means to increase the capacity and capability of the community, either via an active presence on the internet or social media or through e-commerce and e-learning (Leclair and Warren 2007). The argument for use of these emerging digital technologies recognises the tradition of technology adoption and adaptation by indigenous communities. Thus, the use of ICT becomes part of contemporary indigeneity. In the Arctic, Aporta and Higgs (2005) argued that the Inuit have, since time immemorial, used new technologies, from adopting the rifle to the snowmobile and, more recently, global positioning system (GPS) technology. They argued that the Inuit's recent use of GPS within traditional Inuit wayfinding represents a consistent system of socio-technological relationship with the world based in knowing the land. Therefore, it is how the adoption of technology is integrated into practice and culture so that the complexity and multidimensionality of relationships between individuals and the communities they exist in are maintained and even enhanced (Orlove 2005). For example, residents of Clyde River, Nunavut, Canada, worked with engineers and cartographers to develop customised GPS weather station technology with an Inuktitut interface, allowing hunters to document their observations and contribute to research of interest to them through active use of their environment (Gearheard *et al.* 2011).

Whether ICT empowers individuals and communities in maintaining and strengthening culture, improving economic well-being, and passing knowledge from elders to youth, or acts as another mechanism of assimilation, diluting individual and collective senses of indigeneity, depends on the extent to which it is appropriated. Meanwhile, an increasing number of projects are utilising technology to these ends because it is the mode that affected communities are using. For example, the Sea Ice for Walrus Outlook project has adopted Facebook as a primary interface between indigenous communities and other project participants (e.g. sea ice scientists; Lovecraft *et al.* 2012). If we consider technological change from a youth perspective, cultures are always evolving and young people tend to use the technology of their time (Rasmussen 2008). In Makkovik, one of this project's research communities, the social media tool Facebook is the main way that the youth communicate with each other and know what is going on from one day to the next. Additionally, research shows that technology can work to bridge across generations (Crate 2006c), and in the last decade that youth are computer savvy and knowledge savvy (Herman 2008). Considering the issues of ICT and indigenous groups, it is critical that initiatives follow the direction of the communities with respect to how they want to adopt (or not) new technology, maintain language and culture, and document their lives, using a variety of theoretical and methodological techniques.

Conclusion

I argue in this chapter that anthropology plays a central role in facilitating community-based adaptation to unprecedented change, most notably, the local effects of climate change. These community-based and community-monitored and maintained responses are critical tools for effective adaptation to climate change. In the community context, inhabitants share a local knowledge of place and all its cultural, biophysical, political, and historical intricacies. By working in a community collaborative partnership to develop intranet (within the communities) atlases of community change, inhabitants can monitor change, develop plans of action, and move forward with appropriate responses. Furthermore, the atlas technology was designed in a way that community members can directly add content and control access to content. The pilot atlas technology initiated during PHENARC established a system that has the potential to facilitate communication and linkages within and across the communities, integrating aspects of the complexity of change, and also to effectively store, manage, and disseminate the various pieces of related data in a way that meets the needs communicated by the respective communities. In these initial pilots, it was also clear that the atlases gave communities a relevant way to monitor how their local environment was changing because of global climate change. The processes presented many challenges; however, significant progress was made and the prototypes developed drove sufficient community interest to warrant further development.

Note

1 National Science Foundation (NSF), Office of Polar Programs (OPP) grant #0902146 Understanding Climate-Driven Phenological Change: Observations, Adaptations and Cultural Implications in Northeastern Siberia and Labrador/ Nunatsiavut (PHENARC). PI: Susan Crate $640,000, 1 September 2009 – 31 August 2013.

References

ACIA, 2005. *Arctic Climate Impact Assessment*. Cambridge: Cambridge University Press.

Agrawal, A., 1995. Indigenous and scientific knowledge: Some critical comments. *Development and Change*, 3 (3), 7–8.

Agrawal, A., 2002. Indigenous knowledge and the politics of classification. *International Social Science Journal*, 54 (173), 287–97.

AHDR, 2004. *Arctic Human Development Report*. Akureyri, IS: Stefansson Arctic Institute.

Aporta, C., 2010. The sea, the land, the coast and the winds: Understanding Inuit sea ice use in context. *In*: I. Krupnik, *et al.*, eds, *Siku: Knowing our ice: documenting Inuit sea ice knowledge and use*. Dodrecht, NL: Springer, 165–82.

Aporta, C., and Higgs, E., 2005. Satellite culture: Global positioning systems, Inuit wayfinding, and the need for a new account of technology. *Current Anthropology*, 46 (5), 729–53.

Arctic Council, 2013. *Arctic Resilience Interim Report 2013*. Stockholm: Stockholm Environment Institute and Stockholm Resilience Centre.

Argent, N., and Walmsley, J., 2008. Rural youth migration trends in Australia: An overview of recent trends and two inland case studies. *Geographical Research*, 46 (2), 139–52.

Barthel, S., Crumley, C., and Svedin, U., 2013. Bio-cultural refugia: Safeguarding diversity of practices for food security and biodiversity. *Global Environmental Change*, 23 (5), 1142–52.

Berkes, F., 2008. *Sacred Ecology*. 2nd edition. New York: Taylor & Francis.

Berkes, F., Berkes, M., and Fast, H., 2007. Collaborative integrated management in Canada's North: The role of local and traditional knowledge and community-based monitoring. *Coastal Management*, 35 (1), 143–62.

Bryceson, D., 1996. Deagrarization and rural employment in sub-Saharan Africa: A sectoral perspective. *World Development*, 24 (1), 97–111.

Cajete, G., 1999. *Native Science: Natural laws of interdependence*. Santa Fe, NM: Clear Light Publishers.

Carson, D., *et al.*, 2011. *Demography at the Edge: Remote human populations in developed nations*. Farnham: Ashgate.

Crate, S., 2002. Viliui Sakha oral history: The key to contemporary household survival. *Arctic Anthropology*, 39 (1), 134–54.

Crate, S., 2006a. *Cows, Kin and Globalization: An ethnography of sustainability*. Lanham, MD: Alta Mira/Rowan and Littlefield Press.

Crate, S., 2006b. Investigating local definitions of sustainability in the Arctic: Insights from post-soviet Sakha Villages. *Arctic*, 59 (3), 294–310.

Crate, S., 2006c. Elder knowledge and sustainable livelihoods in Post-Soviet Russia: Finding dialogue across the generations. *Arctic Anthropology*, 43 (1), 40–51.

Crate, S., 2011. Climate and culture: Anthropology in the era of contemporary climate change. *Annual Review of Anthropology*, 40 (1), 175–94.

Crate, S., 2012. Climate change and ice dependent communities: Perspectives from Siberia and Labrador. *Polar Journal*, 2, 61–75.

Crate, S., 2014. An ethnography of change in northeastern Siberia: Whither an interdisciplinary role? *Sibirica*, 13 (1), 30–74.

Crate, S., 2015. Towards imagining the big picture and the finer details: Exploring global applications of a local and scientific knowledge exchange methodology. *In*: J. Tischler and H. Greschke, eds, *Grounding Global Climate Change: Contributions from the social and cultural sciences*. Berlin: Spring-Verlag.

Crate, S., and Fedorov, A., 2013a. A methodological model for exchanging local and scientific climate change knowledge in northeastern Siberia. *Arctic*, 66 (3), 338–50.

Crate, S., and Fedorov, A., 2013b. *Alamai tiin: Buluu ulustarigar klimat ularitigar uonna atin kihalghar* (Alamai tiin: Climate change and other change in the Viliui regions). Yakutsk, RU: Bichik.

Crate, S., and Nuttall, M., eds., 2009. *Anthropology and Climate Change: From encounters to actions.* Walnut Creek, CA: Left Coast Press.

Crate, S., and Nuttall, M., eds., 2016. *Anthropology and Climate Change: From actions to transformations.* New York: Routledge Press.

Crumley, C., 2012. A heterarchy of knowledges: Tools for the study of landscape histories and futures. *In*: T. Plieninger and C. Bieling, eds, *Resilience and the Cultural Landscape: Understanding and managing change in human-shaped environments.* Cambridge: Cambridge University Press, 303–14.

Danielsen, F., *et al.*, 2009. Local participation in natural resource monitoring: A characterization of approaches. *Conservation Biology*, 23 (1), 31–42.

Dearing, J.A., *et al.*, 2010. Complex land systems: The need for long time perspectives to assess their future. *Ecology and Society*, 15 (4), 21.

Field, C.B., *et al.*, eds, 2012. Managing the risks of extreme events and disasters to advance climate change adaptation. *In*: IPCC, *Climate Change 2012: A special report of Working Groups I and II of the Intergovernmental Panel on Climate Change.* Cambridge: Cambridge University Press.

Garcia, J., and Gonzalez, M., 2004. Rural development, population ageing and gender in Spain: The case of rural women in the autonomous community of Castilla y Leon. 44th European Congress of the European Regional Science Association: 'Regions and Fiscal Federalism', Porto, 25–29 August.

Gearheard, S., *et al.*, 2011. The Igliniit project: Inuit hunters document life on the trail to map and monitor Arctic change. *Canadian Geographer/Le Géographe Canadien*, 55 (1), 42–55.

Glendinning, A., *et al.*, 2003. Rural communities and well-being: A good place to grow up? *Sociological Review*, 51 (1), 129–56.

Gregory, T.A., 2006. An evolutionary theory of diversity: The contributions of grounded theory and grounded action reconceptualizing and reframing diversity as a complex phenomenon. *World Futures*, 62 (7), 542–50.

Hamilton, L.C., and Seyfrit, C.L., 1993. Town-village contrasts in Arctic youth aspirations. *Arctic* 46 (3), 255–63.

Hansen, K., Rasmussen, R., and Roto, J., eds, 2012. Nordic perspectives on demography: A background report for the project on coastal societies and demography. *Nordregio Working Paper* 2012, 12.

Heikkilä, K., and Fondahl, G., 2012. Co-managed research: Non-indigenous thoughts on an indigenous toponymy project in northern British Columbia. *Journal of Cultural Geography*, 29 (1), 61–86.

Herman, R.D.K., 2008. Reflections on the importance of indigenous geography. *American Indian Culture and Research Journal*, 32 (3), 73–88.

Houghton, J.T., *et al.*, eds, 2001. The scientific basis. *In*: IPCC, *Climatic Change 2001: Contribution of Working Group I to the Third Assessment Report of the Intergovernmental Panel on Climatic Change.* Cambridge: Cambridge University Press.

Hovelsrud, G., Krupnik, I., and White, J., 2011. Human-based observing systems. *In*: I. Krupnik, *et al.*, eds, *Understanding Earth's Polar Challenges: International Polar Year 2007–2008.* Edmonton, AB: CCI Press, 435–56.

IPCC, 2007. *Climate Change 2007: Impacts, adaptation and vulnerability: Working Group II: summary for policymakers.* Cambridge: Cambridge University Press.

Krupnik, I., and Jolly, D., eds, 2002. *The Earth is Faster Now: Indigenous observations of Arctic environmental change*. Fairbanks, AK: Arctic Research Consortium of the United States.

Krupnik, I., *et al.*, 2005. Social sciences and humanities in the International Polar Year 2007–2008: An integrating mission. *Arctic*, 58 (1), 91–101.

Krupnik, I., *et al.*, eds, 2010. *SIKU: Arctic residents document sea ice and climate change*. Berlin: Springer.

Leclair, C., and Warren, S., 2007. Portals and potlatch. *In*: L.E. Dyson, M. Hendriks, and S. Grant, eds, *Information Technology and Indigenous People: Issues and perspectives*. Hershey, PA: IGI Global, 1–13.

Lovecraft, A.L., Meek, C., and Eicken, H., 2012. Connecting scientific observations to stakeholder needs in sea ice social–environmental systems: The institutional geography of northern Alaska. *Polar Geography*, 36 (1–2), 105–25.

Lundholm, E., and Malmberg, G., 2006. Gains and losses: Outcomes of interregional migration in the five nordic countries. *Geografiske Annaler: Series B, Human Geography*, 88 (1), 35–48.

Maffi, L., and Woodley, E., 2010. *Biocultural Diversity Conservation: A global sourcebook*. London: Earthscan.

Marino, E.K., 2015. *Fierce Climate, Sacred Ground: An ethnography of climate change in Shishmaref, Alaska*. Fairbanks, AK: University of Alaska Press.

McCarthy, J.J., and Martello, M.B., eds, 2005. Climate change in the context of multiple stressors and resilience. *In*: *Arctic Climate Impact Assessment (ACIA)*, Cambridge: Cambridge University Press, 946–88.

McGranahan, D., Cromartie, J., and Wojan, T., 2010. Nonmetropolitan outmigration counties: Some are poor, many are prosperous. *Economic Research Report No. ERR-107*.

Murphy, B., 2011. From interdisciplinary to inter-epistemological approaches: Confronting the challenges of integrated climate change research. *Canadian Geographer/Le Géographe Canadien*, 55 (4), 490–509.

NORDBUK, 2006. *Strategy for Children and Young People*. Nordic Committee for Children and Young People of the Nordic Council of Ministers, Copenhagen. ANP 2006, 723.

O'Brien, K.L., and Leichenko, R.M., 2000. Double exposure: Assessing the impacts of climate change within the context of economic globalization. *Global Environmental Change*, 10 (3), 221–32.

Orlove, B., 2005. Time, society, and the course of new technologies. *Current Anthropology*, 46 (5), 699–700.

Ostrom, E., 1990. *Governing the Commons: The evolution of institutions for collective action*. Cambridge: Cambridge University Press.

Ostrom, E., 2009. A general framework for analyzing sustainability of socio-ecological systems. *Science*, 325 (5939), 419–22.

Pearce, T., *et al.*, 2009. Community collaboration and climate change research in the Canadian Arctic. *Polar Research*, 28 (1), 10–27.

Pielke, R.A., *et al.*, 2012. Dealing with complexity and extreme events using a bottom–up, resource-based vulnerability perspective. *In*: A. Surjalal Sharma, *et al.*, eds, *Extreme Events and Natural Hazards: The complexity perspective*. Geophysical Monograph Series [online], 196. Available from: http://onlinelibrary.wiley.com/doi/10.1029/2011GM001086/summary [Accessed 30 August 2017].

Rasmussen, R., 2008. Gender, generation and social characteristics of internal and external migration patterns in Greenland. *Conference Proceedings*, ICASS VI, Nuuk, Greenland.

Rasmussen, R., 2009. Gender and generation: Perspectives on ongoing social and environmental changes in the Arctic. *Signs*, 34 (3), 524–32.

Rasmussen, R.O., Barnhardt, R., and Keskitalo, J., 2010. Education. *In*: J.N. Larsen and G. Fondahl, eds, *Arctic Social Indicators*. Copenhagen: Nordic Council of Ministers, 67–90.

Sillitoe, P., 1998. The development of indigenous knowledge: A new applied anthropology. *Current Anthropology*, 29 (2), 223–52.

Smith, E.A., and Wishnie, M., 2000. Conservation and subsistence in small-scale societies. *Annual Review of Anthropology*, 29, 493–524.

Stenseth, N., *et al.*, 2002. Ecological effects of climate fluctuations. *Science* [online], 297, 1292–95. Available from: www.sciencemag.org/cgi/content/full/297/5585/1292 [Accessed 30 August 2017].

Steward, A.S., 2007. Nobody farms here anymore: Livelihood diversification in the Brazilian Amazon, a historical perspective. *Agriculture and Human Values*, 24, 75–92.

Stockdale, A., 2006. Migration: Pre-requisite for rural economic regeneration? *Journal of Rural Studies*, 22, 354–66.

Sveiby, K-E., 2011. Collective leadership with power symmetry: Lessons from Aboriginal prehistory. *Leadership*, 7, 385–414.

Virtanen, P.K., 2012. *Indigenous Youth in Brazilian Amazonia: Changing lived worlds*. New York: Palgrave Macmillan.

Wyn, J., and Harris, A., 2004. Youth research in Australia and New Zealand. *Young*, 12 (3), 271–89.

14 Professionalising the 'resilience' sector in the Pacific Islands region

Formal education for capacity-building

Sarah Louise Hemstock,
Helene Jacot Des Combes,
Leigh-Anne Buliruarua, Kevin Maitava,
Ruth Senikula, Roy Smith, and Tess Martin

Introduction

Climate change and a changing environment are the Pacific region's greatest contemporary challenges. Both are affecting Pacific societies and cultures in ways that are far-reaching and rapid. Geographic remoteness, ecological fragility, rapid population growth, waste disposal needs, limited land resources, depleted marine resources, exposure to natural hazards, and global fluctuations in climate all contribute to the increasing vulnerability of small island developing states in the Pacific Islands region (Woods *et al.* 2006; IPCC 2014). The Pacific Islands countries and territories have come to represent the 'front line' or the 'canary in the coalmine' in raising awareness globally on the potential for negative consequences of climate change and impacts on environmental security (Smith and Hemstock 2011). A recent United Nations Development Programme study (Nunn 2013) established that most Pacific island populations lack climate change awareness and knowledge of appropriate adaptation strategies, leaving them unable to make informed choices about adaptation to climate change impacts affecting their livelihoods and resources. A lack of formal training programmes run by competent staff at well-resourced and well-equipped training institutions is a key barrier to improving energy security status and resilience to climate change impacts in these countries (Buliruarua *et al.* 2015). Most global policy frameworks dealing with climate change adaptation and disaster risk management, such as the 2015 Sendai Framework on Disaster Risk Reduction (UNISDR 2015), identify the central role of training and capacity development for achieving sustainable development (Hemstock *et al.* 2016).

In the Pacific Islands region, many young people continue to acquire workplace skills by informal means and non-formal training.[1] This is despite the many policy dialogues and agreements on the requirement of education per se to improve resilience to climate change and disasters. Although the role of action at the local level is recognised in policy dialogue – such as the Framework for Resilient Development in the Pacific (FRDP) – there are no formal qualifications accessible at this level. Most opportunities occur at postgraduate level, which is not appropriate for the majority of stakeholders, including communities. In that regard, regional technical and vocational education and training (TVET) qualifications aligned with Levels 1 to 4 of the Pacific Qualifications Framework would be most appropriate (Sanerivi *et al.* 2016; Hemstock *et al.* 2017). Since most of the current regional training delivery is carried out on a project basis, usually by short-term consultants, it is unsustainable in terms of national capacity to deliver. Ad hoc training and lack of national capacity to deliver training sustainably also means that many projects fail if the individuals trained on those project activities leave the community (Woods *et al.* 2006). These issues lead to the conclusion that national capacity to deliver quality-assured regional qualifications in climate change adaptation and disaster risk management should follow a more sustainable approach.

Recognising and validating the learning outcomes from non-formal and informal learning help identify the knowledge, skills and competences acquired within the informal sector to promote decent employment and labour mobility (UNESCO Institute for Lifelong Learning 2015). In this regard it is also noted that a lack of formal qualifications, certification, or professional recognition of an individual's skills makes workers vulnerable and fosters social inequality (Asian Development Bank *et al.* 2015). The lack of an accredited skills recognition process for informally acquired skills in the Pacific Islands region also compounds the 'poverty of opportunity' that is deemed to exist there (Tuvalu Ministry of Finance, Economic Planning and Industries 2005). Mobility of the labour force in the Pacific region has long been a focus for Pacific leaders. An education and training system that incorporates recognition and validation of competences across the region will contribute to this regional objective. It is also contended that when enforced migration due to climate change becomes a wider reality, people should be able to 'migrate with dignity' – whereby they should have the means to participate in the job market of the place to which they migrate. One way to achieve this is to have recognised, accredited qualifications.

Findings from Buliruarua *et al.* (2015) indicate that formal educational pathways and the professionalisation of climate change adaptation and disaster risk management sectors should be established as a matter of urgency since the region currently has little capacity to absorb the funding for climate-change-related activities entering the region. The UNFCCC COP21 Paris Agreement agreed to commit a minimum of US$100 billion per year in climate finance for all developing countries by 2020. Adapting to climate change is central to major development efforts for Pacific ACP (African, Caribbean and Pacific Group of States) (PACP) countries. Financial resources for adaptation are already flowing into PACP countries, totalling US$2,148 million in 2013, with almost half of this (48 per cent) funded by Australia (OECD 2017). Over 70 per cent of these aid flows are linked to climate change and disaster risk management activities.

The situation in Tuvalu provides a good illustration of why local capacity in climate change adaptation and disaster risk management is desperately needed to take full advantage of aid flows into the region. In 2008, Tuvalu's GDP was US$32 million, with 50 per cent of this in the form of development aid. Approximately US$4 million was spent on external technical assistance (Smith and Hemstock 2011) because of a lack of in-country capacity, a staggering 12 per cent of Tuvalu's GDP is spent on external experts from consulting companies and multilateral organisations. These results support comparable findings in a study of the water sector in Kiribati (Storey and Hunter 2010).

Professionalising the resilience sector (i.e. climate change adaptation and disaster risk management) requires accredited qualifications and on-the-job training. Formal education in disaster risk management is currently only offered in the region at postgraduate level (Levels 8 to 10 on the Pacific Qualifications Framework). This is because most adaptation efforts to date have largely been top–down in their process and approach, which means little attention has been given to integrating community experiences of climate change into adaptation actions, including the knowledge and views of community members on how to cope and adapt to locally changing environmental conditions (Reid *et al.* 2009; McNamara *et al.* 2012). Although capacity-building workshops are often offered as components of climate change adaptation or disaster risk management projects, these take place on an ad hoc and non-formal basis.

As a response to these gaps, the European Union Pacific Technical and Vocational Educational and Training in Sustainable Energy and Climate Change Adaptation project (EU PacTVET) was devised. Its aim is to overcome the lack of formal training programmes and qualified staff at the local level in the PACP country grouping. EU PacTVET is the third component of the larger European Union Tenth European Development Fund programme: Adapting to Climate Change and Sustainable Energy. EU PacTVET is a €6.1 million project currently being implemented by the Pacific Community (SPC) and the University of the South Pacific (USP). The wider programme aims to enhance sustainable livelihoods, strengthen countries' capabilities to adapt to the adverse effects of climate change, and enhance their energy security at the national, provincial, and local/community levels in all 15 PACP countries: Cook Islands, Federated States of Micronesia, Fiji, Kiribati, Nauru, Niue, Palau, Papua New Guinea, Republic of the Marshall Islands, Samoa, Solomon Islands, Timor Leste (East Timor), Tonga, Tuvalu, and Vanuatu. The purpose of EU PacTVET is to enhance and/or create regional and national capacity and technical expertise in these countries to respond to climate change adaptation and sustainable energy challenges.

This chapter outlines the EU PacTVET initiatives that support global, regional, and national frameworks and policies that prioritise building resilience to climate change and natural hazards through human resource development facilitated by accredited qualifications. It also outlines the recommendations guiding future policy formation that EU PacTVET activities have initiated. Responsive and accredited regional qualifications that integrate local knowledge should ensure that the interventions managed by practitioners having these qualifications do actually support sustainable development, thereby limiting the impacts of climate change and natural hazards, empowering locals to become actively involved in their own development, and limiting maladaptation and the generation of new risks.

History of EU PacTVET and methodology

EU PacTVET activities were guided by an initial training needs and gaps analysis. In aiming to maximise its effectiveness and ensure it captured the opinions of many stakeholders[2] and relevant information, a mixed-methods approach was employed. This included literature survey, policy analysis, and in-country consultations for all 15 PACP counties. Prior to in-country consultations, questionnaires were forwarded to government ministries and departments responsible for energy, climate change, and education, energy utilities, and TVET training institutes. This ensured that stakeholders and existing formal qualifications and non-formal training were identified. A consultative workshop was held in the first two days of most in-country missions. This involved a consultation with stakeholders at a venue where the agenda for discussion was available to all parties simultaneously. One-to-one interviews were conducted with key stakeholders that were unable to attend the workshops. Workshops and interviews took place between February and September 2015.

Methodologies and participating stakeholders in all 15 PACP countries were as reported by Buliruarua *et al.* (2015) and Hemstock *et al.* (2017). Research revealed that formal qualifications were required for professionalisation in the areas of sustainable energy and climate change adaptation. And that particular emphasis should be placed on the recognition of 'resilience' (climate change adaptation and disaster risk management) as an important employment sector – especially for small island developing states such as Tuvalu, where the government is the largest employer. Professionalisation of the resilience sector was clearly urgent (Buliruarua *et al.* 2015).

EU PacTVET has worked with stakeholders from all 15 PACP countries via a partnership with the Fiji Higher Education Commission to develop qualifications at Levels 1 to 4 on the Pacific Qualifications Framework in Resilience (climate change adaptation and disaster risk management) and Sustainable Energy, 'thus allowing Pacific Islanders to benefit from the opportunities of globalisation and actively engage in all forms of productive livelihood activities' (EQAP 2011). There is no other example of a regional approach to TVET educational qualification development and accreditation. The regional frameworks, especially the Framework for Pacific Regionalism, and the size of the Pacific Islands region facilitate a position that can provide global leadership in the area of regionally accredited qualifications. The EU PacTVET initiative is also the first ever development of TVET qualifications in the subject area of resilience.

Some stakeholders, especially representatives from national education ministries or agencies, were initially resistant to the project. The main issue was the perceived use of regional qualifications. Five PACP countries have national accreditation authorities and they did not see the need to have regional accreditation while they could provide accreditation at the national level. Representatives from these accreditation authorities were concerned about losing ownership and 'sovereignty' under a regional accreditation process. The solution was to accredit the qualifications nationally and regionally for these countries.

Another challenge was the creation of the 'resilience' sector, since this is extremely broad and cross-cutting compared with other TVET sectors. As a result, identifying stakeholders to provide input for all sectors covered during the qualification development process (such as for agriculture, coastal management, water resources, etc.) was problematic because there is no 'professional organisation' for this sector. Bringing these stakeholders together to discuss qualifications, a topic with which they were unfamiliar, was difficult and time-consuming. Including traditional knowledge was another challenge since it is rarely thought to add value to the 'modern science' that is the main approach for most training in the Pacific Islands region. Some aspects of traditional knowledge may also be restricted to a single community or even a single family. As a result, education professionals were initially sceptical about how traditional knowledge could be included in the qualifications. In fact, what is included is a methodology that recognises the value of traditional knowledge-based solutions in specific local contexts and ensures that these solutions are included in resilience-building strategies.

Resilience in the Pacific context

Pacific island countries face many challenges (Kelman *et al.* 2015) – natural hazards and climate change being considered the most important. Most of the natural hazards to which PACP countries are exposed are either hydro-meteorological or climatic, and both are likely to be influenced by climate change (IPCC 2013). Development, risk management, and climate change adaptation are highly linked. Countries have limited resources to implement climate change adaptation and disaster risk reduction programmes in parallel; however, there is duplication in the data collected and some solutions developed for communities to address both these issues.

As a result, countries have started to develop joint national action plans to integrate these issues and mainstream them into their development plans. Following these developments at national level, the regional frameworks for climate change (*Pacific Islands Framework for Actions on Climate Change 2006–2015*: SPREP 2005) and disaster risk management (*Regional Framework for Actions 2005–2015*: SOPAC 2005) were merged by the Pacific community's member countries and territories in 2016 to form an integrated framework: the *Framework for Resilient Development in the Pacific 2017–2030* (FRDP; SPC *et al.* 2016).

In developing the FRDP, it was soon realised that the phrase 'integrated climate change adaptation and disaster risk management' was too long. So a new term was used – one that was shorter, more neutral, and not too climate change- or disaster-oriented and so relevant for both communities of practice. The term was 'resilient development'. It was defined as follows: 'Development processes and actions that address the risks and impacts of disasters and climate change while progressing to stronger and resilient communities' (SPC *et al.* 2016).

In the context of the FRDP, resilient development corresponds to development processes and actions that address the risks and impacts of disasters and climate change while progressing to stronger and more resilient communities (SPC *et al.* 2016). The rationale for integrating disaster risk management and climate change adaptation in the Pacific Islands countries and territories is based on several similarities: both aim for the same goal (making communities or countries more resilient); both use comparable approaches (risk assessment, vulnerability assessment, and ecosystem-based actions); both support development activities; the most frequent disasters in the Pacific island countries are caused by hydro-meteorological hazards (cyclones, floods, droughts); and the projected impacts of climate change include more intense and/or more frequent extreme weather events.

It is important to note that the approach chosen for resilient development does include the concept of progress, in contrast to the definition of resilience adaptation, which implies a return to the status quo (Pelling 2011). Although not mentioned explicitly in the FRDP, or in the TVET qualifications, adaptation in the Pacific context considers not only the physical and natural aspect of risk but also vulnerability based on socio-economic conditions (especially sources of income, gender issues, and the traditional social structures and practices in communities and families) and aims to work within the existing system, adjusting its rules where necessary (Pelling 2011). For example, in the EU PacTVET context, building resilience focuses on reducing community exposure and addresses local drivers of vulnerability such as monocrop culture and limited diversification of household incomes. Global drivers of vulnerability such as market-driven production are not addressed.

The TVET qualifications on resilience were developed to support the implementation of FRDP, as well as global frameworks such as the Sendai Framework for Disaster Risk Reduction, the Paris Agreement on Climate Change and the Agenda 2030 Sustainable Development Goals (SDGs) in the 15 PACP countries. The overall aim of integrating climate change adaptation and disaster risk management with an emphasis on disaster risk reduction is to improve the resilience of Pacific communities to climate change and disaster impacts via the effective, appropriate, and integrated methods of risk and vulnerability assessment, planning, adaptation activities, and monitoring. This integration, in the context of the TVET qualifications developed under EU PacTVET, includes participatory processes to identify with the affected community the best resilience-building strategies, based on 'Western science'-based methods but also on the experience and traditional knowledge of community members. The qualification also covers other issues such as natural resource management, ecosystem services, socio-economic drivers of vulnerability, and pollution. Key stakeholders for training are governments (national and local), the private sector, civil society organisations, rural communities, regional organisations, and disaster management officers (Hemstock *et al.* 2017). This approach through local TVET providers, including rural organisations, is expected to help integrate the views of different stakeholders and to facilitate the inclusion of traditional knowledge and skills, for example concerning food production and preservation.

Once the content of the qualifications was agreed, they needed a title. To be completely aligned with the FRDP, 'resilient development' could have been chosen. However, this term was considered problematic for two reasons. First, sustainable development in the FRDP includes low carbon development and this topic is covered by the sustainable energy qualifications developed under the EU PacTVET project rather than the resilience qualifications. Second, the terms 'development' and 'economic growth' are often confused (Cannon and Müller-Mahn 2010) and there was a risk that people could think the TVET qualifications included skills to support economic growth. As a result, 'resilience' was chosen, using the United Nations Office for Disaster Risk Reduction (UNISDR) definition:

> The ability of a system, community or society exposed to hazards to resist, absorb, accommodate, adapt to, transform and recover from the effects of a hazard in a timely and efficient manner, including through the preservation and restoration of its essential basic structures and functions through risk management.
>
> (UNISDR 2017)

However, as for the FRDP, in the context of the TVET resilience qualifications, resilience is not only seen as the return to previous conditions after a crisis/disaster but also the addition of changes and adjustments, especially for addressing the socio-economic drivers of vulnerability mentioned in the UNISDR definitions of underlying disaster risk drivers and vulnerability (UNISDR 2017), with a view to be better prepared for the next crisis/disaster.

Local policy context and EU PacTVET response

To a large extent, the process by which climate change adaptation and disaster risk management are included across the Pacific Islands region is by integrating climate change into regional and national development policy (Hemstock *et al.* 2017). Mainstreaming has culminated in the development and support of the FRDP (SPC *et al.* 2016), which provides a set of voluntary guidelines for the Pacific Islands region.

An analysis of national guiding policy documents from the 15 PACP countries indicated a strong shift towards the integration of climate change adaptation and disaster risk management into one policy since 2010, when Tonga led the region in the development of its joint national action plan (SPREP 2013). As outlined in the Table 14.1, all countries have also used national policy to highlight the need to strengthen capacities in-country, and at all levels. However, implementation of these policies to build capacity in climate change adaptation, disaster risk management, and sustainable energy is limited (Buliruarua *et al.* 2015). For example, in its climate change policy (Government of the Republic of Fiji 2012), Fiji highlighted the need to integrate climate change into school curricula, tertiary courses, and vocational, non-formal education and training programmes, while Palau, in its Climate Change Policy for Climate and Disaster Resilient Low Emissions Development (Government of Palau 2015), highlighted the need for formal and informal disaster risk management education programmes to be offered through different training providers.

All countries indicated a lack of capacity and the need to strengthen existing capacity to provide early warning systems for all hazards, and most highlighted the need for project management skills (i.e. proposal development, reporting, administration/management, monitoring, and evaluation). Most countries also identified sector-specific-type training needs, for example, fisheries and aquaculture expansion training (Nauru) and capacity-building and training in agro-forestry and sustainable forest management systems to improve capacity and knowledge of forests (Timor Leste).

An EU PacTVET stakeholder and Regional Industry Standards Advisory Meeting in October 2016 confirmed that competencies covering all aspects of disaster risk management should also be integrated into the resilience qualifications at Levels 1 to 4 on the Pacific Qualifications Framework. However, the skills and competencies required for disaster management (e.g. logistics, humanitarian response) differ from those needed in disaster risk reduction and climate change adaptation and will be integrated into the resilience qualifications at a later stage.

The call for formal qualifications and professionalisation was loud and clear from stakeholders in all 15 PACP countries. This is illustrated by the situation in Vanuatu and Tuvalu, both of which were hit by Tropical Cyclone Pam just before their national stakeholder meeting took place. Both countries recommended that disaster risk management should be

Table 14.1 Key national policies on climate change adaptation (CCA) and disaster risk management (DRM) and an examination of their requirements for related learning

Country	Key policy	CCA	DRM/DRR	Non-formal training	Strengthen capacity (general)	Education (formal assumed)
Cook Islands	Cook Islands Joint National Action Plan for DRM & CCA	✓	✓		✓	✓
Fiji	Fiji National CC Policy 2012 & National DRM Plan 1995; National Disaster Management Act 1998; Climate Change Adaptation and Disaster Risk Reduction Strategies 2013	✓	✓	✓	✓	✓
Federated States of Micronesia	Joint State Action Plan for CC & DRM and 2nd National Communications report to the UNFCCC	✓	✓		✓	✓
Kiribati	Kiribati Joint Implementation Plan for CC and DRM 2014–2023	✓	✓		✓	✓
Nauru	Republic of Nauru Framework for Climate Change Adaptation and Disaster Risk Reduction 2015	✓	✓		✓	✓
Niue	Niue's Joint Action Plan for DRM & CCA	✓	✓		✓	✓
Palau	Palau Climate Change Policy: For Climate & Disaster Resilient Low Emissions Development 2015	✓	✓		✓	✓
Papua New Guinea	The National Development Strategic Plan (DSP) (2010–2030)	✓	✓		✓	✓
Republic of the Marshall Islands (RMI)	RMI Joint Action Plan for CCA & DRM; Vision 2018 (2003–2018); National Climate Change Policy Framework 2011; Ministry of Education Strategic Plan (2013–2016)	✓	✓		✓	✓
Samoa	Samoa National Action Plan for DRM 2011–2016	✓	✓	✓	✓	✓
Solomon Islands	National Development Strategy 2011–2020; Solomon Islands Climate Change Policy (2012); Solomon Islands National Disaster Risk Reduction Policy (NDRRP 2010)	✓	✓	✓	✓	✓
Timor Leste	National Adaptation Programme of Action (NAPA 2010) on Climate Change Adaptation; National Disaster Risk Management Policy 2008	✓	✓	✓	✓	
Tonga	Tonga National Climate Change Policy and Joint National Action Plan for CCA & DRM 2010–2015	✓	✓		✓	✓
Tuvalu	Tuvalu National Strategic Action Plan for CCA & DRM 2012–2016	✓	✓	✓	✓	✓
Vanuatu	Vanuatu Climate Change and Disaster Risk Reduction Policy 2016–2030	✓	✓	✓	✓	✓

integrated with climate change adaptation into competencies and qualifications at Levels 1 to 4 on the Pacific Qualifications Framework. One stakeholder, a former government official and community resident from Tuvalu, commented that '[i]f people in communities were equipped with recognised post-disaster assessment skills already we wouldn't have to wait for assessors to visit communities post-disaster and disaster responses could be faster'. Some community members in Tuvalu had received non-formal training on post-disaster assessment, but their assessments were not considered relevant by relief agencies in the aftermath of Cyclone Pam, delaying relief efforts by up to a week. Tuvalu stakeholders therefore determined that recognised and accredited qualifications in climate change adaptation and disaster risk reduction would provide a professional aspect to the training offered. It was concluded that all training should be aligned toward the overall professionalisation of disaster risk management, including identifiable career paths with sequential learning stages.

The policies listed in Table 14.1 call for professionalisation via formal education. However, the problem is that these policy calls are not being implemented. At the recent Third Regional Meeting of Pacific Ministers for Energy and Transport (Nuku'alofa, Tonga, 24–28 April 2017) (SPC 2017), ministers recommended the following: (1) the region's capacity-building and training on sustainable energy to be based on formal accredited TVET qualifications and support to continuing research and development in the area of sustainable energy; (2) while encouraging a national approach, we also support a regional approach to accreditation of sustainable energy competency-based qualifications and skill sets in the vocational educational sector – including a system for incorporating quality assurance/accreditation/recognition of formal and informal learning (project-based training) and recognition of prior learning; and (3) support an industry-driven demand-based TVET system for sustainable energy through national and regional professional industry associations.

The EU PacTVET project is a sequential project, whereby activities are based on stakeholder consultations, the training needs and gap analysis, regional steering group endorsement, policy recommendations, and ministerial directives. From this basis, the project opted for regionally devised and accredited qualifications to ensure that adaptation measures limit the impacts of climate change and natural hazards; empower locals to become actors in their own development; and limit maladaptation and the generation of new risks. In addition, for EU PacTVET to ensure applicability across all stakeholder groups, from grassroots community members to government and private sector managers, qualifications were constructed around a 'competency' and 'skill set' approach. A list of competencies and skill sets is available within the qualifications (e.g. how to perform or interpret a cost–benefit analysis). Completing a range of skill sets will build into a full qualification. Countries can deliver different aspects of the qualifications according to their specific capacity needs. National providers (e.g.

Tuvalu Maritime Institute) have been identified to deliver different skill sets and, where necessary, staff are being trained to deliver the qualifications. Since the qualifications are to be accredited regionally, skill sets will be mutually recognised and can be built upon by completing competencies/ skill sets at more than one educational provider. The competencies and skill set approach allows the development of a range of location-specific teaching resources. While learning outcomes remain the same across the region, learning resources are specifically developed for each country, in local languages and with local examples. For example, one unit of the competencies has as a learning outcome the skill to conduct a vulnerability assessment. Some countries have developed their own vulnerability assessment, such as the Reimaanlok in the Marshall Islands (Reimaan National Planning Team 2008), while a new integrated vulnerability assessment is under development in Fiji. Students enrolled in this unit in both countries will have the skills to conduct a vulnerability assessment, but will be trained to use different ones.

Developing resilience qualifications

The training needs and gaps analysis showed that all countries wanted capacity development at TVET Levels 1 to 4 to cover climate change adaptation and disaster risk management (Buliruarua *et al.* 2015). Two options were available: one qualification on climate change adaptation and another on disaster risk management, or integrate both into a new topic.

Following the policy developments at the national and regional level, especially the endorsement of the FRDP 2017–2030 (SPC *et al.* 2016), PACP countries decided to develop a single set of qualifications, integrating climate change adaptation and disaster risk management. Because 'climate change adaptation and disaster risk management' would be a long and impractical title, the term 'resilience' was chosen by PACP country representatives.

Phase 1: climate change adaptation and disaster risk reduction

The EU PacTVET project partnered the Fiji Higher Education Commission to establish the Resilience Industry Skills Advisory Committee (RISAC), which comprises sector stakeholders, professional associations, licensing agencies, educational institutions, and government representatives. RISAC decided to organise the TVET qualifications in eight streams covering specific sectors of importance for PACP countries at Levels 3 and 4, while Levels 1 and 2 are generic.

RISAC agreed to integrate climate change adaptation and disaster risk reduction skills because they are very similar, the main difference being the source of information on the risks communities are facing: historical records of previous disasters for disaster risk reduction and projections of future climate for climate change adaptation. In the context of the PACP countries, the common skills for climate change adaptation and disaster risk reduction were identified as risk assessment skills (including vulnerability assessment), identification of action for resilience-building through a participatory process, resilience-building implementation skills, communication skills, and project management skills.

Phase 2: inclusion of disaster response and recovery

During discussions with RISAC, it was clear that although climate change adaptation and disaster risk reduction skills were similar, the skills required for the other phases of the disaster cycle, namely disaster response and recovery, were very different. They were thus added to the resilience qualification in a second phase.

Discussion included two main questions: as the skills are different, is it necessary to create a specific unit for disaster response, or even a specific qualification? What skills should be included in the qualification?

To have a specific qualification for 'disaster response', also sometimes called 'disaster or emergency management', would defeat the goal of integration and create more separation between stakeholders focusing on disaster risk reduction and stakeholders focusing on disaster management. The inclination to work in silos was identified and ways to address this were discussed during the World Humanitarian Summit in the resilience section (United Nations 2016). Including a new unit would significantly affect the distribution of credits over the qualifications and affect the balance between core units and elective units.

Sustainability: the Pacific Regional Federation of Resilience Practitioners

Based on policy calls and previous projects, the EU PacTVET project is the starting point for various initiatives to professionalise the resilience (climate change adaptation/disaster risk management) sector. These include the establishment of the Pacific Regional Federation for Resilience Professionals (PRFRP) to encompass practitioners and provide business models that promote sustainability (Hemstock *et al.* 2016) and so to advance the recognition and professionalisation of this employment sector in the Pacific region. The establishment and functions of the PRFRP were agreed by all countries at a high-level meeting in May 2016. It will be a standalone organisation that will continue to maintain, update, and provide industry recognition for the delivery of the qualifications after the EU PacTVET project cycle ends in June 2021. It will certify practitioners based on current competency and prior learning, and will be a united and diverse Pacific regional industry association for resilience. It is also intended to achieve sustainable outcomes in skills development, education, training, and employment for the climate change adaptation and disaster risk management sectors. The PRFRP will align closely with regional/national needs and priorities via national policy and the FRDP, with the aim of enhancing the professionalism of practitioners in the diverse fields of climate change adaptation and disaster risk management.

This will be achieved through several approaches. Transition from ad hoc and non-formal training provision on climate change adaptation/disaster risk management will be facilitated by promoting the formal provision of relevant PRFRP-recognised qualifications or nationally validated training providers. An industry certification scheme for practitioners that sets the benchmark of quality for the resilience sector will be based on qualifications and experience and will include recognition of current competencies and prior learning. Since all previous education and training in this sector has occurred on an informal ad hoc project basis, it is important to develop and implement an appropriate system of recognition of previous learning as a valid and quality-assured process for certification. A register of certified professional resilience practitioners will be maintained and a code of ethics will be developed for resilience practitioners. RISAC will be administered to facilitate reviews and updates of education and training curricula and practices in resilience, about every three years. The EU PacTVET qualifications will be maintained by RISAC, thus ensuring that they continue to meet industry requirements. Standards and environmentally sound practices for sustainable climate change adaptation/disaster risk management products and services – including use of appropriate strategies, technologies, and resources – will be adopted and promoted. This will be achieved by integrating current best practices into the qualifications when they are updated. A collective, collaborative, and effective representation of the 'resilience sector' in industry and government affairs is expected to occur, to promote relationships with relevant stakeholders (including multilateral and bilateral donors), international agencies, and government ministries and departments with the aim of ensuring the use of best practices in climate change adaptation/disaster risk management.

PRFRP currently has around 100 members. Among others, membership is anticipated to include non-governmental organisations and community groups, education and training institutes, universities, private sector green and sustainable environment-focused businesses, industry associations, utilities, government departments, multilateral and bilateral donors, international agencies, and individuals (practitioners).

Concluding remarks

Capacity development is a foundational aspect of successful overseas development assistance and effectiveness in meeting long-term development and climate change adaptation goals.

The EU PacTVET project has built on existing regional climate change adaptation and disaster risk management initiatives such as the USP and SPC European Union Global Climate Change Alliance projects, in order to develop a framework to create a set of region-wide qualifications for vocational training in climate change adaptation and disaster risk management. It is important to note that while setting regional minimum standards, validation, and accreditation processes, there is still sufficient flexibility within this educational regime to allow national providers to access the skill sets or competencies that are most relevant to the needs and priorities of their territories.

The project has developed the competencies for Levels 1 to 4 on the Pacific Qualifications Framework. Broad regional stakeholder engagement has been important in this development so that the core competencies of qualifications can be accepted as having common applicability across the region, while the elective competencies can provide the bespoke characteristics that are most appropriate within each island state. This flexibility will make it possible to meet a wide range of national and regional needs simultaneously. Some countries intend this training to be delivered predominantly, although not exclusively, at the community college level with a view to the qualifications gained being a potential precursor to degree-level education. An innovative aspect of this project is that the material and qualifications can be used equally by other stakeholders, such as government departments, which may wish to use this for capacity-building staff development.

Having a regionally accredited set of qualifications enhances employability mobility, although the intention is that capacity built via this training (especially at Levels 1 and 2) will primarily benefit the communities within which the training took place. In order to achieve this it is clear that employment opportunities will need to be available for those taking these qualifications, to make the most of their enhanced capacity. Thus, engagement with the private sector and aligning with industry standards has also been an integral part of the design and delivery of this project.

It is expected that the cohort of graduates with a TVET qualification in resilience will support the integration of top–down and bottom–up approaches while acknowledging local and traditional knowledge with other forms of knowledge. This was identified by Kelman and West (2009) as the best way forward to support the Pacific Islands countries and territories to adapt to climate change. The qualifications developed in this project are also expected to help strengthen biophysical and social resilience (Storey and Hunter 2010) since both aspects are included in the qualifications.

Notes

1 The definitions of formal and non-formal learning adopted in this chapter are as outlined by the UNESCO Institute for Lifelong Learning (2015): formal learning takes place in education and training institutions, is recognised by relevant

national authorities, and leads to qualifications; non-formal learning is learning that has been acquired in addition to or instead of formal learning. It usually takes place in community-based settings, the workplace, and through the activities of civil society organisations.

2 Stakeholders in the EU PacTVET context include national and local governments, non-governmental organisations, the private sector, development partners (donors and international agencies), civil society organisations, education professionals, and any other organisations implementing climate change adaptation and disaster risk management projects in the Pacific island countries.

References

Asian Development Bank, International Labour Organization and Organisation for Economic Co-operation and Development, 2015. *Building Human Capital through Labor Migration in Asia.* ADB, ILO & OECD [online]. Available from: www.oecd.org/migration/building-human-capital.pdf [Accessed 3 November 2017].

Buliruarua, L.-A., *et al.*, 2015. *P-ACP Training Needs and Gap Analysis: Reports for Fiji, Cook Islands, the Federated States of Micronesia, Kiribati, Marshall Islands, Nauru, Niue, Palau, Papua New Guinea, Samoa, Solomon Islands, Timor Leste, Tonga, Tuvalu and Vanuatu.* The Pacific Community and the University of the South Pacific, Suva, Fiji. EU PacTVET – FED/2014/347–438.

Cannon, T., and Müller-Mahn, D., 2010. Vulnerability, resilience and development discourses in context of climate change. *Natural Hazards,* 55 (3), 621–35.

EQAP, 2011. *The Pacific Qualifications Framework.* Secretariat of the Pacific Board for Educational Assessment (now EQAP – Educational Quality Assessment Programme). Suva, Fiji: Secretariat of the Pacific Community, 6.

Government of Palau, 2015. *Palau Climate Change Policy: For climate and disaster resilient low emissions development.* Palau.

Government of the Republic of Fiji, 2012. *Republic of Fiji National Climate Change Policy.* Suva, Fiji: Secretariat of the Pacific Community.

Hemstock, S.L., *et al.*, 2016. Accredited qualifications for capacity development in disaster risk reduction and climate change adaptation. *Australasian Journal of Disaster and Trauma Studies,* 20 (1), 15–33.

Hemstock, S.L., *et al.*, 2017. A case for formal education in the technical, vocational education and training (TVET) sector for climate change adaptation and disaster risk reduction in the Pacific Islands region. *In*: L.F. Walter, ed., *Climate Change Adaptation in Pacific Countries: Fostering resilience and improving the quality of life.* Climate Change Management. Berlin: Springer International Publishing, 309–24.

IPCC, 2013. Summary for policymakers. *In*: T.F. Stocker, *et al.*, eds, *Climate Change 2013: The physical science basis: contribution of Working Group I to the Fifth Assessment Report of the Intergovernmental Panel on Climate Change.* Cambridge: Cambridge University Press.

IPCC, 2014. *Climate Change 2014: Impacts, adaptation, and vulnerability. Part B: Regional aspects: contribution of Working Group II to the Fifth Assessment Report of the Intergovernmental Panel on Climate Change.* V.R. Barros, *et al.*, eds. Cambridge: Cambridge University Press.

Kelman, I., and West, J.J., 2009. Climate change and small island developing states: A critical review. *Ecological and Environmental Anthropology,* 5 (1), 1–16.

Kelman, I., Gaillard, J.C., and Mercer, J., 2015. Climate change's role in disaster risk reduction's future: Beyond vulnerability and resilience. *International Journal of Disaster Risk Science*, 6 (1), 21–7.

McNamara, K., Hemstock, S.L., and Holland, E., 2012. *Practices of Climate Change Adaptation in the Pacific: Survey of implementing agencies (phase II)*. Pacific Centre for Environment and Sustainable Development (PaCE-SD). Suva, Fiji: The University of the South Pacific. (USP EU-GCCA: FED/2010/258–661).

Nunn, P.D., 2013. *Climate Change and Pacific Island Countries*. Asia Pacific Human Development Report. Background Papers Series 2012/07. New York: United Nations Development programme. HDR-2013-APHDR-TBP-07.

OECD, 2017. *Development Aid at a Glance: Statistics by region – Oceania* [online]. Available from: www.oecd.org/dac/stats/documentupload/Oceania-Development-Aid-at-a-Glance.pdf [Accessed 3 November 2017].

Pelling, M., 2011. *Adaptation to Climate Change: From resilience to transformation*. London: Routledge.

Reid, H., *et al.*, 2009. Community-based adaptation to climate change: An overview. *Participatory Learning and Action*, 60 (1), 9–11.

Reimaan National Planning Team, 2008. *Reimaanlok: National conservation area plan for the Marshall Islands 2007–2012*. N. Baker, ed. Melbourne: Reimaan National Planning Team.

Sanerivi, L., *et al.*, 2016. *Changing Climate for Quality Assured Regional Qualifications in the Pacific: An innovative collaboration (EU-PacTVET & EQAP)*. Asia Pacific Quality Network (APQN) Conference 2016.

Smith, R., and Hemstock, S.L., 2011. An analysis of the effectiveness of funding for climate change adaptation using Tuvalu as a case study. *International Journal of Climate Change: Impacts and Responses*, 3 (1), 67–78.

SOPAC, 2005. *A Framework for Action 2005–2015: Building the resilience of nations and communities to disasters*. SOPAC Miscellaneous Report 613. Suva, Fiji.

SPC, 2017. *Third Pacific Regional Energy and Transport Ministers' Meeting Communiqué*. Nuku'Alofa, Tonga, 26–28 April 2017. The Pacific Community (SPC).

SPC, SPREP, USP, PIFS, UNISDR, UNDP 2016. *Framework for Resilient Development in the Pacific: An integrated approach to address climate change and disaster risk management (FRDP) 2017–2030*. Pacific Community (SPC), Secretariat of the Pacific Regional Environment Programme (SPREP), the University of the South Pacific (USP), Pacific Islands Forum Secretariat (PIFS), United Nations Office for Disaster Risk Reduction (UNISDR) and United Nations Development Programme (UNDP), the Pacific Community, Geoscience Division, Suva, Fiji.

SPREP, 2005. *Pacific Islands Framework for Action on Climate Change 2006–2015*. Apia, Samoa: Secretariat of the Pacific Regional Environment Programme.

SPREP, 2013. *JNAP Development and Implementation in the Pacific: Experiences, lessons and way forward*. Apia, Samoa: Secretariat of the Pacific Regional Environment Programme.

Storey, D., and Hunter, S., 2010. Kiribati: An environmental 'perfect storm'. *Australian Geographer*, 41 (2), 167–81.

Tuvalu Ministry of Finance, Economic Planning and Industries, 2005. Te kakeega II: *National Strategy for Sustainable Development 2005–2015*. Funafuti, Tuvalu: Tuvalu Government, Economic Research and Policy Division, Ministry of Finance, Economic Planning and Industries.

UNESCO Institute for Lifelong Learning, 2015. *Global Inventory of Regional and National Qualifications Frameworks*. Hamburg: UNESCO Institute for Lifelong Learning.

UNISDR, 2015. *Sendai Framework for Disaster Reduction 2015–2030*. Geneva: United Nations International Strategy for Disaster Reduction (UNISDR).

UNISDR, 2017. *Terminology on Disaster Risk Reduction*. Geneva: United Nations International Strategy for Disaster Reduction (UNISDR).

United Nations, 2016. *Restoring Humanity: Global voices calling for action: synthesis of the consultation process for the World Humanitarian Summit*. Executive summary. New York: United Nations.

Woods, J, Hemstock, S.L., and Bunyeat, J., 2006. Bio-energy systems at the community level in the South Pacific: Impacts and monitoring: greenhouse gas emissions and abrupt climate change: positive options and robust policy. *Journal of Mitigation and Adaptation Strategies for Global Change*, 4, 473–99.

Part VI

Conclusion

15 Conclusion

The politics in critical adaptation research

Sybille Bauriedl and Detlef Müller-Mahn

This peer-reviewed volume presents a collection of articles focusing on adaptation research from a critical perspective. Being mostly based on empirical case studies, the contributions to the book cover a wide range of geographical and thematic foci, and do so from diverse disciplinary backgrounds, scalar perspectives, and conceptual approaches. In their multifaceted views they mirror the current state of adaptation research, which has become a thriving field of scientific activities with an enormous publication output. Against the backdrop of an existing large body of literature it is legitimate to ask what this collection of case studies can contribute to the debate, what is new, and what makes this new publication unique.

A first answer to this question is already indicated by the title of the book, which calls for a denaturalisation and a 'critical' reading of climate change and adaptation. Being critical in the social sciences basically means to disagree with conventional positions, to view things differently, to explore alternative ways of understanding phenomena that are also studied by conventional science, and finally, to disclose the epistemologies and institutional structures of knowledge production. Examples of critical positions in terms of explicit 'disagreements' have been reported by Hulme (2009) in his influential book *Why We Disagree about Climate Change*, in approaches to deconstruct apocalyptic discourses of climate change and ensuing 'catastrophism' (Swyngedouw 2010), the inherent securitisation of climate policymaking (Bettini 2013; Hayes and Knox-Hayes 2014; Dalby 2016), and in studies of the de-politicised micro-geographies of climate summits (Weisser and Müller-Mahn 2017).

By taking a critical perspective, the authors in this book address a fundamental dilemma that is symptomatic of a large part of ongoing debates about adaptation. On the one hand, there is an almost anonymous agreement that adaptation is essential in the face of ever advancing climate change, especially in the Global South. On the other, the present chapters give striking examples of prevailing misunderstandings and gaps in adaptation research. Being critical therefore aims at two directions: scrutinising the weaknesses of scientific approaches to understand what adaptation means and how it can – and should – be brought about, and as a consequence, bringing politics back into the analysis of how adaptation is framed, negotiated, and translated into action. It is in this sense that we understand the common message of all contributions, which has already been outlined in Chapter 1: adaptation is *not* a neutral driver of action but carries political and ontological implications.

Two arguments appear most relevant for a critical perspective in adaptation research: first, adaptation is itself a normative goal, a contested political process, formulated by institutionalised scientists of the Global North, and second, adaptation is mostly told as a single story, disregarding multifaceted knowledge systems. Having studied various regions and communities affected by climate change, the authors of this anthology state that adaptation to environmental risks is not a new phenomenon for most people – especially in tropical regions. Nonetheless, these people are not regarded as adaptation experts, and local understandings of climate change adaptation are not recognised as resources for sustainable answers to risks, uncertainties, and vulnerabilities. A striking outcome of all studies on regional adaptation in this book is that vulnerabilities caused by climate change are not the only (and often not even the main) problem, but an additional pressure on scarce environmental resources by increasing tourism (see Chapter 5), industrialised agriculture, extensive biomass production for carbon trade-offs (see Chapter 8), water management, and rigorous fisheries and environmental protection policies (see Chapters 6 and 10), regulations for the mobility of pastoralists (see Chapter 2), or forest extraction and mining (see Chapter 7).

Against this background, this conclusion focuses on two aspects. First, it highlights the importance of structural factors and asks what makes people vulnerable in a world of uneven development. Second, it explores the critical potential of adaptation research, in the sense of its political impact for local and global environmental justice and equity. These are grounding issues in the spirit of the early works of political ecology. We aim to promote this approach for critical adaptation research with reference to recent conceptual debates.

In Chapter 1, the editors asked for a cultural, social, and political diversity of adaptation politics and a re-politicising of climate change adaptation. In this concluding chapter, we will approach this goal along with the following questions:

1. How can adaptation research become more socially and politically reflexive?
2. What is the consequence of criticising mainstream adaptation research as deterministic, and as creating an incomplete, biased picture of the problem?
3. What are the impacts of a technocratic understanding of adaptation that is based on the dominant knowledge system of the Global North, with its Eurocentric moral and ethical dimension related to adaptation?

4. How can the concept of adaptation overcome post-colonial ideas of development, and the failure to address the root causes of vulnerability?
5. How can a post-development approach be adopted for critical adaptation research?
6. And finally, should adaptation research not in any case be critical, given that adaptation is always an act of criticism on the unsustainable use of nature?

Negotiating adaptation to climate change

Finalisation of this book coincided with the UN Climate Change Conference in Bonn (COP23), where more than 20,000 delegates and observers from all over the world convened to discuss progress on implementing the Paris Agreement. During the two-week summit, adaptation was at centre stage in high-level negotiations and numerous side events, largely linked to questions and actors from the Global South. That the conference took place under the presidency of Fiji, one of the countries most seriously affected by climate change impacts, helped focus attention on adaptation. From the view of the small island states and other low-income countries, the issue of adaptation is not only about finding appropriate responses to adverse weather effects and climatic impacts, but is first and foremost a matter of compensation and cost recovery. Who pays for the adverse effects of climate change in poor countries? How and for whom shall that money be used? Who decides? And what does adaptation mean under these conditions?

At a global scale – in the context of earth summits and climate agreements – the struggle over climate change and adaptation is largely determined by negotiations over funds and finance. In her opening speech at COP23, the German Federal Minister for Environmental Affairs, Barbara Hendricks, highlighted the importance of the issue: 'Adaptation measures will be required in many countries, which is why adaptation to climate change is an equally important second pillar of the Paris Agreement.' As an expression of its good intentions, the German Government announced an additional €100 million to support developing countries in adapting to climate change. However, many delegates from southern nations commented that adaptation was not only a question of announcing additional funds, but of actually putting these funds to work. This means making the promised payments actually available, making the funds locally accessible, and first and foremost developing refined visions of what adaptation means in practice.

International adaptation policies are deeply entangled with international development policies. By focusing primarily on adaptation in the Global South, the funds and programmes set aside for this purpose revived the old-fashioned classification of the world into 'developing' and 'developed' countries. These notions are geographical imaginaries of bordering and ordering. They define a hierarchical division of the globe with categories of states of economic growth and classifications of more resilient, and more vulnerable, global regions. The present global climate governance results from a specific policy formation and global economy of the 1990s with a deep belief in free markets, technological opportunities, and management solutions. Therefore, critical arguments in adaptation research have been driven for two decades by the radical emphasis of political economy upon social justice (see Chapter 4).

Enlarged visions of adaptation

This book aims at a deconstruction – as a practice of critical science – of adaptation by addressing it as a normative concept with political and onto-logical implications that have been largely shaped by natural sciences and technocratic perspectives. In our view 'critical' adaptation research is dis-tinguished from other forms of adaptation research by making the political framing of science more transparent and taking a critical approach to the unquestioned use of science as a neutral backdrop to politics. In this sense 'critical adaptation research' presents the appropriate foundation for a new approach to adaptation research that addresses a wide range of climate policy problems resulting from the separation of science and politics. Rec-ognising the political character of environmental science does not question the reality of environmental problems, but strengthens our capacity to address them.

Over recent years, much research has gone into analysing how indi-viduals and societies adapt to climate change, what support may be pro-vided, and which obstacles and constraints are encountered in the process of adaptation (Adger *et al.* 2009; Schipper and Burton 2009). However, little has been said so far about the constraints that are caused by exclud-ing alternative discourses of sustainable development, such as non-capitalist, post-patriarchal or beyond-growth discourses. While there is growing understanding that adaptation planning should be considered first and foremost a political process (Eriksen and Lind 2009), these issues rarely receive much attention in research and political practice (Naess *et al.* 2011).

As early as 2003, Tim Forsyth had argued that the ecological 'laws' underlying much of the political debate on climate change, mitigation, and adaptation should be considered part of environmental politics (Forsyth 2003). He challenged orthodox views about the environment such as an assumed equilibrium within ecosystems and adaptation as practice to cope with a system imbalance. In line with other political ecologists, he stated that many scientific prescriptions were based on orthodox explanations that have not only been ineffective against environmental problems, but have even further aggravated precarious livelihoods. This critique is turned against conventional adaptation researchers themselves, arguing that technocratic and Eurocentric approaches in adaptation research are part of the problem by legitimising or causing uneven development. Acknowledging this entanglement, Forsyth calls for more locally determined forms of environmental management and greater public participation in the formulation of environmental science and politics (Forsyth 2003; see also Chapters 11 and 14).

Adaptation as a path-breaking strategy?

From its original root in evolutionary biology, the idea of adaptation reflects the necessity for organisms to constantly adjust to changes in their external environment as a means to bring themselves into line with newly arising challenges, constraints, and opportunities (Taylor 2015: 3). Similar to the concept of resilience, adaptation research will only consider system elements, not unsustainable systems themselves. From a critical social science perspective, adaptation is primarily a strategy within unjust social structures. Incremental adaptation is always embedded in dominant normative paths. Critical adaptation research therefore reflects the contribution of adaptation research to path stability of visions of growth and progress, and visions of social justice. Adaptation represents a structure conservative solution. The imperative to adapt to climate change does not lead to fundamental transformations of socio-ecological relations or general debates on nature exploitation (Park *et al.* 2012).

Adaptation develops its particular significance in the face of a society whose predominant logic of change – the logic of making profit, accumulating capital, and expanding economic activities – produces even stronger and less controllable crises. In other words, growth itself has become a destabilising factor. The continuous growth in producing (short-life) goods and services also causes potential and real instability. The required resources must be secured, which is not always free of conflict, and climate change also generates many uncertainties, including 'tipping points' of the local or regional climates.

Marcus Taylor argued in his recent book *The Political Ecology of Climate Change Adaptation* that climate change represents a discursive biopolitical project that seeks to render lives and livelihoods governable in ways that do not threaten the liberal democratic and capitalist institutions that have largely been responsible for producing vulnerability in the first place (Taylor 2015). He stated that we ought not to tell people to live more adaptable lives, to be more resilient individuals, in the same milieu that caused their problems in the first place. Julie Cupples sought to use a biopolitical approach informed by the work of Gilles Deleuze and Felix Guattari to offer a new way of understanding adaptation as part of a process of becoming, in which both humans and non-humans live in practices of capitalist exploitation (Cupples 2011).

Non-biased and reflexive climate adaptation knowledge

The climate discourse is an illuminating example for a practice of othering non-scientific knowledge and universalising scientific experiences, observations, and interpretation. 'Indigenous' or synonymously 'local' as well as 'traditional' climate knowledge is a prominent reference to generate climate information – as additional knowledge. In adaptation research so-called 'indigenous knowledge' is usually understood as time-, place-, and culture-specific (Speranza *et al.* 2010: 296), as related to societies with deeper (spiritual) relations with their environment, such as pastoralists or hunter-gatherers, with a high awareness of weather variability. In these specific contexts, indigenous knowledge is viewed as the other knowledge that complements scientific climate knowledge. The Fourth Assessment Report of the Intergovernmental Panel on Climate Change (IPCC) had a specific chapter on indigenous knowledge for adaptation to climate change (Parry *et al.* 2007), where 'indigenous knowledge' is used in distinction to scientific knowledge.

But does a purely indigenous or locally constituted knowledge actually exist? Can we even think of a locally bound or culturally fixed knowledge? Knowledge production is always a translation process in which ideas undergo reinterpretation, modification, and appropriation. With reference to the climate debate of the past decade, we argue that scientific and non-scientific types of knowledge are not the relevant categories to identify fundamental oppositions in climate knowledge production. First, indigenous and scientific knowledge systems are not separate and mutually unaffected spheres, and second, other oppositions are more relevant for disintegrated climate knowledge. Climate knowledge in the Global South matches experiences, needs, and interests at multiple scales by different actors – especially in post-colonial societies. According to Derek Gregory, local knowledge is not local any more (Gregory 1994: 9). This also applies to climate knowledge. The observers and the observed are in constant and interactive motion. Differentiation of local knowledge, indigenous knowledge, and scientific, universal knowledge is not accurate when trying to understand causes and impacts of climate change within complex global and local human–nature interrelations, histories, and possible futures. At best, climate researchers are aware of a hierarchical and non-objective knowledge production and contribute to a reflexive climate knowledge (see Chapters 1 and 13).

Non-governmental organisations (NGOs) often play a special role in knowledge transfer and translation of climate knowledge. Most have an advocacy agenda, aiming at communicating national policies to the local level and raising awareness for community problems at the national level. Their intermediate position and capacity to access green climate funds and international donors led to an 'NGO-isation' of community-based adaptation activities, which goes along with a universalised vocabulary of adaptation as a donor-oriented articulation of adaptation needs and capacities (see Chapter 3).

Adaptation of humans and non-humans

While social justice is essential for sustainable adaptation, we argue that critical adaptation research must attend arguments for rights of nature more carefully. The ability to adapt is a fundamental capacity of nature. Many people believe that humans must respect the uniqueness of nature and its regenerative capacity and should stop treating it as an object (GARN 2017). Therefore, critical adaptation research must engage with the theoretical and substantive problems of representing biophysical agency. Adaptation is a strategy not only for adjusting individual practices in everyday life to the reality of volatile environments, but is also a way for changing human–environment relations to reduce future impacts of climate change. Effectively understanding the desire for past natures also requires that adaptation researchers and all people adapting to environmental changes simultaneously re-imagine their current and future relationships between the human and non-human world. This includes allowing the non-human world to flourish, to have autonomy, and for human–environment (as human–non-human) relationships to be non-hierarchal (see Chapter 12).

Sara De Wit (Chapter 2) pointed out that the Cartesian dichotomy denies the basic idea that humans (society, culture, language, etc.) are not just *outside* their climates, but are an integral part of them. Rethinking climate and society as bounded and co-produced impels us to explore climatic change in terms of the shifting couplings of human and meteorological forces through which our lived environments are actively formed (Taylor 2015: 5). Analysing the co-production of nature and society is the fundamental perspective of political ecologists (Bauriedl 2016). Scholars of this non-determinist approach move beyond epistemological concerns and call into question the ontological grounding of climate change adaptation (Taylor 2015; Watts 2015). Rather than being seen as an obvious social solution to a natural problem, climate change adaptation as a paradigm is seen as problematically resting on and upholding a dualism between human and natural worlds. In doing so, it becomes a negative biopolitical project that seeks to regulate and constrain emergent forms of life by defining the ways in which people can adjust their lives in response to actual or potential environmental risks and traumas (Mullenite 2017).

Decision-making for suitable and sustainable adaptation strategies

Which and whose experiences of adaptation practices are recognised in adaptation research? Who is involved in the contested process of developing suitable and sustainable adaptation strategies? Whose voices have been heard in recent processes of local, regional, national, and international adaptation policy? Most studies of critical adaptation research highlight the unequal representation of actor types within adaptation governance, and problematise the insufficient representation of civil society (see Chapters 3 and 9). One repeated argument in critical adaptation research is the dominance of market-related actors in climate negotiations, who prefer technological innovations and centralised management instead of social innovation or sufficiency strategies (Bauriedl 2011).

Climate adaptation policies of international institutions such as UNEP and UNDP, as well as national governments of 'developed and developing countries' created a mantra of win–win options for investments in local infrastructure and pro-poor development ('climate compatible development'). But as in the case of climate adaptation, climate change too will generate burdens. But who should carry the burdens of adaptation? This question is not trivial, since the burdens of adaptation are entangled with the burdens of capitalism, racism, sexism, and other systems of oppression and exclusion. Critical adaptation research delivers increasing knowledge of power structures within the intersection of race, class, and gender, not only in the bias of Global North and Global South or local and global levels (Arora-Jonsson 2011; Sultana 2014; see also Chapter 1).

We must also ask honest questions about the final state of adaptation. Where does adaptation end? Adaptation is tied to a very low standard of development and livelihood. Is everybody adapted if nobody starves or lives without shelter after a drought or a flood? Or should goals of adaptation be linked to an equal global distribution of risks and benefits? The answers to these questions touch on contradicting visions of a just global development and are fundamental to making different ideas of welfare and wealth explicit.

Despite the inherently political nature of international negotiations on climate change, much of the theory, debate, and evidence-gathering assume a largely apolitical and linear policy process. It is timely to propose an approach to critical adaptation research in which explicit attention is given to the way that ideas, power, and resources are conceptualised, negotiated, and implemented by different groups at different scales.

Riskscapes: geographical imagination of vulnerability

As the previous section explained, adaptation aims at reducing the risks of future climate change, but may at the same time produce new risks. This paradox is addressed by the concept of 'riskscapes' (Müller-Mahn and Everts 2013). The notion of riskscapes connects the perception of risks and opportunities and ensuing practices of risk-taking with the material landscape of spatially differentiated risks. Riskscapes combine symbolic and physical dimensions, the first with regard to perception and imagination, and the second with regard to the materiality of specific risks at particular places. The two dimensions are connected through individual practices of risk-taking and risk-avoidance, which also have consequences for other actors and thereby influence the constitution of risk in a given territory. Riskscapes emerge from spatial imaginations and their influence on human agency. This phenomenon can be seen in the way that the perception of risks and opportunities in the context of climate change is currently reconfiguring development agendas.

How do geographical imaginations of climate vulnerability frame possible development options and therefore enable and/or constrain possible transformations for a sustainable future? For example, the African climate discourse is filled with narratives, maps, and images that represent a geographical imagination of poor people living in arid areas, suffering from climate-change-induced hazards. Gregory (1994) formally defined geographical imaginations as the spatialised cultural and historical knowledge that characterises social groups, implicating a framing of possible societal relations within imagined spaces. They conventionally occupy a location somewhere between the domains of the factual and fictional, the subjective and objective, the real and representational (Manzo 2010). Geographical imaginations are powerful and at the same time instruments of power because they localise social inequality. Most people have a particular geographical imagination of the planet as a world which is essentially divided into localities or territories, within each of which dwell local people with local problems and rights. From this perspective, climate vulnerability appears as the space-bound problem of local people. Doreen Massey called this practice 'the localisms of the powerful' (Massey 2007: 47). She asked for a deconstruction of the imaginations of locality that incorporates the geometries of power in a highly unequal world (ibid.: 49).

Two discursive practices still frame the climate debate: victimisation and territorialisation. All the publications of the United Nations and international development institutions evoke images of specific people within specific spatial settings, who are suffering most by climate change. They all live near the equator and are all poor – and mostly female. Climate vulnerability and climate adaptation are associated with 'tropicality', with specific views and visions of the tropical world, evolved during the period of most intense European penetration into the geographic spaces and human worlds that bestride the equator (Cosgrove 2005). In adaptation discourses, tropical regions in the Americas, the Pacific, Africa, and South Asia are linked with poverty, underdevelopment, and thus vulnerability (see Chapter 1). Adaptation policy is absolutely focused on rural and indigenous communities living in this region (Mannke 2011: 17). And these regionalised adaptation discourses are dominantly informed by scientific knowledge produced by scholars of the Global North.

This practice of space-making is the essential of international adaptation research. The Fifth Assessment Report of the IPCC takes into consideration climate change predictions and other factors of vulnerability such as food security, ranging from diversification of food production to access to markets or food supply systems. These regionalised factors were aggregated to 'regional climate risks', 'most vulnerable regions', and 'regions with best adaptation capacities' (IPCC 2014). In general, the entire African continent is declared the most climate-vulnerable. The generalisation and condensation of climate knowledge into notions such as 'vulnerable Africa' and the homogenisation of persons of different age, gender, and bodies living in tropical areas as 'vulnerable people' is compatible with the dominant (under)development discourse. International climate policy has been observed in many countries as a relabeling of older concepts of development policy (Weisser *et al.* 2013).

For the past decade, the European adaptation discourse has amplified the entangled observation of adaptation and poverty by climate war scenarios: climate change predictions for Africa suggest increasingly scarce water resources associated with a high risk of violent conflict (Adano 2012: 65). The notion of 'climate wars' has generated several bestsellers (Dyer 2008; Welzer 2012) and is reserved for violent conflicts in Africa. Especially in Europe the narratives of massive, abrupt, and unavoidable 'flows of climate refugees' in the near future is very popular (WBGU 2007). Such dystopian narratives, either framed within humanitarian or 'national security' agendas, relegate the concerned populations to the status of victims (either to protect or to fear) (Bettini 2013: 63). The authors of this book all criticise the narrative of a Global South as naturally 'vulnerable', disaster-ridden, poverty-stricken, and disaster-prone.

Adaptation as future-making

Using the terms 'adaptation' or 'resilience' in policy circles often invokes a discursive practice that aims at keeping control over the future by ruling out the possibility of surprise (see Chapter 5). However, social-ecological transformation is not only about redistributing resources or control over nature. It implies a redefinition of nature and nature–society relations, changing aspirations of the future use of natural resources. The idea of environmental management on a sustainable path of development and growth implies that ecosystem responses to human use are linear, predictable, and controllable, and that human and natural systems can be treated independently. Evidence from diverse regions all over the world suggests that natural and social systems behave in non-linear ways, exhibiting marked thresholds in their dynamics, and interacting within coupled social-ecological systems (Folke *et al.* 2002).

Are there alternative approaches to understanding adaptation? The contributions to this book give ample evidence that adaptation should not simply be viewed as a predetermined goal, but as an aspect of transformative processes and practices.

Conceptualising adaptation in terms of 'response to climatic stimuli', as the notion was defined in the Fourth Assessment Report of the IPCC (Parry *et al.* 2007), completely misses the essential role of human agency. Even though recent definitions have become more sophisticated in this regard, adaptation still carries the legacy of a concept that has originally been used in biology, and was later transferred to other spheres of life. Uncritically applying it to human societies and their relations with nature risks falling into the trap of 'adaptationism' (Bargatzki 1984), which is none other than outright environmental determinism. Adaptationism implicitly assumes that humans are not much different from other species in how they react to changing environments. This view ignores the often complex societal relations with nature. Instead, it tends to naturalise society, and to 'reduce the future to climate' (Hulme 2011).

In line with the other contributors to this book, we conclude that adaptation and adaptive action are far too complex to leave them to natural science and modelling approaches alone.

Instead, adaptation should be seen as a complex transformative process that is tied to a web of enabling and constraining factors, economic incentive structures, different knowledge systems, and diverse patterns of environmental governance. Understanding adaptation as human agency requires taking into account different forms of knowledge, environmental perception, cultural backgrounds of values and norms, contested settings of interests, and the institutional regulation of societal decision-making. This is one of the key messages of this book: understanding how decisions in the context of climate change are made requires the acknowledgement of the political dimension of adaptive processes. Denaturalising the explanations of climate change adaptation means to reinvigorate the political in these processes, that is, to politicise adaptation research.

Understanding adaptation as a transformative process that links the present to the future clearly has a timeframe that points into the future, and it is perhaps from this side that adaptation research may gain some innovative ideas. Approaching it with a strong focus on human agency, adaptation may be understood as a way of active future-making. This implies a future that does not simply emerge out of changing climates and responsive actions, but one that is actively shaped by imaginations, visions, desires, (climate) knowledge, enabling and constraining structures, negotiations, and adaptive practices.

Adaptive future-making may be understood in two ways: one defined by probabilities, and one searching for possibilities (Appadurai 2013). The first is one that is narrowed down to the assumption that the future is more or less predetermined by changing climates. Such a reduction of the future to climate is, as Hulme (2011) argued, a form of climate determinism. Alternatively, and that is the second option, the future may be understood as one that is open to be shaped according to visions and imaginations of 'desirable futures' (Jasanoff and Kim 2015). It is in this context that we suggest viewing adaptation to climate change: as a driver of future-making.

References

Adano, W.R., *et al.*, 2012. Climate change, violent conflict and local institutions in Kenya's drylands. *Journal of Peace Research*, 49 (1), 65–80.

Adger, W.N., Lorenzoni, I., and O'Brien, K., 2009. *Adapting to Climate Change: Thresholds, values, governance.* Cambridge: Cambridge University Press.

Appadurai, A., 2013. *The Future as Cultural Fact: Essays on the global condition.* London: Verso.

Arora-Jonsson, S., 2011. Virtue and vulnerability: Discourses on women, gender and climate change. *Global Environmental Change*, 21, 744–51.

Bargatzki, T., 1984. Culture, environment, and the ills of adaptationism. *Current Anthropology*, 25 (4), 399–415.

Bauriedl, S., 2011. Adaptive capacities of European city regions in climate change: On the importance of governance innovations for regional climate policies. *In:* W. Leal Filho, ed., *The Economic, Social and Political Elements of Climate Change.* Berlin: Springer, 3–14.

Bauriedl, S., 2016. Politische Ökologie: Machtverhältnisse in Gesellschaft/Umwelt-Beziehungen. *Geographica Helvetica*, 71, 341–51.

Bettini, G., 2013. Climate barbarians at the gate? A critique of apocalyptic narratives on 'climate refugees'. *Geoforum*, 45, 63–72.

Cosgrove, D., 2005. Tropic and tropicality. *In:* F. Driver and L. Martins, eds, *Tropical Visions in an Age of Empire.* Chicago, IL: University of Chicago Press, 197–216.

Cupples, J., 2011. Wild globalization: The biopolitics of climate change and global capitalism on Nicaragua's Mosquito Coast. *Antipode*, 44, 10–30.

Dalby, S., 2016. Framing the anthropocene: The good, the bad and the ugly. *Anthropocene Review*, 3 (1), 33–51.

Dyer, G., 2008. *Climate Wars.* New York: Random House.

Eriksen, S., and Lind, J., 2009. Adaptation as a political process: Adjusting to drought and conflict in Kenya's drylands. *Environmental Management*, 43 (5), 817–35.

Folke, C., *et al.*, 2002. Resilience and sustainable development: Building adaptive capacity in a world of transformations. *Ambio: A Journal of the Human Environment*, 31 (5), 437–40.

Forsyth, T., 2003. *Critical Political Ecology: The politics of environmental science.* New York: Routledge.

GARN (Global Alliance for Rights of Nature), 2017. *International Rights of Nature Tribunal in Bonn.* Press release, 10 November. Available from: https://therightsofnature.org/wp-content/uploads/Press-release-Bonn-Tribunal-final-2.pdf [Accessed 25 November 2017].

Gregory, D., 1994. *Geographical Imaginations.* Oxford: Blackwell.

Hayes J., and Knox-Hayes, J., 2014. Security in climate change discourse: Analyzing the divergence between US and EU approaches to policy. *Global Environmental Politics*, 14 (2), 82–101.

Hulme, M., 2009. *Why We Disagree about Climate Change.* Cambridge: Cambridge University Press.

Hulme, M., 2011. Reducing the future to climate: A story of climate determinism and reductionism. *Osiris*, 26, 245–66.

IPCC, 2014. *Climate Change 2014: Impacts, adaptation, and vulnerability: Working Group II.* Cambridge: Cambridge University Press.

Jasanoff, S., and Kim, S.-H., eds, 2015. *Dreamscapes of Modernity: Sociotechnical imaginaries and the fabrication of power*. Chicago, IL: University of Chicago Press.

Mannke, F., 2011. Key themes of local adaptation to climate change: Results from mapping community-based initiatives in Africa. *In*: W. Leal Filho, ed., *Experiences of Climate Change Adaptation in Africa*. Berlin: Springer, 17–32.

Manzo, K., 2010. Imaging vulnerability: The iconography of climate change. *Area*, 42 (1), 96–107.

Massey, D., 2007. *World City*. Cambridge: Polity Press.

Mullenite, J., 2017. Can climate change adaptation be a desirable goal? Book review. *Human Geography*, 10 (2), 87–94

Müller-Mahn, D., and Everts, J., 2013. Riskscapes: The spatial dimensions of risk. *In*: D. Müller-Mahn, ed., *The Spatial Dimension of Risk: How geography shapes the emergence of riskscapes*. London: Earthscan, 22–36.

Naess, L.O., Polack, E., and Blessings, C., 2011. Bridging research and policy processes for climate change adaptation. *IDS Bulletin*, 42 (3), 97–103.

Park, S.E., *et al.*, 2012. Informing adaptation responses to climate change through theories of transformation. *Global Environmental Change*, 22, 115–26.

Parry M., *et al.*, eds, 2007. Cross-chapter case study. *In*: IPCC, *Climate Change 2007: Impacts, adaptation and vulnerability: contribution of Working Group II to the Fourth Assessment Report*. Cambridge: Cambridge University Press, 843–68.

Schipper, E., and Burton, I., 2009. *The Earthscan Reader on Adaptation to Climate Change*. London: Earthscan.

Speranza, C.I., *et al.*, 2010. Indigenous knowledge related to climate variability and change: Insights from droughts in semi-arid areas of former Makueni District, Kenya. *Climatic Change*, 100, 295–315.

Sultana, F., 2014. Gendering climate change: Geographical insights. *The Professional Geographer*, 66 (3), 372–81.

Swyngedouw, E. 2010. Apocalypse forever? Post-political populism and the spectre of climate change. *Theory, Culture and Society*, 27 (2–3), 213–32.

Taylor, M., 2015. *The Political Ecology of Climate Change Adaptation: Livelihoods, agrarian change, and the conflicts of development*. New York: Routledge.

Watts, M. 2015. Now and then: The origins of political ecology and the rebirth of adaptation as a form of thought. *In*: T. Perrault, G. Bridge, and J. McCarthy, eds, *The Routledge Handbook of Political Ecology*. New York: Routledge, 19–50.

WBGU (German Advisory Council on Global Change), 2007. *World in Transition: Climate change as a security risk*. London: Earthscan.

Weisser, F., and Müller-Mahn, D., 2017. No place for the political: Micro-geographies of the Paris Climate Conference 2015. *Antipode*, 49 (3), 802–20.

Weisser, F., Bollig, M., Doevenspeck, M., and Müller-Mahn, D., 2013. Translating the 'adaptation of climate change' paradigm: The politics of a travelling idea in Africa. *The Geographical Journal*, 180 (2), 111–19.

Welzer, H., 2012. *Climate Wars: What people will be killed for in the 21st century*. Cambridge: Polity Press.

Index

Page numbers in **bold** denote tables, those in *italics* denote figures.

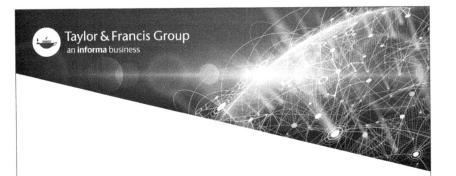

For Product Safety Concerns and Information please contact our EU
representative GPSR@taylorandfrancis.com
Taylor & Francis Verlag GmbH, Kaufingerstraße 24, 80331 München, Germany

www.ingramcontent.com/pod-product-compliance
Ingram Content Group UK Ltd.
Pitfield, Milton Keynes, MK11 3LW, UK
UKHW021621240425
457818UK00018B/670